BY THE SAME AUTHOR

The Heroic Temper
Oedipus at Thebes
Oedipus the King (translation)
Word and Action

ESSAYS
Ancient & Modern

Bernard Knox

THE JOHNS HOPKINS UNIVERSITY PRESS   BALTIMORE

© 1989 Bernard Knox
All rights reserved
Printed in the United States of America

Hardcover edition originally published 1989
Johns Hopkins Paperbacks edition, 1990

The Johns Hopkins University Press, 701 West 40th Street,
Baltimore, Maryland 21211

The paper used in this book meets the minimum requirements of
American National Standard for Information Sciences—Permanence of Paper
for Printed Library Materials, ANSI Z39.48-1984.

Library of Congress Cataloging-in-Publication Data
Knox, Bernard MacGregor Walker.
Essays ancient and modern / Bernard Knox.
p. cm.
Bibliography: p.
ISBN 0-8018-3789-8 (alk. paper)—ISBN 0-8018-4107-0 (pbk.)
1. Books—Reviews. 2. Greek literature—History and criticism.
3. Greece—Civilization—To 146 B.C. I. Title.
PA85.K69A5 1989
814'.54—dc19 88-46122
CIP

To Bianca, *sine qua non* . . .

When you start on the journey to Itháki,
Pray that the road you take will be a long one,
Full of adventures, full of things to learn.
                                CAVAFY

Contents

Introduction xi

The Ancient World

Greek Literature & Society

Work and Justice in Archaic Greece: Hesiod's *Works and Days* 3

Dogs and Heroes in Homer 23

Triumph of a Heretic 35

The Freedom of Oedipus 45

The Greek Polis

Ancient Slavery and Modern Ideology 63

The Toilers Find a Voice 71

Greece à la Française 77

Thucydides and the Peloponnesian War: Politics and Power 92

Invisible Woman 110

The Socratic Method 116

The Modern World

Survivals & Transformations

The Life of a Legend 129

Oedipus Rex 137

The Greek Conquest of Britain 149

Visions of the Grand Prize 162

The Scorpion's Sting 176

On Poets & Poetry

Subversive Activities 185

Closet Modern 195

CONTENTS

Siegfried Sassoon 206
W. H. Auden 216
Forster's Later Years 224

From Madrid to the Garden of the Finzi-Contini
Everybody but Shakespeare 243
Remembering Madrid 250
The Spanish Tragedy 272
One Woman's War 292
The Triumph of the Italian Jews 298

Introduction

A collection of essays and reviews that deals with ancient Greek literature and society, the program of the Ecole des Beaux-Arts, English writers of the 1930s, modern Italian novelists, and the Spanish civil war can hardly fail to provoke speculation about the connections, if any, between these subjects, as well as a pardonable curiosity about the author's background. This introduction attempts to supply enough of that background to throw some light on the connections.

I was born a British subject and educated at a London grammar school, a private school that had been founded by that interesting character St. John Bolingbroke early in the eighteenth century (it has since disappeared, abolished in the reorganization of the British educational system that followed the Second World War). It was not a famous school, but it was a very good one. We began French at the age of twelve; it was taught by an eccentric master who insisted on cramming into our heads, or rather our throats and tongues, a correct pronunciation before going on to reading and spelling. This was not the usual practice in British schools, which regularly turned out people who spoke French fluently and grammatically but with blatantly upperclass British vowels and consonants—a phenomenon recorded for posterity in Ophuls' *Le Chagrin et la pitié*, where Sir Anthony Eden answers the interviewer's questions in impeccable syntax with an impossible accent. My French, brought to fluency by frequent visits to Paris, was to prove invaluable later on in the Bataillon Commune de Paris of the XIth International Brigade at Madrid and, later still, among the Maquisards of Finistère in the summer of 1944.

In our second year at school (1927 in my case) we were given a choice: Latin or German. The teachers of these subjects addressed us in the school gymnasium, each one advocating the merits of his language. I don't remember what the case for German was, and all I remember about the case for Latin is the claim of superior utility. The example given was its use by General Napier, conqueror of the Indian province of Sind, who saved money on the telegram announcing his victory to the War Office by sending the single Latin word *peccavi,* "I have sinned." I doubt that this can have been the reason for my decision, but I chose Latin.

Progress in both languages was rapid but balanced, fortunately for me, by a pitiful incompetence in mathematics, chemistry, and physics. I say fortunately because English schoolboys of that day (have they changed? I wonder) viewed any outstanding academic performance as "crawling" or, more coarsely, "sucking up" to the enemy, the enemy being the masters, who, it is true, handed out corporal punishment on the slightest pretext and with a practiced hand. Not content with Latin and French, I began dabbling in other languages in secondhand books bought from a bookstore near the school: Italian in a bilingual edition of Dante's *Inferno* (this, too, was to prove useful later); Russian in a primer printed in Moscow—its linguistic examples were all slogans, "Foreign Languages for the Masses," for example—and lastly, and to the immediate exclusion of the others, Greek. I started with *Doctor Smith's First Greek Book,* a beaten-up Victorian volume bought for twopence, and was soon exploring with awe the apparently unending paradigms of the verb *luo* and the mysteries of the dual, the middle, and the optative. This was all done on my own time; the school, much stronger in the sciences than in the humanities, did not offer Greek.

One morning in a study session, I had finished the English composition we had been set and went to work on my Greek. I got so absorbed that I failed to notice the silent approach of the supervising master, who was patrolling the room making sure that his charges were not drawing caricatures of the headmaster (an irresistible subject), playing noughts and crosses, or copying out pornographic texts. He was on me before I could hide Doctor Smith and the papers covered with Greek characters. The material was confiscated and I was told, in words that usually signaled six of the best, to come and see the master after class. When I did, he produced no cane but sent me to the Latin teacher, to whom he had passed on my book and papers. The result of this interview was an offer: if I would like to go on with Greek, he would be glad to tutor me. Of course, I would have to give up some other subject. "Algebra?" I asked hopefully. No, I would have to pass that subject to matriculate. But chemistry might perhaps be dispensed with. And chemistry it was.

Introduction

Early in 1933 I went up to Cambridge to take the scholarship examinations and was awarded a handsome scholarship in classics at St. John's College; a supplementary grant from the London County Council meant that all my expenses for the three years of resident undergraduate study would be amply provided for. In the fall I went up for the Michaelmas term, was assigned a suite of two rooms (but no bath) in a corridor leading off the magnificent Jacobean second court of St. John's, and settled down to the privileged existence of a Scholar of the College, my only duties to take my turn with the other Scholars at reading the lesson in the college chapel and the Latin grace before dinner in Hall. John's was notorious for the length of its grace, and I won a certain popularity by being able to speak it trippingly upon the tongue and get it over with faster than my colleagues.

This happy life was not the only thing I had my school to thank for. It had also prepared me for what was to come after Cambridge. Like most private schools in the England of those days, it was the recipient of a large grant from the War Office for the maintenance of a Cadet Corps, a military training program designed to turn out junior officers for the next war. Membership was compulsory; training, which occupied Friday afternoons and two weeks of camp on the Isle of Wight, was thorough. In addition to the usual interminable drill, we practiced infantry tactics (in a local park), signaling (Morse and semaphore), and under the supervision of professionals from a local Territorial Regiment to which the corps was attached, range firing with the Lee-Enfield rifle and also the Lewis gun, a World War I weapon that was still, in those days, the standard light machine gun of the British Army. Even though, with a bunch of disreputable companions, I was a subversive element in the corps, turning up on parade with unpolished buttons and regularly ending up on Friday doing extra drill on Defaulters Parade, I gave fervent silent thanks for my days in the Cadet Corps when, in November 1936 at Madrid, General Kléber presented the small English section of the Compagnie Mitrailleuse of the Bataillon Commune de Paris with a pair of Lewis guns.

After London, Cambridge was an enchanted country. The colleges, strung out along the river Cam, were a feast for the eye, and St. John's with its three red-brick Jacobean courts and, across the river, a Victorian Gothic extravaganza that somehow harmonized with its neighbors, was a delightful place to live. And live there one did: the gates were locked at ten, and any student coming in after that paid a fine; those coming in after twelve had to see the dean and face stiffer penalties. The university's program allowed the undergraduate freedom to enjoy the amenities of the place; attendance at lectures was not compulsory, and meetings with one's tutor to read him an essay or a Latin or Greek prose were not so frequent as to be a burden on the soul. All one had to do was pass the examinations given at the end of each year. These were not based on course material but covered every aspect of one's field of study; in fact they were set by outside examiners, and the last two were particularly formidable. "We give you enough rope . . . ," said one of the college Fellows to me one day; he had a sardonic grin on his face.

Though my main interest was Greek rather than Latin, the Fellow of the college who showed most interest in me was a Roman historian, Martin Charlesworth. He was extraordinarily kind to me even when, falling behind in my academic work and doing less well than expected in the second-year examinations, I had my scholarship reduced and was demoted from my position as senior scholar. In the opening months of 1936 Charles, as his friends were invited to call him, had just returned from a visit to the United States, an unusual initiative for a Cambridge don in those days. When not giving lectures he had spent his time traveling round the country on long-distance buses and been fascinated by the people he met on the way. In fact he packed me off to the local cinema to see *It Happened One Night*, which he had already seen twice. I told him that though I had not been to America, I had heard voices speaking, or rather singing, from New York. My father (who died in 1926 just before I started grammar school) was a professional pianist, who after service in the Flanders trenches in 1917–18 joined one of the first jazz bands organized in England; it played at Murray's River Club in the fashionable resort of Maidenhead on the Thames, a favorite haunt of the Prince of Wales. A telephone had been installed in our London flat, and every now and then someone would call from New York (an extraordinary event in those years) and sing the latest American hit song for my father to take down. He would then orchestrate it for the band, which would perform it weeks before the sheet music became available in England. Charles asked me if I could remember any of the songs; I could produce only one. It was "Barney Google, with his Goo-goo-googly Eyes." I asked Charles what he had been doing in America, apart from riding the buses. He had given the Martin Lectures at Oberlin

College, a distinguished lectureship in the classics. Neither of us could possibly have foreseen at that moment that almost fifty years later I would be invited to Oberlin to give the Martin Lectures myself.

As a matter of fact, at that moment in 1936 there was some question in both our minds whether I would be able to scrape through the coming final examination, Part II of the Tripos, with anything better than a third class. I had long since given up even a faint pretense that I was working for the examination; my time was entirely devoted to politics, those of the Cambridge Socialist Club. I was, of course, not alone in this, though none of my contemporaries turned their backs so decisively on academic work. My friend John Cornford, for example, won a starred first class in Part II of the History Tripos at the end of the year, and he was even more deeply involved in politics than I. Perhaps the difference had something to do with our respective disciplines; the study of history, especially of English history, did not seem so alien to an engagement with contemporary political realities as did the investigation of detailed problems in Greco-Roman language, culture, and literature.

The obsession with politics characteristic of the students of those years is not hard to understand in the light of the catastrophic condition of the British economy in the 1930s and the growing menace of Fascism—Italian and, more recent but more frightening, German. Adolf Hitler came to power in 1933, the year I went up to Cambridge, and by 1936 German rearmament was in full swing; Hitler's intentions were clear to anyone who took the trouble to read *Mein Kampf*. But the British government, far from protesting strongly against this open threat to European stability (not to mention the brutal repression of the German opposition and the persecution of the Jews) gave increasingly clear signals that its attitude toward Nazi Germany and Fascist Italy was conciliatory, by the most charitable interpretation, and might even be thought of as friendly. In May 1935 it signed the Anglo-German Naval Agreement, which conceded to Hitler the right to build submarines, a move bitterly regretted in the desperate days of the Battle of the Atlantic in 1941. In that same year, it sponsored the Hoare-Laval pact, which if it had not been withdrawn in the face of outraged protests, would have given Mussolini everything he wanted in Abyssinia. And it was mainly due to British pressure that France took no action when Hitler reoccupied the Rhineland in March 1936. The British government already had its feet firmly set on the road that led to the cynical betrayal of the Czechs at Munich, a bargain that brought not "peace in our time" but rather the Wehrmacht to the Channel ports and the Luftwaffe over London.

At home, the situation was equally dismal; the Depression seemed to have become a permanent condition. Even the professional optimists among the economists could offer little hope of recovery. The Depression was a more dispiriting phenomenon in England than in the United States; the Roosevelt New Deal was no economic panacea, but it was at least evidence of official concern, whereas the so-called National Government's policy of retrenchment was a defiant manifesto of indifference to widespread distress. In 1933, unemployment in England reached a record level of three million (23 per cent of all insured workers); the unemployment benefits on which these families had to live were just enough to keep them from outright starvation on a diet of bread and margarine, potatoes, and tea. Looking back on it in 1966, Harold Macmillan, who was a junior Conservative M.P. in the 1930s, remembered his conviction that "the structure of capitalist society in its old form had broken down. . . . Perhaps it could not survive at all without radical change. . . . Something like a revolutionary situation had developed."

There were towns in the industrial north where men had been out of work and subsisting on the dole, as it was known, for up to six years; in the mining villages of South Wales some of the pits had not been reopened since the General Strike of 1926. As if the misery of living on starvation allowances were not enough, the government decided, in 1931, to apply to workers who had been on unemployment compensation for more than twenty-six weeks a Means Test, which was to be administered by the local Poor Law authorities. This meant that any income accruing to any member of the family—war pension, widow's pension, money from odd jobs—would be deducted from the government payments. The Means Test was administered without regard for the rights and dignity of the individual; a Trades Union Conference Report published in 1932 spoke of "prying inquiries into domestic circumstances" and investigating officers who "assume the right to enter houses and make remarks about the furniture"—presumably suggesting it should be sold if it looked too good for the unemployed. When the government proposed cuts in the already inadequate allowances, the National Unemployed Workers Movement organized a series of Hunger Marches, bringing contingents of unemployed men, many of them veterans of the 1914 war, on foot from all over the country to present a petition to Parliament. The Hunger Marchers were enthusiastically welcomed, housed, and fed at stops along the way (Cambridge was one, and our Socialist Club took the lead in organizing food and shelter for them), but when they finally reached London they were welcomed by police horse and baton charges.

Meanwhile a different response to the breakdown of the traditional capitalist system appeared on the right: the formation, in the fall of 1932, of the British Union of Fascists under the leadership of Sir Oswald Mosley. It was amply funded—in part, as we now know, by Benito Mussolini—and received an enthusiastic welcome from most of the press; its members, dressed in black uniforms and boots, rose to some twenty thousand in less than two years. Its program was militaristic, authoritarian, antiunion, antidemocratic, and not at first but very soon, antisemitic. In the Jewish district of London's East End, the Fascists held provocative meetings, beat up Jewish shopkeepers, smashed the windows of their shops, and whitewashed on the walls the letters P.J.—"Perish Judah."

The Blackshirts held several rallies in Cambridge, which we Socialists attended to voice our opposition. One of them was addressed by a man with a fearsome-looking scar down one side of his face; his name was William Joyce, and years later he became famous in England as Lord Haw-haw of the Nazi radio and was duly hanged as a traitor. I was one of several in the crowd who had been primed to shout awkward questions at intervals; like my fellow club members who had the same assignment, I was grabbed, hauled away, and kicked out by the Blackshirt goon squad. But the B.U.F. did not arouse much enthusiasm in Cambridge. In fact, at the last of their meetings there, which took place on an open green common with the remarkable name of Christ's Pieces, they managed to make themselves look ridiculous. As a crowd gathered round the speaker's platform, the Blackshirt squad seemed to be having an agitated discussion. Suddenly they formed fours, sprang to attention, and at the word of command marched smartly off across the green. The crowd took this to be a preliminary display of Blackshirt discipline and military precision; they were going to do some close-order drill. But the squad kept going right across the green and we began to wonder what they were up to. As it dawned on us that they were heading for the gentlemen's lavatory at the far end of the green, we all burst out laughing, and the Blackshirt cause was lost in Cambridge.

But it was still a menace elsewhere. In October 1936 Moseley organized a national rally of his Blackshirts, which was to end with a march through the heart of the East End. In spite of protests from the local authorities and a petition signed by a hundred thousand residents calling for a ban on the march, permission was granted. When it became clear that there would be counterdemonstrations, all police leave was stopped and six thousand foot police and the whole of the mounted division were mobilized to clear a path for the Blackshirts. On the day, their way was blocked by a crowd estimated at three hundred thousand, and in spite of repeated horse and baton charges the march had to be called off. The contrast between the police action on this occasion and that of the arrival of the Hunger Marchers was an illuminating commentary on the government's claim that its action was impartial.

Meanwhile, across the Channel, a similar polarization was taking place in France. A movement similar in many ways to the British Blackshirts and the Nazi Sturmabteilungen had made a spectacular debut in February 1934 in riots outside the Chambre des Députés in which fifteen people were killed and more than a thousand injured. There had, of course, been powerful anti-Republican organizations in France for some time—Camelots du Roi, Action Française—but the emergence of an avowedly Fascist group, Les Croix de Feu, under the leadership of Colonel de la Roque, was a danger signal that had much to do with the willingness of Radical and Socialist parties to cooperate with the Communists in the formation of the Front Populaire, which won a stunning electoral victory in May 1936. Under pressure from sitdown strikes in the factories, the new government of Léon Blum introduced a long overdue program of reforms—the forty-hour week, paid vacations, the nationalization of the munitions industry; it also banned Fascist organizations. I had friends in Paris and spent many weekends there in those days; they were days of jubilation and hope. For the first time since the Depression began, a government was breaking out of the pattern of retrenchment and repression. But the hope was not to be fulfilled. Internally the government had to face a massive flight of capital. Externally it had to deal with German pressure and the reluctance of the British government to oppose

Hitler in any way; with the collapse of the League of Nations, signaled by the Italian occupation of the Abyssinian capital in July; and finally, with the military revolt in Spain against the newly formed government of the Frente Popular. Political sympathy, popular demand and considerations of national security all spoke strongly for immediate sales of arms to Spain, but Blum yielded to British insistence on nonintervention, which, since Hitler and Mussolini continued to supply the rebels, amounted to a form of cooperation with the Fascist regimes.

When the war broke out in Spain in July I was back in London. I had my Cambridge degree and had somehow managed to get a 2.1 (a position in the upper half of the second class); my examiners must have been in a charitable mood. The best I could hope for was a job in some dreary provincial private school teaching elementary Latin and possibly Greek, and I was in no hurry to take that road. John Cornford came home in September (he had been fighting on the Catalan front) and asked me to go back to Spain with him and another Cambridge friend, MacLaurin. He had decided to recruit a small English unit which would set an example of discipline and cleanliness on a front manned almost entirely by Anarchist units who lived up to their name. Partly from political conviction but more from surrender to Cornford's personal magnetism, I said yes without a second thought. I said a long farewell to Greece and Rome and sold my classical books to have money for the equipment I would need. (I still have two survivors of that clean sweep, volumes lost in corners; they are an odd couple, a school edition of Juvenal and an annotated edition of the Acts of the Apostles.)

John's plan for a small English unit on the Catalan front was soon discarded as, once in Paris, we found ourselves part of a stream of volunteers from all over Europe en route to Albacete, the training base for the new International Brigades. There we were assigned to the machine-gun company of the Bataillon Commune de Paris, also known, after its commander, as the Bataillon Dumont. (Dumont survived the war but, much later, was shot by a German firing squad for his activity in the French Resistance.) Our assignment to a French unit (there were only twenty-one of us, not enough to form a separate contingent) thrust me into an unwanted position of responsibility; since I was the only fluent French speaker in the bunch, I had to handle relations with the French and began at once to experience the sad fate of all interpreters—to become a target for the complaints and accusations of both linguistic parties.

We had no weapons; training consisted of drill and route marches. When the weapons did arrive—rifles but no machine guns—we were immediately sent up to Madrid, where Franco's spearheads were already in the suburbs. We got our machine guns there, on November 7, and for the best part of the next six weeks were engaged in the heavy fighting on the northwestern sector, first in the University City, where we defended a building called Filosofia y Letras and later at Humera and Aravaca on the western flank. After some days in the trenches in the Casa de Campo and the Parque del Oeste we went back to the University City, where many of the buildings, overrun by Franco's Moors, had to be retaken, some of them room by room. We were then sent in to help stem a powerful Franco offensive at Boadilla del Monte, a village northwest of Madrid; in that battle I and two others of our English section were wounded.

I had been shot in the neck and shoulder; my recovery was slow and left me with a malfunctioning right arm. The news that John had been killed while I was in hospital persuaded me to follow the doctor's recommendation that I should go home and seek expert treatment. I was now the only survivor of our Cambridge group of three; MacLaurin had been killed during the very first days at Filosofia y Letras.

For the next year and a half I drifted from one temporary job to another, growing steadily more pessimistic about the prospects for Spain and for Europe. In France the Front Populaire had come apart, and Paris was meekly following London's policy of appeasement; the Fascist powers were building their military strength and raising their territorial demands from month to month. But it was near the beginning of this period that a meeting changed the whole course of my life, a meeting with an American girl I had known at Cambridge, where she was reading English at Girton. We had been friends at the university, but this time we fell in love. Hopeless though my prospects seemed, we planned to get married and, if the British government persisted in its policy of surrender to Hitler and Mussolini, to move to America. Munich made it clear that there was to be no change, and in any case a decision was forced on us by her parents' insistence that she return to the United States. Once there she enlisted her parents and a friend from Cambridge days in an effort to get me through the process of applying for an immigration visa; it was granted early in 1939, and in April of that year we were married in New Jersey across the river from New York City. Unlike many academic couples of my acquaintance, we are still married to each other.

Jobs were no easier to find in New York than in London, but eventually my Cambridge degree, knowledge of Latin, and above all, English accent landed me a position of the kind I had always hoped to avoid. I was hired as a sort of junior Mr. Chips by a small private school in Connecticut. There, for fifty dollars a month and all found, I taught Latin (and occasionally things I knew less about) while my wife worked on her first novel. But, of course, we were just marking time; the war was bound to catch up with us. And catch up it did, with us and everybody else, on December 7, 1941. After protracted negotiations with the War Department, which did not want to accept noncitizen volunteers, I was inducted into the United States Army as a private at exactly the same rate of pay and allowance I had been receiving as a civilian; the only difference was that army food was much better. Meanwhile my wife, her novel finished and in the press, signed up, at a much higher rate of pay, as a sheet-metal mechanic building fighter planes for the United States Navy.

I was selected for officer training after a few months in the ranks, but my time as an enlisted man was invaluable for me. It was my first real contact with Americans. I had so far lived in the middle-class Anglophile atmosphere of a New England private school; now I was suddenly thrown into close, one might even say intimate, contact with men from all over the country, men from every type of ethnic background, most of them working men—mechanics, bricklayers, farmhands. With them I was shunted on troop trains from state to state, from Florida to Kansas, from Colorado to Alabama and Texas. Though my accent quickly earned me the nickname "Limey," I began to think of myself as an American, so that when my citizenship papers came through in 1943, the swearing-in ceremony seemed almost anticlimactic.

It took place on an American base in England; I had been stationed for some months on a B-17 field in East Anglia, where I was defense officer. Once I had drafted a plan for defense of the field against German paratroop attack (unlikely, to say the least, in 1943, but the military mind relentlessly contemplates the worst case), there was little for me to do except train my antiaircraft machine-gunners and inspect the crews from time to time. Boredom was relieved by a visit to nearby Cambridge, where Charles took me in to lunch at High Table and for coffee afterwards in the magnificent Tudor-Jacobean Combination Room of St. John's. He enquired about my plans for "after the war," and I had to tell him that they did not include the classics. My Greek was more than a little rusty after eight years of disuse, and teaching elementary Latin had not done much for my mastery of that language either. I told him I rather enjoyed the army and might try to stay in it as a career soldier.

Back once more at the base, however, I found myself bored and frustrated; my mood was not helped by a feeling of guilt as I watched the B-17s take off for Germany and counted the battered survivors as they returned. I was also exasperated that my knowledge of French was not being put to use. I pestered the adjutant day after day, asking him to get me a more interesting assignment. One day he showed me a telex that asked for officer volunteers with command of European languages. My name was sent in, and I soon received orders to report to an address in London; it was just off Grosvenor Square.

The officer who conducted the interview wore an American uniform that could only have been cut by a Savile Row tailor. Next to him sat a smartly dressed young woman (a rarity in the drab England of 1943) whose deferential air marked her as a secretary. The major, for such the elegant bronze oak leaves embroidered on his shirt collar proclaimed him, asked me if it was true that I spoke fluent French. Assured that it was, he turned to the woman at his side and said: "Miss King, carry on." "Bonjour, mon lieutenant," said Miss King, in a French that made it clear that King was a nom de guerre. "Il paraît que vous parlez couramment français. Où l'avez-vous appris?" After five minutes or so of question and answer she turned to her boss and announced: "He's O.K., Major." And was dismissed with thanks.

This Hollywood scenario turned out to be my introduction to the Office of Strategic Services. The operation I was being invited to join was a joint effort of the American OSS, the British Special Operations Executive, and the French Forces Françaises de l'Intérieur. Its code name was Jedburgh. The idea was to send in to occupied France, by parachute, three-man teams (Anglo-American-French) which would arm, train, and direct the activities of the French Maquis, so as to coordinate their operations with those of the advancing Allied armies after the landing. These teams (and others with Belgian or Dutch officers) would go in in uniform with an initial load of light arms; once established, they would organize fresh arms drops to equip as many Maquisards as the local Resistance networks could produce. Activity against the Germans was to be held to a minimum; the signal for full-scale attack would come from London whenever it seemed most useful to the advancing Allied armies.

In the fall of 1943 the volunteers, the "Jeds" as they came to be called, began to assemble at the training base, Milton Hall, a large country house and estate near Peterborough, and as might be expected of men who would volunteer for such a wildcat operation, they were a remarkable crew. I do not know how the British and French chose their personnel, but the U.S. Jeds were selected with the help of psychologists and psychiatrists who tested for a specific set of character traits. The problem in choosing men for such an operation, of course, is that once they are landed in enemy territory, you can no longer control them. They may do the obviously sensible thing: go to ground in a safe hiding place, do nothing to attract attention to themselves, and wait for the arrival of friendly troops. The psychological and psychiatric tests the Jeds were subjected to had one basic objective: to select men psychologically incapable of remaining quiet—troublemakers, in fact; people who could be relied on to upset applecarts. I have no great admiration for psychology as taught and practiced in the United States, still less for psychiatry, but I have to admit that the men in charge of selecting the Jedburghs delivered the goods. I have never known such a bunch of troublemakers in my life. Douglass Bazata, for example, was famous among us for a brazen audacity, both physical and verbal, that took people's breath away and enabled him to get away with actions and remarks that were, in a military milieu, outrageous. He used to address full colonels, for example, as "Sugar." (He also ended the war with a Distinguished Service Cross and three Purple Hearts.) René Dussaq astonished the British instructor who was briefing him on how to jump out of a barrage balloon canopy (you let yourself down through a hole in the floor) by making a swan dive over the side. (He had been a professional stunt man in civilian life.) There was Lou Conein, who had served in the French Foreign Legion and, in a later war, was to become a legend in Vietnam. William Colby and Jack Singlaub were also to distinguish themselves in later life. Many of the British Jeds came from colorful outfits famous for their independence and idiosyncrasy—Commandos, Special Air Service, Long Range Desert Group; one came from a fabled outfit known as Popski's Private Army. The French volunteers were all of them men who had broken their connection with Vichy France, cutting themselves off from their roots; they assumed noms de guerre to prevent reprisals against their families, and in many cases we did not learn their true names until after the war. I had been recruited because of my fluent French (a rarity among the U.S. Jeds), but was not subjected to the psychological and psychiatric tests. I suppose I was assumed to be slightly crazy like the others on the basis that at the age of twenty-one I had gone to Spain to fight for the Republic in the Civil War.

I was immediately appointed an instructor, put through jump and demolition schools, and set to initiating the French officers into the mysteries of plastic explosive, detonators, and Bickford fuse. Fifty years later, at a reunion of the Jeds in Paris, a tall, distinguished Frenchman whose face was vaguely familiar came up to me, took me by the hand, and addressed me as "Maître." I was taken aback at such an honorific title. "Pourquoi maître?" I asked, and he replied: "You taught me how to blow up railroad trains." I gathered later that his record in that line was an enviable one.

Milton Hall was no ordinary school. The curriculum (some of it taught at other secret locations) included courses in knife fighting, burglary, demolitions, industrial sabotage, and a fearsome type of unarmed combat known simply as "Australian barroom fighting"; it offered also an "assassination" pistol range, an obstacle course that had been designed by a malevolent fiend, opportunities to detect and defuse mines and booby traps, and above all, "schemes." These were exercises that simulated combat conditions; Jedburgh teams were jumped into Scotland or Wales and told to make their way undetected back to Milton Hall, armed and in uniform, through areas in which the police, the Home Guard, and the Boy Scouts had been alerted and supplied with descriptions (it was usually the Boy Scouts who spotted us; they were, as we say now, highly motivated, and willing to stay up all night).

The instructors in all these exotic arts were mostly British; SOE had been perfecting their techniques ever since Winston Churchill, in 1941, gave them the signal to "set Europe ablaze." The burglary school was especially memorable. Not all of us were sent there; I like to think that the selection of my name was due to purely random factors. We were greeted in our first class by a plainclothes CID inspector who introduced the instructor, a gentleman who was serving a life sentence in Pentonville prison. "He's the super cracksman of the century," said the CID man proudly. "We had to lock him up for life—he can open any safe ever made." Our teacher cleared his throat and held forth in a ripe East London accent. "Gen'lmen, I'm only doin' my bit, like all o' you. . . ." He taught us, among other things, how to diagnose the checks and tremors of safe combinations, feeling through the steel the fall of the tumblers. I was flunked early in that course because my fingertips were not sensitive enough. "You 'aven't got the touch, sir. You better stick to the dynamite." As a graduation present at the end of the course we were all fingerprinted and photographed, "just in case you gentlemen should think of putting what you have learned here to use after the close of hostilities." Luckily, none of us had to burgle a German HQ, though most of the things we were taught at Milton Hall and in the other schools did indeed prove useful when we went in.

On July 3, 1944, my team, code named Giles, was alerted, and I went to draw weapons and equipment from the supply sergeant at Milton Hall. I was issued a .45 pistol and .30-caliber carbine, with ammunition, grenades, field glasses, medical supplies (including enough syringe tubes of morphine to kiss myself goodbye with in case I had to be left behind badly wounded), a commando fighting knife, compass, map case, down sleeping bag, canteen, pocket rum flask, and an enormous money belt, which was later stuffed with eight million francs in thousand franc notes (printed in London, of course). I checked the equipment and got out my pen to sign for it. "You don't have to sign for it, sir," said the sergeant. I couldn't believe my ears. Like every officer in the United States Army, I had signed my life away, to use the fashionable phrase; I had never received a penny, a pair of socks, or a round of ammunition without signing for it; never left a post without signing out at the mess, the PX, supply, and everywhere I might have owed money or materiel; never departed without obtaining my successor's signature for every piece of equipment handed over, down to the last nail. If I was not expected to sign for all this equipment, it could mean only one thing: they didn't expect me to come back; they thought they would never see any of this stuff again. Nor did they. I still have most of it, though after the war I had to sell the field glasses to a bird-watching professor when I was short of cash in graduate school at Yale.

As it turned out, the gloomy prognostications of higher headquarters were ill-founded; our losses were not heavy. In my area, Finistère, the westernmost department of Brittany, we had five teams at work but only one casualty—Major Colin Ogden-Smith of the British Army, who was killed in a German raid on his team's hiding place. all the Americans in the area came out unharmed—Phil Chadbourn and John Summers to the north. Shirley Trumps to the south. Trumps urged on his partisans in a fluent French spiced by his native Cajun; Chadbourn had gone to school on the Riviera and had an impeccable French accent (he had in fact been recruited to go in as an agent but opted for the Jedburghs). Summers spoke no French at all nor did his radio operator Zielski; they were dependent for local contacts on the French officer of the team. This team had the toughest assignment—the flat area adjacent to Brest with few places where a Maquis could find cover. On one occasion they had to move packed, with all their equipment, into wine barrels that were transported on a horse-drawn cart. They passed some anxious moments when, at a German roadblock, the sentries asked for a sample of the wine; luckily the driver had some bottles handy up front.

In Finistère we were all in position by mid-July. From then until Patton's armor came racing for Brest in August we organized massive drops of arms and ammunition in the area, trained the locals in their use, and kept our rapidly growing strength in reserve as far as possible, waiting for the day when it could be unleashed to maximum advantage.

The drops were arranged with London via our portable Jed radio; we transmitted coordinates for the grounds and a code message for the BBC. After the BBC news in French (which everyone listened to, including the Germans) the announcer would say: "Et voici maintenant quelques messages personnels." He would then go on to recite a string of apparently meaningless phrases—"la lune brille sur le dolmen, le cancre s'ennuie, méfie-toi de Cécile"—which were announcements to the Maquis that there would be a drop that night on grounds *dolmen, cancre, Cécile*. All they had to do was be on the field with flashlights or fires lined up to guide the four-engine bomber in and enough men to protect the ground and collect and empty the six-foot containers that came plunging down through the night on oversized parachutes. The Germans rarely intercepted these drops; there were too many of them, and the grounds had been chosen for their inaccessibility to motorized troops. When in August the signal came from London to launch a general attack on the Germans, thousands of armed young Frenchmen were ready and able to respond. My citation for the Croix de Guerre (and it is typical) speaks of "arms drops which enabled four thousand men of the Maquis to take part in the liberation of Brittany." And my team was only one of twelve operating in Brittany, only one of the more than eighty that jumped into France, Belgium, and Holland.

What had seemed the craziest thing about the project (perhaps the basis for the official conviction that few of us would come back) was the decision that we were to run around in German-occupied territory doing our stuff in uniform. (Just to make sure that nobody got the wrong idea, I had a six-by-four-inch American flag sewn on my upper left sleeve.) Uniformed Allied groups were far from rare in the mountains of Greece and Yugoslavia, but France, especially in the areas where we would do the most good, was thickly settled, well equipped with road networks and modern communications. From the moment team Giles arrived in central Finistère everyone in the countryside knew where we were, even though, for the first three weeks, we moved, sometimes twenty miles, every night. The whole countryside knew, but no one told the Germans, in spite of rewards offered for information about the "imitators of Lawrence of Arabia" featured on German posters. And, as it turned out, the appearance of Allied soldiers in uniform many miles behind the German lines was, from the propaganda point of view, a master stroke. It came to the French in the summer of 1944 as a guarantee of victory, an announcement that liberation was imminent; it emboldened those already committed to resistance, made up the minds of the hesitant, and warned the collaborationists that it was time to change sides or look for a rat hole.

The BBC message we had been waiting for came in August, as Third Army's tanks came round the bend at Avranches, heading for Brest. For a hectic week we harassed units of the German Second Parachute Division as they moved east to meet the American advance and then attacked them again as they fell back on Brest.[1] Overrun at last by American troops, we and our French irregulars, now well organized, armed, and disciplined, were assigned a role in General

Middleton's siege of Brest: we fought our way along the Presqu'île de Crozon, the long southern peninsula that curves round to protect the wide expanse of the bay in which the harbor of Brest is set. With some U.S. reconnaissance armored cars serving as our light artillery, we took the heights of the Menez-Hom, a hill that surveys the whole sweep of the Rade de Brest and that had served the Germans as the principal O.P. for their guns, the formidable 88s.

At this point the Jed teams were recalled to London (team Giles went back on a British Navy minesweeper) for debriefing. After writing reports on our activities in France we were kept on hold in London week after week, playing interminable games of poker for high stakes and keeping the proprietors of the local black-market nightclubs happy. At one point we were alerted to take part in Operation Market Garden, the ill-fated attempt to seize the Dutch Rhine crossings, but in the end the teams with Dutch officers jumped in, ahead of the main body. Finally we were loaded into a Liberty ship that had been (very poorly) converted for troop transport; it tied up in the Hudson River one night in late November.

We were to disembark next morning and entrain for Washington—so we were told by an OSS colonel who came aboard to brief us. Buses would take us to Pennsylvania Station; once there we would board a special train. Under no circumstances were we to try to communicate with relatives or friends; this was a *secret* troop movement. Nobody questioned this ridiculous announcement; we were by now familiar with the comic cloak-and-dagger routines of our employers. But the moment we reached the station the next morning everyone ran for the public telephones. My wife was living in an apartment uptown; as soon as I got through to her she said, "I'm coming down there right away," and rang off. She told me afterwards that she tore out of the apartment with nothing but her purse. About twenty minutes later, as we milled around on the platform and the porter started calling, "All aboard," I heard a sudden commotion and voices calling: "Hey, Bernie, here's your wife." And there she was. It had been almost two years since we had seen each other. The train started to move, and we swept her aboard to join the secret troop movement. Later I had to introduce her to the colonel. He took it very well, acted as if she had just happened to be in Penn Station at the time. In fact, once we reached Washington he got us a room in a downtown hotel;

the rest of the Jeds were whisked off to the OSS base Area X (otherwise known as the Congressional Country Club).

Most of the Jeds were sent off to the China-Burma-India theater, where, on missions similar to those they had accomplished in France, they were jumped into China, Burma, and what was later to be known as Vietnam. But a few, and I was among them, were sent back to Europe. Apparently I was needed in a hurry; I was flown over. (It took longer in those days than it does now; on our way to Casablanca we stopped for refueling at Gander and the Azores.) My orders were sealed, and on the outside of the envelope there was a typed notice: "Not to be opened until the aircraft reaches a height of 10,000 feet." "Hollywood again," I thought, as I asked the sergeant flight attendant to let me know when we reached 10,000 feet. He thought I was crazy until I showed him the envelope, and then he thought, and stated his opinion in no uncertain terms, that the people running the war were crazy. But he got on the intercom to the pilot. About five minutes later he gave me a thumbs-up signal. I opened the envelope. "Your destination," the orders began, "is Naples, Italy." Apparently the OSS moguls in Washington figured that anyone who could speak French could also speak Italian. I saw why they had insisted on keeping me in the dark until I was off and away; they knew that if I had read the orders at the field before takeoff I would have rushed to a phone to tell them they had made a mistake.

As it turned out, I learned Italian quickly; Latin, French, and an early immersion in Dante were a great help (though my Spanish was a hindrance, continually leading me astray with near resemblances—*frente* for *fronte*, *fuego* for *fuoco*, and so on). And I was soon—after a long trip north to Florence through a devastated landscape of blown bridges and wrecked buildings, dismal in the winter rains—in charge of a large Italian partisan formation in the mountains that divide Tuscany from the Po Valley. I was not behind the lines this time but, so to speak, between them. On the west-central sector of the front facing the German Gothic Line, German demolition squads had blocked the few passes through the mountains; no serious offensive was feasible, for either side. The main battle, when it came in April 1945, took place on the coast, above Viareggio and, more important, on the approaches to the Futa Pass into Bologna. American Fifth Army was short of men, since it had been stripped of some of its best divisions for the invasion of southern France the previous summer; it did not want to waste its meager reserve watching the long mountain line. So the partisans, who had come over from the Po Valley after their premature rising in the summer of 1944 had been suppressed, were armed, fed, clothed (in G.I. uniforms but without insignia), and put under the supervision of OSS units to hold the front from Barga in the west to Porretta Terme in the east.

My base was at San Marcello Pistoiese, a winter resort in peacetime; our forward positions were mountain peaks that faced the even higher peaks held by the Germans. At night our partisans, many of whom had been smugglers before the war and knew unmapped paths through the mountains, ran patrols deep into the German rear areas; occasionally we came back with prisoners. We were given a role in the April offensive: to capture the heights immediately opposite and occupy the small town of Fanano. We did this without too many casualties and then pushed on northward through the mountains on foot, wading across rivers, fighting German rearguard units left in the villages; it seemed like a war from an earlier century—no gas-driven vehicles, no aircraft, no radio or telephone communications. We did not link up with American troops until we reached Modena in the valley.

It was in one of those rearguard actions that I was suddenly reminded of the classical heritage I had turned my back on. Taking cover in a ruined house (the Germans had a heavy machine gun covering the street, and we were waiting for a flanking party to take it out), I saw in the debris a handsome, gilt-edged book lying under a patina of brick dust and broken glass. One word of its long title was legible: MARONIS. It was a text of Virgil, printed on expensive heavy paper, one of a series of classical texts issued by the Royal Italian Academy to celebrate the greatness of ancient (and modern) Rome; the title page bore the improbable heading, in Latin, IUSSU BENEDICTI MUSSOLINI—"By Order of Benito Mussolini." My first idle thought as I reached out for the book was: "I wonder if I can still read this stuff." And then I remembered that in medieval Europe, when Virgil was thought to have been a great magician, people used his book as a sort of I-Ching. The *Sors Virgiliana*—Virgilian lottery—it was called. You opened the book at random, and the passage you put your finger on foretold your future. King Charles I once consulted Virgil in the Bodleian Library at Oxford, where driven from London by the Parliamentarians, he was holding court during the civil war. He drew a passage from Dido's curse on Aeneas, in Book IV; except for the final detail—"lie unburied"—it was an accurate forecast:

> May he be harried by war, by a people daring in arms, be exiled from his lands, and beg for help as he sees his closest friends die untimely deaths. And then, after he submits to the conditions of an unjust peace, let him not even then enjoy the throne or even dear life but let him fall before his time and lie unburied on the sand.

Hoping for better luck than that, I opened the book and stabbed my finger at a line. What I got was not a prophecy; it was a cry of agony—the last lines of the first Georgic.

> Here right and wrong are reversed; so many wars in the world, so many faces of evil. The plow is despised and rejected; the farmers marched off, the fields untended. The curving sickles are beaten straight to make swords. On one side the East moves to war, on the other, Germany. Neighboring cities tear up their treaties and take to arms; the vicious war god rages the world over.

> Quippe ubi fas versum atque nefas; tot bella per orbem
> tam multae scelerum facies, non ullus aratro
> dignus honos, squalent abductis arva colonis,
> et curvae rigidum falces conflantur in ensem.
> Hinc movet Euphrates, illinc Germania bellum;
> vicinae ruptis inter se legibus urbes
> arma ferunt; saevit toto Mars impius orbe.

These lines, written some thirty years before the birth of Christ, expressed, more directly and passionately than any modern statement I knew of, the reality of the world I was living in: the shell-pocked, mine-infested fields, the shattered cities and the starving population of that Italy Virgil so loved, the misery of the whole world at war. And there was in fact a sort of prophecy in it. "On one side the East moves to war." I did not know it yet, but the unit in which I served was to be selected for a role in the main Japanese landing, which was already in the planning stage. In this case, luckily for all of us, the Virgilian oracle was wrong.

It was time to move up. I tried to get the book into one of my pockets, but it was too big and I threw it down. But as we ran and crawled through the rubble I thought to myself: "If I ever get out of this, I'm going back to the classics and study them seriously."

The German surrender found us in Verona; the Adige, swollen by spring rains, raced past the piers of its dynamited bridges. Eventually, as planned, we were shipped home for a month's leave, with orders to report to APO San Francisco for the Far East and the coming Japanese landing. The military authorities had decided that since we had done such good work with what they called the "party-jans" in Italy (they had given our unit a citation), we could do equally well in Japan. Our commanding officer had come back from an interview with the commanding general shaking his head in wonder. When he had asked what we were supposed to do, the general had looked at him as if he were a moron and said: "Same thing you do here, son. You hit the beach with the first wave and make contact with the party-jans." Luckily for us, we didn't have to try; the Japanese surrender and the atomic bomb saved us. I was demobilized in September 1945 and, taking advantage of the generous terms of the G.I. Bill, began graduate work in classics at Yale in the spring of the next year. In 1948 I was awarded a doctorate and appointed instructor in the classics department. And so, though no fatted calf was produced (instructors' salaries in 1948 were not exactly princely), the prodigal son returned after ten years in a far country.

Virgil was my obsession and the subject of my first scholarly article. I sent an offprint of it to Charles, only to have it returned with a note from the college saying he had died of a heart attack a few months before. He had written a letter to back up my application to Yale in 1945 (my record did not look especially brilliant at that point), and I was saddened to think that he had not lived to see some evidence that his confidence had not been misplaced nor his many kindnesses wasted on me.

As I moved through the ranks of instructor and then assistant professor, teaching, for the most part, the classics in translation, the same shock of recognition I had experienced in northern Italy recurred, even stronger this time, as I read and taught Thucydides in the forties and fifties as the Greek civil war reenacted the heroism and horrors of the Peloponnesian War and, on a global scale, the Cold War aligned the opposing camps in the tense, fragile balance analyzed so brilliantly in Thucydides' introductory book. It seemed to me that there was no better key to an understanding of the modern world's power

Introduction xxxiii

struggles than this unfinished history of a war fought twenty-five hundred years ago between two states whose combined population was less than half a million. And in Greek tragedy, which became the focus of my scholarly work and teaching, I found the same modernity, the same immediacy. The figure of Oedipus, the man who knew the answer to the riddle of the Sphinx but not his own identity; Prometheus, champion of mankind's material progress, crucified on a mountainside but unyielding in his defiance of oppressive power; Antigone, a girl who without help or encouragement challenged the power of the state and buried her brother's body, though she knew the penalty was death—all these were compelling images of the human condition in the twentieth century. I remembered often the man in Lewis Carroll's poem who "thought he saw a rattlesnake, / that questioned him in Greek. / He looked again and found it was / The Middle of Next Week." Though it had taken me a long time, I had finally realized that when you read Thucydides, or Sophocles, or any of the great Greek writers, you may think you see an ancient text that speaks to you in Greek. You look again, and find it is The Middle of Next Week.

Postscript

William Casey's account of his service as head of the London and Paris offices of the O.S.S. in World War II—*The Secret War against Hitler* (Washington, D.C.: Regnery Gateway, 1988)—contains the following sentence (p. 129): "The stone viaduct at Morlaix was held by Bernard Knox's Jedburgh team Giles, beefed up by 100 SAS troops." This statement is inaccurate in every particular. The only SAS personnel in our sector were three French officers who had been parachuted onto one of our grounds (we knew them only by their code names— Egalité, Equivalence, for example), and the first time I saw the viaduct at Morlaix was in 1953, when I returned to Brittany after the war. Morlaix was in any case in the territory of team Hilary, Captain Philip Chadbourn of the U.S. and Captain Edgar Mautaint of the French Army.

Mr. Casey, as Director of the C.I.A., must have had access to the detailed operations reports submitted by the U.S. Jeds immediately on their return to London; in any case, they have since been published in microfiche form. A glance at my report or Phil Chadbourn's would have been enough to get the record straight. I suspect, however, that what he used was a secondary source.

In a volume entitled *The Commandos* by Russell Miller, published in 1981 as one of a series of Time-Life Books (Alexandria, Va.) on World War II, there is an account of SAS and Jedburgh operations in Brittany in the summer of 1944. The relevant passage begins on page 158.

> On August 2, some 100 French commandos from the 3rd SAS were dropped near Morlaix to seize the great stone viaduct spanning the gorge at the town's edge. They attacked immediately and after a brief fire-fight took the viaduct.
>
> At dawn the next morning about 1,000 men from the German 2nd Parachute Division moved towards Morlaix with orders to recapture and destroy the viaduct, blocking the American advance on Brest. Shortly before 10 A.M., as the column was leaving the little town of Châteaulin, it ran into an ambush organized by Jed officer Bernard Knox.
>
> Knox had 2,000 maquis hidden in the bushes on both sides of the road. Before dawn he and his men had scattered hundreds of "tire busters"—mines disguised as cow dung—across the road. Knox held his men in check as the Germans came trudging up the road behind their slow-moving trucks and guns. When the lead vehicle struck the first mine and burst into flames, the maquis attacked with bazookas, light machine guns and grenades. Within minutes, 30 Germans lay dead and 20 had been wounded. Those who fled into the fields were pursued by maquis killing squads, on forays they referred to as "Boche hunts." The shattered German column was forced to abandon its mission and the viaduct remained in the hands of the SAS and the maquis. American armor rolled on to Brest.

This sounds more like what actually happened, though the writer has tarted his account up with some of the clichés of the Hollywood Resistance film, in which the lead vehicle always bursts conveniently into flames. We did not use tire busters on this occasion; the Germans, for one thing, were no longer deceived by them, and for another, they were now so short of gasoline that most of their transport was horse drawn. We did not have anything like two thousand Maquisards concentrated in one place until much later in the campaign, when the Germans had retreated into Brest and Lorient, and we were advancing up the Presqu'île de Crozon. We certainly did not place Maquis troops on both sides of the road; if we had done so, they would have been shooting each other as well as the Germans. And the idea that a force of one thousand seasoned troopers of the 2nd Parachute Division, veterans of many months on the Russian front, could be routed and dispersed in panic after an engagement in which they sustained a mere fifty casualties is downright ludicrous. The Germans were much tougher than that; they did turn back on this occasion, but after the initial surprise, they rallied, reformed, and fought their way out.

Otherwise, this account is accurate enough, though I did not at the time suspect (and am not completely convinced even now) that this particular German unit was headed for Morlaix. What does seem likely, since this is the only evidence for a connection between team Giles and Morlaix, is that Mr. Casey's sentence is based on a blurred reminiscence of the passage in the Time-Life book.

Greek Literature & Society

Work and Justice in Archaic Greece: Hesiod's Works and Days

If you take the road north from Athens, not the new double highway, the so-called NATO road, but the old road, the Sacred Way, you come first to Eleusis, once the home of the Mysteries and now the site of a huge cement works, its tall plumes of white smoke visible for miles. Here you turn north into the hills. The road rises, gently at first and then more steeply. The ruins of a fourth-century fortress on the right-hand side of the road—Yiftokastro (Gypsy Castle) the Greeks call it, but it was once called Eleutherae or Panakton—remind you that you are in a frontier area. And soon you come to the frontier. From the summit of the pass of Dryoskephali (Oaktop pass), 650 meters above sea level, the road plunges down in a series of zigzags and hairpin bends to the plain below. This was indeed a bitterly contested frontier for centuries; control of this pass and of others to the southwest was disputed by Thebes and Athens as long as the two cities were independent city-states. From the high escarpment on which you stand you can see to the west the summit of Kithairon (where Oedipus was sent to die but was saved by shepherds); far off to the northwest, the great bulk of Parnassos, Apollo's mountain, is faintly visible (though his famous shrine at Delphi is hidden on the southwestern slope). Below you is the territory of Boeotia; directly ahead, to the north, lies its principal city, the legendary seven-gated city of Thebes. Its inhabitants, according to the Athenians, were stupid and crude in manner—"Boeotian pigs," they called them (and the adjective *Boeotian* can still be used in English as a literary insult); but from this area came two of the greatest poets of Greece, Pindar and Hesiod. And to the west, as you stand at the summit of the pass, is the mountain mass of Helikon, where, so Hesiod tells us in the *Theogony*, his account of the birth of the gods, the Muses summoned him to the profession of poetry as he tended sheep on the lower slopes.

This essay originally appeared in *Thought* 57, no. 226 (1981).

The *Theogony* is not the only product of this meeting between poet and Muse; Hesiod also composed a long poem about men, the *Works and Days*, which deals with the unceasing labor demanded by the land—plowing, sowing and reaping—and also the signs which announce the proper seasons for those operations. The language and meter of both poems is that of the Homeric epics; Hesiod, like Homer, draws on the formulas created by many generations of illiterate oral bards. But though he composed for oral recitation (he tells us himself of a prize he won for singing at the funeral games for a king), there is one feature of his poetry which suggests strongly that it was written down during the lifetime of its author. He is the first Greek poet to insist on his own identity; he does so firmly and repeatedly and he also expresses personal opinions on moral and social problems. It is the nature of fully oral poetry that the singer recreates the song at each performance; he does so as the anonymous servant of the Muse, who is the repository of age-old knowledge and the techniques of the oral tradition. Hesiod's solid presence in his work (the *Theogony* begins with an account of his meeting with the Muses on Mount Helikon and the *Works and Days* is addressed to his lazy, greedy brother, Perses) suggests that he expected the poems to be handed on in the form he had given them, securely identified as his work. The most reasonable explanation for such confidence seems to be that the text of the poems was fixed in writing.

There is another feature of the *Works and Days* which speaks tellingly for the idea that it was composed to be written down. The oral epic bard has at his disposal not only the formulas, themes and set scenes which can be combined with improvisations as he makes the song new; he has also a firmly fixed story line, a narrative thread to follow. Once he starts he knows where he is going, and so does his audience. When at the court of Alcinous, Odysseus asks the bard for a song, he says:

> Come to another part of the story, sing us
> the wooden horse, which Epeios made with Athene helping,
> the stratagem great Odysseus filled once with men and brought it
> to the upper city, and it was these men who sacked Ilion.
> If you can tell me the course of all these things as they
>   happened,

> I will speak of you before all mankind, and tell them
> how freely the goddess gave you the magical gift of singing.
> (VIII 492–98)[1]

The story was *there;* you could ask for any part of it, start anywhere. "Beginning from somewhere here, goddess," says Homer to the muse at the beginning of the *Odyssey*—and everyone knew where it was going. But suppose you asked an oral bard: "Sing me the song of Hesiod and his brother Perses, begin where . . ." Yes, where? The thing has no real beginning or end; there is no story line to guide the bard. The only way to preserve such a song in an oral tradition is to learn it by heart. Which means that the text was fixed, and there is only one sure way to fix it—by writing.

There is no doubt, however, that as a poem it is lacking in that architectonic quality which strikes every reader of the Homeric epics. Those poems may sometimes seem to digress, sometimes dwell too long on one scene, sometimes repeat a theme a little tediously, but that they have a beginning, middle and end in the full sense of Aristotle's famous definition no one can doubt. About the *Works and Days* on the other hand, there is plenty of room for doubt. Pausanias, who in the second century A.D. wrote the first guidebook to Greece, tells us (IX.31.4) that "the Boeotians living around Helikon hand down the tradition that Hesiod wrote nothing but the *Works and Days* and even from that they take away the prelude to the Muses, saying that the lines about strife are the beginning of the poem" (that is, our line 11). So much for the beginning; as for the end, the *Days,* one critic after another condemns these lines as spurious. To quote a recent influential history of Greek literature, they are "in form and narrow superstitious spirit so strikingly at variance with their context that they cannot be assigned to Hesiod."[2] Nor has the middle been spared; the latest edition, the Oxford text of Friedrich Solmsen,[3] comes with an *apparatus criticus* which abounds with such notes as *suspecta,*

---

1. All translations from Hesiod and Homer cited in this essay are by Richmond Lattimore: *Hesiod* (Ann Arbor: University of Michigan Press, 1959), and Homer, *The Odyssey* (New York: Harper & Row, 1965).

2. Albin Lesky, *A History of Greek Literature,* trans. (from the German) J. Willis and Cornelius de Heer (New York: Crowell, 1966), p. 103.

3. *Hesiodi Theogonia Opera et Dies Scutum,* ed. F. Solmsen (New York: Oxford University Press, 1970).

expulsit, traiecit, damnavit, delevit, proscripsit, dubitavit, seclusit. Scholars have for years tried to make a logical discourse of this poem by cutting, rearranging and rewriting.

The trouble is they are asking too much of it. They are asking it to be a logical progression (as the Homeric poems are a narrative progression); they are treating it as if it were a practical handbook on agriculture or a poem about justice with a consistent argument. And judged by that criterion it fails to live up to elementary standards of logic, structural coherence, inner consistency and relevance. It must be judged, of course, by quite other standards. It is the first attempt in Western literature to compose a large-scale work without the armature of a given narrative line. It is, in fact, an extraordinarily bold venture; what we should do is admire its successes, not chastise its defects. In his other long extant poem, the *Theogony,* Hesiod had a genealogical line to follow which was itself a sort of narrative thread; in the *Catalogue of Women,* he simply added one story of a famous mythical woman to another. Such a poem needed no structure and could obviously go on as long as anyone wished to hear it; what is more, the episodes could be arranged in any order. But the *Works and Days* has a purpose: to explain why life is a ceaseless round of labor and to offer advice which will make that labor profitable and tolerable. It does this in a dramatic framework: Hesiod's quarrel with his brother Perses.

For this extraordinary poem a recent editor, M. L. West,[4] has provided an illuminating context: the genre known as "wisdom literature." It is familiar to most of us from the Old Testament, but Professor West has assembled parallels also from the Sumerian, Akkadian, Egyptian, Persian and Indian literatures of the ancient world as well as more modern examples from Medieval Irish, Middle English, Old French, Norse and Finnish—not to mention exotic specimens from Basutoland, Uganda and the Torres Straits of New Guinea. In many of these texts there is a dramatic framework: the proverbial advice and instructions are presented as spoken by a father to a son, for example. But some of the texts are phrased as advice to a ruler and still others purport to be the complaint of a victim of injustice.

All this comparative material suggests that Hesiod is either follow-

4. M. L. West, *Hesiod. Works and Days* (New York: Oxford University Press, 1978).

ing a Middle Eastern model (as we know he did in a famous passage of the *Theogony*) or else that some such dramatic form is an almost inevitable medium for this kind of discourse. In Hesiod's hands, however, the device becomes much more dramatic and alive; instead of a fictional vizier, father or the like, he speaks in his own person, identifying himself, his home and his father; the recipient of his advice is his lazy brothers Perses, who has wronged him. Some of the advice is directed at the kings, who have supported Perses by giving crooked judgments. Hesiod thus manages to combine all three of the elements characteristic of this type of literature—advice to a relative, address to a king, from a victim of injustice. And he provides a setting for the advice which, unlike the barely sustained, almost impersonal fictions of the Eastern father or vizier, is extraordinarily effective: the lazy brother Perses, hanging around the agora listening to quarrels with an eye to his advantage, and Hesiod's father, who:

> used to sail in ships, for he wanted to live like a noble,
> and once on a time, leaving Kyme of Aeolis, he came here
> in his black ship, having crossed over a vast amount of water;
> and it was not comfort he was fleeing, nor wealth, nor prosperity,
> but that evil poverty that Zeus gives to men for a present;
> and settled here near Helikon in a hole of a village,
> Askra, bad in winter, tiresome in summer, and good at no season.
>
> (*Works and Days* 634–40)

Some critics have of course assumed that Perses and the story of the quarrel is a fiction, but no one has gone so far as to doubt the existence of this father; and it seems unlikely that Hesiod would add a fake brother to a real father. And the quarrel between brothers over inherited land is so constant an element of Greek life, from the mythical quarrel of Eteocles and Polynices to the orations of Isaeus in the law courts of the fourth century, that nothing in fact could be more true to life.

So much for the framework; the content however is still advice and rather unwelcome advice at that: to acquiesce in the grim necessity of unceasing labor. To this is added some instruction which will help to avoid the irremediable disaster of a crop failure. But the first part of the poem is concerned with the necessity for hard work, which, far from being welcomed as good for the soul, is viewed as a curse. This is the gruelling year-round business of working the land: hard, brutalizing labor, monotonous, exhausting—demanding, too, for a mistake or neglect in the fall can mean starvation in the spring. This is the incessant round of toil which mankind in the modern world has turned its back on whenever and wherever it could, to flock into cities where life may be poor, miserable and unsafe but no longer consists of uninterrupted manual labor—that peasant existence which has been the lot of the unsung majority of the human race for most of its history, that bondage which Karl Marx, in a rare compliment to the bourgeoisie, condemned as "the idiocy of rural life."[5]

In the first part of his poem Hesiod attempts to explain why this hard labor is the destiny of man before he goes on to suggest ways in which it may be endured. The explanation will of course be expressed in mythical terms, but Hesiod begins with some admonitions to his brother Perses, who is summoned to settle fairly the issue already joined between them. Perses has taken more than his fair share of the estate inherited from their father and has bribed the kings, the local nobility, to judge unfairly in his favor. But suddenly, without any logical transition, Perses and the corrupt judges are dismissed as fools "who have never learned how much better than the whole the half is." It is obviously not; what this proverbial phrase (for so it became) must mean is that those who try for the whole will end with nothing; "half a loaf," in our proverb, "is better than no bread." *How* the gift-eating kings will come to nothing is not revealed; Hesiod leaves us only with the repeated declaration of faith in the ultimate justice of Zeus.

Half, says Hesiod, is better than the whole, than nothing; this half is characterized as "living on mallow and asphodel." Mallow is not the marshmallow of the type roasted by Girl Scouts; it is a rather un-appetizing plant that could serve as a substitute for bread but only in poverty or famine. And no one should be misled by the English poetic associations of asphodel—Milton's "to inbathe / in nectared lavers strewed with asphodel" or Pope's "happy souls who dwell / in yellow meads of asphodel / or amaranthine bowers"; it is a spiky, rattail-

---

5. "Die Bourgeoisie hat die Zahl der städtlichen Bevölkerung gegenüber der ländlichen in hohem Stande vermehrt und so einem bedeutenden Teil des Bevölkerungs dem Idiotismus des Landlebens entrissen." *Das Kommunistisches Manifest,* 1848.

shaped plant which grows on stony ground; its root, a huge, hard onionlike affair, could, according to the ancient physician Galen, be made edible by repeated boiling and soaking, but nobody ate it except as a last resort. This half that is better than the whole is no picnic; rogues may come to grief in the end, but meanwhile honest men starve. It could have been better, says Hesiod. You might have been able to work one day and eat all year on the produce, hang up your steering oar, stay at home content. But the gods decided otherwise. They have hidden the good life and keep it hidden.

The reason for their decision is contained in the famous myth of Prometheus, Epimetheus and Pandora. Zeus hid the secret of an easy life in anger at Prometheus, who had cheated him; he made the division of the sacrificial animal's flesh in such a way that Zeus got the bones concealed under a layer of fat and mankind got the meat. Zeus punished mankind by hiding fire, but Prometheus stole it and gave it back to them. For Prometheus, Zeus devised a spectacular punishment, but he did not forget the human race. For them he created Pandora, the first woman. And she is responsible for the present state in which good living is hidden, as fire once was, and has to be won, if it can be won at all, by unceasing work.

Woman as the source of all our ills is of course a familiar idea because it is a powerful and influential Hebrew myth, which through the Fathers of the Church (who compared Eve to Pandora) was grafted onto Christianity (I say grafted, because there is no trace of misogyny in the sayings of Christ in the New Testament—quite the contrary). But this misogynistic mythology is not the exclusive property of the Greeks and Hebrews. It is typical of peasant societies and reflects a peasant attitude: though a woman is necessary if one is to have a son, she may also produce a daughter (or even two) who besides being a useless mouth will also require a dowry if she is to be married off. But of course woman has her attractions too, and Zeus in fact calls her "an evil all men shall fondle . . . close to their hearts, and take delight in." Made from the earth by the smith god Hephaestus, she has the face of an immortal goddess, the weaving skills of Athene, the sexual attraction of Aphrodite, but the mind of a hussy—and a treacherous nature. She has everything—so she is called Pandora, All Gifts, because all the gods gave her a gift. And she was accepted as a gift by Epimetheus (Afterthought), the foolish brother of Prometheus. Once inside the house she took the great lid off the storage jar, and all the evils men have been plagued with ever since flew out into the world. The lid was closed down before Hope (the Greek word is *Elpis*) could get out, but all the others did—troubles and sicknesses which come silently in the night.

The story is one of the most familiar Greek myths, though it has been popularly known for centuries in a distorted form. Pandora's box, we say—*la boîte de Pandore*, say the French, and the Germans, *Die Büchse der Pandora*—and it is often imagined (and portrayed in art) as a small box Pandora brings with her from Zeus. In the Greek it is a *pithos* and nobody arrives bringing a *pithos;* it is a storage jar, one of those huge jars, over five feet high and set in the ground, which can still be seen in the palace at Knossos. The box is due to Desiderius Erasmus, who made a widely read Latin version of the story in his *Adagia* and translated *pithos* as *pyxis;* Dora and Erwin Panofsky have published a fascinating book about the strange fortunes and immense influence of this mistranslation in European art.[6]

The *pithos* means that the evils were already there; what Pandora did was to let them out. We are not told why she took the lid off; unlike the Hebrew Eve, she is given no motive. She does not need one; it was the will of Zeus that man should live in toil and trouble. "There is no way," Hesiod concludes the story, "to avoid what Zeus intended." And what about hope? There have been prodigies of interpretation lavished on this passage to make it mean something more than what it plainly states. Since *Elpis*, a Greek word which means something like "expectation," can be either a good thing, sustaining courage in adversity, or a bad thing, leading men on to rashness and disaster, some have thought that Hope was the bad kind and the fact that she was shut in the *pithos* and did not escape with the other evils is a mercy. Others take it that Hope is a good—the only thing that can sustain mankind in a world of evils—and that it is loose among men. This means however that while the evils are among men because they got out of the *pithos*, Hope is among men because it got shut in. It is hard to see how such a position can be maintained, and I prefer to believe that Hope is indeed a good thing for man and that it is denied him, shut in the jar—his position is hopeless. For this is, after all,

---

6. Dora and Edwin Panofsky, *Pandora's Box* (Princeton: Princeton University Press, 1962).

the situation described at the end of the next myth, the story of the five ages.

The Prometheus story is a grim one if that is what it means. But this myth has at least one advantage over the Hebrew version. The misery in which man lives is not his own fault; it was the will of Zeus. The cause of that ill will was the action of Prometheus, who was not a man, and the instrument of disaster was a creature made by Zeus expressly to bring it about. It was not even a man who let Pandora in; it was another Titan, Epimetheus. The myth absolves man of any responsibility for the evil of the world; it is enough that he has to live in it. Whereas the myth of Eden puts the blame squarely on the shoulders of the human race: we have only ourselves to blame. The development of that theme by Hebrew prophets and Christian theologians helped to produce that sense of sin, that burden of responsibility, which is one of the chief differences between the modern Western outlook and the ancient.

Not content with one explanation of the misery of the world, Hesiod announces that he will give us another. This is the famous myth of the five ages. It is a creation myth; Zeus and the Olympian gods create five successive generations of mortal men, of which we, the iron age, are the latest. The first, the golden age, was one of leisure, of no hard work or pain; the land yielded its harvest of its own accord. Next came the silver age: but now men were a hundred years a-growing and, when fully grown, raged in senseless crime against each other; they lived only a short time and did not worship the gods, so Zeus destroyed them. Third was the age of bronze, born from ashwood spears. They had bronze weapons and bronze houses, and they worked as bronzesmiths. But they destroyed each other and left the sunlight forever. Then Zeus created a fourth generation—the race of heroes, half gods—those who fought at seven-gated Thebes and at Troy. And then the fifth age, the iron age, our age. Hesiod wishes he had died before it or that he could be born after it. It gives no rest from work and pain, no end to weariness in the night. But Zeus will destroy this generation too when the time comes. He will do so when the genetic clock, so to speak, has run down, when children are born with gray hair. And when all civil order has vanished, to be replaced by turmoil, violence, envy, mockery. ("And there shall be no defense against evil.") We are back at the same point from which we started, where the first myth ended: with Hope shut in the jar, man's situation desperate.

These five ages have been a scholarly battleground ever since modern interpretation began. Is there a real historical memory behind it? Is it merely an adaptation of Near Eastern myths which also tell the story of degeneration in successive ages identified with metals? If so, what is the nonmetallic heroic age, the fourth, doing in the list? There is not much use pretending that Hesiod is thinking in modern terms of the Bronze and Iron ages; for one thing his own age used bronze as well as iron and so, clearly, did the Homeric heroes of the fourth age. And the gold and silver ages have to be passed over in silence. As for the Near Eastern parallels, though some of them are attested later than Hesiod, there is obviously some influence here; the resemblances can hardly be coincidental. The same four metals in the same order turn up in a Zoroastrian myth, and in the book of Daniel there is a statue made of five different metals, which, starting with gold, symbolize the degeneration of human life over five successive ages.[7] Given the other undeniable evidences of Hesiod's use of Near Eastern myth, we must assume that he is using some such model here. But, in typical Greek style, he tinkers with it. He wanted a symbolic scheme of degeneration to explain, as the Pandora myth does, why human life is so hard, but the Eastern metal-age myths ran smack into the difficulty that the Greek vision of the immediate past was a heroic one—the great heroes and demigods who fought at Thebes and Troy and who were the ancestors of kingly houses. Hesiod might have identified them with his third, bronze age, but that would not do; the heroes were "better and nobler," a "wonderful generation of hero men," and furthermore, after their death, they went to "a dwelling place in the islands of the blessed." So he simply inserted them where the Greeks always thought they came, immediately before the present generation. And although this disturbs the pattern of progressive degeneracy which is the essence of the Eastern models, it reinforces his main point—the misery of the present age, which emerges as all the more intolerable against the bright background of the heroic time of Troy. It suits his purpose, which is not to write a history of mankind but to put the harsh reality of the present world

---

7. West, pp. 174–75.

in a perspective which will justify the body of the poem, the grim lesson that only relentless, back-breaking work will guarantee survival. There is a poetic structure called a priamel, a list of good things capped by a supreme good—as in the opening lines of one of Sappho's poems: "Some say the finest thing on earth is a troop of horsemen, some say footmen and some a fleet of ships but I say it is the one you love." Hesiod's myth of the five ages is a priamel in reverse; he is saying: "the golden age was fine, but the silver was bad, and the bronze was worse and now iron is the worst of all." And his insertion of the heroes into the series just ahead of the iron age of labor in which he lives—and wishes he did not—makes the contrast even more painful.

We are in the iron age, not the final, apocalyptic stage of it but the one in which, though there is no end of work, pain, weariness and anxiety, yet, says Hesiod, there are some good things mixed with the bad. What they are he does not say yet, and he goes on to tell a story which makes the picture even darker. He has explained, speaking to Perses, the reasons for the hard way in which we live now; he follows with a story meant for the kings, one he says they will understand. It is the fable of the nightingale and the hawk. And it is a reminder that it is no use struggling against the powerful. "What is the matter with you?" says the hawk to her victim. "Your master has you. You shall go wherever I take you . . . for all your singing." With this mention of the kings, those gift-eating kings, we are returned to the framework of the poem, the quarrel with Perses, who has enlisted the corrupt kings on his side. And Hesiod now launches at last on an argument which brings some gleam of comfort in this world of despair he has sketched for us: the ways of justice, and his belief that Zeus somehow stands, in the end, for justice between man and man. For without some such belief, there would be nothing for it but to echo the wish with which he opened his description of the fifth, the iron age:

> I wish that I were not any part of the fifth generation
> of men, but had died before it came, or been born afterward.
> For here now is the age of iron.
>
> (*WD* 174–76)

With this fable Hesiod seems to have reinforced the lugubrious lesson taught by the myths of Pandora and the five ages: Zeus has abandoned men to a world in which might is right, justice the will of the powerful. "He is a fool," says the hawk, "who tries to match his strength with the stronger." And then, as if he had not ruled justice out of the world, Hesiod begins to talk about it, addressing his brother. "As for you, Perses, listen to justice. Do not try to practice violence."

The Greek word translated "justice"—*dike*—is a troublesome one, a word with a long history, an obsessive theme in archaic Greek literature. Its etymology is obscure, but when we first meet it, in Homer, it means something like "the way things are, the way things go." "This is the *dike* of godlike kings," says Penelope in the *Odyssey*. "They hate one man and love another." That's the way kings are. And the shade of Odysseus' mother says to him, in the world of the dead, "This is the *dike* of mortals when they die. The sinews no longer hold the bones and the flesh together." From this basic idea—the way things are, the way they regularly are—there seems to have developed an additional nuance: "the way they ought to be." What is normal, what is expected, is right; departures from regularity are wrong. And along these same lines the word *dike* (and also its plural) came to signify "rules of right, principles of what is right"; later the word described the process of setting to right—a trial, a law case—and it also came to mean the frequent result of such a trial, a law case—punishment, "justice" in the punitive sense. In Hesiod most of these senses are latent in the word; yet its basic meaning can be deduced from its opposites—*bia*, "force" and, as here in the advice to Perses, "violence." The Greek word for this is *hubris*, and although it came to mean simply physical violence, it also describes the mentality which allows and encourages violence—an overweening pride and sense of superiority, of invulnerability, of contempt for the rights of others. For the Greeks of Hesiod's peasant society (as for the peasant societies of the modern Greek countryside, and in fact the Mediterranean in general—Spain, Sicily, North Africa), this is the supreme, intolerable evil. For all such societies foster in the individual a fierce sense of his privileges, no matter how small, of his rights, no matter how confined, of his personal worth, no matter how low. And *hubris* is the mood which drives one man to deny another these elementary rights, to treat him as nothing, to show disrespect for his dignity as a man, to deprive him of his honor. These are the terms, of course—*honor, rispetto, philotimo*—which still govern relations between man and man in Mediterranean agricultural societies. And that is one reason why *hubris* brings retribution in the end: it drives its victims to desperation—they will think of nothing but revenge.

This *hubris*, says Hesiod, is dangerous for a weak man; it is not for such as Perses. But even the kings cannot indulge in it with impunity; they may fall prey to delusions, go too far—even for a king. For it is Justice which wins over violence when it comes out in the end. That phrase is enigmatic, in the Greek as in the English. And, of course, there is nothing to indicate when the "end" comes—in our lifetime? Or is it in the next generation that retribution comes for violence? But come it does, says Hesiod. And the foolish man realizes the truth after the suffering comes to him in his turn.

This is cold comfort for the present spectacle of injustice, graphically presented in the next few lines as Justice is dragged off and molested by bribe-taking judges who give crooked decisions, but it is at least a flash of light in the gloomy picture conjured up by the myths of Pandora and the five ages. And in the succeeding lines this flash becomes a steady gleam as Hesiod contrasts two communities: one "where men issue straight decisions," justice, to their own people and strangers, another "where men like harsh violence and cruel acts." In the first, where men deal in justice and do not step off the road of just action, the city flourishes and the people in it. They enjoy the blessings of peace "who bring boys to manhood," they escape famine and they do the work that they must do as if it were a holiday. The earth gives them great livelihood, their oaks give acorns and honey, their flocks are heavy with wool, their women bear children who resemble the fathers. They are so prosperous, in fact, that they do not need to go to sea to supplement their livelihood.

There is more than one touch in this radiant picture which recalls the happy state of the golden age, and the end of the iron age is recalled in the picture which follows—the fate of the city "where men like harsh violence and cruel acts." Zeus ordains their punishment—it is the same word *dike*—and often not for the crimes of the community, but for the crimes of one man. Famine and plague, the deaths of the people, the barrenness of women, the destruction of the city's army, fleet and fortifications in war—all these are the punishment inflicted by Zeus. The reminiscences of the first and last of the mythical ages are no accident; Hesiod here is posing the results of communal justice and injustice against each other in the extreme form appropriate for moral examples, and such dramatic pictures tend to take mythical shape. In real life nothing is so clear cut; but the plea for justice is best served by this pushing of the contrast to extremes.

Hesiod goes on to be more specific about the manner in which injustice is punished. It is not an automatic, natural process; it is brought about by the agents of Zeus, thirty thousand of them, immortal spirits who watch what men do. "Invisible in the darkness they hover over the whole earth." And Justice herself, Zeus's daughter, goes to his throne to complain when she is violently used and punishment comes. "Beware," says Hesiod to the kings, "of such spirits . . . , for the eye of Zeus sees everything. He is watching us right now; . . . he does not fail to see what kind of justice this city keeps inside it." Hesiod is so sure of this that he can conclude with a ringing declaration of faith:

> Now, otherwise I would not myself be righteous among men
> nor have my son be so; for it is a hard thing for a man
> to be righteous, if the unrighteous man
> is to have the greater right.
> But I believe Zeus of the counsels will not let it end thus.
>
> (*WD* 270–73)

And now, turning to Perses, he clinches this long tormented meditation on justice with a statement of the law as Zeus has established it for human beings:

> As for fish, and wild animals, and the flying birds,
>   they feed on each other, since there is no idea of justice among
>   them;
> but to men he gave justice, and she in the end is proved
>   the best thing they have.
>
> (*WD* 277–80)

This long discussion of the superiority of just dealing to injustice is hardly a logical argument; it seems at times even contradictory, but it is nonetheless a remarkable and moving poem. Armed only with poetic language and techniques which the epic bards developed for heroic narrative, Hesiod is struggling with concepts that border on the abstract; he is writing, in effect, ethical, not epic verse. And we can see the wandering progress of his mind at work. He announces in the prologue the power of Zeus, but it is power with only the slightest hint of ethical direction. When he tries to explain in mythical terms the present state of mankind bound to the incessant labor of the soil, he presents us with a Zeus who punishes mankind with the gift of Pandora, one who creates five successive races of which ours is the last and most miserable. But the fable of the hawk and the nightingale brings Hesiod out of the mythical world into the real one, a world of unjust decisions. And here the personified figure of Justice, as victim and avenger, is the daughter of Zeus, who favors the just and punishes the unjust. Late it may be, but in the end punishment comes. And even kings must beware of the ministers of Zeus.

This may not be logic but some such end to his argument is necessary, for he is now to return to the theme with which he started—work. And there is no point in working in a world without justice. Or perhaps we should say, in a world where it is impossible to believe in justice. For Hesiod can give us no proof that the justice of Zeus exists, only his firm belief. In this belief he turns to Perses now with advice which he will give over and over again: work "so that famine will avoid you" and so that your barn will be filled. It is from work that men grow rich. Work is no disgrace; in fact the disgrace is not working. Gains made without work, unjustly made, by force, stealing or lying, will not last; Zeus makes such men pay a bitter price. Work is the way to riches and so to nobility and honor. We have come all the way from work as a curse inflicted as punishment for the tricks of Prometheus to work as the mainstay of human life and the way to prosperity and honors. And here, too, the conclusion is not a logical development from what went before. It is the conclusion only in the sense that it is the final statement.

We should not, however, be looking for logic here. Aristotle has not yet invented the syllogism or excluded contradictions. Hesiod does not have to hand the distinctions which Plato was to work so hard at in the Socratic dialogues, the distinction between a particular instance and an underlying universal principle, for example. He has in fact no developed method of thinking at all. He is, like all his contemporaries, at a stage of development for which the French anthropologist Lévy-Bruhl once coined a phrase: "prelogical."

To present-day anthropologists of course that is a dirty word. It is felt to be condescending; "there are no superior societies" is the banner under which we march today. Actually Lévy-Bruhl did not claim his "prelogical" societies were inferior, only that they were different from us, that they thought differently. Faced with the obvious fact that the methods of thinking of many undeveloped tribes are indeed different from ours, modern anthropologists have tried hard to find and claimed to have found a logic in their apparently chaotic and arbitrary accounts of themselves and their societies; the classic example is the investigation by Claude Lévi-Strauss of the myths of the Bororos of Brazil and the Indians of the southwestern United States, in which, through breathtaking maneuvers and brilliant insights, he reveals a logic which is mathematical in its systematic rigor. Once the effect of the undoubtedly dazzling exposition has worn off, however, it is difficult to remember the stages of the argument or even, indeed, the conclusion. And it should also be added that the myths in question, especially those of the Bororos, are so arcane, arbitrary and chaotic that they resemble second-rate surrealist art or for that matter psychotic ramblings. To make any sense of them at all you *have* to produce some extraordinary system of interpretation like that of Lévi-Strauss.

Hesiod's myths and sayings are not like this; they are trying to say something clear and in our terms. But the discourse is "prelogical" in the pure, uncondescending sense Lévy-Bruhl gave the word: Hesiod is struggling with problems for which methods of thought have not yet been devised. And he is struggling with a problem which we, with all our logical resources, have not solved either: the existence of evil, of sorrow, of injustice in human life and society.

Hesiod can work only with the tools in hand, with myths for example. And if one doesn't fully explain the facts, he will give us two. He can combine with these elements stories and parables, proverbial expressions, gnomic precepts—"the half is better than the whole," "Give is a good girl, but Grab is a bad one"—to fight his way through to an attitude which enables him to go on living and to encourage others to do so. There *is* an ultimate justice in the world, he claims, and so labor is not a waste of effort; but the way that justice works he cannot explain and for its existence he can offer no real proof.

Work, of course, the *Works* of the title of the poem, means work on the land. For the context of Hesiod's poem is the countryside, the village of Askra, a remote village in a valley below Mount Helikon.

No one knows today exactly where it was; it was not big enough to leave any remains for the archaeologists to disinter. It is not what the later Greeks will call a *polis*. In fact the world evoked by Hesiod's poem is that of the age before the characteristic Greek state organization, the *polis*, based on a central place of refuge and the concentration of temples and places of business, came into existence.

The word does occur in the poem but never in any context involving its real business, work on the land; it appears always in general statements, as in the comparison of the two communities where, Hesiod says, Zeus will punish the unjust, "wreck their city with its walls, or their ships on the open water." This phrase suggests a picture widely different from that farming community Hesiod writes of, and some commentators think it is a reference not to any actual city, but to the mythical, epic city of Troy. It is true, in any case, that in Hesiod we are not in the world of the Greek *polis*. For the great ideal of that world is not work, but its opposite, *schole:* leisure, the leisure to walk in the city squares, to talk in the covered porches—those *stoas* which gave shade in summer and shelter in winter—to attend the assembly and listen to the orators, to follow the proceedings of the law courts—all those things in fact which Hesiod warns Perses against:

> Put all this firmly in your heart.
> Nor let that strife who loves mischief
> keep you from working
> as you listen at the meeting place
> to see what you can make of the quarrels. . . .
> Walk right on past the blacksmith's shop
> with its crowds and gossip. . . .
> (*WD* 27–29, 493–94)

Only in the exhausting heat of full summer, for a few weeks in June and July, when nothing can be done in the fields, does Hesiod allow leisure. All the rest of the year is work, which was, for the later Greeks of the *polis*, a thing to be avoided by any and every means. The necessity for work becomes in fact the class distinction which ranges the poor man with the slave over against the privileged *kaloi kai agathoi*—the good and beautiful people—the gentlemen, the young men who frequent the gymnasium and talk philosophy with Socrates, who drink and sing on the red-figure vases, who train for the great athletic contests. Hesiod's world is still a peasant world in which those who do not work do not eat. Except, of course, for those who lie, cheat and use violence.

And yet in this peasant society, before the full emergence of the *polis,* that Greek political unit which was to revolutionize the history of the West by its development of democratic concepts of law, Hesiod is already, more instinctively than by any process of thought, feeling his way toward such concepts, though he expresses them not explicitly, but in semimythical terms. How far he has come can best be seen by comparing the passage where he describes the just community and its prosperity with a similar passage in another work which must date from about the same period, Homer's *Odyssey.*

In Book XIX of that poem, Odysseus, disguised as a beggar, pays a compliment to his wife Penelope, who does not know who he really is:

> Lady, no mortal man on the endless earth could have cause
> to find fault with you; your fame goes up into the wide heaven,
> as of some king who, as a blameless man and god-fearing, . . .
> upholds the way of good government, and the black earth yields him
> barley and wheat, his trees are heavy with fruit, his sheepflocks
> continue to bear young, the sea gives him fish, because of
> his good leadership, and his people prosper under him.
> (*Odyssey* XIX.107–14)

This is doctrine older than Homer and very widespread in early times, the notion that the king's righteous conduct or divine favor or both was responsible for the prosperity of the land—and its converse, not mentioned in the *Odyssey,* that the king is also responsible for the sorrows of the land. (Among the Burgundians he could be deposed in case of defeat in battle or failure of the crops, and in Ireland a crop failure or a cattle blight was proof that the king must be a usurper, a false claimant to the throne.) Hesiod, too, could envisage a just king, as he does, not in this poem but in the *Theogony,* a king from whose mouth

> the words run blandishing, and his people
> all look in his direction as he judges their cases
> with straight decisions, and, by an unfaltering declaration
> can put a quick and expert end even to a great quarrel. . . .

as such a one walks through an assembly, the people adore him
like a god, with gentle respect . . .
(*Theogony* 84–87, 90)

But the kings of the *Works and Days* are not like that; they are the kings that devour gifts. And in Hesiod's vision of the righteous community there is no king at all.

But when men issue straight decisions to their own people
and to strangers, and do not step at all off the road of rightness,
their city flourishes, and the people blossom inside it. . . .
peace . . . is in their land nor does Zeus . . .
ever ordain that hard war shall be with them.
Neither famine nor inward disaster comes the way of the people
who are straight and just; they do their work as if work were a
  holiday;
the earth gives them great livelihood; . . .
their sheep . . . are weighted down with fleecy burdens.
(*WD* 225–34)

All the blessings the good king brings in the Homeric passage are here the blessings and the reward of a just people; in these lines justice is won by those who work, without benefit of kings or rulers of any kind.

It is only a vision, for in the next lines he addresses the kings, those eaters of bribes who have judged for his brother and against him, but it is a vision of the future, of a community making its own laws and dealing justly with its own citizens. And it is toward that ideal that the scattered Greek communities, as they grew and formed the political shape we know as the *polis*, struggled unevenly: the high point of the process was to be the Periclean democracy of late fifth-century Athens.

In Hesiod that is all far in the future; the present is a time of incessant toil on the land. And to the rules and seasons that govern that work he now turns, in the body of the poem, the part which gives it its name. He begins with some general precepts: work brings prosperity but prosperity obtained by theft and violence will not last and is punished by Zeus, as are a whole host of transgressions against accepted morality. One should refrain from such actions and sacrifice to the gods; the motivation for this piety is typical for a peasant mentality:

so they may have a complacent feeling and thought about you;
so you may buy someone else's land, not have someone buy
   yours.

                                                         (*WD* 340–41)

Cultivate your neighbors; they are quicker to come to your aid than relatives are. When you deal with your brother be pleasant—but get a witness (Hesiod should know; it is his brother who has cheated him). Don't let any sweet-talking woman beguile you; "It's your barn she's after." Have one son only; if you have more you had better live long to accumulate enough wealth for them. And in any case—work. "Keep on working, with work and more work." *ergon ep' ergo ergazesthai.*

This is the harsh reality of a world which is only rarely glimpsed in the rest of Greek literature. In the *Odyssey* the nearest we get to it is in the hut of the swineherd Eumaeus, but even he was once a prince, and he does not plow or reap. And in the great poets of the sixth and fifth centuries we lose sight of the land and its works and days; only in cosmopolitan Alexandria, among scholars and courtiers in the third century, will the country be the locale of poetry once again, but it is an artificial country, a bucolic fairyland. And yet we should not forget that under the brilliant surface of all Greek literature—Homer's heroic song of the wrath of Achilles, the aristocratic poetry of Sappho and Alcaeus, the celebrations of athletic victories in Pindar and Bacchylides, the tragedies of Aeschylus, Sophocles and Euripides—underneath all this, the indispensable condition of its existence, is the yearlong work on the land. And for the men who did that work, who scanned the night skies for the stars which marked the changing seasons, Hesiod was the supreme poet, the one who taught, as Aristophanes said later, "the day-after-day cultivation of the fields, the seasons, and plowings"[8] and who also, in the dim beginnings of Greek history, asked questions, still unanswered, about work and justice.

8. *Frogs* 1033–34.

Dogs and Heroes in Homer

It is a remarkable testimony to the fierce vitality of the literature which has survived from ancient Greece that no interpretation of it, however magisterial, goes unchallenged for very long; each new generation sees its own problems reflected in the ancient mirror and brings to the formulation of that vision the insights and terminology of new sciences, new critical vocabularies. Sometimes these reevaluations are attempted from the inside, by Greek scholars whose fresh understanding of the material in the light of modern psychological or anthropological insights is based on mastery of the Greek language and control of the vast scholarly literature which has increased in volume year by year since the Renaissance. E. R. Dodds's epoch-making *The Greeks and the Irrational* is such a book, and G. S. Kirk's work in the field of Greek mythology presents the same stimulating combination of professional expertise and new perspectives.

But often, too, the attempt is made from the outside, by social scientists whose knowledge of Greek is minimal or nonexistent and whose erratic maneuvers in the wilds of classical bibliography resemble the frantic struggles of a June bug trapped behind a window. Some malignant daimon always seems to guide these unfortunates to the most incompetent translations and the most diluted and vulgar popularizations of the subject. The results are all too like the familiar volume produced by the anthropologist or social scientist who has spent his sabbatical year with an African tribe or in a modern Greek village and, totally ignorant of the language, comes back to present to the world a series of pompous generalizations based on information supplied by the local English speaker, who is, by that very fact, a tainted source. Rhetorical balance demands, at this point, some names, but charity forbids; any Greek scholar can think of at least one recent production of this kind which, imposing itself on the un-

This essay originally appeared in the *New York Review of Books*, April 29, 1976.

suspecting public by the arrogance which cloaks its ignorance, proves once again that P. T. Barnum was a profound student of human nature.

James M. Redfield, who describes his *Nature and Culture in the Iliad*[1] as "an essay which stands between the humanities and the social sciences," is a professor in the Committee on Social Thought and the college at the University of Chicago. His father, Robert Redfield, was a famous professor of anthropology at the same university; he himself uses for his work the image of the social scientist in the field: "I have lived with these Homeric heroes so long that I have come to think of them the way an ethnographer thinks of his tribe—as 'my people' and"—he adds disarmingly—"I find much wisdom in them."

His claim to have lived long with them is fully vindicated by his performance. He knows the Homeric texts well; the literal translations (sometimes of long excerpts) are his own and they are, with some minor exceptions, accurate. (One interesting exception is his version of XXII.496, where he has mistaken for a feminine genitive form, with the sense "flourishing," a nominative which, ironically enough, is a technical kinship word meaning "a man with both parents living.") Redfield also knows his way around in the vast scholarly literature; his citations, from scholars writing in German, French, and Italian as well as English, are carefully chosen and economically deployed; they are always exactly what he needs to make or defend his point and no more. In addition, his own discussions of the Homeric words which denote psychological processes or social values are penetrating and useful. This book, which will hold the general reader's attention by its bold interpretations and the elegance of its prose, must also be taken seriously by the professional scholar.

It is an ambitious book. In addition to a fascinating exploration of the themes implied by the "nature" and "culture" of his title (deftly summarized on the dust jacket as "the role of the warrior and of women, the relations between humanity and the gods, the power of institutions and ceremonies, of games, assemblies, and funerals"), Redfield proposes a literary interpretation of the *Iliad* (based on a new reading of Aristotle's *Poetics*) which expands into nothing less than a general theory of the relation of tragedy (Redfield's subtitle is *The Tragedy of Hector*) to culture and society. The argument is long, subtle,

---

1. *Nature and Culture in the "Iliad": The Tragedy of Hector* (Chicago: University of Chicago Press, 1975).

and complicated, a structure of interlocking components so logically interdependent that the following attempt to present it in outline can hardly avoid omissions and consequent distortions, for which the reviewer apologizes in advance.

Redfield begins with the great speech of Achilles in which he refuses the offers of Agamemnon and his invitation to return to the battle. He rejects two current interpretations of Achilles' obstinacy, Bowra's and Whitman's, which claim respectively, in Redfield's paraphrases, that Achilles' refusal is a departure from the norms of his society, "a deviance properly punished and repented," and that "Achilles is a kind of existential hero who leaves the safe bounds of social convention and sets off on a quest for his true self—and who thus comes to confront the Absolute and the Absurd."

Redfield on the contrary sees Achilles in terms which "throughout the poem direct attention away from the hero's personality." Achilles' "actions are dictated by his situation." And this viewpoint is asserted for all the Homeric characters; they are seen as "embedded in a social fabric; they are persons whose acts and consciousness are the enactment of the social forces which play upon them." If this analysis seems to deprive Achilles of his significance as the central figure of the *Iliad*, "perhaps the problem is with us, with our conception of heroic grandeur." Taking now the viewpoint of the poet, he directs attention from character to plot, "that implicit conceptual unity which has given the work its actual form."

This rejection of the "pervasive assumption that the classic narrative must center on the inner experience of a single hero" is, as Redfield says, "somewhat parallel" to the approach of John Jones in his controversial *On Aristotle and Greek Tragedy*[2] and, like Jones, he finds support for his position in Aristotle's *Poetics* which, Jones says (and Redfield agrees), has been subjected "to systematic misreading." They both take their stand on Aristotle's sentence: "Tragedy is the imitation, not of human beings, but of action and life," and Redfield, quoting Jones's description of Aeschylus' Orestes as "isolated by his status-determined circumstances," suggests that the solitude of Achilles is similarly "status-determined."

There follow sixty-eight pages which in two chapters ("Imitation" and "Tragedy") go carefully over the all too familiar ground of the

2. New York: Oxford University Press, 1962.

Platonic theory of imitation and Aristotle's definition of tragedy—error, pity and fear, catharsis—in an attempt to trace "certain aspects of the problematic of narrative art from Homer down to Aristotle." There is much in these chapters which is new and which in its abstract but careful formulation has implications for literary criticism reaching far beyond the particular work under discussion (the section entitled "Nature and Culture in Fiction" is especially suggestive), but no adequate summary can be attempted. The most relevant point for Redfield's interpretation of the *Iliad* is recapitulated in a passage on page 91.

> The interpretation of error is the focus of the poet's inquiry. In his error the actor enacts the limitations and self-contradictions of his culture; through his imitation of error, the consequences of error, and the healing of error, the poet leads us, not to a rejection of culture, but to a reaffirmation of it on a new level of troubled awareness.

But the story of Achilles, though "certainly a tragedy in several meanings of that polyvalent term," is not a "tragic action in the narrow Aristotelian sense," for though "Achilles makes errors . . . the poet has not been at pains to construct a clear relation of cause and effect. . . . The crucial errors in Achilles' story . . . are the errors of others—of Agamemnon, of Nestor, of Patroclus." His tragedy is "not so much a tragedy of action as of reaction." Further, Achilles is "a marginal figure, half god, half man, suspended between the worlds." In fact, the "end of the *Iliad* is a ceremonial recognition of the monstrous singularity of Achilles"—he is "drawn into the divine community."

Hector's story however "is a tragic action in the classic mold, . . . the story of a man somewhat better than ourselves who falls through his own error. . . . the true tragic hero of the poem is a secondary character." Everyone will recognize the justice of the phrase Redfield uses to describe Hector, "a hero of responsibilities." Homer shows him in his relations with his wife and son, with his father and mother, with Helen and Paris, with all the Trojan warriors and their wives—all of these people dependent on him for their safety. In his tenderness to his wife, his kindness to Helen and even his brotherly scolding of Paris, we are shown a man as clearly supreme in the ways of peace as the brooding figure of Achilles on the beachhead, now isolated even from the male society of his fellow soldiers, is supreme in the ways of war. But Hector's duty now is to fight, and he does not shirk it. He "embodies the ideal norm of Homeric society."

But what is his error? Redfield finds it in the overconfidence he shows as, fulfilling in ignorance the will of Zeus, he carries the offensive into the Greek camp. He rejects the advice of Polydamas—who interprets an omen as a signal to retreat—leads an attack on the Greek ships, refuses advice to retreat into the city after killing Patroclus. According to Redfield he "has lost contact with that social order which defined and generated his heroism." Achilles now returns to the battle and the Trojans are routed. Hector, alone before the wall facing Achilles, rejects the appeal of his parents to take shelter; his knowledge that he has caused a Trojan defeat fills him with *aidos*, "shame"— "the characteristic emotion of the social man"—and he elects to fight Achilles, though he must know it means his death. "A hero who is preeminently responsive and responsible," Redfield sums up, "he is here defeated by his own characteristic goodness."

The last chapter, "Purification," deals with the resolution of the tragic dilemma posed by the action: the ransoming of Hector's corpse by Priam. Through an involved and brilliant discussion of ceremonies of purification (of which the funeral is the ultimate example, for it "purifies the dead man by setting a definite period to his existence and converting him into something not subject to change; . . . by the funeral the community purifies itself") Redfield proceeds toward his objective: "The Problem of Ending the *Iliad*." Earlier in the chapter Redfield makes the point that the threats to give the enemy's body to the dogs and birds, made ever more frequently as the fighting grows more savage, are the poet's introduction of "the limiting case of impurity" from which however he "draws back. . . . In the event, the two heroes most threatened with defilement—Patroclus and Hector— are properly mourned and buried."

The dog, in Homer, is a predator and scavenger; he is "the most completely domesticated animal . . . but . . . he remains an animal. The dog thus represents man's resistance to acculturation" and "stands for an element within us that is permanently uncivilized." The danger run by the warrior, who, according to Redfield, "stands on the frontier of culture and nature," is that he may become a dog—a transformation suggested often in the similes—and more, a cannibal. This is a theme often hinted at and finally brought into the open in Achilles' wish that he could bring himself to chop Hector's flesh and eat it raw (XXII.347).

> The dog is thus an emblem of the impurity of battle. The warrior becomes a mad dog as he enacts the inner contradiction of battle. On behalf of a human community the warrior is impelled to leave the community and act in an inhuman way. He becomes a distorted, impure being; great in his power, he is at the same time reduced to something less than himself.

Hector was a mad dog in the rage of battle but he is now a corpse. "To the passive impurity of Hector—marked by the impure condition of his body . . .—corresponds the active impurity of Achilles—marked by his inability to find any limit to his act."

The purification of both the dead man and the living hero is a problem beyond human capacity; it is brought about by divine intervention. Achilles is persuaded by his goddess-mother's entreaty and the command of Zeus to accept the ransom brought by old Priam in the night. And in his reconciliation with Priam, his recognition of their common loss, Achilles comes "to know his situation and no longer merely experience it." He "surveys and comprehends his world and himself. That is the purification of Achilles."

By this purification through the ceremony of their common meal (Achilles' first since the death of Patroclus), "culture is overcome." The community had failed to move Achilles; "the reconciliation takes place on the level of nature, outside the human world; it is a ceremony founded on a universal concept of man *qua* man." And it is contrived by the poet: "the *Iliad* comes to a conclusion, not because the action imitated reaches a resolution, but because the poet has conferred on the event, in the manner of his telling it, a form and an ending." And now Redfield returns us to Aristotle. "In tragic art, the pains and terrors of life are transformed from experiences to objects of knowledge; tragic art attains to form when it makes a lucid theoretical statement of the practical opacities of the human condition. In this sense tragic form is a 'purification of these experiences.'"

This is a painfully inadequate outline of an argument which is both intensely theoretical and richly concrete; the book must be read in its entirety to yield the wealth of insight it offers. But the summary may serve as the base for some critical observations.

Redfield starts out by begging a question—a very big one, the Homeric question itself. His "premises are broadly Unitarian," he says, but so are those of almost everyone nowadays; there is general agreement that "Homer" is the monumental composer who at a late stage of a centuries-old tradition of oral composition gave the *Iliad* something like the shape in which we now read it. But when? It is a difficult problem. As Redfield points out, M. I. Finley, in his *World of Odysseus* (see pp. 35ff.), an attempt to reconstruct a "society" from Homer's *Odyssey* (which he salutes as "one of the foundations of the present essay") has difficulty locating his reconstructed society in historical time. In view of Redfield's concern with the relation between poetry and culture one expects that he will at least tackle the problem. Instead he repudiates it in Olympian style.

> Homeric culture . . . is transmitted to us only in poetic imitation. We should not speak of the "background" of the poems, as though we could reconstruct Homeric society and then apply this reconstruction to interpretation of the poems. On the contrary, we discover the society by interpreting the poems.

That there are dangers involved in this procedure Redfield is the first to admit, but he is confident that they can be avoided.

> No doubt we often go wrong. Yet I allow myself one hypothesis which establishes an important control: I assume that the poem is a success. The poem can serve to interpret the culture if we assume that the poem is successfully founded on exactly that culture, so that any understanding of the implicit system of meanings will enable us to see this particular poem as more of a poem.

Since, however, "the understanding of the implicit system of meanings" is the interpretation of the poem Redfield is trying to establish, this hypothesis is not a very impressive control. How do we know that this undefined and imaginary culture, conjured out of the poem by Redfield, would have agreed with his reading of it? In fact the only reason why this argument cannot be characterized as circular is that it never gets off its base.

There is a much better "control." Though we know next to nothing from outside sources about the dark centuries during which oral bards fashioned and refined the formulas and themes which the monumental composer transformed into the *Iliad*, we do know a great deal about later centuries, from the sixth on, for which Homer, "the poet," as they called him, was the dominant literary and cultural influence; one has only to read Plato's *Ion* to see how hypnotized the Greeks were by Homer in performance as late as the fourth century B.C. And Greeks of this culture saw the *Iliad* very differently from Redfield. The story of Achilles does not seem to have suggested to them that "the action of the *Iliad* is an enactment of the contradictions of the warrior's role. The warrior on behalf of culture must leave culture and enter nature. . . . That others may be pure, he must become impure."

On the contrary, Achilles, throughout the historical period, is the beau ideal not only as the supreme warrior but also as the model of aristocratic breeding and conduct (as he is in Pindar); he is cited as an example of devotion to duty (his insistence on fighting Hector though he knows it will mean his own death) by, of all people, Plato's Socrates, as he refuses to buy his life at the price of silence. Alexander, when he started out to conquer the world, had a bedside copy of the *Iliad* with him, and the prelude to his march south in Asia Minor was a ceremony in which he and his friend Hephaestion laid wreaths on the tombs of Achilles and Patroclus at what was thought to be the site of Troy and then, naked and anointed with oil, ran a race around them. On the other hand, except for an unflattering portrait in the second-rate drama called *Rhesus*, which is doubtfully attributed to Euripides, there is hardly an echo of Hector in later literature.

This is not by any means the only point on which the understanding of the *Iliad* by Redfield's presumed Homeric culture differs sharply from that of the historic Greek culture we know. For him, the gods of the *Iliad* are a problem; they are "generally frivolous, unsteady creatures, whose friendship or enmity has little to do with human justice. They do not appear in the narrative as guarantors of human norms or as the sources of natural process." This is perhaps too strongly stated but it is basically correct. According to Redfield's principle (that "we discover the society by interpreting the poems"), this fact should be accepted and given its place in the interpretation of the poem as a whole. But Redfield cannot accept it and his attempt to deal with "The Problem of the Gods" (as this section of his book, pages 75ff., is called) involves him in methodological contradictions. He contrasts with the gods of the *Iliad* those of Hesiod (who "are guarantors of moral norms; they punish the guilty") and prefaces this contrast with a sentence which begins: "If, however, we assume (as seems reasonable) that Hesiod's *Works and Days* represents actual religious belief at the time of Homer—or something very like it . . ."

So there *is* a "background" to the poem, and it is Hesiod! And a particular poem of Hesiod at that, for the same poet's *Theogony* presents the gods indulging in crude antics (such as castrating each other and eating each others' children) which make Homer's divine crew look angelic by comparison. Undeterred by this violation of his own ground rules, Redfield goes on to claim that since "actual religious belief at the time of Homer" is represented by the gods of the *Works and Days*, the gods of the *Iliad* "belong to the conventional world of epic and were understood as such by the audience. Just as the epic tells, not of men, but of heroes, so also it tells stories, not of gods conceived as actual, but of literary gods."

Such neoclassic literary sophistication ("O how convenient is a machine sometimes in a heroic poem," says Dryden of Mercury's intervention in *Aeneid* IV) is really unimaginable in "Homeric culture." And once again, the reaction of historical Greece speaks against the thesis. "What all men learn is shaped by Homer from the beginning," says Xenophanes, and he goes on to castigate both Homer and Hesiod for "ascribing to the gods all that is a reproach among men—thieving, adultery, lying to each other." One of the principal reasons why Homer is attacked in Books II–III of Plato's *Republic* and banned from the ideal city in Book X is precisely his picture of the gods. Some fifth-century exponents of Homer took the opposite tack and (providing a model for the Fathers of the Church who had to defend some unsavory passages in the Old Testament) explain that Homer's gods were moral and cosmological allegories. Neither of these reactions is comprehensible if Greek culture, at any time, had taken Homer's gods to be "literary gods" and "epic conventions."

Redfield's discussion of Achilles in the poem (as opposed to some of the conclusions drawn from it) is on the whole admirable, though he does devote a great deal of attention to minute character analysis which comes strangely from one who cites Aristotle on the importance of action as opposed to character. With his rejection of the idea, very fashionable today, that Achilles in his speech in Book IX repudiates the heroic ideal, I am in full agreement; but there is at least one speech of Achilles which argues strongly against Redfield's view of the hero as "status-determined." When Achilles sends Patroclus out to battle and instructs him not to go beyond driving the Trojans back from the ships, he expresses an astonishing wish. "If only," it runs in Lattimore's translation,

> if only
> not one of all the Trojans could escape destruction, not one
> of the Argives, but you and I could emerge from the slaughter
> so that we two alone could break Troy's hallowed coronal.

It is an almost manic vision of a world which consists of nothing but himself and his own glory, for Patroclus is an image of himself, sent out to fight in his armor. This sounds more like Whitman's "existential hero" than Redfield's "persons whose acts and consciousness are the enactment of the social forces which play upon them." And Redfield's discussion of the passage is, to say the least, unsatisfactory. "This prayer is so strange that most of the Hellenistic grammarians omitted it from their texts. But we should notice that it is in a way granted. When Patroclus dies, Achilles in a way dies with him." Since Achilles is clearly praying for the death of everyone in both armies except himself and his friend, I find Redfield's remark incomprehensible.

And there are other passages which are difficult to follow. Redfield himself qualifies one of his formulations as a "dark saying" but he has no such comment on the following sentence, which I find impenetrable even in its context. "That which baffles ethical forming, when further formed through imitative art, becomes itself a source of aesthetic form. As the forming of art is a further forming of forms already present in nature and culture, so it follows that artistic form is inclusive of culture and nature." And it is almost as hard to follow the series of metaphorical transfers by which Aristotle's baffling word *catharsis* is made to yield, through a discussion of ceremonial purifications, the sophisticated literary idea with which he ends his discussion.

The proponent of a theory which ranges widely and swiftly over different fields of thought and knowledge to create a general theory of the relation between culture and nature and the relation of literature to both is subject to one great temptation: his dazzling vision of the whole which he is engaged in constructing may blind him to the nature of some of the parts, and even to the existence of others. To borrow a phrase from MacNeice, he may reach the stage where he "can't see the trees for the wood." To be more accurate, in Redfield's case, he often sees the trees but only through the distorting spectacles of his vision of the wood.

One link in the chain of his interesting argument about impurity, for example, is the discussion of the *Keres*—those spirits of death which surround men in battle, are assigned to individuals at their birth, and, in a scene on the shield of Achilles, drag dead and living men off the battlefield. It is important for Redfield's argument that these horrific creatures should be imagined by the poet and his audience as shapes combining the salient features of dogs and birds, those scavengers to whom the warriors threaten to expose each other's corpses. There is of course no hint of this in Homer's description of the shield; Redfield has to cite two passages from another poem, a second-rate product called *The Shield of Heracles*, attributed to Hesiod, where the *Keres* do "gnash" and "clash their teeth," clasp the dead in their claws and suck their blood. "The *kēres* in Hesiod," says Redfield,

> eat the wounded; to die—at least in battle—is to be eaten by a *kēr*. It seems clear that the same idea pervades the *Iliad*, even though Homer, with quite characteristic tact, never tells us so. Sarpedon speaks of the "countless winged keres" (XII.326–27) ... and the dead Patroclus says "the *kēr* gaped for me, the hateful one, allotted to me at my birth" (XXIII.78–79). Each man has his own *kēr* who watches him hungrily. The coward at the moment of danger "thinks of the *kēres*, and his teeth chatter."

Redfield then proceeds: "The *kēres* have teeth; they also have wings and talons. They are thus a composite of dogs and birds."

Redfield must have been very dazzled by his overall vision here. If we "should not speak of the background of the poems" we should certainly not drag in a poem by another hand which was certainly composed much later. And the hints that he finds of this picture of the *Keres* are nearly all from his own creative imagination. Sarpedon does not speak of "winged" *Keres*, only of "*Keres* which stand over us" (*ephestasin*); the adverb "hungrily" has no basis in the text; the teeth belong to the coward, not the *Ker*. The only support for his interpretation is Patroclus's word, "gaped round me," which does suggest some kind of jaws, but since the word occurs only here in Homer, no certainty is possible. Even if this point should be conceded, the *Keres*, wingless and toothless and talonless, do not live up to their billing as a composite of dogs and birds.

But Redfield is not often so careless. And the book is an intellectual tour de force which, flawed though it may be, commands respect. It should send many readers back to the *Iliad*, with a renewed appreciation of the splendors and terrors of what is still, after all these centuries, the greatest epic poem ever composed.

Triumph of a Heretic

In 1954 a young American scholar who was later to become professor of ancient history at Cambridge published a book—*The World of Odysseus*—which in a limpid, hard-hitting prose and with a bare minimum of footnotes attempted to draw "a picture of a society, based on a close reading of the *Iliad* and *Odyssey,* supported by study of other societies." This is how Professor Finley characterizes the book now, in the preface to a revised edition[1] which makes only minor changes in the original text but adds two valuable and stimulating appendices replying to criticism and bringing the argument up to date. He goes on to claim that "the social institutions and values make up a coherent system" which, however strange to us, is "neither an improbable nor an unfamiliar one in the experience of modern anthropology." The fact that the later Greeks and the nineteenth-century scholars found it incomprehensible on its own terms he dismisses as "irrelevant" and adds that "it is equally beside the point that the narrative is a collection of fictions from beginning to end."

The ideas here stated in uncompromising terms were implicit in the work from the start. And at the time of its first publication they were not greeted with enthusiasm by the world of Homeric and Bronze Age scholarship. Far from believing that "the narrative was a collection of fictions," most scholars of the subject found in the Bronze Age remains excavated on the Homeric sites a confirmation of the historicity of the tale of Troy, at least in its main outlines, and went on to search the text of the poems for objects described that might match the objects discovered. Almost simultaneously with the publication of Finley's book, the decipherment of the Linear B tablets by Ventris and Chadwick seemed to provide the definitive proof that the Homeric poems preserved historical facts of the thirteenth century B.C. Here were clay tablets, inscribed in a form of Greek that bore striking re-

This essay originally appeared in the *New York Review of Books,* June 29, 1978.

1. M. I. Finley, *The World of Odysseus,* rev. ed. (New York: Viking, 1978).

semblances to the Homeric literary dialect, which contained lists of chariots, corslets, and helmets and such Homeric names as Hektor, Achilleus, Aias, Pandaros, and Orestes. John Chadwick recently took a wry backward look at the euphoria of those early days:

> The revelation of the Mycenaean archives fostered wild hopes that one day we might come across, let us say, the muster of ships at Aulis for the expedition against Troy or an operation order for the attack of the Seven against Thebes.[2]

Finley remained one of what he calls a "heretical minority"; and it soon became apparent that the decipherment of Linear B, far from confirming the thesis that the Homeric poems were a reflection of Mycenaean society, had in fact dealt that thesis a fatal blow. It is hard to think of Homer's Agamemnon as living in the same world with that *wanax* of Pylos, whose scribes duly recorded that "Kokalos repaid the following quantity of olive oil to Eumedes: 648 liters; from Ipsewas 38 stirrup-jars." The bureaucratic inventories of the Bronze Age palaces resemble the detailed records of the Near Eastern civilizations which preceded them and the intricate accounting of the later Ptolemaic papyri, but anything more alien to the mentality of illiterate freebooters such as Achilles and equally illiterate pirates such as Odysseus can hardly be imagined.

The tablets also demonstrated that the precise geographical description of Nestor's kingdom at Pylos which is offered in Book II of the *Iliad* bears practically no relation to the Mycenaean facts; the conclusion, that the poet or poets knew little or nothing of western Greece, might already have been surmised from the confused and confusing Homeric descriptions of the hero's homeland, Ithaca. And meanwhile, quite apart from the tablets, it was becoming steadily clearer to all but the most stubborn that there was very little in the archaeological record which would serve to connect the world of the poems with the Bronze Age.

Finley, in the preface to the new edition, contents himself with a very restrained, "I told you so"; he "cannot resist pointing out that proper concern for social institutions and social history had anticipated what philology and archaeology subsequently found." In *The Mycenaean World*, John Chadwick heads his penultimate chapter,

---

2. John Chadwick, *The Mycenaean World* (Cambridge: Cambridge University Press, 1976), p. 159.

"Homer the Pseudo-Historian," and concludes it with the sentence: "to look for historical fact in Homer is as vain as to scan the Mycenaean tablets in search of poetry; they belong to two different universes."

Oral heroic poetry is not a medium that preserves historical fact—as Finley pointed out, with a reference to the *Chanson de Roland*, which made out of a Basque attack on Charlemagne's rear guard an assault by Muslim beys and pashas, all carefully identified by names which are "German, Byzantine, or made-up." A modern example, from the Second World War and from Greece itself, strengthens his case and gives a fascinating glimpse of epic "history" in the making.

In 1953 the late Professor James Notopoulos was recording oral heroic song in the Sfakia district of western Crete, where illiterate oral bards were still to be found. He asked one of them, who had sung of his own war experience, if he knew a song about the capture of the German general and the bard proceeded to improvise one. The historical facts are well known and quite secure. In April 1944 two British officers, Major Patrick Leigh Fermor and Captain Stanley Moss, landed on Crete from a submarine, made contact with Cretan guerrillas, and kidnapped the German commanding general of the island, one Karl Kreipe.

The general was living in the Villa Ariadne at Knossos, the house Sir Arthur Evans had built for himself during the excavations. Every day, at the same time, the general was driven south from the villa to the neighboring small town of Arkhanes, where his headquarters were located. He came home every night at eight o'clock for dinner. The two British officers, dressed in German uniforms, stopped the car on its way home to Knossos; the Cretan partisans overpowered the chauffeur and the general. The two officers then drove the car through the German roadblocks in Heraklion (the general silent with a knife at his throat) and left the car on the coast road to Rethymo. They then hiked through the mountains to the south coast, made rendezvous with a British submarine, and took General Kreipe to Alexandria and on to Middle East Headquarters in Cairo.

Here, in Notopoulos's summary, is the heroic song the bard produced:

> An order comes from British and American headquarters in Cairo to capture General Kreipe, dead or alive; the motive is re-

venge for his cruelty to the Cretans. A Cretan partisan, Lefteris Tambakis (not one of the actual guerrilla band) appears before the English general (Fermor and Moss are combined into one and elevated in rank) and volunteers for the dangerous mission. The general reads the order and the hero accepts the mission for the honor of Cretan arms. The hero goes to Heraklion, where he hears that a beautiful Cretan girl is the secretary of General Kreipe.

In disguise the partisan proceeds to her house and in her absence reads the [English] general's order to her mother. When the girl returns he again reads the general's order. Telling her the honor of Crete depends on her, he catalogues the German cruelties. If she would help in the mission, her name would become immortal in Cretan history. The girl consents and asks for three days' time in which to perform her role. To achieve Cretan honor she sacrifices her woman's honor with General Kreipe in the role of a spy. She gives the hero General Kreipe's plans for the next day.

Our hero then goes to Knossos to meet the guerrillas and the English general. "*Yiassou* general," he says. "I will perform the mission." The guerrillas go to Arkhanes to get a long car with which to blockade the road. Our hero, mounted on a horse by the side of the blockading car, awaits the car of Kaiseri (that is what the bard calls Kreipe). The English general orders the pistols to be ready. When Kreipe's car slows down at the turn he is attacked by the guerrillas. Kreipe is stripped of his uniform (only his cap in the actual event) and begs for mercy for the sake of his children (a stock motif in Cretan poetry).

After the capture the frantic Germans begin to hunt with dogs (airplanes in the actual event). The guerrillas start on the trek to Mount Ida and by stages the party reaches the district of Sfakia (the home of the singer and his audience; actually the general left the island southwest of Mount Ida). The guards have to protect the general from the mob of enraged Sfakians. Soon the British submarine arrives and takes the general to Egypt. Our bard concludes the poem with a traditional epilogue—that never before in the history of the world has such a deed been done. He then gives his name, his village, his service to his country.[3]

So much for epic history. Nine years after the event the British protagonists have been reduced to one nameless general whose part

3. James Notopoulos, "The Genesis of an Oral Heroic Poem," *Greek, Roman, and Byzantine Studies* 3 (1960): 135ff.

in the operation is secondary, and there can hardly be any doubt that if the song is still sung now the British element in the proceedings is practically nonexistent—if indeed it managed to survive at all through the years in which Britain, fighting to retain its hold on Cyprus, became the target of bitter hostility in Greece and especially among the excitable Cretans.

It took the Cretan oral tradition only nine years to promote to the leadership of the heroic enterprise a purely fictitious character of a different nationality. This is a sobering thought when one reflects that there is nothing to connect Agamemnon, Achilles, Priam, and Hector with the fire-blackened layer of thirteenth-century ruins known as Troy VII A (the archaeologists' candidate for Homer's city) except a heroic poem which cannot have been fixed in its present form by writing until the late eighth century, at least four illiterate centuries after the destruction.

Finley's professional interest in the poems lies in their value as a source for knowledge of the Dark Ages (so called because we know almost nothing about them) which intervene between the destruction of the Mycenaean palaces around 1200 B.C. and the beginning of a new literacy some time in the late eighth century. If the poems contain no memory of historical events of the Bronze Age and, furthermore, do not reflect the civilization, customs, social relationships, or even the material objects of the Bronze Age, what *do* they have to tell us? Finley's answer was (and still is) that the poems preserve, with the anachronisms and misunderstandings inevitable in a fluid oral tradition, the social institutions and values of the early Dark Ages, the tenth and ninth centuries B.C. "The choice," as he poses the question in the new edition, "lies between that period and the poet's own time, now that the ground beneath a supposed Mycenaean world of Odysseus has been removed by the Linear B tablets, assisted by continuous archaeological excavation and study."

The "poet's own time" he takes to be the mid-eighth century (a date with which few will quarrel) and makes the claim that the poems fail to reflect the known social conditions of that period. "The *polis* (city-state) form of political organization" was "widespread in the Hellenic world by then, at least in embryonic form. Yet neither poem has any trace of a *polis* in its political sense." Further, the "Phoenician monopoly of trade" in the *Odyssey* is a reflection of "the period before

800 B.C., for by that date the presence of Greek traders in the Levant is firmly attested." Finley sees no reason to find in Homer's picture of the sea lords of Phaeacia a "reflection of the Greek western colonization movement contemporary with Homer," as many have done: "Magical ships that powered themselves were not instruments of the westward colonization, nor did magic gardens await the migrants on arrival."

The epic poets are the guardians, preservers, and renewers of a heroic tradition and though they often admit anachronistic details or misunderstand the use or nature of archaic objects, they maintain intact, so Finley insists, the social context in which the heroes can live their larger life. From that context he constructed a model, to use his own formula, "imperfect, incomplete, untidy, yet tying together the fundamentals of a political and social structure with an appropriate value system in a way that stands up to a comparative analysis." The most striking and original feature of this presentation (organized in chapters headed: "Wealth and Labor"; "Household, Kin, and Community"; "Morals and Values") is his discussion of the "institution of gift-exchange."

No reader of the *Odyssey* can have failed to be amazed and puzzled by the central role gifts play in the social relationships of the characters. Telemachus at Sparta, a young provincial with very uncertain prospects visiting the splendid court of Menelaus and Helen, is offered a parting gift of horses. He declines, on the grounds that his native island is no place to graze horses, and asks for something else: "Give me something that can be stored up." Menelaus is delighted with his frankness and gives him a bowl made of silver and gold. There are many such encounters in the Homeric poems, and readers seeking some explanation of the generosity and especially of the unashamed claims made on it usually found themselves fobbed off with a discussion of Homeric hospitality and the guest-friend relationship. Finley put it firmly in a familiar anthropological context.

> The word "gift" is not to be misconstrued. It may be stated as a flat rule of both primitive and archaic society that no one ever gave anything, whether goods or services or honors, without proper recompense, real or wishful, immediate or years away, to himself or to his kin. The act of giving was, therefore, in an essen-

tial sense always the first half of a reciprocal action, the other half of which was a counter-gift.

His persuasive analysis of the working of this form of exchange in the poems was widely accepted; those who objected that it reflected not a society but a "heroic ideal" are given short shrift in the new edition.

The system of gift-giving which Finley identified in the poems was already familiar to anthropologists and sociologists; Marcel Mauss in his *Essai sur le don*[4] had analyzed its operation in a wide variety of societies ancient and modern (though not in ancient Greece, to which he made only some half-dozen tangential references in his footnotes). If, as Finley says, "the practice . . . 'does not reflect a society' but an 'heroic ideal,' we are driven to the conclusion that, by a most remarkable intuition, Homer was a predecessor of Marcel Mauss, except that he (or his tradition) invented an institution which nearly three thousand years later Mauss discovered to be a social reality." Since, he goes on to say, "Tamil heroic poetry of South India reveals a comparable network of gift-giving," Homer is not the only "instinctive, premature Marcel Mauss."

Finley's arguments from the system's internal coherence and its recorded existence in real societies are compelling, but a lingering doubt may remain. Speaking of the belief in the historical reality of the Trojan War and the Catalogue of Ships firmly held by some scholars who reject his sociological model he asks: "In what respect do they differ from gift-giving in their inherent credibility?" A skeptic might answer: "Not at all. Both the Trojan War *and* the gift-giving system may be equally unhistorical." If the epic Muse can forget the palaces, inventories, and geography of Mycenaean Greece, remember the chariots but not how they were used, and fabricate not only a war but the names and personalities of chieftains on both sides, how can we trust her to preserve intact the memory of an intricate social system long since obsolete? Finley's case would be stronger if the comparative method, to which he so often appeals, could produce a parallel: an oral epic poem which, celebrating heroes of a bygone age, garbles time, place, and material objects but preserves, in recognizable form, a complex system of primitive social institutions.

4. "Essai sur le don, forme archaïque de l'échange," *Année Sociologique*, n.s. 1 (1925): *The Gift*, trans. Ian Cunnison (1954; New York: Norton, 1967).

There is one oral epic which goes far toward meeting these specifications, the Turkish *Book of Dede Korkut*. The full text has only recently been made available in an English version[5] (which may be the reason why Finley, whose mastery of the enormous Homeric literature is demonstrated in his useful critical bibliography, does not seem to be aware of it). The text on which modern editions are based was written in the last quarter of the sixteenth century, but there is in existence a summary of the poem which was written down before 1332, and the text contains numerous traces of original versions dating from the tenth century. The book recounts, in a mixture of prose and verse, the deeds of the Oghuz, a tribe which, over many centuries, migrated from lands which are now in the Kazakh, Uzbek, and Turkmen Soviet Socialist Republics to become the ancestors of the Seljuk and Ottoman Turks in western Asia Minor.

In their original home their raiding expeditions were aimed at their neighbors to the north, the shamanistic Kipchaks; the Oghuz were recently converted Muslims (though sometimes pre-Islamic customs remain embedded in the narrative). But the sixteenth-century version retains only occasional reminiscences of the Kipchaks and the geography of the Samarkand area; in it the Oghuz beys now live, hunt, and plunder in western Anatolia, a thousand miles to the west; their infidel enemies "worship a god made from wood" and have churches with monks in them—one of their strongholds is Trebizond, which remained in Byzantine hands until 1461.

The Oghuz nomadic beys are given a nonexistent history; at the same time, the known participation of their descendants in major historical events is utterly ignored. "No reference is made," say the translators, "to the well-known involvement of the Oghuz in the affairs of the Ghazmanide Dynasty . . . nor is there any mention whatever of the successive stages by which the Seljuks, of Oghuz origin, conquered Iran and most of Anatolia . . . during the remainder of the eleventh century." The action of the epic is, as the translators put it, "mainly fiction" but, as they go on to say, "so well do the legends reflect the pattern of early Oghuz life that they must also be considered documents of cultural and social history."

One of the institutions of the Oghuz is a spectacular variation of the gift-giving system. Their king, Bayindir Khan, commands the al-

5. Trans. Faruk Sürner, Ahmet E. Uysal, and Warren S. Walker (Austin: University of Texas Press, 1972).

legiance of the beys, the heroes of the epic; they deliver the booty from their brigand raids to him. Periodically he invites them to sumptuous feasts, at which he "distributes the wealth of the Oghuz, usually in the form of gifts to the beys." But occasionally the feast was a "plunder banquet." On these occasions, at the high point of the feast, the khan would take his wife by the hand and leave; the beys would then help themselves to any of his possessions they fancied. It was, in the story, his failure to invite the Outer Oghuz to a plunder banquet which caused a fratricidal war, the "*Götterdämmerung*" episode which concludes the saga.

In the years since its first appearance, Finley's "model" has won wide acceptance; his reconstruction of a Dark Age society from the epic text has even, as he says in his preface, "been the acknowledged starting-point of studies by other historians of society and ideas"— among them J. M. Redfield's *Nature and Culture in the Iliad* (see pp. 23ff.). But Homer is a subject on which no two people can be expected to agree entirely, and it may be objected, without impugning the validity of his main thesis, that Finley pushes too hard against the evidence in his claim that there is no trace in the *Odyssey* of the "*polis* in its political sense" and his denial that the wanderings of Odysseus are "a reflection of the Greek western colonization movement contemporary with Homer."

On the first point he is of course right to rule out the imaginary city of the Phaeacians and also right to deny that the presentation of "walls, docks, temples, and a marketplace" can be treated as "Homer's recognition of the . . . rise of the *polis*." But the equally imaginary city of Troy in the *Iliad* does seem to prefigure some features of later social organization—in the procession of the women to the Temple of Athena in Book VI, the debate in the assembly in Book VII, above all in Hector's devotion to Troy and its people, his sense of his duty to the community. Hector is unique in his loyalty to a larger social unit than the *oikos,* that extended household which, "together with its lands and goods," was the basic nucleus of Homeric society.

As for the western wanderings, it is true that there is nothing in the poem "that resembles eighth-century Ischia or Cumae, Syracuse, Leontini or Megara Hyblaea." There is not very much in Shakespeare's *Tempest* which resembles early seventeenth-century Bermuda either, but no one can doubt that the play reflects an age of maritime exploration. The fantastic adventures of Odysseus contain several features which suggest that this part of the poem was originally the saga of a voyage to the East, the voyage of the Argonauts, in fact; why should it have been adapted for a western sea tale except to please an audience interested, if not in the actual founding of colonies, at any rate in the voyages of exploration which must have preceded their foundation?

These are minor cavils. It is an unmixed pleasure to welcome this new edition of a book which has become a classic in its field, as indispensable to the professional as it is accessible to the general reader.

The Freedom of Oedipus

Oedipus the King is universally recognized as the dramatic masterpiece of the Greek theater. Aristotle cites it as the most brilliant example of theatrical plot, the model for all to follow, and all the generations since who have seen it staged—no matter how inadequate the production or how poor the translation—have agreed with his assessment as they found themselves moved to pity and fear by the swift development of its ferociously logical plot. The story of Oedipus, the myth, was of course very old in Sophocles' time and very well known to his audience. It was his use of the well-known material that made the play new. He chose to concentrate attention not on the actions of Oedipus that had made his name a byword—his violation of the two most formidable taboos observed by almost every human society—but on the moment of his discovery of the truth. And Sophocles engineered this discovery not by divine agency (as Homer did) and not by chance, but through the persistent, courageous action of Oedipus himself. The hero of the play is thus his own destroyer; he is the detective who tracks down and identifies the criminal—who turns out to be himself.

The play has also been almost universally regarded as the classic example of the "tragedy of fate." To the rationalist critics of the eighteenth century and still more to the firm believers in human progress of the nineteenth, this aspect of the play was a historical curiosity, to be discounted; but our own more anxious age has seen in the situation of Oedipus an image of its own fears. In the very first year of our century Sigmund Freud in his *Interpretation of Dreams* offered a famous and influential interpretation of the destiny of Oedipus the King:

> There must be something which makes a voice within us ready to recognize the compelling force of destiny in the *Oedipus*, while we can dismiss as merely arbitrary such dispositions as are laid down in . . . modern tragedies of destiny. And a factor of this kind is in

This essay originally appeared in the *New Republic*, August 30, 1982.

fact involved in the story of King Oedipus. His destiny moves us only because it might have been ours. . . . It is the fate of all of us, perhaps, to direct our first sexual impulse towards our mother and our first hatred and . . . murderous wish against our father. Our dreams convince us that this is so.

This passage is of course a landmark in the history of modern thought, and it is fascinating to observe that this idea, which, valid or not, has had enormous influence, stems from an attempt to answer a literary problem—why does the play have this overpowering effect on modern audiences?—and that this problem is raised by an ancient Greek tragedy. As a piece of literary criticism, however, it leaves much to be desired. If the effect of the play did indeed depend on the "particular nature of the material," then one would expect modern audiences to be just as deeply moved by a performance of Voltaire's *Edipe*, whereas, in fact, the play is rarely produced, and then only as a museum piece. At any rate, though the primordial urges and fears that are Freud's concern are perhaps inherent in the myths, they are not exploited in the Sophoclean play. And indeed Freud himself, in a later passage in the same work, admits as much: "the further modification of the legend," he says, "originates . . . in a misconceived secondary revision of the material, which has sought to exploit it for theological purposes." This "further modification" is the Sophoclean play.

Sophocles' play has served modern man and his haunted sense of being caught in a trap not only as a base for a psychoanalytic theory that dooms the male infant to guilt and anxiety from his mother's breast, but also as the model for a modern drama that presents to us, using the ancient figures, our own terror of the unknown future that we fear we cannot control—our deep fear that every step we take forward on what we think is the road of progress may really be a step toward a foreordained rendezvous with disaster. The greatest of these modern versions is undoubtedly Jean Cocteau's *Machine infernale*; the title alone is, as the French say, a whole program. Cocteau also worked with Stravinsky on an operatic version of the Sophoclean play (the text in liturgical Latin), and for a recording of this work he wrote a prologue that sums up his compelling vision of man's place in a strange and haunted universe. "*Spectateurs*," says the author in his forceful, rather nasal voice, "*sans le savoir* . . . without knowing it, Oedipus is at grips with the powers that watch us from the other side of death. They have spread for him, since the day of his birth, a trap and you are going to watch it snap shut." This is of course much more explicit (and much more despairing) than the Sophoclean play; it stems, like the beautiful and terrifying second act of the *Machine infernale*, in which the Sphinx and Anubis play their fiendish game with Oedipus, out of a modern vision of a death-haunted universe, from the obsessed imagination that gives us also, in the film *Orphée*, the unforgettable images of Death at work: her black-uniformed motorcyclists, enigmatic radio messages, and rubber gloves.

Parallel with this modern adaptation of the Oedipus story, serving new psychologies and mythologies of the irrational, goes a reinterpretation of the Sophoclean play itself by scholars and critics. Yeats, who translated the play for production at the Abbey Theatre in Dublin, described his reaction to a rehearsal in the words, "I had but one overwhelming emotion, a sense as of the actual presence in a terrible sacrament of the god." Taking his cue from the work of Frazer and Harrison, who emphasize the religious, tribal, and primitive aspects of the Greek tradition, Francis Fergusson, in his brilliant book *The Idea of a Theater*, gives us a vision of the Sophoclean masterpiece as an Athenian mystery play, a solemn rite of sacrifice that purges the community of its collective guilt by punishing a scapegoat, one man who perishes for the good of the people.

All this is a reaction, predictable and perhaps even necessary, against the nineteenth-century worship of the Greek rational "enlightenment"—a vision of ancient Greece dear to the hearts of optimistic Victorians who found in Greece, as each successive generation in the West has done since the Renaissance, their own image. But the reaction toward the mysterious, the irrational has gone too far. For Sophocles' play, read without preconceptions of any kind, gives an entirely different impression. There is not one supernatural event in it, no gods (as there are in so many other Greek plays), no monsters—nothing that is not, given the mythical situation, inexorably logical and human. Destiny, fate, and the will of the gods do indeed loom ominously behind the human action, but that action, far from suggesting primeval rituals and satanic divinities, reflects, at every point, contemporary realities familiar to the audience that first saw the play.

The voice of destiny in the play is the oracle of Apollo. Through his priests at Delphi, Apollo told Laius that he would be killed by his own son, and later told Oedipus that he would kill his father and marry his mother. At the beginning of the play Apollo tells Creon that Thebes will be saved from the plague only when the murderer of Laius is found and expelled. This Delphic oracle, which for modern poets—Yeats, for example—can conjure up mystic romantic visions, was, for Sophocles and his audience, a fact of life, an institution as present and solid, as uncompromising (and sometimes infuriating) as the Vatican is for us. States and individuals alike consulted it as a matter of course about important decisions. Sparta asked Apollo if it should declare war on Athens in 431 B.C. (it was told to go ahead and was promised victory). The oracle promoted revolutions, upheld dynasties, guided the foundation of colonies. Its wealth and political influence were immense.

Its power was based on a widespread, indeed in early times universal, belief in the efficacy of divine prophecy. The gods knew everything, including what was going to happen, and so their advice was precious; the most famous dispenser of such advice was Apollo, son of Zeus. Private individuals and official representatives of state had for centuries made the journey by land and sea to Apollo's temple in its magnificent setting on a high plateau below Mount Parnassus; in gratitude for the god's advice, kings and cities had lavished gifts on the sanctuary and even built treasuries on the site to house their precious offerings.

But in the second half of the fifth century B.C., particularly in Athens, this belief in prophecy and with it belief in the religious tradition as a whole was under attack. Philosophers and sophists (the new professional teachers of rhetoric, political theory, and a host of allied subjects) were examining all accepted ideas with a critical eye: the fifth century in Athens was an age of intellectual revolution. Among the younger intellectuals, prophecies, especially those peddled by self-appointed professional seers (a class of operator common in ancient Greece but not unknown in modern America), were viewed with skepticism if not scorn; inevitably some of the skepticism spread to embrace the more respectable oracular establishments that claimed to transmit divine instructions. Thucydides, the historian of the Peloponnesian War, dismissed prophecy contemptuously in a couple of cynical sentences, and Euripides attacked it, sometimes lightheartedly, sometimes bitterly, in one play after another. The philosophical attack on it was more radical; the dictum of the sophist Protagoras—

"the individual man is the measure of all things, of the existence of what exists and the nonexistence of what does not"—subjected prophecy, and for that matter the gods themselves, to a harsh criterion that found them wanting.

When he chose as the subject of his tragedy a story about a man who tried to avoid the fulfillment of a prophecy of Apollo, believed he had succeeded and cast scorn on all the oracles, only to find that he had fulfilled that prophecy long ago, Sophocles was dealing with matters that had urgent contemporary significance; prophecy was one of the great controversial questions of the day. It was in fact the key question, for the rationalist critique of the whole archaic religious tradition had concentrated its fire on this particular sector. Far more than prophecy was involved. For if the case for divine foreknowledge could be successfully demolished, the whole traditional religious edifice went down with it. If the gods did not know the future, they did not know any more than man. These are in fact the terms of the Sophoclean play. When the chorus hears Jocasta dismiss divine prophecy and Oedipus agree with her, they actually pray to Zeus to fulfill the dreadful prophecies they have just heard Jocasta and Oedipus report. They identify prophecy with the very existence of the gods. Never again, they say, will they go reverent to Delphi or to any oracular shrine of the gods

> unless these prophecies all come true
> for all mankind to point toward in
>   wonder. . . .
> They are dying, the old oracles sent to
>   Laius,
> now our masters strike them off the rolls.
> Nowhere Apollo's golden glory now—
> the gods, the gods go down.[1]

By this emphasis Sophocles gave the age-old story contemporary and controversial significance, and he had other ways besides to make his audience see themselves in the ancient figures he brought to such disturbing life on stage. The play opens, for example, with a citizen delegation begging a ruler for relief from plague. The Athenians were all too familiar with plague; in the second summer of the war, in a city

---

1. Translations throughout the essay are from Robert Fagles's *Three Theban Plays* (New York: Viking, 1982).

overcrowded with refugees from the Spartan invasion of Attica, plague had raged in the city, and it had recurred over the next three or four years.

But more important for the play's impact on the audience than this grim setting is the characterization of the play's central figure, Oedipus the King. The poet's language presents him to the audience not as a figure of the mythical past but as one fully contemporary; in fact he is easily recognizable as an epitome of the Athenian character as they themselves conceived it and as their enemies saw it too. One trait after another in the character of Sophocles' Oedipus corresponds to Athenian qualities praised by Pericles in his Funeral Speech or denounced by the Corinthians in their attack on Athenian imperialism at the congress in Sparta before the war.

Oedipus is quick to decide and to act; he anticipates advice and suggestion. When the priest hints that he should send to Delphi for help, he has already done so; when the chorus suggests sending for Tiresias, the prophet has already been summoned and is on the way. This swiftness in action is a well-known Athenian quality, one their enemies are well aware of. "They are the only people," say the Corinthians, "who simultaneously hope for and have what they plan, because of their quick fulfillment of decisions." But this action is not rash, it is based on reflection; Oedipus reached the decision to apply to Delphi "groping, laboring over many paths of thought." This too is typically Athenian. "We are unique," says Pericles, "in our combination of the most courageous action and rational discussion of our plans." The Athenians also spoke with pride of the intelligence that informed such discussion: Pericles attributes the Athenian victories over the Persians "not to luck, but to intelligence." And this is the claim of Oedipus, too. "The flight of my own intelligence hit the mark," he says, as he recalls his solution of the riddle of the Sphinx. The riddle has sinister verbal connections with his fate (his name in Greek is *Oidipous,* and *dipous* is the Greek word for "two-footed" in the riddle, not to mention the later prophecy of Tiresias that he would leave Thebes as a blind man, "a stick tapping before him step by step"), but the answer he proposed to the riddle—"Man"—is appropriate for the optimistic picture of man's achievement and potential that the figure of Oedipus represents.

Above all, as we see from the priest's speech in the prologue and the prompt, energetic action Oedipus takes to rescue his subjects from the plague, he is a man dedicated to the interests and the needs of the city. It is this public spirit that drives him on to the discovery of the truth—to reject Creon's hint that the matter should be kept under wraps, to send for Tiresias, to pronounce the curse and sentence of banishment on the murderer of Laius. This spirit was the great civic virtue that Pericles preached—"I would have you fix your eyes every day on the greatness of Athens until you fall in love with her"—and that the enemies of Athens knew they had to reckon with. "In the city's service," say the Corinthians, "they use their bodies as if they did not belong to them."

All this does not necessarily mean that Sophocles' audience drew a conscious parallel between Oedipus and Athens (or even that Sophocles himself did); what is important is that they could have seen in Oedipus a man endowed with the temperament and talents they prized most highly in their own democratic leaders and in their ideal vision of themselves. Oedipus the King is a dramatic embodiment of the creative vigor and intellectual daring of the fifth-century Athenian spirit.

But there is an even greater dimension to this extraordinary dramatic figure. The fifth century in Athens saw the birth of the historical spirit. The past came to be seen no longer as a golden age from which there had been a decline if not a fall, but as a steady progress from primitive barbarism to the high civilization of the city-state. One of the new teachers, the sophist Protagoras, was particularly associated with this idea; and there is a clear reflection of his ideas in that chorus of *Antigone* that sings the praise of man the resourceful. "Man the master, ingenious past all measure . . . / he forges on. . . ." Three of the most important achievements of man celebrated in that ode are his conquest of the earth, the sea, and the animals. And Oedipus, in the images of the play, is presented to us as hunter, sailor, and plowman. He is the hunter who follows "the trail of the ancient guilt"; the sailor who, in the chorus's words, "set our beloved land—storm-tossed, shattered—straight on course"; and he is also the plowman—"How," sings the chorus when the truth is out at last,

> how could the furrows your father
> plowed bear you, your agony,
>   harrowing
> on in silence O so long?

But Oedipus speaks too in terms that connect him with more advanced stages of human progress. Among these—the culmination of the *Antigone* ode—was the creation of the city-state, "the mood and mind for law that rules the city." Oedipus is a ruling statesman; he is a self-made man who has won and kept control of the state, a master of the political art, and he is conscious of his achievement and its value. And, as head of the state, Oedipus is the enforcer of the law. He is, in the play, the investigator, prosecutor, and judge of a murderer. In all these aspects he represents the social and intellectual progress that had resulted in the establishment of Athenian democracy and its courts of law, a triumph of human progress celebrated in the last play of Aeschylus's *Oresteia*.

The figure of Oedipus represents not only the techniques of the transition from savagery to civilization and the political achievements of the newly settled society, but also the temper and methods of the fifth-century intellectual revolution. His speeches are full of words, phrases, and attitudes that link him with the "enlightenment" of Sophocles' own Athens. "I'll bring it all to light," he says; he is like some Protagoras or Democritus dispelling the darkness of ignorance and superstition. He is a questioner, a researcher, a discoverer—the Greek words are those of the sophistic vocabulary. Above all Oedipus is presented to the audience as a symbol of two of the greatest scientific achievements of the age—mathematics and medicine. Mathematical language recurs incessantly in the imagery of the play—such terms as "measure" (*metrein*), "equate" (*isoun*), "define" (*diorizein*)—and at one climactic moment Oedipus expresses as a mathematical axiom his hope that a discrepancy in the evidence will clear him of the charge of Laius's murder: "One can't equal many." This obsessive image, Oedipus the calculator, is one more means of investing the mythical figure with the salient characteristics of the fifth-century achievement, but it is also magnificently functional. For, in his search for truth, he is engaged in a great calculation to determine the measure of man, whom Protagoras called "the measure of all things."

Functional too is the richly developed image of Oedipus as a physician. Hippocrates of Cos and his school of physicians had in this same century founded Western medicine; their treatises and casebooks are still extant, and in them we can see the new methods at work: detailed observations of hundreds of cases, classification of symptoms, plotting of the regular course of individual diseases and then diagnosis, prognosis (these are Greek words, their words). In the play the city suffers from a disease and Oedipus is the physician to whom all turn for a cure.

And all these images, like the plot, like the hero, have what Aristotle called their *peripeteia*, their reversal. The hunter catches a dreadful prey, the seaman steers his ship into an unspeakable harbor—"one and the same wide harbor served you / son and father both"—the plowman sows and reaps a fearful harvest, the investigator finds the criminal, and the judge convicts him—they are all the same man—the revealer turns into the thing revealed, the finder into the thing found, the calculator finds he is himself the solution of the equation, and the physician discovers that he is the disease. The catastrophe of the tragic hero thus becomes the catastrophe of fifth-century man; all his furious energy and intellectual daring drive him on to this terrible discovery of his fundamental ignorance. He is not the measure of all things but the thing measured and found wanting.

The reversal of the tragic hero is singled out for praise by Aristotle because it comes about through recognition, in this case Oedipus's recognition of his own identity. But he recognizes also that the prophecies given to his father and to him by Apollo were true prophecies, that they had been fulfilled long ago, that every step taken to evade them, from the exposure of the child to the decision never to go back to Corinth, was part of the pattern of their fulfillment. And this poses, for the modern reader as for the ancient spectator, the question of fate and, though those spectators could not have expressed the idea in abstract terms, of free will and human freedom.

This basic theme has often been discounted on the grounds that the opposition of fate and free will, providence and chance, determined and open universe, was not explicitly formulated until much later than Sophocles' time, in the philosophical discussions of the late fourth and third centuries. This is true, but it does not necessarily follow that because a problem had not yet been given philosophical expression, it could not be conceived. The myth of Oedipus itself—like the stories of attempts to escape a predicted fate so frequent in the *Histories* of Sophocles' friend Herodotus—poses the problem in poetic form, and one of the functions of myth in preliterate socities, as Lévi-Strauss has so brilliantly demonstrated, is to raise deeply disturbing problems that will later demand more precise formulation.

Even though what remains of early Greek literature shows no verbal consciousness of the ideas we associate with freedom of the will, there is abundant evidence, from the earliest times, for a related concept that is in fact almost inseparable from it: individual responsibility. No one can be held fully responsible for actions committed under some kind of external constraint, and in early Greek belief such constraint might be exerted by a host of nonhuman powers. When Agamemnon, in Homer's *Iliad,* makes his apologies to Achilles for the harsh treatment that led to the death of so many heroes, he tries to evade responsibility: he is claiming, in other words, that he did not act freely: "I am not responsible / but Zeus is, and Destiny." The context suggests that this is merely an excuse. But the negative implication of this is clear: that a man *is* responsible for those actions that are not performed under constraint, which are the expression of his free will. The question of Oedipus's responsibility for what happens (and what has happened) is, as we shall see, posed in the play; it is also discussed much later, in *Oedipus at Colonus,* which deals with Oedipus's old age and death.

It is interesting to note that in those later centuries, when the stoic philosophers do pose the problem in abstract form, they start from this same mythical base, the oracle given to Laius. Chrysippus uses this oracle to illustrate his almost completely determinist position (the only freedom he allows man is that of a dog tied to a moving cart); Carneades reinterprets the oracle to allow man a little more freedom; Alexander of Aphrodisias takes up the challenge on the same ground, and Cicero debates the meaning of this same oracular prophecy. As long as Greek philosophy lasts, the discussion of Oedipus's freedom or his subjection to fate goes on—even in the commentaries on Plato by Albinus in the second and Calcidius in the sixth century A.D.

The end of Greek philosophy and the triumph of Christianity brought no end to the argument, only new terms in which to phrase it. St. Augustine wrote his book *On Freedom of the Will* (*De Libero Arbitrio*) just as Cicero had written his *On Fate* (*De Fato*); Augustine is no longer concerned with the oracle given to Laius, but he is just as tormented (as he claims all humanity is) by the contradiction between our free will and God's foreknowledge that we will sin. It was of course an argument that was to go further; Bergson, Croce, and Friedrich Engels, to name only a few, continue it into modern times.

It has become much more complicated and sophisticated with the years; the terms of the opposition can be, and have been, continually redefined in philosophically elegant formulas that are designed, and may even seem, to abolish it; and of course modern analytical philosophers can dismiss the problem as a mere verbal misunderstanding. But to the ordinary man, now as in Sophocles' day, there is a problem in the coexistence of predictable pattern and free will, whether that pattern be thought of as divine providence, the will of history, or the influence of the stars.

There are two obvious ways of avoiding the contradiction, both of them extreme positions and at opposite poles; one might call them, to use a political metaphor, the right and the left. The right is all for order and pattern; it escapes the dilemma by dispensing with freedom altogether. It sees history, individual and general, as a rigidly determined succession of events in time. If you take such a view, whether Christian with St. Augustine—that all history is God's providential preparation of two cities, one of God, one of Satan, and that certain souls are predestined for salvation (or with Calvin, that other souls are destined for damnation); or materialist and atheist with Marx and Engels, denying the freedom of history to all classes but the proletariat—"Freedom," wrote Engels, "is the recognition of necessity" (which is a German version of Chrysippus's dog tied to a cart)—if you take either of these determinist views, you have no antinomy, no contradiction. But you have no freedom, and unless you happen to be one of the Christian or the Marxist elect, you have no future either.

What we have called the left, on the other hand, is all for freedom. To the devil with pattern and order; they are for anarchy, the human will is absolutely free and nothing is predictable; there is no pattern of order in the universe, which is merely the operation of blind chance. If you deny the possibility of prediction and the existence of order, whether as an "atomic" theorist like Democritus, or out of sheer desperation, as Jocasta does in the play—"What should a man fear? It's all chance, chance rules our lives"—you have abolished the logical contradiction. But you accept a blind, pointless, meaningless universe—the universe of the absurd.

Both of these extremes are of course repugnant to the human spirit and especially to that of the West, which is that of the Greeks.

We want both the freedom of our will and the assurance of order and meaning; we want to have our cake and eat it too, and in this non-Christian and Christian are alike. But no matter what subtle distinctions we invent and refine, the basic contradiction remains. Insofar as any meaningful pattern or divine providence exists, it must encroach to some extent on human freedom; if human freedom is unlimited, the possibility of pattern or order is denied.

As a logical proposition, the two concepts are irreconcilable. The only way to believe in the pattern and the freedom at once is not as a logical proposition but as a mystery; the medium of exploration is not philosophy but religion—or art. We can say, as Tertullian is supposed to have said (but almost certainly didn't), "I believe it precisely because it is absurd," or we can express the contradiction in poetic terms that transcend logic. It is significant that Plato's main discussion of the problem is not phrased in the cut and thrust of dialectic, but in the great myths, as in the myth of Er, where Socrates is no longer subject to questioning. Only a mood of religious humility or a work of art can hold in precarious coexistence the irreconcilable concepts. But for one form of art, the drama, this is a particularly dangerous subject. For the power of drama depends on our feeling that the actors are free, that their choice of action is significant. The dramatist who, like Sophocles, dares to base his drama on a story that seems to question if not rule out freedom of action is walking a perilous tightrope.

The soul of drama, as Aristotle says, is plot—the action that demands and succeeds in engaging our attention so that we are no longer detached spectators but are involved in the progress of the stage events. Its outcome is important for us; in the greatest plots (and the plot of this play by Sophocles is perhaps the greatest) it is for the moment the most important thing in the world. But this engagement of the audience proceeds from an identification with the figures on stage, and this is not possible if we are made to feel that the action of the characters is not free, not effective. We expect to be made to feel that there is a meaningful relation between the hero's action and his suffering, and this is possible only if that action is free, so that he is responsible for the consequences.

The hero's will must be free, but something else is needed: it must have some causal connection with his suffering. It is the function of great art to give meaning to human suffering, and so we expect that if the hero is crushed by a bulldozer in Act II, there will be some reason for it, and not just some reason but a good one, one that makes sense in terms of the hero's personality and action. In fact, we expect to be shown that he is in some way *responsible* for what happens to him.

If so, the hero obviously cannot be "fated," predestined or determined to act as he does. And Oedipus in Sophocles' play *is* a free agent, and he is responsible for the catastrophe. For the plot of the play consists not of the actions that Oedipus was "fated" to perform, or rather, that were predicted—the plot of the play consists of his discovery that he has already fulfilled the prediction. And this discovery is entirely due to his action.

He dismisses Creon's politic advice to discuss the Delphic response in private; he undertakes a public and vigorous inquiry into the murder of Laius. He is the driving force that, against the reluctance of Tiresias, the dissuasion of Jocasta, and the final supplication of the shepherd, pushes on triumphantly and disastrously to the discovery of the truth. If it had not been for Oedipus, the play persuades us, the truth would never have been discovered, or at least it would not have been discovered *now*. This presentation of the hero's freedom and responsibility, in the context of the dreadful prophecy already unwittingly and unwillingly fulfilled, is an artistic juxtaposition, a momentary illusion of full reconciliation between the two mighty opposites, freedom and destiny. It is an illusion because of course the question of responsibility for what happened *before* the play, of Oedipus's freedom in the context of divine prophecies fulfilled, is evaded. But it makes the play a triumphant tour de force. Oedipus is the free agent who, by his own self-willed action, discovers that his own predicted destiny has already been fulfilled. This is why the play moves us as a spectacle of heroic action and why the figure of Oedipus, dominating the stage, arouses our admiration as well as our sympathy. It is noticeable that in Cocteau's masterpiece, where Oedipus is deliberately portrayed as a marionette in the hands of demonic powers, the greatest dramatic excitement is generated by the action and speech not of Oedipus but of those divine powers, Anubis and the Sphinx.

Oedipus's heroic achievement is the discovery of the truth, and that discovery is the most thoroughgoing and dreadful catastrophe the stage has ever presented. The hero who, in his vigor, courage, and intelligence stands as a representative of all that is creative in man, discovers a truth so dreadful that the chorus that sums up the results of the great calculation sees in his fall the reduction of man to nothing:

> O the generations of men
> the dying generations—adding the total
> of all your lives I find they come to
> > nothing

The existence of human freedom, dramatically represented in the *action* of Oedipus in the play, seems to be a mockery. The discovery to which it led is a catastrophe out of all proportion to the situation. Critics have tried, with contradictory results, to find some flaw in Oedipus's character that will justify his reversal. But there is nothing in his actions that can make it acceptable to us. The chorus's despairing summation, "come to nothing," echoes our own feelings as we watch Oedipus rush into the palace.

But this estimate of the situation is not the last word; in fact, it is contradicted by the final scene of the play. Oedipus's first thought, we are told by the messenger, was to kill himself—he asked for a sword—but he blinds himself instead. This action is one that the audience must have expected; it was mentioned in the earlier *Antigone*, for example, and Oedipus as the blind, exiled wanderer seems to have been one of the invariable elements in fifth-century versions of the myth. But, though the blindness was foreseen by Tiresias, Oedipus's action did not figure in the prophecies made to and about him by Apollo. When the messenger comes from inside the palace to describe the catastrophe, he uses words that emphasize the independence of this action: "terrible things, and none done blindly now, all done with a will." And as Oedipus, wearing a mask with blood running from the eye sockets, stumbles on stage, he makes the same distinction when the chorus asks him what power impelled him to attack his eyes:

> Apollo, friends, Apollo—
> he ordained my agonies—
> these, my pains on pains!
> But the hand that struck my eyes was mine,
> mine alone—no one else—

These two passages suggest that in his decision to blind himself Oedipus is acting freely, that the intricate pattern of his destiny was complete when he knew the truth. To that terrible revelation some violent reaction was inevitable; the choice was left to him. He resisted the first suicidal impulse perhaps (though Sophocles is silent on the point) because of a latent conviction, fully and openly expounded in the last play (*Oedipus at Colonus*), that he was not to blame. He chose to blind himself, he tells the chorus, because he could not bear to see the faces of his children and his fellow citizens. But his action has, in the context of this play, an impressive rightness; the man who, proud of his far-seeing intelligence, taunted Tiresias with his blindness, now realizes that all his life long he has himself been blind to the dreadful realities of his identity and action.

The messenger's description of the horrors that took place inside the palace has prepared the audience for the spectacle of a broken man. So Oedipus seems to be at first, but very soon this bloodstained, sightless figure begins to reassert that magnificent imperious personality that was his from the beginning. He reproaches the chorus for wishing him dead rather than blind, defends his decision to blind himself, issues instructions to Creon, and finally has to be reminded that he is no longer master in Thebes. The despairing summation based on the fate of Oedipus—the great example (as the chorus calls him) that man is equal to nothing—is corrected by the reemergence of Oedipus as his old forceful self. Formidable as of old he may be, but with a difference. The confident tone in which the blind man speaks so regally is based on knowledge, knowledge of his own identity and of the truth of divine prophecy. This new knowledge, won at such a terrible price, makes clear what it was in the hero that brought about the disaster. It was ignorance.

In spite of his name *Oidipous*, with its resemblance to the Greek word *oida* ("I know")—a theme that Sophocles hammers home with continual wordplay—Oedipus, who thought he knew so much, did not even know who his mother and father were. But ignorance can be remedied, the ignorant can learn, and the force with which Oedipus now reasserts his presence springs from the truth he now understands: that the universe is not a field for the play of blind chance, and that man is not its measure. This knowledge gives him a new strength that sustains him in his misery and gives him the courage needed to go on living, though he is now an outcast, a man from whom his fellow men recoil in horror.

The play, then, is a tremendous reassertion of the traditional religious view that man is ignorant, that knowledge belongs only to the gods—Freud's "theological purpose." And it seems to present at first sight a view of the universe as rigid on the side of order as Jocasta's was anarchic on the side of freedom. Jocasta thought that there was no order or design in the world, that dreams and prophecies had no validity; that man had complete freedom because it made no difference what he did—nothing made any sense. Jocasta was wrong; the design was there, and when she saw what it was she hanged herself. But the play now seems to give us a view of man's position that is just as comfortless as her acceptance of a meaningless universe. What place is there in it for human freedom and meaningful action?

Oedipus did have one freedom: he was free to find out or not find out the truth. This was the element of Sophoclean sleight of hand that enabled him to make a drama out of the situation which the philosophers used as the classic demonstration of man's subjection to fate. But it is more than a solution to an apparently insoluble dramatic problem; it is the key to the play's tragic theme and the protagonist's heroic stature. One freedom is allowed him: the freedom to search for the truth, the truth about the prophecies, about the gods, about himself. And of this freedom he makes full use. Against the advice and appeals of others, he pushes on, searching for the truth, the whole truth, and nothing but the truth. And in this search he shows all those great qualities that we admire in him—courage, intelligence, perseverance—the qualities that make human beings great. This freedom to search, and the heroic way Oedipus uses it, makes the play not a picture of man's feebleness caught in the toils of fate, but on the contrary, a heroic example of man's dedication to the search for truth, the truth about himself. This is perhaps the only human freedom, the play seems to say, but there could be none more noble.

ESSAYS
The Ancient World

The Greek *Polis*

Ancient Slavery
and Modern Ideology

In 1939 Louis MacNeice, then professor of Greek at the University of London, wrote in his *Autumn Journal* what turned out to be a definitive farewell to his career as, to quote his own words, "impresario of the ancient Greeks." In the ninth section he ended a brilliant and witty catalogue of those aspects of ancient Greek life he could never hope to understand with the lines:

> And how one can imagine oneself among them
> I do not know;
> It was all so unimaginably different
> And all so long ago.

In the list of exotic phenomena which drove him to this melancholy conclusion, the final item, singled out by its position and elegant metrical phrasing, consisted of the words: "and lastly / I think of the slaves."

Most of the scholars and teachers whose talents have been invested in what has been called the Associated Bank of Greece and Rome try not to think of the slaves or to do so as little as possible. The great Wilamowitz-Moellendorf, as M. I. Finley points out in his *Ancient Slavery and Modern Ideology*,[1] devotes one paragraph and a few scattered phrases to the subject in his *Greek State and Society* (214 large pages in the German edition); in the index to Werner Jaeger's three-volume survey of Greek civilization, *Paideia*, the word "slave" is conspicuous by its absence. But slavery is not a matter that can be swept under the rug. Reliable figures for ancient population are nonexistent but modern estimates of the proportion of free to slave in Sophocles' Attica range from one to one to one to four. Finley squarely (and rightly) rebuts any attempt to wish the consequences away: "There was no action or belief or institution in Graeco-Roman antiquity," he says in the remarkable first chapter from which the book takes its

---

This essay originally appeared in the *New Republic*, September 27, 1980.

1. New York: Viking, 1980.

title, "that was not in one way or the other affected by the possibility that someone involved *might* be a slave."

His first chapter, a penetrating and occasionally acerbic survey of modern treatments of the subject since the eighteenth century, may initially daunt the reader not versed in the intricacies of ancient historiography, but perseverance will be richly rewarded. Modern ideologies, as Finley brings out clearly in his selective, brilliantly organized review, have been at play in every approach to the problem. "The matter of the relationship between Christianity and slavery," for example, was ground fiercely contested for many years, with the battle lines going now this way, now that; this is, as Finley says, "a prime example of what happens when the past is summoned as a witness in a moral or theological disputation." By 1875 it had become a dogma (it is still a popular belief) that the early church was opposed to slavery, and in spite of the careful refutation of this theory by Millar in the eighteenth, Overbeek in the nineteenth, and Westermann in the early twentieth century, Joseph Vogt, the director of a large-scale research program into ancient slavery organized at Mainz in 1951, holds to the dogma of fundamental opposition by Christianity from the outset. He does so in the teeth of the evidence; Finley cites only two telling items—the series of papal and conciliar rulings from as late as the fifth century restricting and even forbidding the manumission of slaves who were the property of the church or of clerics; and an inscribed bronze slave collar, discovered in Sardinia, naming the owner as Felix the archdeacon.

This is not the only failing of Vogt and the school of Mainz; the ten pages in which their shortcomings are dealt with is in fact what the whole chapter has been leading up to. (Along the way the great Eduard Meyer, cited by Vogt as his authority and generally regarded as little less than a god by ancient historians, is criticized in detail and then disposed of in a sentence which begins: "In sum, Meyer's lecture on ancient slavery is as close to nonsense as anything I can remember written by a historian of such eminence.") Of the two views of the historical process Finley outlines at the beginning of the chapter, Vogt adopts the "moral or spiritual" rather than the "sociological." Like Wilamowitz and Jaeger, he considers the Greek achievement a miraculous creation for which slavery and its attendant loss of humanity were part of the sacrifice which had to be paid. Wilamowitz and Jaeger turned their Olympian backs on the realities of the sacrifice, but

Vogt insists it must be faced: "human society must be portrayed as it really is without concealing or extenuating its negative aspects." On examination, Finley sarcastically remarks, "human society as it was turns out to be not all that bad"; the whole exercise, he concludes, is a "kind of 'saving the phenomena,' rescuing 'classical humanism' by certain concessions."

It also, and here Finley's ideological preoccupations emerge clearly, involved a large-scale attack on the Marxist approach to the problem—a facet of the bitter hostility between the two Germanies. Finley's indictment of the Mainz school on this point is overwhelming; most of their anti-Marxist polemics are aimed at straw men—"absurdities in Soviet writing on the subject between 1933 and 1953," for example. A product of the school which deals directly with the subject, Backhaus's *Marx, Engels und die Sklaverei* (1974), starts with a quotation from Stalin and goes on to produce what Finley calls "a caricature of the current situation in Marxist thinking." It entirely ignores the Marxist work on the ancient world which has been "appearing in the West at an accelerated rate" and which is for the most part, "groping, tentative and mutually polemical."

Finley's own analysis, organized in three chapters headed "The Emergence of a Slave Society," "Slavery and Humanity," and "The Decline of Ancient Slavery," does not claim to be Marxist itself but clearly owes much to Marxist thinking; his emphasis throughout is on the ancient economy and the nature and organization of its labor force. The prose, however, owes nothing, mercifully, to Marxist writing—Finley does not take refuge in technical jargon and his categories and concepts are lucidly defined. In the spare but flowing style and with the logical economy his readers have come to expect of him, Finley proceeds to conduct, in a little more than seventy pages, a searching examination of the questions raised by that slave system which formed the base of Greco-Roman civilization.

There have been only five genuine slave societies, two of them in antiquity (classical Greece and classical Italy), three in the New World (United States, the Caribbean, and Brazil). One of the problems faced by ancient historians is the paucity of the evidence and the enigmatic nature of much of what does exist, but no solutions can be expected from the comparative method; the differences are so great that the New World cannot be brought in to explain the riddles of the Old. Finley does indeed adduce a fascinating modern parallel (Captain

Cudjoe and his Marroons on Jamaica), which serves to validate Athenaeus's account (usually dismissed as fiction) of the activities of the rebel slave leader Drimachus on Chios, but this is exceptional. One obvious and decisive difference is that ancient slaves, though foreign, were for the most part not colored; consequently, the children of emancipated slaves could climb the social ladder with no telltale sign of their origin. This was especially true in Rome, where manumitted slaves became full citizens. The poet Horace, whose position in Augustan society was so secure that he was asked to become the private secretary of the emperor Augustus and could decline the honor without losing the emperor's friendship, was the son of a man who had started life as a slave.

On Finley's first problem, the origins of the slave system, the reason why "something new and wholly original in world history" was established first in Greece and Italy, the New World experience throws no light; the vast quantities of available land, the absence of a sufficient native labor force, and the availability of highly desirable export crops are factors missing in the Mediterranean situation. After a careful definition of slavery (distinguishing it from other forms of nonvoluntary labor which existed all over the ancient world), Finley rejects the popular theory that "war and conquest" were "a necessary condition for the creation of a slave society." He points out that there is solid evidence for the "growth of slavery . . . in Rome" considerably earlier than the last two centuries before Christ, the great ages of conquest and mass enslavement. "The demand for slaves," Finley concludes, "precedes the supply." And he lists three necessary conditions for the existence of that demand: an economy predominantly agrarian, the land held as private property in units large enough to require extrafamilial labor; a sufficient development of commodity production and markets (imported slaves have to be paid for); and unavailability of internal labor supply. Admitting that the Roman evidence is not decisive, Finley explores the situation of sixth-century Athens, where, after the Solonian reforms which abolished prevailing forms of involuntary labor (debt bondage, for example), all three of his preliminary conditions are to be found. "The free man," he says,

> was one who neither lived under the constraint of nor was employed for the benefit of another: who lived preferably on his an-

cestral plot of land, with its shrines and ancestral tombs. The creation of that type of free man in a low-technology pre-industrial world led to the establishment of a slave society. There was no realistic alternative.

He does not of course mean to imply (in fact he explicitly denies) that the predominance of slave labor was the result of deliberate choice; he posits only "general acquiescence in the shift to slave labor." In his last chapter, on the gradual dissolution of the system, he is equally anxious to avoid giving the impression that there was a "thought-out change in policy." What took place in the late centuries of the Roman empire was rather

> a slow process of shifting practices, locality by locality. . . . Only later, centuries later, did it become evident that the labor regime had been undergoing a basic transformation, specifically in those central regions that had long been genuine slave societies.

The process which ended in the replacement of a slave-based by a feudal society was in fact probably not complete, as Marc Bloch argued and Finley agrees, until the time of Charlemagne.

His analysis of the process—"a slow quantitative decline in slaves, . . . a changeover . . in the status and organization of labor"— begins by dismissing some of the conventional explanations, Stoic or Christian influence, for example, and, more important, the same "conquest" theory which has been used to explain the origin of slavery, this time in reverse. Finley has only to point out that most of the Roman conquests were completed by the death of Augustus in A.D. 14; if the theory is correct, the supposed deficiency in the supply of slaves should have shown up centuries earlier than it did. In any case, systematic slave breeding was a sufficient substitute for foreign sources, as the American southern states found out in the early nineteenth century, when the slave trade was formally prohibited. The reasons for the fact that "in the late Empire, on the whole, the employers of labor were not successful in maintaining a sufficient complement of slave labor" must lie, Finley concludes, within the society itself.

His attempt to explain this phenomenon is, as he says himself, speculative and tentative, as it must be in view of "the extraordinary difficulty of the enterprise." He takes up, each in turn, the three conditions he isolated as necessary for the establishment of a slave system to see if there were changes in one or more of them. Changes there certainly were. Private ownership of land continued, but with a steady trend toward more middle-sized and large estates at the expense of free, small landholders. This, Finley concludes, is not of itself sufficient to explain the decline in the predominance of slave labor, but his second prerequisite, commodity production and markets, is more helpful. He believes the evidence shows that over the empire as a whole there was a significant decline in commodity production; he attributes this to an accelerated expansion of the "practice of payments in kind to (and by) the state," the flight of the wealthy from the cities, and a decline in the urban population in general. However, he is on controversial ground here and he moves with more confidence to condition three, the absence of an internal supply of free labor. He argues that the most decisive factor in the gradual replacement of slave labor was "the fundamental change in the political-military structure." The Augustan imperial system, with its professional armies, relieved the citizen small farmer of the burden of military service, but at the same time deprived him of his only effective leverage against the state. Over the centuries of imperial administration, with, as the situation at the frontiers grew more serious, increasing taxation, the pressure on the sector that was economically and politically weak increased. The result, in Finley's careful formula, was "a gradual erosion in the capacity of the lower classes to resist working for the benefit of others under conditions of less than full 'freedom of contract.'" In the late centuries of the empire, to the already existing slave system and the forms of dependent agricultural labor inherited by the Romans in territories taken over in the East, there was added a significant new element, as "the status of many once free rural people—peasants, tenants, agricultural laborers—was steadily being depressed into one of dependency, of 'unfreedom.'" The word *colonus*, as he points out, began by meaning "farmer," came to mean "tenant farmer," and was defined in the early fourth century as "slave of the land." The world of late antiquity, despite the continued presence of slaves in large numbers, was no longer a slave society.

In his third chapter, as its title indicates, Finley discusses the matter not as an economic but as a human problem. One reason our sources are so unsatisfactory is that to the ancient writers on whom we depend for information, slavery was such a fact of everyday life that it seemed perfectly natural, as indeed Aristotle said it was, and so not a matter for discussion or investigation. Classical humanists therefore have found it not too difficult to ignore or discount the unpleasant realities of ancient slavery; in this chapter Finley pulls the skeleton out of the classical cupboard and takes a good look at it. It is not a pretty sight. Slaves were subject to an indignity no free man endured—corporal punishment. They were, to quote Demosthenes, "answerable with their bodies for all offenses." Their evidence in court could be accepted only if extracted under torture; they were available, without restrictions, for the sexual pleasure of their owners. They were liable to be sold and so separated from their families, which were, of course, the property of their masters. Those slaves employed in the mines were worse off still; anyone who has tried to crawl through the narrow tunnels cut in hard rock at Laurion, the ancient Athenian silver mines, realizes that for the thousand slaves leased to the city as miners by Nicias, the great Athenian aristocrat of the late fifth century, life must have been brutal and mercifully short. Our sources preserve many individual incidents which illustrate the magnanimity of masters or the loyalty of slaves; they are irrelevant not only because the literature represents "the views and hopes of the owning classes" but also because, as Finley rightly points out, there is a distinction between "more or less humane treatment of individual slaves . . . and the inhumanity of slavery as an institution." Sometimes he presses the evidence a little too far, in the matter of slave evidence and torture, for example. It was standard practice in an Athenian lawsuit to make a point of the fact that you were willing to hand over your slaves for torture to the other party or of the fact that the other party refused to do so. We have no hard evidence, however, that testimony normally was extracted in such fashion; most scholars assume it was an exceptional practice, but Finley (pointing out that in Rome there is evidence for it) assumes the opposite. But it seems like a double-edged weapon (if I can torture evidence against you out of your slaves, you may retaliate in kind), and it would certainly result in damage to property. It seems more likely that the purpose of the law was to rule out slave testimony altogether; if a man's slaves could bear witness against him in court, few masters would sleep sound of nights. Yet in the main Finley is on solid ground: the realities of slavery were appalling and he could have cited much more shocking evidence than he saw fit to print. Those of us who assume the role of impresario of the ancient Greeks must not attempt to suppress the truth about the foundations on which the most influential of Western civilizations was built.

That does not mean that we have to abandon it. It is a strange paradox that the Greeks, who first developed the idea of individual and political freedom, denied any such freedom to a huge population which performed the menial tasks of their society. But that does not detract in the least from the stature of Pericles' funeral speech as the original and perhaps the noblest and most humane statement of the democratic ideal. Anyone who thinks it does should remember the slave families owned by the author of the Declaration of Independence.

The Toilers Find a Voice

"Jesus knows all about the class struggle"—the words are those of an irreverent ballad sung by British hunger marchers of the 1930s—"'E was there when it first begun. . . ." Geoffrey de Ste. Croix, in his *Class Struggle in the Ancient Greek World*,[1] has some interesting things to say about Jesus and the class struggle, but he traces the theme much farther back—to Hesiod and archaic Greece of the eighth century B.C.—and forward—to the Arab conquest of what had been the eastern provinces of the Byzantine Empire in the seventh century A.D. To make clear on which side of the class struggle the author's sympathies lie, a frontispiece reproduces, in the authentic gloomy colors, Van Gogh's *Potato Eaters;* they represent

> the voiceless toilers, the great majority—let us not forget it—of the population of the Greek and Roman world, upon whom was built a great civilization which despised them and did all it could to forget them.

As the title suggests, this is an avowedly Marxist book and its author is at some pains to make clear what he means by the terms of Marxist analysis, particularly the words "class" and "struggle"; the first 275 pages, in fact, are devoted to "conceptual and methodological problems." True to type, Ste. Croix spends quite some time dealing roundly with other would-be, pseudo-, or mistaken Marxists who have written on the ancient world before he tackles the problems himself. That there are real problems is clear from the fact, unknown to the countless readers who have quit long before they got there, that the fifty-second chapter of volume three of *Das Kapital*, entitled "Classes," breaks off after scarcely more than a page, leaving the world with no authoritative definition of that crucial category. A defi-

This essay originally appeared in the *New Republic,* May 28, 1982.

1. G. E. M. de Ste. Croix, *The Class Struggle in the Ancient Greek World: From the Archaic Age to the Arab Conquest* (Ithaca: Cornell University Press, 1981).

nition has to be abstracted from scattered passages in the sacred writings; unfortunately, they seem to mean different things to different readers. In any case, as Ste. Croix himself points out, even Marx and Engels sometimes confuse "class" with "status," the Weberian concept which is currently fashionable in non-Marxist analyses of Roman imperial society.

Ste. Croix's definition of class and class struggle turns on the concept of exploitation, "the appropriation of part of the product of the labor of others." A "class" is "a group of persons . . . defined above all according to their relationship (primarily in terms of the degree of ownership or control) to the conditions of production." In a class society "one or more of the smaller classes, in virtue of their control over the conditions of production . . . will be able to exploit . . . the larger classes." He uses the "expression *class struggle* for the fundamental relationship between classes . . . involving essentially exploitation, or resistance to it." This class struggle, however, turns out in the event to be a very peculiar form of "struggle"; Ste. Croix applies the term to "situations in which there may be no explicit common awareness of class on either side, no specific political struggle at all, and perhaps even little consciousness of struggle of any kind." Such a definition of "struggle" would seem to belong to the realm of metaphysics rather than economics, but it is certainly an ingenious way to deal with the major difficulty facing Marxist historians of ancient society. That difficulty is, briefly, that the political struggles of the ancient world, democrat versus oligarch in Greece, patrician versus plebeian in early Rome, and *nobiles* versus *populares* in late, Republican Rome, were clearly not class struggles at all, since both sides belonged essentially to the same class, one united in its dependence on and repression of the slave population which did the heavy work of the society.

Ste. Croix admits that his use of the term "class struggle" "is not a very happy one for such situations" but insists on it nonetheless; the alternative would lead, he says, to a contradiction of the opening sentence of the *Communist Manifesto* and its full development "would make nonsense not merely of the *Communist Manifesto* but of the greater part of Marx's work." That of course is an argument which will have more force in some quarters than in others.

With his ideological and methodological foundations thus firmly laid, Ste. Croix proceeds to Part Two, which consists of four chapters;

they deal in turn with (1) the class struggle in Greek history on the political plane, (2) "Rome the Suzerain," (3) the class struggle on the ideological plane, and lastly (4) "the 'decline and fall': an explanation." The chapter on Roman history is of course dictated by the fact that the Greek-speaking Near East became, in the second century B.C., part of the Roman Empire.

Early Greek history gets very little attention (five and a half pages from Hesiod to Pisistratus); there is in any case very little evidence. The great age of Athenian democracy (fourth and fifth centuries B.C.) is discussed at more generous length and also, unlike all the other regimes discussed in this book, with a large measure of approval, since "democracy played a vital part in the class struggle by mitigating the exploitation of poorer citizens by the richer ones." However, it is hard to see why Athenian democracy gets such very high marks for its performance in the class struggle, since "it was only adult male citizens of a small *polis* who could indulge effectively in class struggle on the political plane" and since only citizens could own land ("the most important means of production") and could therefore "be considered a distinct class of landowners," and since furthermore both rich and poor "exploited" not only their slaves (more than twenty thousand deserted to the enemy in the last years of the Peloponnesian War) but also the subject "allies" of the Athenian Empire. Perhaps it is because after the extinction of Athenian democracy by Macedonian and later by Roman rulers (completed, no doubt, with the active collaboration of the Athenian upper classes, as Ste. Croix insists), there is no break in the monotonous record of oligarchic and autocratic rule.

In the history of Rome—which in the second century B.C. established dominion over the Greek east that outlasted by centuries the fall of Rome itself to the Germanic "barbarians"—there is not much evidence for class struggle on a political level. The best Ste. Croix can do is to equip the earliest of the *populares*, the Gracchi (but not their later leaders Marius and Julius Caesar), with somewhat hesitant credentials: they "served, *faute de mieux* and sometimes against their will, as leaders of what was in a very real sense a political class struggle: a blind, spasmodic, uninformed, often misdirected and always easily confused movement." The strengths of this chapter are the closely argued case that the transition from republic to principate was in no sense a "revolution" and the analysis of the ways in which "imperial rule contributed to maintain a massive system of exploitation of the great majority by the upper classes." Here, too, as in the rest of the notes, the wealth, variety, and in many cases the novelty of the material cited in support of the arguments make the book indispensable even for those who remain unconvinced by its main theses.

To such readers, the last two chapters will seem most rewarding. The evidence for class struggle on the ideological plane is of course one-sided; but Ste. Croix's selection from the "psychological propaganda" of the "dominant classes" is brilliantly chosen. Its prize exhibit is a really repulsive piece of class snobbery from Plato's *Republic* (VI.495c), which compares "some poor creature who has proved his cleverness in some mechanical craft" and who presumes to study philosophy to a "bald-headed little tinker, who, having come into some money, has just got out of prison, had a good wash at the baths and dressed himself up as a bridegroom, ready to marry his master's daughter." Slavery was justified by the theory of "natural slavery," a concept elaborated by Aristotle. Unfortunately the Christian church, which in the later centuries of the empire became the dominant and finally the exclusive religious organization, took no stand against this fundamental institution of the ancient economy. "Whatever the theologian may think of Christianity's claim to set free the soul of the slave . . . the historian cannot deny that it helped to rivet the shackles rather more firmly on his feet"—a harsh judgment but backed by the evidence. Ste. Croix adds that he knows of no "general outright condemnation of slavery, inspired by a Christian outlook, before the petition of the Mennonites of Germantown in Pennsylvania in 1668."

Though Jesus himself "accepted slavery as a fact of his environment," his attitude toward property—"Go thy way, sell all thou hast, and give to the poor"—was one which no functioning and governing institution of Roman society (which is what the Christian church became) could possibly accept. But Jesus, as Ste. Croix sees him, was not a denizen of the Greco-Roman world at all. He lived and preached in the *chora,* that countryside which lived its life of agricultural toil and spoke its ancestral language; it was unaffected by the Greek culture of the cities, with their theaters, gymnasia, and stoas, which had been founded in the wake of Alexander's conquests and which lived on the produce and labor of the workers in the fields. When St. Paul, a Greek-speaker and a Roman citizen, carried the message of Jesus to those cities, to Caesarea, Antioch, Philippi, Thessalonica, Athens, Corinth, Ephesus, and finally to Rome, there took place "the transfer of a whole system of ideas from the world of the *chora* to the world of the *polis*." The early Christian attitude to property ownership developed into something very different from Jesus's opinions on that subject, which were, Ste. Croix is "tempted to say . . . nearer to those of Bertolt Brecht than to those held by some of the Fathers of the Church and by some Christians today."

This opposition of *polis* and *chora* is fundamental to the argument of the last chapter, in which Ste. Croix ambitiously claims to "explain and not merely describe . . . the disintegration of large portions of the Roman empire." He has already discussed, with a wealth of detail, the "change in the form of exploitation . . . which came over the Greco-Roman world during the first three centuries of the Christian era," a process by which "the whole of the working agricultural population throughout the Roman empire, inscribed in the tax registers, were tied to the land on a hereditary basis and thus entered into serfdom." This characterization of the "colonate" as "serfdom" is controversial, but his discussion, based on expert knowledge of the sources and the modern bibliography and conducted with his customary combination of firmness and modesty—"if I have analysed it correctly (and I am not quite certain of this)"—carries conviction. He sees the causes of the Roman collapse in the resulting concentration of economic and political power in the hands of the few, the increased rate of exploitation of an "unfree labor," and the consequent indifference of the exploited classes to the fate of the empire, which needed for its defense against growing pressure from outside "large numbers of recruits willing to fight to the death in defense of their way of life (as the free Greeks and early Romans had been)." The empire fell not because, in Gibbon's magnificent phrase, "the stupendous fabric yielded to the pressure of its own weight" but because the "Roman political system . . . facilitated a most intense and ultimately destructive economic exploitation of the great mass of the people . . . and it made radical reform impossible. . . . The propertied classes . . . who had deliberately created this system for their own benefit, drained the life blood from their world and thus destroyed Greco-Roman civilization over a large part of the empire."

This explanation of "Gibbon's problem" must await the detailed critique and judgment of experts; only first reactions can be recorded here. The reference to the "free Greeks and the early Romans" recalls the fact that the kind of free peasantry on which those citizen armies were based had vanished long before the military crisis of the empire in the third century A.D.; already in the fourth century B.C. democratic Athens relied on mercenaries to do much of its fighting, and the free Roman peasantry which had fought the Republic's wars in Italy did not survive the Punic Wars. Yet Roman armies had held and even extended the frontiers for centuries. And, in any case, Ste. Croix's term, "disintegration of the Roman empire," is valid only for the West; the Greek east (his main concern, as his title indicates) maintained the Roman Empire, in one form or another, until the fall of Constantinople to the Turks in the fifteenth century.

Whatever the verdict of the professionals turns out to be, this book is a landmark in the field of ancient history. The notes are a vast storehouse of new materials, of fresh evaluation of passages already well known and of valuable references to modern literature in many disciplines. The ancient historian who fails to consult it will do so at his peril; his work has been made easy for him, for the book concludes with a really admirable analytical index.

One last word. I do not know the author personally but this book makes a personal impression. It is the voice of a man wholly dedicated to the truth as he sees it, but fair-minded in his treatment of opponents and honest in his admission of difficulties, of a man utterly sincere in his sympathy for those "voiceless toilers" his reproduction of the Van Gogh painting brings to our attention. It is the voice, too, of a man concerned with our own world; not that this is an obtrusive note—specific modern parallels are rarely cited—but it is there all the same. This long and depressing analysis of the decay and collapse of a great civilization says implicitly what Gibbon felt the need to say outright: "This awful revolution may be usefully applied to the instruction of the present age."

Greece à la Française

Ever since the turn of the century Paris has been the arbiter of fashion for the English-speaking world, and though since the Second World War the dictates of its couturiers on skirt lengths have not imposed the universal conformity they once did, the methodologies launched by its intellectuals have all, in their turn, found industrious promoters and an enthusiastic clientele. Fashion however is a quick-change artist and some of her intellectual creations no one would now want to be seen dead in. Even the most infatuated of sentimental leftists had long ago to give up trying to explain Sartre's manic switches as he wriggled on the hook attached to the Party line, and almost everyone now realizes that Roland Barthes was too great a wit to have taken his own late work seriously (if *S/Z* is not a gargantuan parody of structuralist criticism there is little excuse for it).

Epigones of Lévi-Strauss, of course, are still constructing diagrams which show the tortuous relationships between questionable opposites, and students of Derrida continue to write critical prose which is often a classic vindication of their master's basic contention that language is not an adequate instrument for the expression of meaning. These fashions too, mercifully, will pass, and there are signs that perhaps Paris is losing its power to impose instant ideologies: what seemed, a year or so ago, to be the distinct possibility that there would be a boom in the Freudian incoherencies of Lacan has turned out to be a false alarm.

In one particular field, however, which might be loosely defined as Greek cultural history, Paris has been exerting an enduring and steadily widening influence on the professional sector in England and the United States. Its source is a group of scholars—Jean-Pierre Vernant, Marcel Detienne, and Pierre Vidal-Naquet—who are not exactly an *école* (the senior member, Vernant, does not function as *maître*) or even an *équipe*, for though they often publish collaborative

This essay originally appeared in the *New York Review of Books*, March 3, 1983.

work they have divergent viewpoints and interests. The main links between them are their cooperation in the direction of the Centre de recherches comparées sur les sociétés anciennes, their teaching and research functions in the Ecole pratique des hautes études (though Vernant moved on to the higher reaches of the Collège de France in 1975), and the general description "structuralist," which appears in the subtitle of a recent selection from their work in English translation.[1]

Vernant, whose training was in psychology (his first collection, *Mythe et pensée chez les grecs*,[2] was subtitled *Etudes de psychologie historique*), attended the seminars of Louis Gernet, whose essays he published (under the title *Anthropologie de la Grèce antique*)[3] after Gernet's death. In the introduction to the volume he writes with admiration and affection of his teacher, a man whose wide interests and original approach evidently did not recommend him to his bureaucratic superios; "*il n'a pas fait carrière*"—in fact he spent most of his life teaching Greek composition at the University of Algiers before he came to the Ecole pratique des hautes études in 1948. This colonial ambience may have stimulated his anthropological interests (among his articles there is one entitled "*You-you, en marge d'Hérodote—le cri rituel*"); he was in any case a friend of the anthropologist Marcel Mauss and a follower of Durkheim. When he died in 1962 he was known to the scholarly world principally as a specialist in Greek law, author of *Droit et société dans la Grèce ancienne*[4] and translator and editor of the private orations of Demosthenes in the Budé series.[5] Since the publication of his selected essays in 1968 his true importance as a pioneer in modern sociological and anthropological analysis of ancient Greek society has been beyond dispute and a recent English translation of the volume edited by Vernant[6] will make this rich mine of informed speculation and revealing interpretation available to a wider audience.

1. *Myth, Religion, and Society: Structuralist Essays by M. Detienne, L. Gernet, J. P. Vernant, and P. Vidal-Naquet*, ed. R. L. Gordon (Cambridge: Cambridge University Press, 1981). This includes translations of five of the essays contained in *Le Chasseur noir*.
2. Paris: Maspero, 1962.
3. Paris: Maspero, 1968.
4. 1955; Paris: Publications de l'Institut de Droit romain de l'Université de Paris, 1964.
5. *Démosthène: Plaidoyers civils*, 2 vols. (Paris: Belles Lettres, 1954–57).
6. *The Anthropology of Ancient Greece*, trans. John Hamilton and Blaise Nagy (Baltimore: Johns Hopkins University Press, 1981).

Vernant defines his own interest as that of Ignace Meyerson—*recherches de psychologie historique*—and his first book, *Les Origines de la pensée grecque*,[7] deals not only with the birth of Greek "rationality" from the conditions of the city-state—"in its limitations as in its innovations it is the daughter of the city"—but also with its nature—it is "inseparable from the social and mental structures characteristic of the Greek city." Since then in collections of essays,[8] and also in a series of conferences he has organized or contributed to,[9] he has established himself as perhaps the leading, certainly the most consistently exciting, investigator of the psychological, political, and religious norms of ancient Greek archaic and classical culture. He is an eclectic "structuralist," as ready to use Georges Dumézil's three Indo-European "functions" as Lévi-Strauss's binary opposites (or to combine them, as in an influential analysis of Hesiod's myth of the five ages); he has learned from Marx as well as from Gernet, Mauss, and Durkheim. But the resulting methodology is very much his own; time and time again, coming across a typically challenging and brilliant formulation one feels: "Only Vernant could have said that!"

Marcel Detienne, his close associate at the Ecole pratique des hautes études and now director of studies in the section dealing with Greek religion, is mainly concerned with developing the analytic methods of Lévi-Strauss; in fact he has even won that rare cachet, an endorsement from the master who has, quite understandably, made very sour remarks about some of his would-be disciples but said of

---

7. Paris: Presses Universitaires de France, 1962. Trans. *The Origins of Greek Thought* (Ithaca: Cornell University Press, 1982).

8. *Mythe et pensée* is now in its sixth edition. *Mythe et tragédie en Grèce ancienne* (Paris: Maspero, 1972) has been translated as *Tragedy and Myth in Ancient Greece* (Atlantic Highlands, N.J.: Humanities Press, 1981). The translation contains an essay by Vidal-Naquet, "The Shields of the Heroes," which was not included in the French edition. As for the other essays, a note to the preface states: "Many of the studies that are reprinted in this volume have been modified or corrected since their first appearance, or even in some cases expanded." *Mythe et société en Grèce ancienne* (Paris: Maspero, 1974) has been translated as *Myth and Society in Ancient Greece* (Humanities Press, 1980). *Les Ruses de l'intelligence: La métis des grecs*, in collaboration with Detienne (Paris: Flammarion, 1974) has been translated as *Cunning Intelligence in Greek Culture and Society* (Humanities Press, 1978).

9. *Problèmes de la guerre en Grèce* (Paris: Mouton, 1968); *Il mito greco: Atti del convegno internazionale, Urbino, 1973* (Rome: Edizioni dell' Ateneo e Bizarri, 1977); *Divination et rationalité* (Paris: Editions du Seuil, 1974); and *La Mort, les morts dans les sociétés anciennes* (Cambridge: Cambridge University Press, 1982).

Detienne's *Jardins d'Adonis*[10] that it is "gripping . . . skillfully organized . . . written with a grace uncommon in scholarly works." This praise is justified; the book is a spectacular performance. One of Frazer's central concerns, the myth of Adonis, is subjected to a structural analysis that stands Frazer's classic interpretation on its head: instead of a vegetarian god whose life and death was an image of the agricultural year, Adonis emerges as a figure representative of illicit, issueless sexuality, a threat to the institution of marriage and its Greek purpose—the begetting of legitimate children. Linked with Adonis is the whole world of seductive spices and perfumes; Detienne's decipherment of the "codes" embodied in the myths makes fascinating reading—who could resist chapters with titles such as "The Perfumes of Arabia," "The Misfortunes of Mint," "From Myrrh to Lettuce"? Even if the reader emerges not convinced on every point, Detienne has opened up for him a strange and alluring new world.[11]

Pierre Vidal-Naquet's name appears as joint author with Pierre Lévêque on the title page of *Clisthène l'Athénien*,[12] and he shares with Vernant the authorship of *Mythe et tragédie*, to which he contributed two brilliant essays, but *Le Chasseur noir*[13] is the first book dealing with classical Greek civilization to be issued solely under his own name. That name, however, has often appeared on books which appealed to readers who do not share his interest in the institutions of the ancient world; he was a leading figure, for example, in the campaign to expose and document the use of torture by the French army

10. *Les Jardins d'Adonis: La mythologie des aromates en Grèce* (Paris: Gallimard, 1972). Trans. J. Lloyd, *The Gardens of Adonis: Spices in Greek Mythology* (Hassocks: Harvester Press, 1977).

11. More recently Detienne has tackled the myths and cults associated with Dionysus in *Dionysos mis à mort* (Paris: Gallimard, 1977), trans. Mireille Muellner and Leonard Muellner, *Dionysus Slain* (Baltimore: Johns Hopkins University Press, 1979). The choice of subject, like that of Adonis, is characteristic of his discretion: here, as in his contribution to *La cuisine du sacrifice en pays grec*, ed. M. Detienne and J.-P. Vernant (Paris: Gallimard, 1979), he has focused attention on the wilder shores of Greek myth rather than the highly sophisticated literary versions which are shaped by the moral and artistic concerns of poets.

12. Paris: Les Belles Lettres, 1964.

13. *Le Chasseur noir. Formes de pensée et formes de société dans le monde grec* (Paris: Maspero, 1981; 2nd corrected ed., 1983). Trans. A. Szegedy-Maszak, *The Black Hunter: Forms of Thought and Forms of Society in the Greek World* (Baltimore: Johns Hopkins University Press, 1986).

and police in Algeria. *L'Affaire Audin*[14] presented the results of an investigation into the case of an assistant professor of mathematics at the University of Algiers who died in the course of an "interrogation" by the paratroops. The book accused the army of the systematic use of torture as well as murder and managed to document its case very effectively. In *Raison d'état*[15] the army's use of torture as a normal practice was meticulously exposed, mainly through demonstration of contradictions in the official records. In the next year Penguin Books, in England, published his *Torture, Cancer of Democracy: France and Algeria 1954–62*, a sobering meditation on the moral and political crises revealed by the public indifference to the use of torture not only in a colonial war but in France itself. This book did not appear in French until 1972[16] and was followed in 1977 by *Les Crimes de l'armée française*,[17] another selection of documents, mostly accounts by men who had served in the campaign, which amply justifies the title.

This book, Vidal-Naquet explains in the preface, is an *aide-mémoire*. For a people's memory, he points out, is not an automatic process, a "natural" phenomenon. It can be wiped out, as in the USSR, or maintained, as in the case of the museums and institutes that preserve the record of Nazi terror, or it can simply cease to function, lulled to sleep by the official voices of government, press, and television. "If the profession of historian has a social function," says Vidal-Naquet, in an ironically appropriate military metaphor, "it is to furnish cadres and benchmarks for the collective memory."

It was with the memory of another, older controversy which divided the French nation that he engaged, "not without illusions," in the polemics of the Algerian war: "in the background was the example of the Dreyfus case." His most recent publication is a long and fascinating account of that "*affaire*" and its effects on French society, a preface to a reissue of Dreyfus's own account of his imprisonment, *Cinq années de ma vie*.[18] Vidal-Naquet had heard about the *affaire* as a child; in fact his great-uncle Emmanuel Vidal-Naquet was a devoted Dreyfusard, but such an interest was in any case natural in a French-

14. Paris: Editions de Minuit, 1958.
15. Paris: Editions de Minuit, 1962.
16. *La Torture dans la république* (Paris: Minuit).
17. Paris: Maspero.
18. Paris: Maspero, 1982.

man of Jewish ancestry, whose parents were "*déportés*" under the German occupation.

A collection of articles, prefaces, and essays, *Les Juifs, la mémoire et le présent,*[19] explores the problem of Jewish identity and destiny all the way from a fascinating discussion of Josephus, the historian of the revolt that ended in the Roman destruction of Jerusalem, to the controversy over the "revisionists," French and American, who dismiss the Holocaust as Zionist propaganda. And in a long preface of over one hundred pages written for a translation of Josephus's *Jewish War,*[20] Vidal-Naquet explores with penetrating political insight and formidable erudition the religious and ideological chaos of first century Palestine, a tangled skein which seems so familiar that it is hardly a surprise to come across a Menahem (who seizes the fortress of Masada in 66 B.C. and returns as king to Jerusalem); one half expects to turn the page and find some form of the name Arafat.

Vidal-Naquet has a talent for writing prefaces and he is often invited to do so. He wrote the introduction to Detienne's book on early Greek philosophy, *Les Maîtres de vérité dans la grèce archaïque,*[21] to translations of Sophocles, the *Iliad,* and Aeschylus.[22] He also contributed to the French translation of M. I. Finley's *Democracy, Ancient and Modern*[23] a substantial essay on the use made of the Athenian democratic tradition by the French revolutionaries of 1789–94. *Le Chasseur noir* does not contain any of these pieces but it does consist entirely of articles that have been previously published elsewhere; "in the Greek area," Vidal-Naquet says in the *avant-propos,* "the article is a means of expression more in my line than the book."[24] The contents were first published, in their original form, over the course of twenty-three years (from 1957 to 1980) and have here been corrected, expanded, and rewritten to take account of criticism, fresh insights, and new data.

The book is, however, not a haphazard collection of Vidal-Naquet's scholarly articles; from his impressive output he has selected those

19. Paris: Maspero, 1981.
20. "Du bon usage de la trahison," preface to *La Guerre des Juifs,* translated by Pierre Savinel (Paris: Editions de Minuit, 1977).
21. Paris: Maspero, 1967.
22. Paris: Gallimard, 1973 and 1982.
23. *Démocratie antique et démocratie moderne* (Paris: Payot, 1976).
24. For translation from the French here, as elsewhere in this review, the reviewer is responsible.

essays which deal with "forms of thought" and "forms of society" in the Greek world, or, rather, which attempt to establish a link between those two subjects, "which are not here studied in themselves and for themselves." The title of the book is that of a chapter on the Athenian institution of the *ephebeia*, the young Athenian's initiation in citizenship and military service; this is a brilliant essay which is already well known, not only in French (1968) but in English (1968) and Italian (1975) versions. It is also the essay that, as Vidal-Naquet states in his preface, marked a crucial stage in his development: "the discovery of structural analysis as a heuristic instrument."

The methods and terminology of "structuralism," particularly of Lévi-Strauss, are plain to see in the contents of the book—in the analysis, for example, of the voyage of Odysseus as a series of contacts with alien cultures, all of them belonging to a world ignorant of agriculture, or in the title of one of the chapters, "*Le Cru, l'enfant grec et le cuit.*" But as Pierre Pachet has pointed out in a thoughtful appreciation of Vidal-Naquet's whole career in *Esprit*,[25] "He has always been at pains to reintroduce into structuralism the historical conscience, to restrict the fields of study, examine the testimony and evaluate its scope, distinguish the authentic from what reactivates or imitates it." Lévi-Strauss himself, somewhat reluctantly one feels, made an exception for the Greeks: myth is timeless but the Greeks "*ont pris le parti de l'histoire*" and Vidal-Naquet is always aware of the fact that the Greeks, who invented history in the modern sense, were also creators of historical myths. He is also fully aware of the danger inherent in applying Lévi-Straussian methods to Greek material which is "furnished to us," as he says, "by a learned tradition" and so deserves "a differentiated treatment."

The introduction, "*Une civilisation de la parole politique*" (an abridged version of an article contributed to the *Encyclopaedia universalis* [Paris, 1970]), presents the "oppositions" which are the object of discussion in the rest of the book. They are, to quote the summary in the preface: cultivated and wild, master and slave, man and woman, citizen and foreigner, adult and child, warrior and artisan. "These," says Vidal-Naquet, "are some of the oppositions which the body of the book will continuously keep in play, without trying to enclose in

---

25. *Critique*, March 1982, pp. 213–230. This article concludes with a full (thought not complete) bibliography of Vidal-Naquet's publications.

them matter which resists the process." They are so basic to the structure of the book, in fact, that its very full and helpful index (an unusual feature in a French scholarly work) is prefaced by a note that warns the reader: "When a pair of opposites is in question, it is located under the word which comes first in alphabetical order; *virilité* for example refers the reader to *femme.*"

The main text is divided into four sections: "Space and Time"; "The Young, the Warriors"; "Women, Slaves and Artisans"; "The City, Vision and Reality" (*La Cité, pensée et vécue*). "Space" is accounted for by the analysis of the "cultures" discovered by Odysseus on his wanderings; Greek conceptions of time are the issue in "Human and Divine Time," while the third essay in the section is concerned, again, with space; it is an attempt to explain Epaminondas' revolution in military tactics, the use of the left wing instead of the traditional right as the main striking force, by new philosophical and technical ideas which challenged the age-old preeminence of the right hand—"Epaminondas the Pythagorean" is the title.

This sociological approach to military matters is even more highly developed in the next section: "The Tradition of the Athenian Hoplite," "The Black Hunter and the Origin of the Athenian *ephebeia*," "The Raw, the Greek Child and the Cooked." In all three essays the key concept is that of initiation into manhood. Part Three opens with a title which is a provocative question: "Did Greek Slaves Constitute a Class?" (the answer proposed is a negative) and continues with a penetrating analysis of the "Greek Historiography of Slavery"; it proceeds, in "Slavery and Gynecocracy," with a careful analysis of the similar but different roles of slaves and women (both excluded from the "citizens' club") in myth, history, and utopian fantasy.

The last essay in this section, "The Artisans in the Platonic City," deals with one of the most striking contradictions of Greek civilization: the fact that its "hero is the artisan, but he is a secret hero." There is a sense in which the creators of epic poetry, the sculptors, the doctors, the builders of the Parthenon and Erechtheum, are all of them artisans, but in classical Athens and especially in Plato's ideal cities of the *Republic* and the *Laws,* artisans play no important political role as individuals, still less as a class. In the final section of the book structural analysis is applied to two of the most puzzling Platonic myths: the Atlantis story of the *Critias* and the strange myth of the *Politicus* in which the whole universe, free of divine control, revolves backward in space and time.

Throughout this long text the argument maintains an unfailingly high level of interest; detailed discussion is not shirked, but it is conducted without pedantry; theory and speculation abound but their formulation is concise and clear. In every case, whether he is dealing with hoplite tactics, initiation periods, utopian fantasies, or mythical cities, Vidal-Naquet never loses sight of the central concern of the book, its method. He states it in the preface.

> The things I bring together could quite legitimately be the object of separate studies and it has happened that I have been able to contribute to research in the two separate domains. What interests me here is their conjunction. Separated from the study of social observances, the structural analysis of myth can bring to completion a magnificent program, arranging the myths in series, making them reflect each other, giving play to their logical articulations. But there is a danger—that of taking refuge in what Hegel used to call "the serene kingdom of friendly appearances. . . ." On the other hand, institutional, social and economic history . . . yields its full value only, as I see it, when it can be combined with the "representations" which accompany, or one could even say which penetrate, the institutions and the observances of the social and political game.

For an example of the method at work one may as well choose what is obviously Vidal-Naquet's favorite piece, since he gives its title to the book. "*Le Chasseur noir*" is an attempt to connect what is known about the Athenian *ephebeia* with comparable institutions elsewhere (especially at Sparta but also in Africa) as well as with a mysterious myth that was supposed to explain the origin of a festival and with a song sung by the chorus of women in Aristophanes' *Lysistrata* about a hunter-hermit called Melanion—*melas* means "black" and this is the Black Hunter of the title. Of the *ephebeia* itself before the fourth century practically nothing is known; our evidence consists of scattered mentions in fourth-century speeches, some inscriptions, and a full description in Aristotle's *Constitution of Athens*, a treatise written in the last third of the fourth century.

At this time the institution was a two-year military training period for the sons of citizens who had reached the age of eighteen: after a year of training they served as garrison troops in the frontier fortresses of Attica; they wore a black cloaklike garment. As soldiers they were not part of the heavily armed infantry line, the hoplites, and were supposed to be used, presumably as light-armed skirmishers, only on home territory. During this period the young men, Aristotle tells us, were excluded from legal proceedings either as plaintiff or defendant, except in cases involving an inheritance, a female relative whose hand in marriage gave title to property, or a hereditary priesthood.

This two-year period has been compared to the period of sequestration, of "latency," which precedes full recognition of manhood in many tribal societies. Vidal-Naquet compares it also to the Spartan *krypteia*, which turned the young initiates out onto the wild hills to live off the land by ruse, robbery, and murder of the helots. Such a life, as Vidal-Naquet points out, is, like many initiation rites, the exact reverse of the mature status to which it is a prelude. The oppositions in this case are many: light- or unarmed against heavily armored hoplite; separate small-group operations as opposed to the massed phalanx; young man on the mountain and fully grown soldier on the level ground; the winter guerrilla and the regular soldier of the summer season; the stealthy assassin of helots as against the frank and loyal warrior of the pitched battle; the young man in the night, the grown man fighting in the light of day.

For the Athenian ephebe there was no such grim hardening process, but Vidal-Naquet finds evidence of the "logical inversion" typical of initiation periods in various Athenian festivals connected with adolescence—the Apaturia festival and, close to it in date, the Oschophoria, in which "the *ephebes* played an important part." The mythical base for the Oschophoria was the return of the young Theseus from his exploits in Crete, a joyful occasion saddened by the suicide of his father Aegeus, who saw his son's ship returning with a black sail—Theseus had forgotten to change it to white if he returned safe, as had been agreed. The black cloak of the ephebe was supposed to commemorate this occasion. And the festival itself contained such features as a procession to a place on the frontier led by two boys disguised as girls and a race between ephebes representing their tribes—the whole festival, says Vidal-Naquet, was based on a series of antitheses—"the most evident the antithesis which opposes male to female."

The Apaturia is the festival at which fathers registered their sixteen-year-old sons as Athenian citizens and members of a "brotherhood" (phratry); from this registration would follow, two years later, their entry into the *ephebeia*. It may have been at this festival that the ephebes took their famous oath (remarkable for its archaic language) to defend "the frontiers of the fatherland, its wheat, barley, vines, olive and fig trees."

The myth that "explained" the festival told of a battle between Athenians and Boeotians (their neighbors to the northeast) which is settled by a duel between the opposing kings, Xanthos (Blond) for the Boeotians, Thymoites for the Athenians. But Thymoites withdraws (too old, says one version) and into his place steps an Athenian called Melanthos (Black). Black wins by a ruse: he calls out to Blond, "You're cheating; there's somebody beside you." And as Blond looks around, Black kills him. In some versions there actually *is* somebody beside him; it is Dionysus—Dionysus of the night and the black goatskin (*nykterinos kai melanaigis*). The model proposed for the young warrior-initiate is a frontier fighter, who wins by cunning and deceit, who is black by name and black by nature. The relation of the mythical model to the real institution of the Spartan *krypteia* is clear.

Vidal-Naquet now goes on to connect this "black" ephebe with the hunt. As in war, so in the chase, there are two worlds. One is the daylight hunt of the adult male, who faces the boar spear in hand, together with his companions—as in the great mythical Calydonian hunt; it is the transposition of hoplite values and organization from the battle line on the plain to the hunt in the woods. Opposed to this ideal is the solitary hunter who uses the net, ruse not courage, and whose snares are set at night. Vidal-Naquet finds him, in literature as in art (though examples are extremely scarce), portrayed as an adolescent. And he turns finally to the strange song in Aristophanes' *Lysistrata*, about Melanion, another "black," a "youth who fleeing from marriage, went off to the wilds, lived in the mountains and hunted the hare with nets he made himself. He never came home—he had such a horror of women." This, says Vidal-Naquet, is a "failed" (*échoué*) ephebe; he remains forever in the initiatory stage instead of proceeding on to maturity.

Vidal-Naquet sums up the results of this fascinating inquiry.

> The ephebe, in archaic and classical Greece, is the pre-hoplite and for that very reason, through the symbolic dramatization afforded

by the rites of passage, he is an anti-hoplite: sometimes black, sometimes cunning hunter, sometimes girl. There is nothing surprising, in any case, that a myth like that of Melanthos should serve as a model for him. Technically, the ephebe is a light-armed combatant and this anti-hoplite ensures the maintenance, often hard to discern, of forms of warfare which are both pre- and anti-hoplite, which will reappear in full daylight during the Peloponnesian War and the fourth century.

"Only connect," said Forster, and there can be no doubt of the brilliance of these connections, which give institutional solidity to a baffling but obviously important myth and insert in a coherent context historical and ritual details which meant little in isolation. *Représentations* are what interests Vidal-Naquet: the ephebe's vision of himself, his image in the eyes of the adult. In one of his contributions to *Mythe et tragédie* he finds such a *représentation* in the literal sense: the figure of Neoptolemus in Sophocles' play *Philoctetes*. The young son of Achilles, as yet untried in battle, is set the task of deceiving the ailing hero Philoctetes, luring him aboard a boat for Troy by acting out an elaborate lie—a typical "ephebic" exploit. He does brilliantly at first but finally, moved to pity by the nobility of his victim, he renounces deceit and emerges as a grown man, a frank and open warrior in the image of his father Achilles.

The theory as a whole is attractive and it is presented with skill and eloquence. But of course it has its flaws. The mythical connections can only be accepted as valid if the institution of an ephebic training period at Athens is at least as old as the mid-fifth century, and they would be stronger still if that date could be pushed further back. But though we have evidence for men of ephebic age mobilized in the Peloponnesian War for specific campaigns, it seems always to be an emergency measure; there is no evidence to show that these men were already in training or on garrison duty. And it seems strange that neither in Aristophanes' fifth-century comedies, so full of allusions to contemporary reality, nor in Plato's early dialogues, in which so many of the characters are ephebes, is any mention of such an institution to be found.

Vidal-Naquet points out that when these youths were summoned to duty for emergencies, for service outside Attica in fact, they served in the same units as noncitizens, as Aeschines did in 370 B.C., or with men recently admitted to citizenship like the Plateans in the campaign at Megara in 424 B.C. But this is frail evidence on which to base the sort of ritual separateness demanded by his thesis, and the fact that the affair at Megara was an *"embuscade nocturne"* does little to help the contrast between cunning nocturnal ephebe and stalwart daylight hoplite since hoplites too, six hundred of them in fact, took part in the operation; they spent the night hiding in a trench from which the bricks for the walls of Megara had been dug—a most unhoplitic situation.

There are other places, too, where the evidence for connections is less than adequate. Melanion the woman-hating hunter is compared to Hippolytus (so far so good—even Wilamowitz-Moellendorf agrees), but it will not do to go on and reinforce the comparison by making Hippolytus, like Melanion, a hunter with the net, in fact the inventor of it. That detail comes from Oppian, who wrote in the late second century A.D. a boring poem on hunting for which the emperor Caracalla is supposed to have paid him a gold piece for every line—the most colossal overpayment in literary history. What his source for the detail about Hippolytus was (if he had one) we have no idea, but the Hippolytus in Euripides' play, produced in 428 B.C., hunts by day "with swift hounds ridding the land of wild beasts," and when Phaedra imagines herself with him she speaks of "hurling the Thessalian lance." Hippolytus in fact is very far removed from the nocturnal sphere; he repudiates the goddess Aphrodite, who "works her miracles by night."

Such awkward details (and there are others—the frailty of the link between the Apaturia and the ephebic oath, for example) may seem unimportant when viewed against the internal coherence of the interpretation as a whole. Taken singly perhaps they are, but their cumulative effect is disturbing and since, in any case, the argument is a chain, the weakness of individual links causes concern. Perhaps it is a matter of temperament which side the reader opts for. Some will be prepared to overlook weak spots in a brilliant interpretation which makes sense of many things that were obscure and connects in a meaningful pattern what previously were isolated and therefore puzzling facts. Others will prefer to settle, reluctantly in most cases, for the old uncertainty and imperfection, to live with unanswered questions and unrelated details rather than allow theory and occasional poetic license the benefit of the doubt.

Perhaps it is even a matter of national temperament. At the final session of an international conference on Greek myth held at Urbino in 1973, Vernant referred to some critical observations that had been made by the Regius Professor of Greek at Cambridge, Geoffrey Kirk, the author of two books on Greek myth which show an intimate acquaintance with and a certain critical distance from structuralist theory.[26] He had written for the *Times Literary Supplement* a review of Vernant and Vidal-Naquet's *Mythe et tragédie* in which he remarked that the authors were both "extremely French."[27] "Coming from a British pen," said Vernant, "the formula is at the very least ambiguous and I am not too sure how to take it. Perhaps I should turn it around and say that in his contribution to the discussion here, my friend Kirk has shown himself, in his positivism and prudence, to be 'extremely English.'" He added that empiricism, even if it is a spontaneous product and a natural inclination, is still as much a philosophy as any other and that it is a form of conceptualization which, if it remains merely implicit, is all the more likely to constrict and deform. He is of course quite right—if, that is, one can call "philosophy" an attitude which, having seen many theories come and go, is on its guard and which is prepared to accept the possibility that in this sublunar world the problems may have no final solution and the data may make less than perfect sense.

But there is one great advantage to being "extremely French": the method is, as Vidal-Naquet says himself, "heuristic"—it discovers things. And not even the most "English" reaction to Vidal-Naquet's book could deny that it contains discoveries; exactly what the connection is between the black ephebic cloak, Melanthos the tricky fighter, and Melanion the woman-hating hunter may be disputed but that there *is* such a connection few readers of this book can doubt.

Discoverers have to be bold: one of Vidal-Naquet's great exemplars, Lafitau, an eighteenth-century Jesuit who lived among the Algonquins, Hurons, and Iroquois, is praised in this book for precisely that quality. In his *Moeurs des sauvages amériquains comparées aux moeurs des premiers temps* (Paris, 1724) he abandoned the customary attitude of writers on the Americas, which was to measure their in-

26. *Myth: Its Meaning and Functions in Ancient and Other Cultures* (University of California Press, 1970); *The Nature of Greek Myths* (Overlook Press, 1975).

27. Vernant quoted these words in the original English; his own remarks were made in French.

habitants by the standard of classical antiquity. With what Vidal-Naquet terms an "incredible audacity" (*une incroyable audace*) he wrote that "if on the one hand the classical authors had helped him understand the savages, the customs of the savages had, on the other hand, lighted his way to an easier understanding and explanation of what was in the ancient authors."

Audacity has been characteristic of Vidal-Naquet's career from the start; it marked his activities as a historian *engagé* in the political struggle; it is visible at work in every page of this book where, however, it is tempered and checked by the historical conscience. As befits a man who has learned from Vernant to reckon with the symbolic and social importance of civic space, the location of his office in Paris is wonderfully appropriate. The rather dilapidated building which accommodates the Centre de recherches comparées sur les sociétés anciennes is located on the curve of Rue Monsieur-le-Prince. Upward the street climbs toward the Odéon, a classic theater named after the building erected by Pericles to commemorate the victory over the Persians. Downward it ends on the Boulevard St.-Germain, where, in the midst of the surging traffic and unnoticed by the pedestrians who wait for the bus, Danton stands on his pedestal, shouting the words engraved below him on the stone: "*De l'audace, encore de l'audace, toujours de l'audace. . . .*"

Thucydides and the Peloponnesian War: Politics and Power

The Greek word *historie* gave us our word *history,* but its original meaning was less precise. It meant "enquiry," "research," and it came to have its present meaning "research into the past" because it was the word used by the first historian, Herodotus of Halicarnassus, to characterize his own work. His book, which deals with the wars between the Greeks and the Persians in the opening decades of the fifth century B.C., is the product of the questions he asked; of the visits he made to cities, temples, and battlefields; of his insatiable curiosity about the past not only of the Greeks but also of the foreign, especially the Eastern, nations with whom they came into contact.

His "history" has an immense scope. It describes not only the Persian invasions of Greece in 490 and 480 B.C. but also everything that led up to them; he ranges far back into the past—in the case of Egypt, thousands of years back. His work is enlivened at every turn by fascinating stories about people, places, and customs; one sometimes has the impression that he was not too much concerned about whether the story was true, so long as it was good. He often gives two or three different versions of one event and declines to choose between them; sometimes he will tell a story that he finds hard to believe. "It is my duty," he says at one point, "to report what people say, but I am not required to believe it." As he approaches his own time, his history becomes more reliable (but remains just as fascinating), and Thucydides, in the next generation, though he does not mention Herodotus by name, pays him the compliment of starting exactly where he left off: the flashback on the foundation of Athenian seapower in Thucydides, Book I, begins exactly at the point where Herodotus's narrative ends.

With Thucydides, however, we enter an entirely different world of thought and feeling. Unlike Herodotus he is a child of the intellectual

This essay originally appeared as the text of the opening lecture for the Strategy Curriculum at the Naval War College in 1972.

revolution; its achievements and also its limitations are reflected everywhere in his work. The charm and endless fascination of Herodotus's stories and his digressions about everything that aroused his interest—the crocodiles in Egypt, the strange sexual arrangements of the Lydians—all this is deliberately avoided. "It may well be," said Thucydides, "that my history will seem less easy to read because of the absence in it of a romantic element." He is quite right. It is less easy to read. But the sacrifice is justified. His purpose was "to be judged useful by those who want to understand clearly the events which happened in the past and which, human nature being what it is, will at some time or other and in much the same way be repeated in the future." And in this he was successful. The events themselves, compared to other wars, especially our own, were small scale. But the profound analysis to which Thucydides subjected them has made them a working model of the dynamics of war and policy for all succeeding generations. He has produced, as he promised, "a piece of writing designed to last forever."

Unlike Herodotus, who wrote of the events of the far and immediate past (he was six years old in 478 B.C., the date at which his history ends), Thucydides writes the history of his own time, contemporary history. For earlier times Herodotus had to rely on local traditions, many of them obviously mythical; his history of the Persian wars was based on the accounts of old men who had fought the war in their youth or the stories their sons remembered hearing from their fathers. Thucydides, on the other hand, fought in his war as a general, or rather an admiral, and could talk to others who had fought it or were still fighting it. He could compare eyewitness accounts, and, unlike Herodotus, he was only interested in them as a means of establishing the truth; he does not report "what they say," no matter how good a story it might have made, but what in his judgment actually happened. The eyewitness accounts, he says, he "checked with as much thoroughness as possible." And the truth, as we all know, is often less spectacular than what the people who fought the battle remember, or claim to remember, long afterwards.

His sources, with the exception of the digression in Book I where he reconstructs the "probable" history of early Greece, were contemporary. He drew, first of all, on his own observation and participation; he probably listened to the speeches of Pericles which he reports in Books I and II, and he was active as a naval commander in the north, where he lost the city of Amphipolis to the Spartan, Brasidas. Secondly, he utilized eyewitness accounts, and since he was exiled for twenty years because of his failure in the north he was able to talk to participants on both sides. Thirdly, he consulted official documents, but these were very rare. Treaties, for example, were inscribed on blocks of stone, and he gives us the texts of some of these; but the paperwork which we associate with war did not yet exist. And lastly, he reports speeches made at important discussions of policy during the course of the war.

This last item, the speeches, calls for some comment. Nobody today, writing a history of the war in Vietnam, would give too much space to the speeches of Presidents Johnson and Nixon and still less to those of President Thieu. The policies governing the war are not hammered out in public speeches; the speeches are merely justifications (sometimes cover stories) for the real bases of policy, which are to be found, if they can be found, in secret memoranda, diplomatic documents, and government position papers. In fifth-century Greece, however, and above all in democratic Athens, it was in public speeches that policy was made. The statesman had to persuade an assembly of his fellow citizens that his proposal was to their interest and also likely to be successful; in the decision to sail to Sicily the speech of Alcibiades undoubtedly was a crucial factor, just as Thucydides reports. The speeches of Greek political leaders were not just an important source, they were essential items in Thucydides' account of the events of the war.

But, as he admits himself, they were a problem for the historian. They were not recorded, taken down in shorthand, nor even published (it was not until the next century that statesmen circulated their public speeches in book form). Thucydides has to rely on memory, his own for the speeches of Pericles and the debates between the Corcyreans and Corinthians in Athens, and other people's memories for speeches in Sparta and elsewhere.

It is true, of course, that in Greek civilization, where literacy was a comparatively recent phenomenon, people's memories were much more reliable than ours. Nevertheless, Thucydides had to admit his limitations here. "I have found it difficult to remember the precise words used in the speeches which I listened to myself and my various informants have experienced the same difficulty." So he compromised. "My method has been, while keeping as closely as possible to the general sense of the words that were actually used, to make the speakers say what, in my opinion, was called for by each situation." What this method enabled him to do was to present, in addition to phrases he remembered, the political and military background of the action under debate, the conflicting opinions, the alternative courses of action—all the material which a modern historian presents editorially as his own analysis.

Some of the speeches fall at times to a level of obvious generalization that tempts one to think Thucydides might better have used the modern method of so-called objective presentation. Nevertheless, most of them combine "what was called for by the situation" with a dramatic personality which clearly reflects the actual speaker. And in the greatest of them—the Corinthians' contrast between Athenian dynamic activism and Spartan conservative isolationism, Pericles' funeral speech with its celebration of Athens' free institutions and cultural magnificence—the method Thucydides has invented for his recreation of the speeches presents intellectal analysis expressed with a passion and a dramatic immediacy which have never been equalled.

From these sources he constructed an account of the war so reasonable, so clear, and, on the surface, so unemotional that it seems to have been written by the pen of a recording angel. He was acclaimed by the historians of the nineteenth century, who were attempting to write history scientifically, as their predecessor, their great example. He was for them the first scientific, objective historian. Today, of course, we realize that there is no such thing as scientific, objective history; the historian is part of the process he attempts to record, or a result of it. Thucydides does have his blind spots and his prejudices. He does not very often express a personal opinion or judgment, but in his treatment of Cleon, for example, he is not exactly fair. Cleon was certainly the most violent of the Athenians (we have other sources to confirm this judgment) but he was not a fool or a coward, and Thucydides presents him as the one in the debates over Pylos and the other in the battle at Amphipolis.

Even when a historian does not express his own opinion, his emphasis and his judgment of what is important will be clear from his selection. Select he must; there is too much data—there was too much even for Thucydides, in an age before the invention of paperwork. Some things have to be left out, some treated in summary fashion, while others are emphasized or presented in full detail. In Thucydides' case it was only too clear what interested him above all other things, indeed to the exclusion of almost everything else. It was war. "Thucydides the Athenian"—this is how the book begins—"wrote the history of the war between the Peloponnesians and the Athenians, how they fought against each other," and there is practically nothing in his history which is not directly relevant to that subject. It is particularly appropriate for a Naval War College to devote some time to him, for he is the only great historian I can think of who concentrates rigidly and exclusively on the dynamics, the methods, the causes, and results of war between sovereign states.

This exclusive emphasis is all the more remarkable since the Athens in which he lived was one of the most intellectually and artistically creative cities the world has ever seen. In his lifetime the great tragedies of Sophocles and Euripides, as well as the comedies of Aristophanes, were staged in Athens; the Parthenon was built, and its great frieze cut in marble; Athenian potters and painters produced masterpieces which are the jewels of our museums; the philosophers worked out an atomic theory of the constitution of matter; the sophists revolutionized political, moral, and social theory. Yet of all this there is not one word in Thucydides except some extremely faint allusions in Pericles' funeral speech. If Thucydides' history were the only document that this century had left us, we could never have guessed what a brilliant cultural life the city possessed. What was important to Thucydides was Athenian power, and power for him was expressed in terms of a capacity to make war. We can be sure he admired the tragedies of Sophocles, but they were not, for his purposes, relevant.

This preoccupation with war and the power to make it is present throughout; it is even the guiding thread of his brilliant reconstruction of early Greek history in the introductory chapters. In the second half of the fifth century the idea of viewing human history as progress was in the air. Protagoras wrote a history of man's conquest of nature and advance to civilized communal living; in the Hippocratic collections we have a text which describes human progress from the doctor's point of view, the advance from savage to civilized diet, the discovery of disease and its treatment. What Thucydides presents us with is a history of Greece in which progress is measured in terms of military and naval power. At first there is nothing but poverty, disorganization, constant migration. Then the first light in the dark: Minos, King of Crete, organized a navy, suppressed piracy, and founded a sea empire. Agamemnon led the united Greeks against Troy, but the expedition was not as important as Homer would have us believe; lacking reserves and supplies, the Greeks were forced to dissipate their military power in cattle raids and piracy. The Trojan War was followed by more confusion, migration, emigration, colonization. But soon progress begins again. "The Corinthians are supposed to have been the first to have adopted more modern methods of shipbuilding"; they built a fleet, put down piracy. Later the Ionians were a great naval power, then Polycrates of Samos, the Phocaeans. But these navies did not possess triremes, fast maneuverable warships. These were used first by the Sicilians; then Themistocles persuaded the Athenians to build a fleet of them. Thus Athenian naval power came into being. After the defeat of the Persians, Athens built up her empire, which in turn set the stage for Thucydides' subject, the Peloponnesian War, the greatest war of all. It is the high point of a history of Greece conceived in terms of the growth of naval and military power.

This exclusive concentration on war is not just a reflection of the fact that Thucydides was himself a general officer in the war, and it does not mean that he was what some people today would call a militarist, if not a warmonger. He is simply taking for granted what most of his fellow Greeks took for granted, that war was a perfectly normal aspect of human life. Their whole history is one of constant war: small repetitive struggles between neighboring cities over borderlands, larger clashes between alliances of cities with common interests, and the great war against the Persian invader in which, characteristically, some Greek cities were neutral, and some even fought on the Persian side. A modern historian, A. R. Burn, has entitled his short history of ancient Greece *The Warring States of Greece,* and that is a very good title. The Greeks accepted war as inevitable. Even their Utopias, the *Republic* of Plato, the perfect state of Aristotle, make full provisions for military training and defense. They would have regarded the maxim of Clausewitz, "War is the continuation of politics by other means," as so obvious that it did not need to be said. War was the most concentrated expression of those competitive values the Greeks so valued in their dramatic festivals and in their athletic contests, and to them as to Thucydides it was a function of human nature, that basic "nature" which the sophistic teachers opposed to conventional law. War revealed human nature in its naked form—in the heights of courage and endurance to which it could rise and the depths of cruelty and degradation to which it could sink. It is in these terms, of war as a crucible in which the elements of human nature are refined and revealed, that Thucydides speaks. Of the men who died heroically in defense of their country he has Pericles say: "The consummation which has overtaken these men shows us the meaning of manliness in its first revelation and in its final proof." And on the hideous massacres at Corcyra he writes: "In peace and prosperity, cities and individuals alike follow higher standards. . . . But war is a violent teacher; in depriving them of the power of easily satisfying their daily wants it brings most people's minds down to the level of their actual circumstances."

This human nature, which Thucydides claims will always behave in the same way in similar circumstances, is described and analyzed in purely secular terms. Homeric man lived in a world full of gods ready at any moment to encourage, warn, threaten, or mislead, but in Thucydides' vision of the human condition there is no divine governing will, no cosmic justice, not even a nameless destiny. Man is alone and, as far as he can see, master of his own fate. With power and foresight there seems to be no reason why he cannot mold events to his own liking. This is the underlying assumption of Pericles' three speeches in which he assures the Athenians that with the right policy they cannot lose the war.

This is a new vision of man's place in the universe; Herodotus saw things differently. Everywhere in his work we are confronted with prophecies made by divine voices, the oracles, and in Herodotus they always turn out to be right even though human beings may not understand them correctly until it is too late. In Thucydides such prophecies are mentioned where they have a psychological effect on those who believe in them (that, after all, is a fact), but it is clear that Thucydides did not. "For those who put their faith in oracles," he says, "here is one solitary instance of their being proved accurate"; he refers to the prophecies which had been in circulation to the effect that the war would last twenty-seven years. The irony of this is that only Thucydides thought it did; his contemporaries and later historians too thought of it as two separate wars, the first lasting ten years, the second eight, with a period of peace in between. Only Thucydides saw that the so-called Peace of Nicias was really a continuation of the war. Equally characteristic is his acid comment on the oracle which was supposed to have predicted the plague. "A Dorian war will come," it said, "and a plague with it." But there had been another version in circulation which, with one vowel slightly different (*limos* instead of *loimos*) predicted a famine. Since the war brought with it a plague, everyone was convinced that what the gods had said was *loimos*, a plague. "But," said Thucydides, "if we get another war with the Peloponnesians and it brings a famine, everybody will claim that the oracle said *limos*, famine."

In Herodotus these oracular voices are the expression of a universal justice which in the rise and fall of individuals and states sees that in the end everything is paid for. It so happens that at one particular point the histories written by the two men intersect, and the contrast between their attitudes to the event is revealing. Herodotus tells how in the opening stages of the great Persian war the Persian king sent heralds to Sparta demanding earth and water, the usual tokens of submission. The Spartans threw the heralds into a well and told them to get earth and water there; their deaths were a violation of the custom of nations, for heralds, as ambassadors, were sacrosanct. The Spartans later found that because of the anger of the long dead hero Talthybius, the patron saint, so to speak, of heralds, their sacrifices were refused. They got the point; they asked for two volunteers to go to the Persian king to offer themselves in exchange for his heralds, and two men at once volunteered. Their names were Spercheius and Boulis. But when they got to Persia, the king refused to kill them; he would not act like the Spartans, he said, and he would not let them get off so lightly. So Spercheius and Boulis came home and lived out the rest of their lives. But, says Herodotus, the anger of Talthybius was not appeased. It fell sixty years later on their sons Aneristus and Nicolaus, who were sent by the Spartans to the Persian king to ask for help against Athens in the Peloponnesian War. They were betrayed to the Athenians in northern Greece and put to death. "This seems to me," says Herodotus, "one of the most plain proofs of divine power. Justice, of course, required that retribution should fall on ambassadors, but that it should fall exactly on the sons of the men who went up to the Persian king, this seems to me quite plainly to be the work of the gods" (VII.137).

Thucydides also records the capture of the two Spartan envoys to Persia. "At the end of the same summer, an embassy consisting of Aristeus from Corinth, Aneristus, Nicolaus, and Stratodemus from Sparta, Timagoras from Tegea, and a man from Argos called Pollis . . .

was on its way to Asia." Herodotus' two men, Aneristus and Nicolaus, are there all right, but they are part of a group of six, and Aristeus of Corinth is in command. Thucydides tells how they were handed over to the Athenians as the result of Athenian intrigue with the king of Macedon; when they arrived in Athens, "the Athenians, fearing that Aristeus, who had done them much harm already, might do more if he remained alive, put them all to death without a trial. . . . They did this in retaliation for the way the Spartans had been behaving—putting to death all the Athenian and allied traders they captured at sea" (II.67).

We know that Thucydides had read Herodotus; he must have realized that he was describing the same incident, but in his account he does not even bother to correct his predecessor, still less to argue with him; he does not even refer to him. The execution of these two Spartans, which for Herodotus was such a firm proof of divine justice, is treated as a detail incidental to the really important matter, the execution of Aristeus of Corinth.

Herodotus's view of the incident may not seem too comforting: gods who exact punishment from the sons whose fathers had escaped it (through no fault of their own) are not exactly merciful gods—they may even seem vindictive. Yet there is an element of comfort in the story: even though the justice of the gods is harsh, there is a justice, and this gives meaning to whatever happens. It is all part of a pattern which we may not understand, but which gives some meaning to our lives and, above all, our deaths. The fate of the two Spartan ambassadors, as Herodotus presents it, is a detail in a pattern of order imposed by the gods; it makes a kind of sense and has a certain dignity. But in Thucydides it simply happened. There is no particular reason for it except that the two men were unlucky to be caught at that time and in that company.

Thucydides proclaimed that his history lacks "a romantic element." It also lacks any religious feeling. There is no heaven above to judge, encourage, or punish; no pattern ordained by divine providence; only the conflicting wills of human beings organized in sovereign states locked in unremitting struggle. In this empty universe things can happen which have no explanation, no possible justification. They are, in fact, pure accidents, and when they are also hideous calamities, the fact that they are meaningless makes them almost too much for the human mind to accept. Thucydides goes out of his way to describe one such incident, one which had no effect on the war one way or the other.

Athens had sent for some Thracian savages to hire as mercenaries. They arrived too late to sail with Demosthenes to Sicily, so they were sent home with an Athenian commander in charge and a roving commission to do some damage to Athens's enemies on the way back. This commander attacked the city of Mycalessus, but his Thracians got out of hand. They began slaughtering the inhabitants; they went berserk, in fact, and killed men, women, children, farm animals, and everything they saw. Particularly horrible was the assault on the boys' school where they killed all the children. "It was a small city," said Thucydides, "but in the disaster . . . its people suffered calamities as pitiable as any which took place during the war." Nobody wanted it to happen this way. There is no rhyme or reason for it. It is an utterly meaningless event.

It is precisely because Thucydides had no religious view, no mystical sense of destiny or divine justice at work in human history that he can observe without preconceptions and analyze so mercilessly that human nature which, he suggests repeatedly, will always be the same. The mainspring of human nature in action, as he sees it, is the will to power, to dominate others, and in the actions of states this will expresses itself as politics and war. "It is a general and necessary law of nature," say the Athenian negotiators to the Melians, "to rule wherever one can. This is not a law that we made ourselves; we found it already in existence and we shall leave it to exist forever for those who come after us." In his examination of the operation of this law, Thucydides presents us with a number of analyses of power politics in action which have been admired and studied ever since as the purest distillation of political experience.

Among them is the famous Melian dialog in Book V. The Athenians bring overwhelming force against a small neutral island and then sit down at the negotiating table. They want no words wasted. "If we have met here for any other purpose than to look facts in the face . . . there is no point in going on with the discussion. . . . We will use no fine phrases" (they do not attempt to justify their actions with the usual appeals—"a great mass of words that nobody believes") and they don't want to hear similar arguments from the other side. "You should try to get what it is possible for you to get, taking into consideration what we both really think." And then this terrible but true statement: "When these matters are discussed by practical people, the standard of justice depends on the equality of power to compel." The United States and the Soviet Union may discuss the justice of their claims against each other, but in the case of the Soviet Union and Czechoslovakia or the United States and, say, Santo Domingo, such discussion is irrelevant. In fact, "the strong do what they may, and the weak accept what they must."

The Melians reply that even in such a case there is a need for fair play, for the superior power may be itself one day defeated. "This is a principle which affects you as much as anybody since your own fall would be visited by the most terrible vengeance." This warning is countered by a cynical but cogent argument. "We are not afraid," say the Athenians, "of being conquered by a power which rules over others as Sparta does. . . . You can leave it to us to face the risks involved." And they are right. When Athens fell at last, she was deprived of her fleet, her fortifications, her empire, and her democratic regime, but she was not destroyed; she did not suffer the massacre and enslavement she had decreed for Mitylene and actually inflicted on Melos and Scione. The Corinthians and the Thebans wanted to raze Athens to the ground, but Sparta would not allow it; not for love of Athens, but because the destruction would have made Thebes and Corinth too powerful, created a power vacuum Sparta was not ready to fill. Furthermore, Sparta, which had won the war with Persian help, now had to face the problem of Persian pressure in the Aegean. After World War II there were many who wanted to destroy Germany and Japan as states, but we did no such thing. On the contrary, we built them up. We needed them against our former allies, Russia and China.

The Melians then ask simply to be allowed the privilege of neutrality, but the answer is negative. Melos is an island, and a neutral island cannot be tolerated by a naval empire. "Our subjects would regard it as a sign of weakness in us." We can translate that into our own terms; "our credibility is at stake." And so it goes on. The Melians appeal to the chances of battle, their hope to save themselves, but the Athenians reject hopes as foolish. They appeal to the gods, but the Athenians claim the gods as power politicians like themselves. The Melians proclaim their reliance on Sparta, but they are told that no help will come from that quarter, and indeed it did not—as no help came from the European democracies to the Spanish Republic or the

Czechs, for as the Athenians say, "good will shown by the party that is asking for help does not mean security . . . what is looked for is a positive preponderance of power." So the Melians went down fighting, and when the city fell the men were slaughtered, the women and children sold into slavery.

Equally penetrating is Thucydides' analysis of the appalling cruelties which accompanied revolution and civil war in Corcyra. Revolutions were not rare in ancient Greece, but this one and the many which followed it were made more brutal by the presence of the war, which invited foreign intervention. "The consequent savagery was the cause of many calamities, as happens and always will happen while human nature is what it is, though, as different circumstances arise, the general rule will exhibit some variety." The collapse of law and moral standards was accompanied by a process of corruption in the language men spoke: "To fit in with the change of events, words too had to change their usual meanings. A thoughtless act of aggression was now regarded as the courage one would expect to find in a party member: any idea of moderation was just an attempt to disguise one's unmanly character." We know this phenomenon very well. George Orwell (who apparently did not realize that Thucydides had anticipated him) satirized the perversion of language for political ends in his chapter on "Newspeak" in his novel *1984*, but the process has continued undeterred. The half of Germany which calls itself the Democratic German Republic is the one ruled by Communist dictatorship, and the "peace-loving nations" are the members of the Warsaw Pact; to come closer home, the word "pacification" is used to describe some activities of ours in Vietnam which have very little to do with peace, and George Orwell would have taken off his hat to the unnamed genius in the Air Force who thought up "preplanned protective reaction."

In these same chapters on Corcyra, Thucydides gives us a lucid analysis of the aftermath of successful revolution; once the safeguards of rule by law have been destroyed, the revolutionaries themselves fall victim to the furies they have unleashed. In the struggle for power among the victors, "those who were least remarkable for intelligence showed the greatest powers of survival. . . . They recognized their own deficiencies and the superior intelligence of the opponents; fearing that they might lose a debate or find themselves out-manoeuvered in intrigue by their quick-witted enemies, they boldly launched straight into action; while their opponents, over-confident . . . were the more easily destroyed."

Truer words were never spoken. In the French Revolution, Danton, the great orator who had roused France to drive out the invaders and whose impassioned oratory dominated the revolutionary Convention, did not imagine that he could be overthrown by a pettyfogging lawyer, a poor speaker, a pedantic schoolteacher named Robespierre—but it was Robespierre who sent Danton and his friends to the guillotine. Leon Trotsky, the fiery speaker, the brilliant writer, the organizer of the first Red Army, the companion of Lenin, had no fear of the crude Georgian peasant who called himself Stalin, but Stalin drove him out of Russia and many years later engineered his murder in Mexico City. The whole passage in Thucydides is the most probing analysis of the effects of violent revolution and civil war ever made; here, if nowhere else, Thucydides justifies his claim to be useful forever.

Armed with this power of surgical analysis and with a fierce devotion to the truth, Thucydides wrote the history of the war which began with Athens at the height of her economic and naval power and ended twenty-seven years later in her total defeat. In the opening books, especially in the speeches of Pericles, he prepares the stage for what seems to be the inevitable victory of Athens. She is invulnerable at home because of the long walls which connected city and harbor—"if only we were an island," says Pericles, and the walls in effect made her so. Her resources in money, ships, and trained naval personnel were infinitely superior to those of her enemies. In order to win she had only to stand pat; the war was an attempt to destroy the Athenian Empire, but it could never succeed as long as Athens retained control of the sea. All she had to do was to avoid large-scale battles on land and refrain from any attempts to extend the empire. If these two restrictions were observed, the war was bound to end in a stalemate, and since the enemy had begun the war as a challenge to the status quo, a stalemate would be an Athenian victory. Such a policy would require great discipline (the Athenians would have to watch the enemy burn their farms), but in Pericles they had a leader who could hold them to it. Yet Athens lost the war. Something was wrong with Pericles' calculations. Why did Athens lose?

Thucydides never poses the question in quite those terms, but his answer to it emerges from his narrative. In Pericles' first speech the strategy is outlined, a calculation of resources made; a supreme confidence is expressed—Athens cannot lose if it follows the Periclean guidelines. A warning note, however, is sounded in the speech of the Spartan King Archidamus as his troops invade Attica. "There is much," he says, "that is unpredictable in war." Pericles was soon to learn that lesson himself. No amount of calculation and preparation can foresee the accidents and combinations of circumstances that war is liable to produce. Pericles had foreseen the Spartan invasion and the destruction of the Athenian crops but not the plague which caused such havoc in the overcrowded city. He admits this in his last speech. "When things happen suddenly, unexpectedly, and against all calculations, it takes the heart out of a man; and this has certainly happened to you," he tells the Athenians, "with the plague coming on top of everything else." The plague dealt a terrible blow to Athenian manpower and morale, but it did something even more damaging: it killed Pericles. And his death opened the way for new leaders who made the mistakes he had feared—involvement in land battles (at Delium and later at Mantinea) and expeditions to enlarge the empire (the disastrous expedition to Sicily). This last mistake came at a time when, strictly speaking, Athens had won the war. When peace was made in 421, she had, it is true, sustained heavy losses in the plague and in the unnecessary land engagement at Delium; she had also lost her subject cities in the north to a Spartan captain of genius, Brasidas, but she had captured, at Pylos, enough Spartan soldiers and officers to induce Sparta to sue for terms. And after all, this was, as Pericles foresaw, the way the war would end. The war was a challenge to Athens's rule over the empire; if the enemy settled for less, he admitted failure. With the return to something like the status quo, a dynamic Athens was now free to rebuild her resources to the level, or above it, of her position in 431.

But the Athenians not only proceeded to engage Sparta in an infantry battle at Mantinea (which they lost); they also gambled their whole fleet and the bulk of their fighting manpower on an attempt to take over Sicily, a place they could hardly expect to hold even if they conquered it.

The fault then lay in the leadership, and this raises the question of Athenian democracy and Thucydides' attitude toward it. Pericles' funeral speech, of course, is one of the great documents of Western democratic ideals. But when Thucydides pays his tribute to Pericles after describing his death, he says something rather disturbing. "In what was nominally a democracy power was really in the hands of the first citizen." True, Pericles had to be reelected to the board of generals each year, but he managed to do so for a period of some fifteen years before his death in 429, and he did it without flattering the people or playing on their prejudices. "He was so highly respected," says Thucydides, "that he was able to speak angrily to them and to contradict them." His successors, however, had no such personal authority. They had to adopt "methods of demagoguery which resulted in their losing control over the actual conduct of affairs." This loss of control by the successors of Pericles resulted in the disastrous abandonment of his strategy; they were unable, unlike him, "to respect the liberty of the people and at the same time hold them in check."

The trouble with Athenian democracy was, of course, that it was a direct democracy. The modern slogan we hear so often from our radical left, "All power to the people," exactly describes it. Policy was decided in an assembly which any citizen could attend; clever orators could play on passions and fears to promote their own interests, as Alcibiades did in his advocacy of the expedition to Sicily. In the last years of the war (Thucydides did not live long enough to describe this incident, though he must have known about it) the admirals at the battle of Arginusae, who in the turmoil of a successful naval engagement failed to rescue the crews of their wrecked ships before a gale made it impossible, were recalled, tried before an assembly whipped up to a rage by their political opponents, and condemned to death. When Thucydides puts into the mouth of Alcibiades at Sparta the statement that democracy is a system which is "generally recognized as absurd," one cannot help feeling, with all due allowance made for the slipperiness of Alcibiades and for the fact that he was addressing a Spartan audience, that Thucydides may have been to some extent in agreement. Periclean democracy was one thing; it was almost like our own democracy in that it had a powerful executive capable of a consistent policy; but the democracy which was to be dominated by Cleon and led to catastrophe by Alcibiades was quite another. In fact, in Book VIII, where Thucydides describes the antidemocratic revolution in Athens which followed the disaster in Sicily, he says of its final phase (an assembly restricted to five thousand property-owning citizens) that "during the first period of the new regime, the Athenians appeared to have had a better government than ever before, at least in my time." For once Thucydides seems to have been in agreement with that Cleon he so despised; Cleon in the debate over Mitylene had said, "A democracy is incapable of governing an empire."

What did Thucydides think of the empire? I, for one, have no doubt that he thought the empire, ruled with tact and wisdom as it was under Pericles, was the justified reward of Athens's crusade against Persia and of her creative energy and administrative skill. He gives a great deal of emphasis to the claim that Athens under Pericles governed her subjects with moderation and benevolence. There is a ring of truth in the words he puts into the mouth of the Athenian representative to the Congress in Sparta before the war. "Those who really deserve praise," he says, "are the people who, while human enough to enjoy power, nevertheless pay more attention to justice than they are compelled to do by their situation. Certainly we think that if anyone else was in our position it would soon be evident whether we act with moderation or not." He goes on to explain that the subject allies complain that lawsuits involving Athenians and allied citizens are tried in Athens, but as he points out, the fact that the cases are tried at all is unusual. Other imperial powers do not bother with such things. "*Our* subjects, on the other hand, are used to being treated as equals; consequently, when they are disappointed in what they think right and suffer even the smallest disadvantage . . . they cease to feel grateful to us for all the advantages we have left them." In Pericles' funeral speech there is a sentence that points in the same direction—the liberal handling of the allies, and their treatment as equals, except insofar as the basic matter of foreign policy is concerned. "We obey the laws," says Pericles, "especially those which are for the protection of the oppressed and those unwritten laws which it is an acknowledged shame to break." But even if Athens's claim to rule with a benevolent despotism which distinguished it from all other ruling powers were to be rejected, the empire, as Thucydides clearly realized, was Athens's only guarantee of security. "It may have been wrong to take it," said Pericles; "it is certainly dangerous to give it up."

Nevertheless it is also clear that Thucydides would have repudiated the reckless doctrine of permanent expansion preached by Alcibiades: "It is not possible for us to calculate like housekeepers exactly how much empire we want to have. The plain fact is that we have reached the stage where we are forced to plan new conquests and forced to hold on to what we have got because there is a danger that we ourselves may fall under the power of others unless others are in our power." This doctrine of limitless expansion was proclaimed in Alcibiades' speech in favor of the Sicilian expedition, the fundamental and fateful departure from Periclean strategy.

Thucydides' attitude toward Cleon's imperial policy is harder to define. There is no doubt that he hated and despised Cleon as a vulgar mob orator and violent demagogue, but it is remarkable that he attributes to him a description of the Athenian Empire which must be a deliberate repetition of a phrase of Pericles. "You hold your empire as an absolute power," they both say; *tyrannis* is the Greek word, a dictatorship, an absolute rule established and maintained by force. Pericles, I feel sure, would not have proposed the slaughter of the male population of Mitylene, but I suspect that if he had been obliged to defend his position against Cleon, he would have used the same line of argument as Diodotus, an appeal, not to humanity, but to Athenian interests. So it is not easy to assess Thucydides' attitude to the Melian dialogue. Would his beloved Pericles have spoken like that? One finds it hard to believe. But he would have recognized the logic of the position. Power over others may be disguised, it may be gently used, it may be beneficial to those who are ruled, it may even be in the interests of humanity at large, but in the last analysis it rests on superior force.

Many historians, great ones among them, have seen Thucydides' history as a repudiation of Athenian imperialism as a whole. He does not specifically condemn it, of course, but a case can be made (and a good one has been) to show that in his dramatic arrangement and emphasis (the cynicism of the Melian dialogue followed immediately by the Sicilian expedition, for example), he is suggesting that Athens had transgressed the moral law and now has to pay the penalty. That, in other words, even though Thucydides excludes divine providence or justice from the world, he still sees a moral law operating which punishes all excess; that his mood after all is not so different from that of Herodotus and the tragic poets. And some critics have gone further to see in his work a condemnation of all power over others in any form and at any time as leading inevitably to the same results.

On the other hand, some students of his work take the opposite extreme and feel that he is simply an analyst of power who believes that in power relationships morality of any kind is irrelevant. This view has recently been put forward in a brilliant book by A. G. Woodhead, *Thucydides and the Nature of Power;*[1] he sums up Thucydides' concern as "power described and illustrated as the object of effort, held and retained by those who have it, envied and hated by those who do not have it, but in itself characterless and without moral content."

My own view is that the truth is somewhere in between. Thucydides, it seems to me, felt deeply that the Athens of Pericles, as described in the funeral speech, was a superior form of society which deserved its preeminent position and was justified in fighting to retain it. It ruled its empire with moderation and gave its subjects much in return for the independence of action it took away. I think that one can even read between the lines a belief that Greece could only be saved from perpetual internecine war by the emergence of a predominant unifying power and that Athens, under Pericles, was uniquely fitted for that role. But the failure of statesmanship, after Pericles' death, left Athenian democracy in the hands of leaders who ruled the empire with the mailed fist without the velvet glove and who launched Athens on a course of mad adventurism. His history, then, is in a sense a tragedy, but the tragedy for him is that Athens lost the war.

1. Cambridge: Harvard University Press, 1970, p. 27.

Invisible Woman

The arresting title—*The Reign of the Phallus*[1]—is explained in the book's first paragraph, a rolling barrage of feminist artillery.

> In the case of a society dominated by men who sequester their wives and daughters, denigrate the female role in reproduction, erect monuments to the male genitalia, have sex with the sons of their peers, sponsor public whorehouses, create a mythology of rape, and engage in rampant saber-rattling, it is not inappropriate to refer to a reign of the phallus. Classical Athens was such a society.

Some of the particulars in this bill of attainder suffer from rhetorical inflation. Monuments with (not *to*) male members, for example, were indeed common in Athens, but these protuberances were details on statues of the god Hermes; whorehouses were regulated, like those of the French Third Republic, but not "sponsored"; and the creation of a "mythology of rape" is understandable in a culture that regarded female sexual initiative as unacceptable but had to explain the large company of heroic sons borne to gods by otherwise respectable mortal women, many of them married. To the main burden of the indictment, however, classical Athens would have to answer, "Guilty as charged."

Only in recent years have scholars been fully awakened to the fact that the Greek *polis*, especially Athens (though perhaps Athens stands out because it is the one we know most about), was an exclusive men's club in which women had no political rights and no legal rights except those exercised through a male relative. Athenian wives were expected to remain at home in a secluded section of the house; in the words of Pericles' famous funeral speech, a panegyric of Athenian democracy, they were to aim "not to be talked about, either for good or

This essay originally appeared in the *Atlantic*, July 1985.

1. Eva C. Keuls, *The Reign of the Phallus: Sexual Politics in Ancient Athens* (New York: Harper & Row, 1985).

for evil among men." This recommendation was so faithfully complied with on the male side that an Athenian wife's name hardly ever surfaces in Greek texts, though women are important threads in the tangled skeins of inheritance suits. One paradigm of female virtue, the young wife of Xenophon's treatise on domestic economy, who in addition to her other duties trains and supervises household slaves, stores and preserves produce from the farm, manages the annual budget, and produces clothes from raw wool, is known to us only as "the wife of Ischomachus." A homosexual culture was an almost predictable result of the exclusion of wives and daughters from social and public life, and one has only to look at Aristotle's cockeyed theory of conception (not to mention Apollo's notorious speech in the *Eumenides* of Aeschylus) to be convinced that Athenian women were not given much credit even for the one thing that made them indispensable.

In this book, written with great verve and a laudable desire to make it "accessible to the general reader," Professor Keuls assembles an enormous body of evidence for the case against Athenian men. Most of the passages that she produces from the literature of the fifth and fourth centuries have not previously been cited in the context of social history. The most original feature of the book, however, is the exploration of the pictorial record: "the panorama of ideals, myths, fantasies and, above all, scenes of daily life that appears on the tens of thousands of Greek vases, scattered in museums all over Europe and the United States." She reproduces more than three hundred of these paintings from the classical period, many of them highly erotic, some grossly obscene. Her interpretation of the pictures (and most of them do need interpretation) is a "major resource" in her investigation of Athenian "phallocracy" in all its aspects—its exploitation of the female sex through marriage, concubinage, prostitution, and slavery; its supporting myths and social fictions (the cultured *hetaera*, for example); and its by-product, the homosexual relationships between grown men and adolescent youths.

She makes an impressive case, but though agreement on its main points can be withheld only by those who cling to sentimental fancies, it is by no means flawless. She sometimes proceeds on the basis of assumptions for which little or no evidence is produced—the idea, for example, that in wailing for the death of Adonis at his yearly festival the Athenian women "lamented their own, loveless lives," and the suggestion, based on vase paintings, that "for marital intercourse wives did not disrobe"—in other words, wives did not even have a good time in bed with their husbands. In the absence of Athenian equivalents of the Kinsey and Hite reports it is useless to speculate about women's feelings on this matter, but Aristophanes' *Lysistrata*, in which wives stop the Peloponnesian War by withholding their sexual favors, would have made no sense, not even comic sense, if the male audience thought of the marriage bed as a place for tiresome duty.

Sometimes, too, she fails to see the evidence in perspective. Many of the vases in her illustrations, for example, show men abusing, beating, and raping women. Such scenes, however, are comparatively rare, as anyone knows who has gone through the vast collections of Attic vases in London, Paris, and Florence or has leafed through the endless plates of the still incomplete *Corpus Vasorum Antiquorum;* and they occur, as Keuls herself points out, mainly on vases of one particular shape—the drinking cups used in the male symposium. These pictures are, in fact, the Athenian equivalent of the porno movies that were the high point of the entertainment offered at stag parties in men's clubs before the sexual revolution made hard-core stuff available to all.

Keuls also tends, as Freudian critics do, to detect a phallus where the uninstructed eye sees only a mundane object. In her discussion of the combat scenes frequent on Greek vases—Greeks versus Amazons or Trojans, for example—she habitually refers to spears and swords as "phallic." But since most weapons, ancient or modern, come to a point or launch projectiles, and in both cases are used to pierce the flesh of an opponent, this description lacks cogency; the only non-phallic weapons would seem to be poison gas and the atomic bomb. One particular erect phallus is proudly announced as a discovery in this book; it has lurked undetected for some twenty-five hundred years on one of the most celebrated pages of Greek, and for that matter world, literature: Plato's account of the death of Socrates.

After Socrates drinks the hemlock, its effect is tested by the jailer, who finds his feet numb and then, moving upward to the thighs, feels him growing cold and rigid (like Falstaff, whose feet were cold to the Hostess' touch—"Then I felt to his knees and so up'ard and up'ard, and all was cold as any stone"). When the chill reaches the area of the groin, Socrates suddenly uncovers his face, sits up, and says, "We owe a cock to Aesculapius. Pay it and do not forget." According to

Keuls, however, what he uncovers is not his face but his groin, and there—hey, presto!—is an erect phallus. A rooster was the standard sacrifice to the healing god Aesculapius, but it was also, as Keuls points out, the conventional homosexual love gift.

Unfortunately, this sensational scenario is based on two questionable interpretations of the Greek text: the word for "uncover" does not specify the part of the body referred to, but its normal usage in the absence of such specification denotes the act of unveiling the face, not the groin; more serious, the Greek word that describes the coldness of Socrates' groin (*psychomenon*) is not likely, considering the solemnity of the context, to be what Keuls calls a pun on the similar word *psychoumenon*, which could also mean "come to life." Obviously, if Plato wished to avail himself of such an ambiguity, all he had to do was use the other word. Her interpretation also rests on the citation of "a known fact that men tend to have erections at the moment of death." This is a fact that does not seem to be known to medical authorities I have consulted (except as a side effect of slow strangulation), and such a phenomenon seems in any case unlikely when the subject is a seventy-year-old man dying from the effects of a paralyzing poison.

There are other surprising revelations offered by the book. One, which is promised in the opening chapter and delivered in the last, is concerned with the item in the full indictment which has not so far been mentioned in this review—the tendency of the Athenian male to "engage in rampant saber-rattling." This jocular formula might pass muster as a pejorative assessment of Athenian imperial policy, but its claim to relevance in a list of male outrages against the female sex may elude readers unfamiliar with the twentieth-century feminist claim that violence, and especially the organized violence known as war, is a function of masculinity, an extension to the political sphere of phallic aggression in sexual relationships. It follows that women are natural opponents of warlike action; this conclusion (which would seem to require modification in the light of the successful wars waged by Indira Gandhi, Golda Meir, and Margaret Thatcher) is the basis for Keuls's characteristically original solution to a notorious problem in fifth-century Athenian history: the identity and motive of those who one summer night in 415 B.C., as the great expedition prepared to sail for Sicily, smashed the face and the erect phallus of almost every stone statue of the god Hermes in Athens.

These images stood outside houses and at crossroads, for the god was a protector of the house and also of travelers; their mutilation was an inauspicious omen for the expedition, a blow to public morale. In spite of a hysterical witch-hunt that produced a wealth of unreliable confessions and even more unreliable denunciations by paid informers, little light was thrown on what was clearly a highly organized act of psychological terrorism. Thucydides records the popular belief that it was the work of oligarchic conspirators who planned to overthrow the democratic regime. There is little evidence for this idea, but it seems likely enough. Athens was an imperial democracy, its public works and social support system subsidized by tribute from subject cities; enemies of the regime were naturally opposed to territorial expansion that would increase its revenues and popular support. Oligarchic conspirators did, in fact, succeed in overthrowing the democracy temporarily after the disaster in Sicily, and some of these same men were among the so-called Thirty Tyrants, who, backed by Spartan troops, ruled a defeated Athens at the end of the war.

But Professor Keuls has a different candidate: the women of Athens. Disgusted with a government that had already waged more than ten years of bloody but indecisive war and was now about to send to a far-off destination the largest Athenian force ever assembled, and deprived of any means of political expression, the women of Athens, in what Keuls calls "an act of impotent rage," attacked the blatant symbol of their oppression.

Like Socrates' final erection, this extraordinary event has gone unrecognized for many centuries, only to be revealed now, in the age of the raised consciousness. It passes belief, however, that no one noticed it at the time—that organized gangs of phallus-bashing women, equipped, presumably, with hammers, roamed the streets of Athens in the dead of night without exciting comment. In the context of the women's life, which Keuls has so skillfully and convincingly recreated from the evidence, respectable women were not to be seen on the streets even by day. Her explanation that women were able to circulate by night during the "counter-cultural" festival of the Adonia will not hold much water: one thing we do know about the festival (and we do not know very much) is that women celebrated it on the roofs of their own houses.

But potential readers should not be discouraged by these aberrations. Pioneering studies like this are all too apt to pursue their new insights far beyond the limits of probability. In this case, once the wilder flights of speculative imagination are discounted, a solid core remains, a rich and memorable survey of the abject condition of women in a society that for creative brilliance in art, literature, politics, and philosophy has hardly a rival in the history of Western culture.

The Socratic Method

When A. E. Housman, toward the end of his life, decided to correct the learned world's misunderstanding of some passages in the Latin poets which deal in detail with the mechanics of homosexual copulation, he published, in a German scholarly periodical, an article entitled *Praefanda*[1] (which means "Dirty Words"). His meticulous explanation of the matter in hand was distinguished by the precise analysis, caustic wit, and elegant prose characteristic of all his writing, but this time the prose was not English but Latin. That was in 1931; in 1932 the New York publishing firm Covici-Friede livened up their list with a translation of Hans Licht's *Sexual Life in Ancient Greece* (Licht's real name was Brandt—he was director of a gymnasium in Saxony). The "thirty-two full-page plates" with which Covici-Friede tried to spice the rather stolid fare served up by Brandt-Licht included such daring images as the Medici Venus, the Hermes of Praxiteles, the Louvre Diana, a Parthenon metope, and for a real thrill, the Naples Aphrodite Kallipygos.

We have come a long way since then. *Eros in Greece*[2] displays a sequence of photographs which illustrate in exquisite color every aspect of Greek erotic activity from alpha to omega and back again. *Eros in Antiquity*[3] offers many of the same photographs, plus a generous coverage of the Pompeian wall paintings and the *curiosa,* most of them coarsely obscene, from the notorious Gabinetto Segreto of the Museo Nazionale in Naples. In *Greek Homosexuality*[4] K. J. Dover, dealing like Housman with specifics, calls a spade a spade but, unlike

This essay originally appeared in the *New York Review of Books,* January 25, 1979.

1. *Hermes* 66 (1931): 402ff. Reprinted in *The Classical Papers of A. E. Housman* (Cambridge: Cambridge University Press, 1972), 3:1175ff.
2. John Boardman and Eugenio La Rocca. Photographs by Antonia Mulas (New York: Erotic Art Book Society, 1978).
3. Photographed by Antonia Mulas (New York: Erotic Art Book Society, 1978).
4. Cambridge: Harvard University Press, 1978.

Housman, in his native tongue. "A man and a boy get into position for intercrural copulation" is one of his photo captions, and another runs: "A hairy satyr masturbates while pushing a penis-substitute into his own anus." And in Dover's text the love that in Victorian England dared not speak its name is examined with a clinical eye, its Greek terminology defined with philological exactness, its physical manifestations unblushingly described, and its role in archaic and classical Greek society soberly appraised.

Eros in Greece (originally *Eros in Grecia* [Milan, 1975]) has a broader scope; only half a dozen of the 160 color illustrations portray homosexual scenes. It is essentially a picture book, one of those quarto volumes which are produced for the coffee tables of the well-to-do and end up, after a decent interval, on the display tables of remainder houses. It is a very distinguished specimen of the genre. John Boardman, a renowned authority on Greek art, contributes an essay on love in Greek art and life which deals gracefully if not in depth with the place of Eros in mythology and cult; he then presents, through the persona of an imaginary youth of the classical period—"Pamphilos we shall call him"—a sketch of the sexual career of the Athenian *homme sensuel moyen:* a liaison with an older youth, marriage with a much younger bride, and extramural consolation with cultured *hetaerae* and the flute girls who entertain guests at the extremely un-Platonic symposia portrayed on red-figure vases. Boardman concludes with a concise but expert discussion of the erotic scenes on these vases which, he reminds us, "are presented without plain wrappers, unromantically, with a smile not a snigger, designed neither to excite nor to embarrass." This is a salutary reminder to the reader who embarks on the following section, a photographic anthology of the erotic art of Greece.

The photographs are extraordinary both in themselves and for the brilliance of their reproduction in color. The erotic pictures are also technically admirable; compared with those featured in *Eros Kalos*,[5] a pioneering predecessor in the Greek sex picturebook field, they show a decided advance in clarity of reproduction, though this is sometimes achieved at the expense of authenticity. On the Boston Corinthian mirror, for example, the outlines of the improbably athletic coupling it portrays emerge with startling emphasis because the dark

---

5. Geneva: Jean Marcadé, 1962.

green of the original bronze surface appears here as off-white. Most of the illustrations, however, are drawn from the vast erotic repertoire of Athenian vase painting (Dover lists some five hundred items) and the colors are faithfully reproduced; in most cases, too, though not in all, the actual dimensions of the object are stated. This is a highly desirable feature in a medium so addicted to reduction and blowup; one carved gem 26 millimeters in width is magnified more than ten times to fill two-thirds of a double spread, and the great metope from Temple E at Selinus, 1.62 meters high, is reduced to a miniature 7 centimeters square. Needless to say, the scene on the gem is highly erotic, that on the metope unobjectionable.

These illustrations cover Greek erotic art from an Etruscan oinochoe with scratched figures cruder than anything to be found in New York public toilets to the sophisticated sensuality of the Aretine bowls, here accentuated by skillful lighting. They are discussed in a critical analysis by Eugenio La Rocca, superintendent of the Capitoline museums in Rome, which deals with the pictures from an art-historical point of view; occasionally he has to justify their inclusion. The bowls made in Arezzo by Marcus Perennius Tigranes, for example, are billed as "the last to show clear evidence of Greek influence." He also discusses possible mythological interpretations (not all of them convincing) and explains what the pictures represent. Such explanation is standard practice in any publication of Greek vase painting, which often features objects unfamiliar to the modern eye and uses artistic conventions which may not be comprehensible at first glance. In the case of erotic pictures, especially those which portray activity which though obviously sexual is not clearly represented or not immediately recognizable, this can pose a delicate problem; Sir John Beazley was a master of precise understatement in this field[6] and Emily Vermeule's publication of the Warren collection—"Some Erotica in Boston"[7]—is a model of its kind.

La Rocca does well enough, but he tends to be evasive when the temperature rises: "Two Men at Exercise" is his heading for the Amasis cup which shows two fat men masturbating and he leaves

6. For example, he supplied for the "most characteristic configuration of homosexual courtship in vase painting"—one in which the suitor reaches for the boy's face with one hand and his genitals with the other—the handy label "the up and down position" (Dover, p. 94).

7. *Antike Kunst*, 1969:9–15.

the baffled reader with no explanation of the strange goings-on represented on the Nikosthenes kantharos (even Vermeule is a little mysterious on this one—"boy tending from the rear a symplegma of boy and girl").[8] La Rocca can also, with that slightly batty irrelevance art historians are prone to, take off at a hilarious tangent to the main line; on the Boston mirror, for example, a picture which will have every reader trying desperately to figure out how the lady can possibly operate in *that* position without breaking her neck, he remarks: "Note the details, especially the extremely fine rosette border of the blanket."

Eros in Antiquity displays its wares unaccompanied by interpretative essay or art-historical commentary; this is a hard-core item. There are very few landscape pictures here; blowups are frequent and spectacular (a votive vulva and a phallos vase, 15 and 8.5 centimeters high respectively, fill each one a quarto page). The Pompeian wall paintings include, besides such well-known items as the bawdyhouse frescoes and the initiation scenes from the House of the Mysteries, a picture of Priapus weighing his truly formidable member on a hand balance. The bronzes, marbles, and terracottas form a monotonous line of phallic grotesques; the prize item is a Mercury who, in addition to a huge bent phallus in the usual place, has two more sprouting from his winged cap and one from each ear. The publisher's blurb claims that "the works in *Eros in Antiquity* come across with such immense visual impact as to make . . . dead civilizations *live*"; unfortunately, this fifteen-page parade of phallic fantasies creates a quite false impression that what the people of Pompeii lived in was an environment something like the inside of an adult books establishment.

Dover's book is a much more serious enterprise; the reader who embarks on it expecting amusement or titillation will be swiftly disillusioned. It is a matter-of-fact, methodical description and analysis of a social phenomenon, central to classical Greek culture, which has been prettily sentimentalized, dismissed as peripheral, or blandly ignored in most presentations of the glory that was Greece. Dover's is an authoritative discussion; he is a philologist of great stature with wide achievement as editor, commentator, and literary critic, and he

---

8. To see what is meant by "tending" the curious reader may consult J. Boardman, *Athenian Red-Figure Vases in the Archaic Period* (London: Thames & Hudson, 1945), fig. 99.

has been working his way toward a full treatment of this subject since the publication of his magnificent edition of Aristophanes' *Clouds*.[9] His witty commentary on the homosexual yearnings betrayed by Right's phraseology in the famous debate scene of that play abolished forever the comfortable doctrine that Right speaks against the sophistic arguments of Wrong in the conservative voice of Aristophanes himself: "it is as if a modern preacher, having thundered 'No girl ever wore trousers in those days' continued 'And sometimes you glimpsed the satiny flesh on the inside of her thighs.'" And in his identification of the physical phenomena Right finds so enchanting in his nostalgic picture of the boys of yesteryear, Dover set a new standard of liveliness in the exegesis of classical Greek texts: "What stimulates Right's aesthetic imagination is the visual and tactile contrast between the matt surface of the penis as a whole and the secretion revealed by pushing back the foreskin; the same kind of contrast as is obtained by taking a small bite at a peach." Since then Dover has dealt briefly with the subject in an article on classical Greek attitudes to sexual behavior[10] and in his book *Greek Popular Morality*;[11] he now presents us with an exhaustive survey of "those phenomena of homosexual behavior and sentiment which are to be found in Greek art and literature between the eighth and second centuries B.C."

The eighth century is now one of the fashionable dates for the late stages of composition of the *Iliad* and *Odyssey*, but Dover, of course, recognizes that "there is no overt homosexuality in these poems." This is a rather remarkable fact, since it is obviously not a case of suppression for reasons of literary decorum; tragedy, as we know from fragments of Aeschylus and Sophocles, dealt unashamedly with this theme and Pindar's "hymns, lords of the lyre" could refer to it without a blush. The historical problem posed by this Homeric silence has been tackled in various ways. Sir William Ridgeway, writing early in the century, identified the Achaeans of Homer as Aryans, "a body of tall, fair-haired invaders," in whose society "there was not likely to be any place for the unspeakable sin which cankered Greek society in historical times." Their descendants were corrupted after the migra-

9. New York: Oxford University Press, 1968.
10. *Arethusa*, Spring 1973.
11. Berkeley and Los Angeles: University of California Press, 1975, pp. 213–16.

tion to the south: "the sin of Sodom in all ages has been endemic in the Mediterranean basin and has never, except sporadically, and that mainly under southern influence, appeared north of the Alps."[12] (It seems hard to believe, but he wrote these words sitting in a Cambridge college midway between King's and Trinity.)

A later theory, basing itself on some passages in Plato's *Laws*, reversed the roles and assigned responsibility for the spread of homosexuality to later invaders, the Dorians. Dover, after a careful review of the evidence, rejects this idea out of hand: "there can be no question of tracing the diffusion of homosexual eros from Sparta or other Dorian states. We can only say that its social acceptance and artistic exploitation had become widespread by the end of the seventh century."

Wherever it may have started, the bulk of our evidence for it (as for almost everything else about classical Greece) comes from Athens. In fact, the "mainstay of the book" (Dover's own description of pages 19–109) is a full exploration of a speech made by Aeschines before an Athenian court, urging that one Timarchus be deprived of his citizenship, in accordance with a law which forbade anyone who had prostituted his body to another male to exercise citizen rights. (The citizen right Timarchus was exercising was the prosecution of Aeschines for treasonous conduct in the course of negotiations with Philip of Macedon.) The number of different issues relevant to homosexuality raised by this speech is, as Dover puts it, "considerable." He proposes "to explore each of them far enough to make what Aeschines said to the jurors in 346 B.C. intelligible in terms of the jurors' attitudes and assumptions."

The reason for Dover's concentration on this particular text (and later on comedy) is the proposition, basic to his book *Greek Popular Morality*, that "works composed for the persuasion or amusement of large audiences" should be treated as the primary "evidence for the moral assumptions made by the average Athenian." And this speech of Aeschines is "the only surviving text which gives us access to the sentiments which it was prudent to profess in public on the subject of homosexuality in Athens during the classical period."

12. *The Early Age of Greece* (Cambridge: Cambridge University Press, 1931), 2:132, 353–54. (This volume was published posthumously; Ridgeway died in 1926 and had been working on it ever since the publication of vol. 1 in 1901.)

Dover's "long and discursive exploration" of this speech investigates the law and the legal issues raised by the case, the Greek vocabulary of homosexual feeling and practice, the Greek view of what was "natural" in these matters, the roles of active and passive partners, the mode of pursuit and flight, courtship and copulation, and (a factor never thoroughly assessed before) the weight of the evidence provided by the abundant artistic representation. What emerges is a general pattern of feeling and conduct which is unique in the history of Western society: a code of male homosexual love openly practiced and socially acceptable.

Aeschines' case against Timarchus is not that he is a homosexual, not even that he was once a homosexual prostitute; it is that having been one, he is breaking the law by prosecuting Aeschines for treason. The orator foresees that the defense will try to confuse the issue by producing a general who will sing the praises of homosexual love (the patriotic lovers Harmodius and Aristogeiton, the heroic lovers Achilles and Patroclus)[13] and point out that Aeschines himself has been the lover (*erastes*) of many and has written "erotic" poems. Aeschines forestalls these arguments by admitting that he has no criticism to make of what he calls *dikaios* ("just" or "legitimate") eros, that he has been an *erotikos*—a man given to homosexual love affairs—and remains one, and that he has even been involved in the contentions and fights which arise from such pursuits. There could be no clearer indication that homosexual relationships, when clear of any suspicion of commercialism, were considered honorable, even admirable. (Incidentally, Aeschines won the case.)

Such relationships had their own peculiar conventions and rituals. They rarely took place between men of the same age; the ideal pair were a fully adult but still young *erastes* and an adolescent *eromenos*, whose beard had not yet grown; the law contained stringent clauses protecting younger boys. There is nothing effeminate about either partner; "in the visual arts of the late archaic and early classical periods, and also in the majority of literary contexts (at any period) in

---

13. Though there is no overt homosexuality in Homer, the classical Greeks, who regularly cited Homer as an ethical standard, had to pretend that there was. Aeschines so interprets the friendship of the two heroes in this speech and Aeschylus produced a play on the subject; a surviving fragment shows that he portrayed the relationship as one of physical as well as emotional passion.

which homosexual eros is expressed directly or described with approval, unambiguously male bodily features and a specifically masculine life-style constitute a homosexual stimulus," though "there may have been a certain shift in taste towards effeminate-looking males during the fourth century." But though the passion of the *erastes*, displayed in the opulence of his gifts, the persistence of his pursuit, and the physical symptoms of his passion, were universally approved and admired, the *eromenos* was expected to play, and be, very hard to get—and even when got, not to enjoy the process. "The boy," says Xenophon, "does not share in the man's pleasure in intercourse, as a woman does; cold sober, he looks upon the other drunk with sexual desire."

Intercourse, when and if it was finally achieved, was, to judge by the vase paintings (our only firm evidence) "intercrural," not anal. And the role of the respectable *eromenos* is summed up by Dover as: "refusal of payment, obdurate postponement of bodily contact until the potential partner has proved his worth, abstention from any sensual enjoyment of such contact, insistence on an upright position, avoidance of meeting the partner's eye during consummation, denial of true penetration." This situation, as Dover wittily remarks, has certain analogies with a heterosexual context: "the presentation of respectable British society in the literature of the nineteenth century."

For the easily won, venal, or prostitute *eromenos*, male society felt contempt, but the successful *erastes* was envied. Housman, in the article referred to above, after informing the German scholarly community that the coarse Latin word for the dominant male partner in one of his aspects (*irrumator*) was not adequately rendered by "*Schweinhund*," went on to lament that it was of course "difficult for people accustomed from boyhood to follow the laws of Paul of Tarsus and the Hebrews to accept the idea, which seemed as perfectly natural to Catullus and Martial as it would to any modern denizen of the slums of Sicily or Naples, that fellators and pathics were obscene, but not their active partners."[14]

The physical aspects of such relationships are fully documented in

14. Scilicet non facile qui Pauli Tarsensis et Iudaeorum norma uti a pueris consueverunt opinionem mentibus comprehendunt quae, ut Catullo et Martiali, ita nunc cuivis de plebe Siciliana vel Neapolitana penitus a natura insita est, obscaenos fellatores et cinaedos, pedicones et irrumatores non obscaenos esse.

the fifty-six crowded pages of black and white illustrations; from the literature we are more familiar with their emotional side. These emotions are of course the context of Socrates' discussions with the young, as they are presented in Plato's dialogues: the physical setting is as often as not a gymnasium, the obvious place to admire and court the fashionable "beauties." We encounter Socrates, as Dover says, "in a strongly homosexual ambience." This phrase occurs in the opening paragraph of a fascinating discussion of Socrates' "exploitation of the Athenian homosexual ethos as a basis of metaphysical doctrine." Dover has already demonstrated, in his analysis of the polite and sometimes euphemistic vocabulary used for public discussion of this subject, that the typical Platonic dialogue is conducted in an athletic, homosexual setting and is rich in imagery drawn from the language of homosexual love; but, though Socrates in the *Charmides* (125b) is made to describe himself as "on fire, absolutely beside myself" as a result of a glimpse inside the cloak of young Charmides, he condemns actual homosexual copulation (*Republic* 403b) and, in a famous scene of the *Symposium*, resists the seductive importunities of the irresistible Alcibiades.

It is Socratic (or more likely Platonic) doctrine that eros, the passion for the physical beauty of another person, is, as Dover puts it, "a step in the direction of absolute Beauty, an aspect of Good." It is only the first step and Diotima, Socrates' mentor (or so he claims in the *Symposium*), describes the rest of the journey: "beginning from these beauties, to ascend continually in pursuit of that other Beauty, going, as it were by steps . . . to end in that study which is a study of nothing other than Beauty itself." That this climb to the metaphysical stratosphere should start from and draw its imagery from earthly sexual passion is a familiar phenomenon from other times and cultures; that in the case of Plato's influential theory of ideas the base passion should be homosexual is a historical accident. In Socrates' world, as Dover points out, "intense eros was experienced more often in a homosexual than in a heterosexual relationship" and the necessary abstinence from copulation was more appropriate for homosexual love, since women's role in society was to bear children, "whereas popular sentiment romanticized and applauded the chastity of an *eromenos* and the devotedly unselfish *erastes*." In fact, of course, such romantic chastity was more honored in the breach than the observance and Plato in his old age ruled homosexual love out of court as "contrary to nature,"[15] a formulation which, as Dover says, was to have a profound effect on the history of morality.

At the end of the book, after a brief discussion of women and homosexuality (brief because the literary evidence is scarce, the pictorial almost nonexistent) and a section on the Dorians, Dover poses the question why the Greeks "developed homosexual eros much more elaborately and intensely than other peoples" and "why its elaboration took certain forms rather than others." He suggests as an answer that "homosexuality satisfied a need . . . for personal relationships of an intensity not commonly found within marriage or in the relations between parents and children or in those between the individual and the community as a whole." He sees the first two deficiencies as consequences of the third: "the political fragmentation of the Greek world" which confronted the Greek city-state continuously with "the problem of survival in competition with aggressive neighbors." The consequent overvaluation of adult male fighters and undervaluation of women produced a situation in which "males tended to group themselves together for military, political, religious and social purposes to a degree . . . which was enough to inhibit the full development of intimacy between husband and wife or between father and son."

This hardly seems an adequate explanation; one thinks at once of other societies that were highly organized for permanent warfare but developed no such elaborate homosexual codes, and in any case, as Dover has already pointed out, the phenomena under investigation are characteristic of the Athenian leisure class (the characters of Plato's dialogues), a world in which unmarried girls were carefully confined in their parents' home until marriage and then just as strictly confined in their husbands'. Such segregation of women was not possible except in a household well equipped with slave labor; the Athenians who manned the war galleys, the mass audience of Aristopha-

---

15. Plato, Dover points out, "appeals to the animal world to establish what is natural and what is not. This argument is weak, if only because Plato knew virtually nothing about animals." A specimen of what Plato did not know about animals is provided in a note to page 99: "The giraffe has developed a courtship technique, exploiting the aesthetic potentialities of his long neck, which he uses in homosexual relations but not in heterosexual mating."

nes, lived in a rougher, coarser, more heterosexual world, as is clear from the comedies themselves.

Dover does not, in any case, intend to indulge in "speculation at more theoretical levels";[16] his "primary object is to describe what is most easily and clearly observed, offering such explanations as are prompted by everyday experience." This he has done, in full measure and with the accuracy, penetrating analysis, and objectivity characteristic of all his work. The subject was one which needed to be exposed to the light of day; we can be thankful that it has been done by a great scholar and one who treats the subject without prejudice either way. "I am fortunate," he says in his preface, "in not experiencing moral shock or disgust at any genital act whatsoever, provided that it is welcome and agreeable to all the participants (whether they number one, two or more than two)." In that parenthesis he gives evidence of another asset which for anyone who writes on this subject is indispensable, a carefully disciplined, but acute, sense of humor.

16. For such speculation, see the interesting article of G. Devereux, "Greek Pseudo-homosexuality and the 'Greek Miracle,'" *Symbolae Osloenses* 42(1967): 69–92.

ESSAYS
The Modern World

Survivals & Transformations

The Life of a Legend

The slightly jarring title of George Steiner's book—*Antigones*[1]—a plural form which is not Greek and does not really sound like English either, was chosen, I suspect, with monitory intent: let no one assume that the author proposes a stroll down such familiar academic lanes as the influence of *Antigone,* some versions of *Antigone,* or the Antigone theme, where he would be following in the footsteps of scholars who, as he points out in his preface, have published articles dealing with this subject as recently as 1974 and 1977. He is dealing not with imitations or reflections of the great original, but with Antigones that stand solid in their own right, with "some of the most radically transformative interpretations and 'reexperiencings' ever elicited by a literary text."

These "reexperiencings" are not the contribution of classical scholars, whose concerns are the establishment and elucidation of the Greek text in the light of what knowledge they can attain of the play's historical background, its intellectual and religious context, and its relation to the work of predecessors and contemporaries. They impose "constraints," as Steiner puts it, on interpretation; they seek, that is, "to determine the limits of possibility within which an Attic mentality of the Periclean Age may reasonably be supposed to have operated." While admitting the validity of such constraints in matters of ascertainable fact ("actual objects and practices"), Steiner points out that major poets are innovators in language and sensibility, and that the drama has been time and again the "testing-ground of lost or future potentials of human utterance and behavior." In fact, as he justly asserts, the reading of a classical text can "press on us a claim of seeming immediacy"; it can "foreshadow, . . . symbolize, . . . speak nakedly to our present condition." The "afterlife of Hellas" consisted of "successive compulsions of identification between ancient and

This essay originally appeared in the *New Republic,* November 19, 1984.

1. New York: Oxford University Press, 1984.

modern"; he cites Ciceronian Atticism, the neoclassicism of the *ancien régime*, the "Sparta" of the French Revolution, Victorian Hellenism, and "Matthew Arnold's observation that Marathon and Salamis were more actual to the governing culture of nineteenth-century England than was the Battle of Hastings."

Such "foreshortenings and claims to relevance" have "taken on peculiar force" in modern times. Philosophy, anthropology, and psychoanalysis have turned back to Greek sources to "make of the archaic the raw material and substance of the continuities of the human psyche," and the relevance of Euripides' *Trojan Women* and *Bacchae* for the turbulence of our times needs no emphasis. In all these foreshortenings the classical scholar is conscious of exaggeration, misunderstanding, even deliberate distortion of the original text. For the literary critic, however, justification lies in Walter Benjamin's "hermeneutic conceit" that "there is that in an ancient text which awaits our discovery, that vital texts perform a millennial pilgrimage towards recognition and interpretation yet to come." The original, says Steiner, is not injured in such a process of discovery: "the integral authority of the classic is such that it can absorb without loss of identity the millennial incursions upon it, the accretions to it, of commentary, of translation, of enacted variation. *Ulysses* reinforces Homer; Broch's *Death of Virgil* enriches the *Aeneid*, Sophocles' *Antigone* will not suffer from Lacan."

That Sophocles' *Antigone* will not suffer from Lacan is something about which I have no doubt whatever—for the simple reason that Lacan is unreadable even now and will be forgotten tomorrow. But the other two cases are impressive examples of works which have "tested the strength of their being" against that of their source. They are among the very few which have survived to "become that enigmatic but undeniable phenomenon, an echo that has life." It is with such echoes that Steiner's book is concerned.

Though adaptations of Sophocles' plot or characters abound in European literature after the first printing of the Greek text (Venice, 1502), it was in the years from 1790 to about 1905 (when "under pressure of Freudian reference, critical interpretative focus . . . shifted to the *Oedipus Tyrannus*") that poets, philosophers, and scholars came to regard the *Antigone* not only as the finest Greek tragedy but also as "a work of art nearer to perfection than any other produced by the human spirit."

Steiner's first chapter is devoted to the Antigones of Hegel, Goethe, Kierkegaard, and Hölderlin. Hegel's reading of the *Antigone* is of course a familiar landmark in the critical literature; Steiner can even speak, justly, of its "notoriety." Both Antigone and Creon are one-sided; both have justice on their side, both act unjustly. "Familial love, the holy, the inward, belonging to inner feeling and therefore known also as the law of the nether gods, collides with the right of the state." It follows that Creon "is not a tyrant, but actually an ethical power. Creon is not in the wrong." Steiner points out that though this passage from the *Lectures on the Philosophy of Religion* may have been Hegel's last word on the subject, it was not his first.

In the unpublished early writings and in the *Phenomenology*, Steiner finds the elements of a different interpretation, a "profoundly original, delicate exegesis. Its focus is Antigone, not Creon, and she is cited as an example of those immaculate, celestial types or presences who preserve within their differences and divisions of self the never-deconsecrated innocence and integrity of their being. . . . Such men and women simply *are.*" Hegel is not a lucid writer; his prose, as Steiner himself says, "does offer difficulties of a peculiar sort." His own exploration of the philosopher's appropriation of Antigone is not easy reading either, but it is brilliantly successful in its attempt "to follow the life of a major text within a major text and the metamorphic exchanges of meaning which this internality brings about."

The Antigone of Kierkegaard is just as complicated, for the "Antigone excursus" in the first part of his *Either/Or* is not only an evocation of the "inmost guises of his being," it is also "embedded in . . . the ironic-reflexive dialectic of hypothetical proposals and self-negations which is Kierkegaard's chosen mode of communication." In any case, Kierkegaard breaks precedent by his radical reshaping of the Sophoclean play; this is not, in form at least, an interpretation of *Antigone* but, to use Steiner's term, a "fantastication," an appropriation of the Sophoclean character for the exploration of Kierkegaard's own tortured conscience. "Some of us," wrote Shelley, "have in a prior existence been in love with an Antigone," but Kierkegaard claimed even closer intimacy. "She is my creation, her thoughts are my thoughts, and yet it is as if I had rested with her in a night of love, as if she had entrusted me with her deep secret."

In Kierkegaard's scenario Antigone alone knows that Oedipus was Jocasta's son, and now that he is dead her resolve to keep that secret forever alienates her from the world and even from the man she loves, from whom, as the keeper of the secret, she would be withholding "the very essence of her spirit." Steiner's brilliant analysis of this Romantic fable exposes its connections not only to Kierkegaard's own anxieties and problems—the secret of his father's guilt, his own abandonment of the woman he loved—but also to a wider concern of nineteenth-century intellectual man: fear of loss of individuality, of "that singular presentness without which there can be no integrity" before the inroads of a "clamorous mass culture." One defense might be "the custody of a secret, a secret grave and spacious enough to guard the soul against dispersal."

Of the four cardinal Antigones of the nineteenth century only one, Hölderlin's, was a translation of the Sophoclean play, but it was in some ways the strangest of them all. To Goethe and Schiller, Hölderlin's versions of *Oedipus* and *Antigone* were "palpable evidence of mental collapse"; it was not until the twentieth century that their real worth was recognized, not only by Heidegger but also by Hellenists as eminent as Reinhardt and Schadewalt. Steiner points out the importance of Hölderlin's *Antigone* in the literary theory of Walter Benjamin (whose "indispensable essay of 1923 on the nature and limits of all translation is an excursus on Hölderlin's Pindar and Sophocles") and the "exemplary function" assigned to it by those students of poetics and of language most in sympathy with Lacan and Derrida. He speaks with authority here; the author of *After Babel* has, as he puts it in his prefatory remarks to the discussion of the Greek text in his third chapter, directed most of his "work and personal life to the study and exposition of the history, of the poetics, of the philosophic-linguistic aspects of translation."

Hölderlin's early translations reflect the ideal of Schiller—to produce versions that are faithful to the Greek but also free, phrased, that is, "in idiom, cadence, and rhetorical conventions . . . natural to the native tongue." In his *Antigone*, however, a different approach is visible—"an intransigent literalism," which results in an "Atticization" of German, a "dislocation of sentence structures, clause dependencies, participial agreements." (Schadewaldt, comparing a typical passage with five other versions, remarks on the paradoxical fact that the result of the "new, audacious demands he makes on the arrangement of German words and clauses, is—a much greater clarity of expression.") But the really revolutionary feature of the work is Hölderlin's conviction, developed by Steiner from cryptic formulations in an 1803 letter from Hölderlin to his publisher, that "latent in the original text are certain truths . . . which are unrealized when it appears in its original embodiment." It is the "translator's" sacred task to call into life "these in-dwelling but hitherto unfulfilled latencies, to 'surpass' the original text in the exact spirit of the text."

Paradoxically, however, what the translator strives to elicit from the text is not those meanings which have over the passage of centuries become apparent with the changes brought about by time, but older layers of thought and feeling that lay behind Sophocles' consciousness—"the Apollonian-passion foundations" constrained within "the Junonian-sober . . . self control." These almost mantic formulas, from Hölderlin's letter to Böhlendorff dated December 1803, are interpreted by Steiner as a program for a return to the "occult source," to "those fonts of tragic meaning and of tragic gesture which Sophocles' continence, Sophocles' Periclean addiction to temperance, had, to some degree, stifled." As Steiner says, "Nietzsche's "famous dichotomy of Dionysian and Apollonian" has its origin here; clearly recognizable also is the twentieth century's return to the "occult source," the search for the roots of fifth-century Athenian civilization in tribal cult and ritual. The opposing forces, Apollonian and Junonian, passion and self-control, are embodied in Antigone and Creon. Both are "radically religious," but their relation to God or gods is different, for Antigone is the *antitheos*, one who, in Steiner's translation of Hölderlin's words, "comports himself as if *against* God in a *godly sense.*" She is a "holy fool," the "holy sinner" of Dostoevsky. But the conflict is not confined to the religious sphere. "The letter of the law (Creon) is challenged by the primal spirit and nascent future of the law (Antigone)." Hegel's antitheses are transformed.

This first chapter, which reaches its high point in the exposition of Hölderlin's "esoteric doctrine," is only one third of this dense and at times difficult book. The second chapter provides a variation of pace: the concentration on four immensely influential nineteenth-century figures is followed by a wide-ranging analysis of Antigones from Robert Garnier's in 1580 to Athol Fugard's *The Island*, staged in 1973, as Steiner considers what subsequent poets and dramatists have made of the Sophoclean prototypes. The focus is no longer steadily on Antigone; Ismene, Haemon, the chorus and, last and at most length, Creon are seen through the eyes of such well-known writers on the theme as Racine, Gide, Brecht, Heidegger, and Anouilh as well as many less familiar (and some surprising) figures such as Maurras, Döblin (in *November 1918*), Conor Cruise O'Brien (in a lecture at Belfast), Ghéon, and, of all people, Houston Stewart Chamberlain, who wrote an opera libretto *Der Tod der Antigone*.

Rich as the material is, it is still "only a small sample." No record of "the matter of Antigone," as Steiner says, can hope to be complete. But it is vast enough to justify the question Steiner raises at the beginning of the chapter: "Why is it that Antigone—together with a handful of other figures—Orpheus, Prometheus, Heracles, Agamemnon and his pack, Oedipus, Odysseus, Medea—should constitute the essential code of canonic reference for intellect and sensibility across Western civilization? Why a hundred 'Antigones' after Sophocles?"

The primacy of Greek myth in the Western imagination, and the dominance of Greek philosophical concepts in Western thought, are partly explicable, of course, in historical terms—the preservation of the classical heritage through Latin in the Middle Ages, its renewal with the discovery of Greek in the Renaissance. Steiner works forward from Heidegger's eloquent celebration of the Western consciousness as formed by "the successive 'experiencings' and interpretations by philosophers, poets, and translators of the Greek verb 'to be.'" From Heidegger's claim that "it is, to a more or less conscious degree, from Greek grammar and from the vocabulary of Greek philosophic and lyric expression that we continue to derive the marks of our communal and personal identity in the West," Steiner moves toward his own highly metaphysical, almost mystical vision of the "'initial' and determinant" Greek myths as *"myths in and of language."*

"We are all Greeks," said Shelley. "Our laws, our literature, our religion, our arts, have their roots in Greece." But Steiner cites Shelley's first four words in a "fundamental sense." The basic operations of our thought and speech are Greek; "to articulate experience grammatically, to relate discourse and meaning as we do, is to 'be Greek,'" for our very conceptions of grammar, of the possibilities inherent in speech, are "organized along Greek lines. . . . So are the syntax of deduction and of inference, of proof and negation, which are the alphabet of rational thought." Steiner goes on to connect the basic work of language at the deepest level with the development of "certain key myths." There is a sense in which "Greek grammar and rhetoric internalize, formalize, certain mythical configurations." Thus primary myths which dramatize uncertainties of kinship can be associated with "the evolution of the grammar of cases; vestiges of this interaction can be made out in the very designation of the 'nominative'—consider the dramatic grammar of uncertain identity in the Oedipus theme, in Odysseus's syntactical ruse in the cave of the Cyclops." The "linguistic leap into unconstrained futurity" may have had its "informing counterpart in the Prometheus motif." Steiner reads in Narcissus "the long history of the first person singular" and in the related myth of Echo "can make out the archaic experiencing of the suggestive sterility of the synonymous."

Whatever else may be said of this theory (which, it should be borne in mind, is offered "in a preliminary, tentative form"), it lacks neither imagination nor originality. We are promised elaboration to come, and must reserve judgment for the appearance of the fully deployed argument. But it is proposed here as an explanation of the firm hold certain Greek myths still retain on the mind of the West and in particular as an answer to the question: "Why a hundred 'Antigones' after Sophocles?" And in the third chapter of his book, where Steiner turns to the Greek text of Sophocles' play, a very different answer to that question begins to take shape in the reader's mind.

There is much in this chapter to engage the attention of classical scholars. As Steiner reads back into the Sophoclean text some of the insights of later poets and thinkers, he is consistently stimulating and sometimes disturbing. One long passage, his discussion of the scenes of confrontation between Antigone and Creon, shows him at his best and also, it seems to me, bears on the problem he raised. These scenes he singles out as "the one literary text" that expresses "all the principal constants of conflict in the condition of man." They are: "the confrontation of men and of women; of age and of youth; of society and of the individual; of the living and the dead; of men and of god(s)." These are not negotiable conflicts; they are permanent in human life. And, in Sophocles' play, "they are made manifest with a perfect economy and natural logic." Steiner's incisive analysis of the scenes along these lines more than justifies his description of them. But this surely is enough to explain the permanence of Antigone in our civilization, her relevance to Belfast and Capetown, to Paris and Berlin, as well as to explain why, to quote the last sentence of Steiner's challenging book, "new 'Antigones' are being imagined, thought, lived now; and will be tomorrow." This permanence has nothing to do with "myth." As Steiner himself has so forcefully demonstrated in his 45-page exegesis of these 140 lines of verse, the thematic richness which gives Antigone such a grip on our minds and emotions is the product of a "literary text." We are obsessed not by the myth of Antigone (whatever *that* may have been) but by the *Antigone* of Sophocles.

And the same distinction must be made for the other mythical figures of his list. If the Aeschylean *Prometheus Bound* had been lost, as its sequel was, the world would know Prometheus only as the trickster god of Hesiod, the Loki of the Olympians. What would Agamemnon mean to us without the *Iliad* and *Oresteia?* Oedipus without the two Sophoclean plays? Medea if we had only Pindar's fourth Pythian and Apollonius Rhodius's *Argonautica?* And how much does the spell Orpheus has cast on poets and musicians ever since antiquity owe to seventy-five lines of the Fourth Georgic, perhaps the most beautiful lines Virgil ever wrote? Steiner himself speaks of a "homecoming" to these myths "made compelling and endurable by the formality, by the narrative coherence, by the lyric and plastic comeliness with which the Greek spirit invested the uncanny and daemonic." But those qualities were the creation not of "the Greek spirit" but of the individual poets who made the canonical versions.

Oedipus Rex

By the middle of the Greek National Theater production of Sophocles' *Oedipus Rex*, at the Kennedy Center in Washington (1985), those members of the audience whose knowledge of modern Greek did not extend much beyond *kaliméra* and *efharistó* had settled into a comfortable acceptance of the play as a suggestive and at times brilliant miming of a familiar plot. They were suddenly galvanized when they heard (or did they?) a whole sentence clearly delivered in English. "Was I hallucinating?" my wife asked me afterwards, "or did I hear English for a second or two in the middle of all that Greek?" It was English all right. The chorus broke off their dance, faced front and took off their masks; their spokesman put a question to the audience. "If such crimes go unpunished, why should I join the sacred performance?" Then they put their masks back on and resumed their collective persona as Greek-speaking elders of ancient Thebes.

The delivery of that sentence in English was a special effect aimed at the mainly English-speaking audiences of Boston, New York, Washington and Los Angeles. The director, Minos Volanakis, wanted to be sure that the radical gesture of the choral dancers should not pass unnoticed. In Greece, where Volanakis first produced the play in 1982 at Epidaurus, he did not need to draw attention to what he was doing; such a deliberate Brechtian rupture of the dramatic illusion for didactic purposes was unprecedented in a revival of classical tragedy.

It is, of course, impossible to imagine Sophocles' chorus removing the mask. But Volanakis is not importing *Verfremdungseffekt* just for the novelty of it; he is attempting to recreate in modern terms a remarkable feature of the ancient play. In the scene before this central ode the chorus learned that Oedipus now had cause to fear that he might in fact be the murderer of Laios and so the cause of the plague and further that, at Delphi, Apollo had predicted a monstrous future for him. They had also heard Jocasta dismiss divine prophecy in

This essay originally appeared in *Grand Street* 4, no. 2 (Winter 1985).

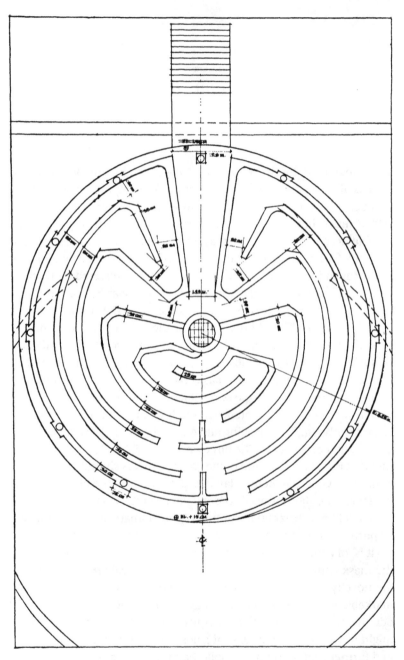

Stage design by Robert D. Mitchell for the production of *Oedipus Rex* at Epidaurus. May 14, 1962.

scornful terms. Their choral chant expresses their distress at these revelations and their shocked disapproval of Jocasta's impiety. They call on Zeus himself to see that on the fulfillment of Apollo's oracle hangs the validity of all religious belief. "If fact and prophecy do not coincide in harmony for all mankind to see . . . I will not go in reverence to the impregnable center of the world [Delphi] nor to the temples at Abae or Olympia. . . . religion is finished." Their question—literally "Why should I dance?"—brings this issue of the truth or falsehood of divine prophecy—and so of the existence or nonexistence of divine omniscience—out of the mythic past and the dramatic illusion into the light of the present day. The whole performance, choral song and dance, actors' speech and movement, was a rite of divine worship, a celebration of the god Dionysos; if "religion is finished," what is the point of the performance? What are we doing here? This question, which makes the validity of the performance itself depend on the outcome of the dramatic action, is in fact a sort of Sophoclean *Verfremdungseffekt;* but for a modern audience, which has no altar in the theater and no priest of Dionysos sitting in the front row, it might pass unnoticed without the kind of emphasis Volanakis has given it.

Volanakis is no stranger to modern theatrical theory and practice. He is said to be the only director to have staged all of Genet in English; his production of *The Screens* in New York won the Critics' Circle Award. He was responsible for the world premiere of Elias Canetti's *The Numbered*[1] and staged the seven-hour version of Berlioz's *Les Troyens* at Covent Garden. For the eight years of the colonels' regime in Greece he worked abroad, mainly in England, but since 1974 he has lived in Athens. He has produced Greek tragedy (and Aristophanic comedy) in his own translations into English and modern Greek. Particularly remarkable must have been a version of Euripides' *Medea* starring Melina Mercouri, staged not in an ancient theater but in a marble quarry on Pendeli, the mountain that hems in modern Athens from the north.

For the *Oedipus* he had no such spectacular backdrop, but he was not content with the stages offered him at Epidaurus and elsewhere; with the stage designer Robert Mitchell, Volanakis created his own. It

---

1. *Life Terms* in *The Plays of Elias Canetti* (New York: Farrar, Strauss & Giroux, 1985).

is a roughly circular, dark brown plate, tilted towards the audience; at the back, ruined walls frame an entrance to the palace. In front of this entrance the opening of a sacrificial pit gives off occasional glare and smoke; on the surface of the plate a labyrinth pattern is etched by dark lines. This labyrinth is important to Volanakis's conception of the play; it represents, as he wrote in his notes to the actors for the 1982 production, "the Hidden Order of the World," a "sacred pattern that lurks beneath the feet of the characters." He refers to "floor patterns," found "from Crete to medieval cathedrals . . . to the Navaho and Pima Indians," patterns that guided "a sacred sequence of steps in the ritual." The labyrinth of his *Oedipus Rex*, like the walls at stage rear, is in ruins. Oedipus, who believes he has evaded the fate predicted by Apollo, and Jocasta, who announces that the universe is governed by blind chance, cannot see the labyrinth and ignore its pat-

Pima basket design

tern in their movements. The chorus, as they pray for delivery from the plague, trace the pattern of the maze on their knees in penitential supplication. But in their premature rejoicing as they foresee that Oedipus will be revealed as the son of a mountain nymph and Apollo, they too ignore the pattern. "Only blind people always follow the patterns on the floor"; Oedipus will follow its windings to make his final exit and Tiresias, in perhaps the most extraordinary entrance in the play, shuffles around its curves, bowed down so that under his cape of animal skin he seems at first to be a beast moving on all fours.

The labyrinth has a special relevance to Oedipus. "Blundering detective and predetermined killer," he walks the "maze with its false turnings and its blind alleys," which will turn out to be the labyrinth "where each step leads inescapably to the next." The only way out of the labyrinth is through the center, where, in Crete, the Minotaur is waiting, in Thebes the dreadful knowledge. Knowing who he is at last and now blind, Oedipus follows the pattern of the labyrinth with unerring steps as he leaves Thebes forever.

This symbolic system could not have been fully comprehensible for those members of the audience who had not read the program notes, but even for them the movements of actors and chorus as acceptance or denial of the labyrinthine pattern may have worked subliminally. And no one could mistake the significance of the placing of Jocasta for the scene in which she undertakes to comfort Oedipus by proving, from her own experience, that prophets and oracles are not worth listening to; her throne is placed squarely over the sacrificial pit which, in the opening scene, had glowed with the flame of sacrificial fires.

The choral dancers were masked, and so, for the opening scenes, were Oedipus and Creon; they wore a projecting half-mask of metal that served also as a crown. Their royal state (Creon is the Queen's brother) was further emphasized by gold, floor-length robes and wide sleeves which, when arms were raised to shoulder level, reached to the ground to create a Byzantine image of regal power, its wings extended in menace or protection. The chorus wore loose, hooded cloaks; Volanakis was aiming at a monastic, Byzantine effect. But I was not the only spectator to be reminded of desert Arabs by the Dionysis Fotopoulos costumes—an impression strengthened by the dark-sand color of the stage, which recalled the gritty surfaces of Pasolini's Moroccan landscape in his *Edipo Re*. I asked Volanakis if he had seen that remarkable film, but although he admired it (with the qualification that "Pasolini filmed the myth, not the play"), he was sure it had not influenced his choice of costume and décor.

The main problem facing the modern director of an ancient tragedy is of course that intractable component the chorus, a group of fifteen (or twelve) masked dancers who marked the spoken dialogue off into separate scenes with intervals of lyric poetry, metrically intricate and chanted to the accompaniment of a sort of oboe, as they danced on the circular floor in front of the stage building. The content of the five choral songs, set to music by Theodore Antoniou, in this play ranges from fervent, despairing appeal to the gods for release from the plague, through agonized brooding over the accusations of Tiresias (ending in a reaffirmation of loyalty to Oedipus), a solemn assertion of faith in divine prophecy and muted repudiation of Oedipus and Jocasta, and a joyful anticipation of the coming revelation that Oedipus will turn out to be of divine birth, to the final solemn lament for Oedipus as the great demonstration that man is equal to nothing. For the original audience, which had an ear attuned to poetry in performance, whether recited by Homeric rhapsodes or sung by individuals at the symposium and by choruses at celebrations of gods or victorious athletes, the complex images and elliptical transitions of tragedy's choral lyrics were elements of a familiar emotional language. But the modern director must somehow restore vibrant life to words which no longer have power to enchant, and his only recourse is an appeal to the eye; he must reinforce words with movement, and precisely because he is compensating for a lost effect, it is to be expected that he will exceed what seems, from what little evidence we have, to have been the choreographic decorum of classic tragedy. Volanakis's chorus is, however, surprisingly restrained. Only in the first stasimon, the prayer for deliverance from the plague, is their dance modern in its kinetic and mimetic energy: as the dancers, on their knees, move around the pattern of the labyrinth in supplication, they are from time to time prostrated as if by the onslaught of the plague or the war god from whom they beg protection. When, at the beat of an off-stage electronic drum, they mime this collapse, their training and expertise are clear to see in the precipitous speed and precise simultaneity of their movement—they are flung to the ground as if flattened by a blast wave from detonating high explosive. After the Tiresias scene, the dancers, torn between awe of the prophet and loyalty to the king, unfold what looks like a length of yellow ribbon which they attempt to lay out as a pattern on the floor. The director's intention is explained in the program notes: "In an almost trance-like effort to work their way through the maze of supposition, their movements nearly create a labyrinth of their own, which being based on logic, is unrelated to the sacred pattern on the floor." This was the less successful of the two experiments with the choral dance, as is clear from the reaction of the reviewers; the concept is perhaps too intellectual for visual expression. Elsewhere, except for the unmasking in the central stasimon, Volanakis has relied almost entirely on the power of the words alone. He could take this risk only because of the extraordinary quality of his own translation of the ancient text into modern Greek.

The merits of the translation meant little to most of the American audience; it was all Greek to them. But it was at least an unusual phenomenon that the director of the play should also be responsible for the text; Volanakis was no more content with the standard versions of ancient tragedy than he was with the pseudoclassical costumes and conventional stage. And in his versions of the choral songs, he succeeded in recreating for a modern Greek audience some semblance of the powerful hold Sophocles' poetry exerted on the emotions of the fifth-century Greeks. The choral songs in the play are all of them functional in their dramatic context, yet they consist essentially of two addresses to the gods, one in supplication and one in joyful (and mistaken) anticipation, two agonized meditations on prophecy and religion and, finally, a grief-stricken lament for Oedipus as the paradigm of man's insignificance before the gods. For the form and language of these songs Sophocles could draw on a vocabulary of cult and hymn familiar to the audience from the rich variety of religious observance, solemn and festal, that marked the progress of the months in the Athenian calendar; Athena, Artemis and Apollo, invoked repeatedly in the opening chorus, were not, as they are for us, mythological figures in a classic play but powers adored, respected and feared in the present. Volanakis has made no drastic alterations; the chorus still addresses prayers to Athena, Artemis and Apollo and their content is unchanged. But he has substituted for the terms of a dead religion those of a living one. Scattered through the prayers at crucial points are words that are for the modern Greek charged with religious energy, words from the Greek Gospels, the Greek fathers and the liturgy of the Greek Orthodox Church.

The first strophe, to take an example, ends with an apostrophe to the voice from Delphi, which will announce, the chorus hopes, some way of escape from the plague—"immortal Voice!" Volanakis used a word, *aphtharsias,* that can indeed suggest immortality (though its literal meaning is "incorruptibility"), but it calls to mind a famous passage in St. Paul's First Epistle to the Corinthians: "When this corruptible shall have put on incorruption" (*aphtharsian*). Similarly, Athena, at the beginning of the following strophe, is described not only as "immortal" but also as "undefiled" (*achrante*), a word associated in sacred texts with the Virgin and also with the elements of the Eucharist. *Achrante,* a word attested in fifth-century tragedy, could perfectly well have been applied to the virgin goddess Athena by Sophocles himself, and as a matter of fact it was so used by one Triphiodorus, who wrote, probably around A.D. 300, a short epic called *The Capture of Troy*. Volanakis's choice of it here enables him to bridge the gap between ancient and modern sensibilities; by this stylistic sleight of hand he can exploit, like Sophocles before him, the emotional potential of contemporary religion and he can do so without linguistic anachronism.

Such effects are possible only because Greek is a language with three millennia of continuous history. Though it has changed considerably over the course of all those centuries, Seferis writes in what is recognizably the same language as Homer. "Earlier stages of the language are . . . accessible to speakers of later stages," as Robert Browning puts it in his invaluable book *Medieval and Modern Greek*,[2] "in a way that Anglo-Saxon or even middle English is not accessible to the speakers of modern English." Such richness of resources offers, of course, temptations as well as advantages. The poet who draws too heavily on earlier stages of the language may well end by sounding pompous, even ridiculous, like the stilted officialese known as *katharevousa*, the antiqued dialect of governmental obfuscation, legal prevarication and old-fashioned professorial pedantry. On the other hand, too close an adherence to the limits of *dimotiki*, the modern spoken language, may sacrifice dignity for liveliness, and Volanakis must maintain the dignity of tragic discourse at all costs. In the choral songs the danger to be avoided is grandiloquence, but in the passionate confrontations of the spoken scenes the risk the poet runs is vulgarity. Volanakis has steered a successful course between Scylla and Charybdis in both areas; the liturgical solemnity of the choral songs is maintained at a consistently high level, never falling into bathos, and in the spoken scenes the actors' lines, phrased in the rhythms and idioms of current speech, combine plainness with elegance.

In his adaptation of the language, Volanakis accepted with respect the obligation to hew close, in content at least, to the Sophoclean text—no place for originality there. But in the staging of the play he felt free, as a modern director, to explore and deploy his own conception of the play's dynamics and meaning. I have seen a great many productions of this play (including one in my own translation) and have wrestled with some of the problems of its original production in print as well as in scholarly argument. But I have not seen a produc-

---

2. London: Hutchinson, 1969.

Survivals and Transformations 145

tion more challenging and stimulating than this one. Even those innovations that mature reflection rejects serve to raise important questions. From the many directional decisions that give the production its shape and rhythm, I single out six, three of minor and three of major importance.

During the opening scenes, Oedipus wears his mask and imperial costume. When he takes them off, the audience can see, what before was partially obscured by the mask, that he is clean shaven. All the other male characters have beards; the clear lines of Oedipus's face emphasize his comparative youth. This effect was intentional. "He is the only young person in the play," Volanakis says. "You have a chorus of old men, two old shepherds and an old prophet; Jocasta is his mother and Creon his uncle." This is true and its visualization points up a slightly sinister aspect of the situation: Oedipus is the younger generation caught in a web spun by his elders, all of whom know part of the truth except Tiresias, who knows it all.

Two more details. In his scene with the king Tiresias is downstage (this theatrical term reassumed its original meaning on Volanakis's raked stage); he faced the audience (why should a blind man look at a king?) and supported himself with his hands on the backs of two kneeling choral dancers. This pyramidal group was reformed later when the blinded king stood with his two small daughters, one on either side of him. And lastly, an extremely effective and affecting gesture from the very last stage of the recognition. The shepherd is on his knees as the last conclusive pieces of the truth are dragged out of him. When Oedipus hears that the baby exposed so long ago was of the house of Laios he sinks to his knees by the shepherd's side as he puts the next question—"A slave? or a member of his family?" And as the shepherd makes his agonized outcry—"Oh God. Here comes the dreadful truth, and I must speak," Oedipus reaches out for the shepherd's hand and clasps it as he replies: "And I must hear it. But hear it I will."

Of the three major innovations perhaps the most spectacular and controversial is the director's treatment of Tiresias. The prophet's entry is a shock for those who have so often seen a tall, venerable figure led on stage by a boy, but the shock is compounded when Tiresias ends his blind shuffle round the labyrinth and faces the audience. His head seems to be tightly encased in some kind of white stocking mask (which presumably represents the confinement imposed by blindness) and his body is naked except for oriental-style tapering trousers. His torso is hung with long necklaces of what look like large sea shells. As, stung to fury by the king's accusations, he names Oedipus as the killer and mouths his dreadful prophecies, he looks like some Buddhist bonze, an Indian gymnosophist, a village guru. "Tiresias is definitely not a member of the Establishment," says Volanakis, when pressed for an explanation. On reflection, there is something to be said for this view. Tiresias is not, as he is often presented on stage, an ancient equivalent of the Archbishop of Canterbury. He lives outside the civilization of the city in a rural solitude where he can read the signs of the future and warnings of the gods in the behavior and voices of the birds. On the tragic stage, when he comes to Thebes, whether summoned, as here, or on his own initiative, as in the *Antigone*, it is never to bring good news; he is a messenger of doom and his regular function is to predict disaster. Sophocles has made him distracted and forgetful—"I knew but forgot. Else I would not have come here"—and this trait suits Volanakis's half-naked dervish better than the venerable hierarch of the usual production.

The second departure from the norm is the exit of this same Tiresias. He turns to leave and Oedipus bids him good riddance. Tiresias then launches into a long speech which repeats his earlier statement that Oedipus is the murderer of Laios and also prophesies, no longer in riddling terms, that Oedipus will be revealed as a native Theban, as brother and father to his own children, son and husband of his own mother, marriage partner and murderer of his father. To this furious tirade the king makes no reply but goes silently into the palace as Tiresias is led off by the boy who guides his steps. That is how the exits at the end of this scene are usually handled in production and explained by scholars.

There is one obvious objection. The last part of Tiresias's speech, which refers with crystal clarity to Oedipus's parricide and incest, corresponds, as we know, to what Apollo prophesied at Delphi—a prophecy that turned Oedipus's steps away from Corinth, the home of those he believed were his parents, and set him on the road to Thebes. If he hears what Tiresias says, how can he fail to make the connection? And if not now, how can he fail to remember Tiresias's words when later he tells Jocasta what Apollo predicted for him at Delphi? It has always seemed to me obvious that Oedipus does not hear the last lines of Tiresias's speech; he moves towards the palace door as he dismisses Tiresias and is offstage by the time the prophet pronounces the crucial words. I have defended this solution in print[3] (not that I am the first to do so) but have failed to convince many of my colleagues. The scholarly consensus is still that Oedipus stands there listening to the whole speech and then stalks off to the palace as Tiresias leaves by the side exit.

One writer who agreed with me that the scene could not be staged in this way was not a scholar, but on the other hand he was a practicing dramatist who was extremely successful on the stage in his own day. His name was Voltaire and the problems raised by this scene were among those that prompted his famous comment: "Cet Edipe qui expliquait les énigmes n'entend pas les choses les plus claires." And when, shut up in the Bastille, he wrote his own *Edipe*, which was to become the most celebrated of his more than fifty plays, he had his Tiresias, the Grand Prêtre, speak to Oedipus in terms of more than Delphic obscurity. I was delighted to see that Volanakis, who has not read the scholarly literature on the subject, simply assumes that Oedipus does not hear the lines in question. After his dismissal of the prophet the king moves to the palace entrance and stands immobile, his back to the theater and his winged sleeves extended as Tiresias, stage front, delivers the prophecy to the audience. The regal figure backstage is fixed in a pose of contemptuous indifference.

And, lastly, Oedipus's final entrance. What comes out of the palace door after the messenger's speech was another shock. Cheeks running with blood or perhaps a mask of sightlessness the audience was prepared for, but they expected to see them on the athletic body of the actor whose decisive movements had dominated the stage action in scene after scene. What they saw instead was a stumbling figure wrapped from head to foot in a white robe, the head encased, like that of Tiresias, in a stocking mask, the sleeves trailing far beyond the ends of the fingers. Oedipus was physically cut off from the world, not one inch of his body exposed to air and light. This was not only a telling image of the isolation blindness imposes (and we hear Oedipus wish that he could have destroyed his hearing too); it also gave visual expression to a powerful motif strongly emphasized in the language of the play but quite alien to modern feeling. Oedipus is a source of

---

3. "Sophocles. *Oedipus Tyrannos* 446: Exit Oedipus?" *Greek, Roman, and Byzantine Studies* 21, no. 4 (1980): 321–32.

pollution. "Get him into the house," says Creon when he sees him. "Even if you have no respect for the feelings of human beings at least show reverence for the flame of the sun that gives life to us all—how can you leave such a polluted object exposed to view? The earth and rain and light reject it." Even an ordinary murderer was thought to transmit *miasma*, a sort of stain, an infection; Oedipus is doubly and triply dangerous. Volanakis's swathed figure made the fifth-century concept of Oedipus as an untouchable intelligible for the modern audience by appealing to a familiar image—the medieval leper.

This was an audacious solution and many of the critics denounced it as mere directorial self-indulgence. Yet, aggressive though it may have been, it has a solid grounding in the Sophoclean text: it is Volanakis's attempt to find a modern emotional correlative for the ancient horror of physical contact with defilement. And this is true of all the innovations in the production. Even the labyrinth, which seems at first to be an extraneous addition to the play's rich imagery, may have been suggested by two passages in the text. Oedipus assures the Thebans that in his concern for their plight he has "gone many ways in wandering of thought." And later, when he hears Jocasta mention the three roads, he experiences, he tells her, "a wandering of the soul." In any case, Volanakis's stage effects are not arbitrary; successful or not, they are, like his translation, honest attempts to recreate for the modern spectator the emotional impact of the original performance, to be faithful to the old play, but at the same time to "make it new."

The Greek Conquest of Britain

A notable feature of Anthony Powell's tragicomic saga of English upper-class life from the twenties of this century through the sixties is the near absence, in a masterpiece distinguished among other things for abundance of subtly controlled allusions to art and literature, of any reference to the literary and artistic legacy of ancient Greece. The few exceptions—a sinister title, *The Kindly Ones,* for example, or the disreputable Mr. Deacon's murky canvas, *The Boyhood of Cyrus*—serve only to highlight the fact, true in real life as in Powell's brilliantly created world, that the English generation which came of age during and just after the First World War viewed with indifference if not with suspicion that Greek experience which had dominated the thought and bewitched the imaginations of their Edwardian and Victorian predecessors.

Perhaps this was a reaction against the education and ideals which had promised enlightened progress and ended in the mud of Passchendaele; Rupert Brooke and many other young products of Oxford and Cambridge, as Richard Jenkyns points out in his *Victorians and Ancient Greece,*[1] had gone to their deaths with Homer's lines ringing in their ears. If so, it was a classic reaction, equal and opposite, for the Victorian obsession with Greek ideals and theory had been almost maniacally complete. *The Tyranny of Greece over Germany* is the title of a well-known study, its dramatic claim not perhaps fully vindicated by its contents. Now Jenkyns and Frank M. Turner, in *The Greek Heritage in Victorian Britain,*[2] have presented us with two lengthy and compendious examinations of the primacy of Greece in English education and intellectual controversy for most of the nineteenth century and the first fourteen years of the twentieth.

Greece had not always been such a power in the land. Ben Jon-

This essay originally appeared in the *New York Review of Books,* June 11, 1981.

   1. Cambridge: Harvard University Press, 1980.
   2. New Haven: Yale University Press, 1981.

son, who sneered at Shakespeare's "less Greek," had none too much of it himself and Samuel Johnson, who said of the young Alexander Pope that "it was not very likely he overflowed with Greek," spoke of the language as a rare commodity: "Greek, Sir, is like lace; every man gets as much of it as he can." The intellectual (and political) model for eighteenth-century England was Augustan Rome; no essay in the *Spectator* or *Rambler* appeared without a quotation (untranslated) from Horace, Virgil, or Ovid as its epigraph.

The Greeks came into fashion and power with the Romantics. Keats saw a new, more "natural" Homer, stripped of Pope's Augustan elegancies, when he first "heard Chapman speak out loud and bold." Wolf's influential thesis that the Homeric poems were put together in a later age from primitive, oral ballads exalted them to the majestic level of Ossian, a poet admired by Goethe and Napoleon, whose work had been translated from the (wholly imaginary) Gaelic by James Macpherson. (It was, according to Samuel Johnson, "as gross an imposition as ever the world was troubled with.")

For Shelley and the young radicals, the Greeks were a revolutionary inspiration, Prometheus a model of heroic defiance, unmoved by the threats and tortures of Zeus-Castlereagh. "We are all Greeks," he proclaimed in the preface to *Hellas* (1822). "Our laws, our literature, our religion, our arts, have their roots in Greece." At the same time the publication of Stuart and Revett's *Antiquities of Athens* and the exhibition in the British Museum of the battered statues a reluctant nation had finally been shamed into buying from Lord Elgin gave the British public new artistic models to replace the Roman copies and adaptations of the old classical canon. And the early decades of the nineteenth century saw the Greek uprising against the Turkish pashas who had misgoverned them for over three hundred years, a struggle which won the sympathy of many who saw the modern Greeks through the lyric haze of Byron's early vision of a regenerate Greece—"when riseth Lacedaemon's hardihood, / When Thebes Epaminondas rears again / When Athens' children are with hearts endued"—rather than with the realistic eye of Byron at Missolonghi—"an intriguing, cunning and unquiet generation."

These exciting developments ushered in a century which saw the firm imposition of Greek on the educational system of the upper classes and the result that, as Frank M. Turner puts it, "knowledge of Greek (even if rarely mastery) and a familiarity with Greek culture were characteristic of a large portion of the British political elite as well as of the leaders and clergy of the Church of England." By 1865 "the major commentator on Homer as well as a major translator of the poet, the chief critic and historian of Greek literature, the most significant political historian of Greece and the authors of the then most extensive commentaries on Greek philosophy either were or had recently been members of the House of Commons or the House of Lords." It was not until after the First World War that Oxford and Cambridge began to admit students who had no knowledge of Greek.

The Yale ecologist Evelyn Hutchinson, who when he enrolled at Emmanuel in Cambridge in 1921 was one of the generation which benefited from this dispensation, tells in his fascinating autobiography[3] of an encounter between his mother and a fierce champion of the requirement, T. R. Glover of John's. "Mother had sat next to Glover at a dinner party on Saturday night and had a heated discussion on the value of compulsory Greek. . . . Next morning he was to give one of a series of Ecumenical sermons at St. Edward's Church . . . so we all trooped down. Arriving (as usual) rather late, we were shown into the front pew. When the time came for the sermon, Glover leaned forward from the pulpit and announced his text: 'And the centurion said unto Paul, Canst thou speak Greek?'"[4]

This same Glover, some thirty years later, dismissed me from a lively tutorial in which I had, in Young Turk style, defended Cleon against Glover's beloved Pericles, with the stern admonition: "Young man, you should go out and get yourself some of the benefits of organized religion."

This bizarre combination of a zealous, muscular, and proselytizing Christianity with an unstinting, almost fanatical admiration for the pagan Greeks to whom, as Paul said, "Christ crucified" was "foolishness," is one of the leading threads pursued by Turner in his attempt "to explore Victorian commentary on antiquity as a means of more

---

3. *The Kindly Fruits of the Earth* (New Haven: Yale University Press, 1979), p. 26.

4. Acts 21:37. Glover was quoting from memory; the Authorized Version runs: "And as Paul was to be led unto the castle he said unto the chief captain, May I speak unto thee? Who said, Canst thou speak Greek?" Glover's point is the *practical* value of Greek; the centurion's question expressed incredulous surprise—he thought Paul was an Egyptian terrorist who had caused trouble in Jerusalem before. Without his Greek Paul would probably have been executed on the spot.

fully understanding Victorian intellectual life itself" and by Jenkyns in his sprightly vindication of what he himself calls "the ambitious claim" that "ancient Greece preoccupied many of the finest minds of the last century, and thus, directly and indirectly . . . became a pervasive influence reaching even to the edges of popular culture."

Like other aspects of the Greek experience which dominated Victorian intellectual debate, the Christian-pagan problem reflected, and influenced in its turn, the changing climates of opinion through the century, and both of these books deal with this central theme. Since the New Testament was written in Greek, it might have been expected that this text would assume a major part in the classical curriculum, but in fact it was studied mainly in divinity schools and did not appear in the influential Oxford "Greats" program, which came into being around the middle of the century. Few attempts were made to justify this embarrassing omission and those cited are vague evasions. The Bishop of Durham, for example, saw the whole of classical Greek literature, Euripides included, as "distinct stages in the preparation for Christianity." The real reason must have been the simple pedagogical fact that students who were being trained to write the pure and elegant Attic of Plato and Demosthenes could not, without grave risk of linguistic corruption, be exposed to the Hellenistic *koine*, the Basic Greek of the Middle East, in which the Gospels are written.

The defense of the pagan texts as essential for an understanding of the Christian message was carried to its paradoxical extreme by no less a person than Gladstone, who found time in between serving as president of the board of trade, colonial secretary, chancellor of the exchequer, and four terms as prime minister, "to write a series of articles on Homer and five books, one of them consisting of three volumes and containing more than 1700 pages." The content of these learned works was remarkable, to say the least. Jenkyns offers a sample:

> The Homeric world, he said, "stands between Paradise and the vices of later heathenism" and he meant it literally: Homer was far closer to the Garden of Eden than the classical Greeks, and Homeric religion contained memories of God's revelation to primitive man. . . . It was evident, he thought, that Jupiter, Neptune and Pluto (he used the Roman names) were a memory of the Trinity. Apollo was a relic of belief in a Messiah, as can be seen from his double character as Saviour and Destroyer (a page is al-

lotted to demonstrating that Apollo's rape of Marpessa was "not of a sensual character"). Was Minerva the Logos or the Holy Spirit? Did Latona represent Eve or the Virgin Mary? How curious that the poems contained no mention of the Sabbath!

Eccentric as these views were, "the eccentricity," as Jenkyns says, "consisted in pushing certain Victorian tendencies to extreme limits." Gladstone was not one for evasions; he was as direct and forceful in his Homeric studies as in his political life. "There are still two things left for me to do," he told Mrs. Humphry Ward in 1888. "One is to carry Home Rule—the other is to prove the intimate connection between the Hebrew and Olympian revelations."

But the evasions prevailed; even Matthew Arnold, who made the famous distinction between "Hebraism" and "Hellenism" could, as Jenkyns points out, translate a passage from *Oedipus Tyrannus* into "a kind of scripture language" and comment: "Let St. Francis—nay, or Luther either, beat that!" Elsewhere, however, Arnold made it clear that he was trying to provide, in "culture" (which included a mammoth portion of Greek literature) a substitute for that "faith" which was now an ebbing tide, its sound a "melancholy, long, withdrawing roar." Others were not so frank; Jowett's eloquent translation of Plato, a minor English classic, went a long way in its "Analyses and Introduction" along the path he had once charted, in strict confidence, to a friend: "Something to be done in the way of making Christianity, *whether under that or some other name*, a reality."

The established Church was not deceived; Jowett had been, early on, prosecuted (unsuccessfully) for having, in an essay on the interpretation of Scripture, "advisedly promulgated . . . certain erroneous and strange doctrines . . . contrary to and inconsistent with the doctrines of the Church of England" (of which he was, like all Oxford dons, an ordained member). The ecclesiastical conservatives succeeded in delaying for ten years a proposal to raise his stipend as Regius Professor to the level of a living wage (a measure which the Bishop of Oxford characterized as "a deadly blow at the truth of God"). Their instinct was correct; Jowett was a sincere Christian all right, but his feelings about the Church were summed up in his advice to a young lady: "You must believe in God, my dear, despite what the clergymen say."

By the time Jowett died in 1893 the Church had more radical

Hellenists to worry about. The subtle rhetoric of Pater's etiolated Platonic fancies cloaked a content more pagan than Christian, and Swinburne was a pagan self-proclaimed—"Thou hast conquered, O pale Galilean; the world has grown grey from thy breath." Symonds was obsessed by visions of a fantasy Greece, a sun-drenched, pastoral landscape full of nubile young boys, and a story (apocryphal, no doubt) about Wilde's *viva* examination at Oxford—surprisingly enough it is not to be found in Jenkyns, who has a keen eye for a lively anecdote—gives a startling impression of the gulf between Christianity and the Hellenic aestheticism of the late seventies. Wilde was given a Greek Testament and told to translate chapter 26 of Luke—the Last Supper; the agony in the garden; the betrayal, arrest, and trial of Christ. He did so with speed and elegance. "Thank you, Mr. Wilde, that will do." "Oh," he said. "Pray let me go on. I want to see how it ends."

The religious question was central to the intellectual battles of the century, and both Jenkyns and Turner give it proper emphasis. In other departments, however, their paths diverge; these are two very different books.

Turner is a modern historian, with a particular interest in the nineteenth century; he is the author of a much admired book on the late Victorian reaction to the new religion of science and technology whose apostles were Huxley and Lewes.[5] His new book is the product of extraordinarily wide reading in the immense flood of Victorian publication; the footnotes are rich in valuable references, some of them to unpublished archives: the Blackie papers in the National Library of Scotland, Jowett's lecture notes in the Balliol Library. His main fields of interest are history and philosophy; the most impressive chapters are those headed: "The Debate Over the Athenian Constitution," "Socrates and the Sophists," and "The Victorian Platonic Revival."

The first of these is a fascinating discussion of the way Greek history, or rather Victorian visions of Greek history, served as a polemical model for the age. The eighteenth-century historians and political theorists complemented their devotion to Rome, and the ideal of factionless order it was made to stand for, with a deep respect for Spartan

---

5. *Between Science and Religion: The Reaction to Scientific Naturalism in Late Victorian England* (New Haven: Yale University Press, 1974).

stability and a sharp mistrust of Athens and its turbulent democracy.

The first major narrative history of Greece, Mitford's, published from 1785 to 1810, carried this prejudicial attitude even farther, including Sparta in the general indictment; "the Greeks were deficient in the . . . science of forming that great machine which we call a government." Mitford found good government in Greece only under monarchies, the Homeric at the beginning and the Macedonian at the end of Greece's existence as an independent nation. But though he criticized Sparta (the British Country Party had always denounced standing armies and Sparta was a whole state organized on military lines), his harshest criticism was reserved for democratic Athens, which, as Turner puts it, "exemplified all the follies of the democratic government that he saw being urged on Britain through calls for parliamentary reform . . . and being undertaken by the former colonies in America."

The rehabilitation of Athenian democracy and its presentation as a model for a modern (imperial) democracy—a model imperfect in some respects (slavery, for example) but in others, especially literature and the arts, hard to surpass or even equal—were the work of an amateur scholar who had been neither to Oxford nor to Cambridge, a banker and liberal reform politician, George Grote. A follower of Bentham and Mill, he took a leading part in the fight for parliamentary reform, before retiring from political life to write his great ten-volume history of Greece, in which Periclean democracy emerged as an enlightened, egalitarian form of government, comparable in many ways (and in some superior) to the parliamentary democracy of Victorian England.

This view of Athens was to retain its hold on the English-speaking world until quite recent times—Alfred Zimmern's influential *Greek Commonwealth* (1911) proclaims, with suitable modifications of Grote's more extreme claims, essentially the same position; it is only with the modern critique of the economic base, slavery and empire, that the splendid eloquence of Pericles' Funeral Speech has lost some of its power to enchant. (Mitford, incidentally, was ahead of his time in this respect: his "sensitivity to the evil of ancient slavery," says Turner, "set him far ahead of the nineteenth-century liberal historians of Greece who turned their eyes from slavery in Greece as they did from the plight of the contemporary poor."

Turner's analysis of exactly what Grote did is one of the most remarkable sections of this closely argued and impressive book.

> Grote portrayed the reforms of Cleisthenes as having in effect vindicated the wisdom of the kind of radical reform program that he had proposed in 1831. . . . Previous antidemocratic writers, such as Mitford, had argued that a modern liberal democratic state would resemble lawless Athens. Reversing the analogy, Grote presented ancient democratic Athens as almost a mirror image of the stable, liberal mid-Victorian polity. . . . Grote's transformation of the character of the Athenian assembly was the single most stunning example of Victorian domestication of Greek life and in large measure accounted for the profound sense of intimacy that later writers perceived between Athens and Britain. . . . Grote described Pericles as the "prime minister" and he portrayed the Assembly as divided between "the party of movement against that of resistance, or of reformers against conservatives."

Grote even managed to present the demagogue and hard-line imperialist democrat Cleon as a sort of leader of Her Majesty's loyal opposition. But though his readers "admired Athens for the resemblance Grote had convinced them the ancient city bore to their own national polity," Grote was in fact the champion of a democracy that, as Turner says, "had no precedent, past or present. His model was the community that under better circumstances Athens might have become after the reforms of Cleisthenes and that Britain might still achieve."

Grote appears in other chapters, too; both in his *History* and his later *Plato, and the Other Companions of Socrates* (1865) he presented a vigorous case for the Sophists, whom the antidemocratic historians (and Plato) had targeted as the destroyers of personal and political morality. Grote (agreeing with Hegel, whom, however, he had not read when he published his first discussion of the subject in the *History*), portrayed the Sophists as the teachers "who immeasurably helped to create a viable democratic culture in the city" and as a force for the stability of the democratic regime, which relied on persuasion, an art of which the Sophists were acknowledged masters.

Not content with this rehabilitation of figures who were blamed by the great German historians of philosophy—Ritter, Brandis, Zeller—as the cause of Athens's decay, Grote included Socrates in their number, on the grounds that he had "awakened 'the analytical consciousness' of his fellow citizens to encourage effective social and political action and he had carried that skill into the study of ethics in the manner normally associated with Bentham."

Grote's "name and achievement," as Turner justly says, "figure more prominently in the Victorian history of Greek studies in Britain than those of any other single author." Grote is discussed in Jenkyns's book, too, but neither as extensively nor as analytically. In fact, analysis is not Jenkyns's strong point; one has the impression that he has read as widely as Turner but not as deeply. His book covers an immense amount of ground and has a wealth of apt quotations (many of them surprising, some hilarious), but his material is organized in rather haphazard fashion (the chapter headed "Homer and the Homeric Ideal," for example, abandons its main line for a discussion of Victorian and Greek athletics), and sometimes, especially when measured against the purposeful economy of Turner's quotations, gives the impression that it is being piled up for its own sake.

Its own sake, I hasten to add, is not to be sneered at. The dust cover reproduces a typically lush Victorian painting on a Greek theme—Hylas being lured into the water by bare-breasted nymphs who look remarkably like English schoolgirls; it promises delights, and the book lives up to the promise. It is a consistently entertaining tour through Victorian Greece, conducted by a guide who has an eye for significant detail, a graceful narrative style, and a polished wit.

The difference between the two books may be in part a difference in emphasis: Jenkyns explores the same territory as Turner but his main interest is not so much intellectual history as art and literature. His most distinguished chapter is the one on George Eliot (who earns only a brief and incidental mention in Turner). Jenkyns demonstrates that time and again what seem like casual allusions to Greek authors in her novels are actually pointers to the fact that she is using ancient myths and plots as a profound commentary on the lives and actions of her modern characters. His discussion of the use she makes of Greek tragedy in *Adam Bede, The Mill on the Floss, Felix Holt, Middlemarch,* and *Daniel Deronda* is an important contribution to the understanding of these novels.

Another Victorian writer who is treated at length and with sympathetic understanding is Ruskin, a figure in whom Jenkyns's two guiding themes, art and literature, combine. Art is the subject of his opening chapter, but it is in "Classical Art in the Later Nineteenth Century" that he hits his full stride. Here they all are, those painters of the hairless Greek female nudes that ruined Ruskin's wedding night, those creators of the chocolate-box canvases that hang in English provincial museums and that, in countless reproductions, imposed on schoolboys a vision of Greece as a place where the sun shone eternally on naked women and not-quite-so-naked men. Here is Crane, whose female nudes had something vaguely wrong with them; his wife would not let him use female models, so "he was obliged to employ a young Italian male, making some rather unconvincing adjustments afterwards." When Leighton saw Crane's *Renaissance of Venus*, he said: "Why, that's Alessandro."

Here is Leighton, whose "studies for the 'Captive Andromache' show that he began by painting the figures in the nude. Then, as though pouring treacle over them, he overlaid these slender bodies with a thick, shapeless layer of something that he was eventually to work up into the form of clothing." (Jenkyns reproduces photographs of *Captive Andromache* before and after.) Here is Alma-Tadema, whose titles defy parody (*Fredegonda at the Death-Bed of Praetextatus*) and whose pictures of ladies in various states of titillating undress were dignified by such classical technicalities as *An Apodyterium, The Frigidarium,* and *In the Tepidarium,* this last "a luscious nude lying with parted lips on a couch and holding up a provocative pair of feathers to cover the last vestige of her modesty."

One reason for this insistence on fake classical themes (or the equally spurious medieval subjects of Burne-Jones and Rosetti) must have been the overpowering ugliness of the Victorian industrial landscape and the appalling conditions in which most people lived. Until after the Second World War the soft-coal fires in London houses turned the winter mists into choking fogs so impenetrable that they stopped all traffic, so poisonous that if you breathed through a handkerchief it turned an oily black after a few breaths. The vast expansion of working-class housing in London and the industrial towns of the north produced a nightmare of congested brickwork which Gustave Doré sketched in an unforgettable illustration for his *London: A Pilgrimage* (1872), and which is given a humorous commentary in a music hall song I remember from my boyhood: "With a ladder and some glasses / You could see to 'Ackney Marshes / If it wasn't for the 'ouses in between." William Morris in the preface to his *Earthly Paradise* advised his readers to "Forget six counties overhung with smoke /

Forget the snorting steam and piston stroke / Forget the spreading of the hideous town."[6] And one way to do so was to dream about Theocritus (a poet who, for reasons unfathomable, came to be associated with homosexual daydreams) and gaze on Alma-Tadema's fancy-dress Greeks lying on sunlit marble. It was better than looking out over the rain-soaked gray slate roofs of Crewe, which stretched in compact rows as far as the eye could see from the longest railway platform in the kingdom.

Jenkyns ends on a somber note; his final chapter is entitled "The Empire and the War." It is a brilliant and moving account of the mood, inspired by Pericles' Funeral Speech, memories of Herodotus's Spartans and, above all, a strangely one-sided reading of Homer's *Iliad*, in which the upper-class youth of England went to their deaths on the Somme and, in sight of Troy, at Gallipoli. "The war," Jenkyns sums up, "destroyed the Homeric ideal and social changes were destroying the way of life which had brought that ideal to birth." He concludes by quoting Matthew Arnold's hope for the future: "If the instinct for beauty is served by Greek literature and art as it is served by no other literature and art, we may trust to the instinct of self-preservation in humanity for keeping Greeks as part of our culture." But that hope Jenkyns sees as vain—in Yeats's phrase, "mere dreams."

This is a premature judgment. After reading these books, one can see why the generation whose history is traced in Powell's *Music of Time* lost interest in Greece; they had had a bellyfull. Yet toward the end of that saga the Greek boy paintings of Mr. Deacon are beginning to rise in value; the Greeks are making a comeback. And it is remarkable how they have returned to the center of the stage in the debates and discussions of the years since the Second World War. We do not have a Homeric scholar for president or a Greek historian for secretary of state, but Robert Kennedy once astonished the impresario of a talk show by saying that his favorite reading was Greek tragedy; and no less an authority than George Catlett Marshall remarked that no one could understand World War II who had not read Thucydides.

6. Quoted by Frances Spalding in her *Magnificent Dreams: Burne-Jones and the Late Victorians* (New York: Dutton, 1978). This book reproduces the Doré illustration on p. 33 and, for those who would like to see Alessandro, a two-page spread of Crane's *Renaissance of Venus*.

He was speaking also of the Cold War, and Thucydides has become as basic a text for discussion of that uneasy confrontation as he once was for the Victorian discussion of the problems faced by an imperial democracy. The armed forces, at any rate, took Marshall at his word; in the last few years I have been invited to speak on Thucydides for the opening sessions of the strategy course at the Naval, National, and Air Force War Colleges. Greek tragedy has never been so much performed, in translation, on stage and screen. Euripides' *Trojan Women* and *Iphigenia in Aulis* were produced as protests against the Vietnam War (and the *Trojan Women* in France as a protest against the war in Algeria); the *Bacchae* as *Dionysus in 69* and in many another iconoclastic version served to voice the outrage of the young radicals of the sixties; the *Medea* is a sacred text of the women's liberation movement. Modern adaptations of Greek tragedy have been even more in the public eye; both Anouilh and Brecht have produced their own versions of Sophocles' *Antigone*.

History plays ironical tricks; in 1853 Matthew Arnold wrote that it was "no longer . . . possible that we should feel a deep interest" in "the conflict between the heroine's duty to her brother's corpse and that to the laws of her country."[7] To the Victorians such barbaric practices as exposing the corpse of an enemy seemed "no longer" possible. But Anouilh had lived in Paris under the German occupation army, which exhibited the corpses of executed Resistance fighters as a deterrent, and Brecht's *Antigone* begins with a prologue—Berlin, April 1945—in which two sisters discover, hanging from a meat hook, the corpse of their brother, a deserter from the front executed by the SS.

Rieu's Penguin translation of the *Odyssey* was one of the greatest best sellers of all time and Lattimore's *Iliad* has gone through countless printings. Plato is as controversial as ever. Karl Popper's attack on him started a running argument, and in this country Eric Havelock's *The Liberal Temper in Greek Politics*,[8] which developed and broadened Grote's defense of the Sophists by connecting them with materialist and "liberal" elements in pre-Socratic thought, provoked a fifty-page

---

7. For an extremely interesting essay on the Antigone theme, see Gerhard Joseph, "The Antigone as Cultural Touchstone: Matthew Arnold, Hegel, George Eliot, Virginia Woolf, and Margaret Drabble," *PMLA* (1980): 22–35.

8. New Haven: Yale University Press, 1957.

blast of furious condemnation from the late Leo Strauss, which appeared, of all places in this world, in the *Journal of Metaphysics*.[9]

But it is not to be wondered at. Shelley was right: we are all Greeks. We are the inheritors of their virtues and vices—their fierce competitive spirit, their intellectual curiosity, their will to action. It is this heritage which defines us, makes us a people different from those who have grown up in the religious faiths and philosophies of the East; it is, for better or worse, the driving force of that civilization we call Western.

9. Volume 12, no. 47 (1959): 390–439.

Visions of the Grand Prize

When we think of the history of European art in the nineteenth century we are thinking almost exclusively of what happened in Paris. Goya had no worthy successor in Spain; Italian painting of the period is known only to specialists; Germany and the Low Countries are a blank page, and England's Constable, Turner, and the enervate pre-Raphaelites cannot challenge the brilliance of the French makers and shakers—from David, Ingres, and Delacroix through Manet and Rodin to the Impressionists and the creative explosion of the nineteenth century *fin de siècle* and the beginning of the twentieth. And yet it was precisely in Paris that throughout the nineteenth century and beyond, painting, sculpture, and architecture were taught to men selected for their talent and supported by the state in an institution which for rigid didacticism, bureaucratic inflexibility, and sheer hidebound conservatism can have had few rivals in the history of the arts.

The Ecole des Beaux-Arts was from the beginning of its long career an official artistic instrument of the modern state; it was the creation of Richelieu, Colbert, and Louis XIV. The Académie Royale de Peinture et Sculpture was founded in 1648; the Académie Royale d'Architecture in 1671; in 1793 they were both suspended by the revolutionary Convention, only to be reconstituted and combined under the First Empire in the Ecole des Beaux-Arts. The school carried on its recruitment and training uninterrupted, except by administrative reform under the Second Empire in 1863, until its radical reconstitution in the aftermath of *les évènements de mai,* the student insurrection of 1968.

A fascinating glimpse at some of the products of these two centuries of academic art has recently (1984) been offered to the public in Paris, Athens, and the United States by two extraordinary traveling exhibitions: "Paris-Rome-Athens," presented in this country by the Museum of Fine Arts, Houston, and the "Grand Prix de Rome,"

This essay originally appeared in the *New York Review of Books,* September 27, 1984.

brought here by the International Exhibitions Foundation. Both exhibitions, in spite of the difference in their titles, were devoted to the work of those students at the Ecole des Beaux-Arts who won the highest honor and award it offered, the Grand Prix de Rome.

Rome, with its classical ruins and its wealth of Renaissance painting, was a mecca for both architects and painters. The French Academy in Rome, to which the winners of the Grand Prix were to be sent, had been founded at the suggestion of Colbert in 1666 for the cultivation of "good taste and the manners of the Ancients" in the arts. But it was not until after the reorganization of the Paris academies as the Ecole des Beaux-Arts in 1797 that winners of the competitions in architecture and painting went regularly to Rome, with a government stipend, to spend from three to five years at the Villa Médicis, the building on the Pincio so lovingly recorded in the sketches of Ingres, who was a young Prix de Rome winner there in 1801 and served as director from 1834 to 1840.

The competition for the Prix de Rome was only the final hurdle of a long series of *concours* the student at the Paris Beaux-Arts had to face. Not everyone made it that far; the early competitions were elimination events. For both painters and architects there was the "perspective contest"; after that architects had to prepare sketches for prescribed building projects, first small units and then large complexes. The painters, meanwhile, entered the "expression contest" (*concours de la tête d'expression*) with female models, and set subjects such as *La Mélancholie, Le Dédain, La Terreur,* and then the torso (*demi-figure peinte*) with male models, and, finally, a sort of dry run for the main event, an oil sketch (*esquisse peinte*) on a mythological or historical subject.

The finalists, restricted by elimination to eight (later ten), had still a few laps to go but their main concern was the *peinture historique,* a subject announced by the judges that might be historical (antique Greco-Roman or Biblical) or mythological (Greco-Roman). "The death of Cato of Utica" was the subject set for 1797. In 1801 it was "Achilles receives the embassy from Agamemnon"; the winner was Jean-Auguste-Dominique Ingres, twenty-one years old. "The death of Demosthenes" was proposed for 1805, and for 1815 "Briseis weeps for Patroclus." In 1827 the subject for the contest was "Coriolanus and the Volscian King" (repeated in 1859). In 1832 Flandrin's version of "Theseus recognized by his father" was given the prize. For the years

1836–39 Biblical subjects held the field but by 1844 the candidates were back in Greco-Roman antiquity—"Cincinnatus receives the envoys of the Senate." They were there again in 1851 with "Pericles at the deathbed of his son."

The candidate's picture had to be completed over a period of seventy-two days during which he was separated from his fellow painters in his curtained *loge* at the Ecole; the final products were varnished and then displayed to the public, the newspaper critics, and finally the judges. After the winner was declared, the paintings were, most of them (a total of over two hundred), stored in the Ecole, where they lay, gathering dust, until they were disinterred for this show.

"This exhibition," as Jacques Thuillier of the Collège de France points out in his introduction to the catalogue,[1] "is unlike any other. Usually an exhibition . . . is . . . an anthology of works carefully chosen from among those most characteristic of a famous painter. In this case there is a complete series of paintings painted by young men in the course of becoming artists." Furthermore, as Philippe Grunchec puts it in the foreword to his detailed discussion of the Beaux-Arts curriculum and the paintings,[2] we are "faced with a selection of works which . . . we did not make but which was made for us by the nineteenth-century board of examiners." What we can discover in it, to quote Thuillier again, is "the image of an *institution*."

This is not to deny that the canvases are, many of them, splendid in their own right. Ingres's Homeric scene, a panorama of male nudity, and Flandrin's *Theseus Recognized by his Father*, against a background of the Acropolis and what was then thought to be the temple of Theseus, as well as Boulanger's *Recognition of Ulysses by Eurycleia*, where Penelope gazes out of the window with her spiky crown looking like the model for the Statue of Liberty, are all dramatically effective compositions and their colors, discreetly restored, brilliant. But the institutional stamp is on every one of these canvases. They are compositions designed to please a professional jury which, to judge by the comments of contemporary critics (Grunchec supplies a liberal selection) was notoriously opposed to originality of any kind. The critics were not entirely wrong; Géricault, Delacroix, Moreau, and

1. *The Grand Prix de Rome: Paintings from the Ecole des Beaux-Arts, 1797–1863* (Alexandria, VA: International Exhibitions Foundation, 1984–85).
2. *Le Grand Prix de peinture: Les concours de Prix de Rome de 1797 à 1863* (Paris: Ecole nationale supérieure des Beaux-Arts, 1983).

Degas, Grunchec tells us, "pulled out of the competition for the Prix de Rome at one level or another."

What the jury was looking for, in fact, was evidence that the student had fully mastered the technical aspects of the training offered by the Ecole and so was a fit candidate for the demanding schedule of work that would be imposed on him at the Villa Médicis in Rome, where he would be expected to proceed along the same antiquarian lines. There the painters would work their way up to the fourth-year project: "a picture . . . with several life-size figures; the subject drawn either from mythology, literature or ancient history, sacred or profane." The architects were expected to produce, in their final year, detailed plans of an ancient building in Italy or Sicily, and later in Greece, and also a *restauration,* a large-scale recreation of the building as it must have been in its original state.

This obsession with classical antiquity was not confined to the academy; it was characteristic of the age. As disgust with the cynicism and corruption of the *ancien régime* began to find expression in the arts and literature, the classical models of virtue and in particular of republican virtue, especially those available to the general public through the much translated *Lives* of Plutarch, served, not for the first or the last time in Western history, as a medium of expression for new ideas. "These subjects were used . . . as a means of exploring values in the political and social realm. Ultimately the same artists would paint in heroic guise with equally compelling implications such contemporary events as the Oath of the Tennis Court or the Death of Marat. . . . These heroic aspects of contemporary life became so closely identified with the achievements of antiquity that the two were at times interchangeable."[3]

This was especially true of the revolutionary years, when one orator after another—Desmoulins, Danton, Robespierre, St. Just—cited Greek and Roman precedents for revolutionary action and the heroes of Plutarch as models of moral conduct. *"La France,"* as Jean Cocteau put it, *"était plutarquisée."* The composition subjects for 1799 were "The oath of Brutus after the death of Lucretia" and "Manlius Torquatus condemns his son to death." These are typical clichés of republican imagery. Later, under the restored Bourbon monarch, such

---

3. Frederick J. Cummings in *French Painting, 1774–1830: The Age of Revolution* (Detroit: Wayne State University Press, 1975), p. 32.

resonance was avoided: the subject in 1816 was "Oenone refuses to help Paris"; in 1817 "Castor and Pollux rescue Helen"; in 1818 "Philemon and Baucis," and so on for the next fifty years or more: mythological and Biblical themes predominate. Sometimes the subjects, like "Zenobia found by shepherds on the banks of the Araxes" (1850), have an exotic flavor that recalls the titles of Anthony Powell's Mr. Deacon—*By the Will of Diocletian, The Boyhood of Cyrus*—and his characterization of his own paintings, in words drawn from Whitman, as "the rhythmic myths of the Greeks and the strong legends of the Romans."

There is another feature of these Beaux-Arts paintings that brings Mr. Deacon to mind: the almost complete absence of female nudes. Mr. Deacon rigidly excluded the female form, draped or undraped, from his canvases; even his sphinxes and chimeras possessed "solely male attributes." The Beaux-Arts painters, though they revel in male nudity, are not so exclusive. But their women stay resolutely clothed. Even bare breasts are a rarity (and the ladies seldom display more than one). That this is not due to the taste and temper of the age is clear from a glance at a nonacademic painting of the period. Regnault's *Judgment of Paris* (1812), for example, and David's *Mars Disarmed by Venus and the Three Graces* (1824) are crowded with luscious female nudes.[4] There is no reason to think, either, that the Prix de Rome winners shared Mr. Deacon's special sexual tastes. In fact, the reason why these canvases display so much male flesh[5] but keep the female form divine under close wraps is the conviction on the part of the Ecole's authorities that the students were indeed perfectly normal. The art critic in the *Journal des débats*, discussing the results of the 1821 contest (subject Samson and Delilah), and remarking that everyone availed himself of a fine opportunity to paint a nude hero surprised in his sleep, went on to complain: "No doubt the same

---

4. *French Painting, 1774–1830*, pp. 221, 279. The David is in Brussels, the Regnault in Detroit.

5. Even so, full frontal nudity is fairly rare. Usually the male member is discreetly wound in a coil of ribbon coming from nowhere in particular or covered by the tip of a scabbard slung (apparently for this precise purpose) improbably high on the chest. In Flandrin's *Theseus Recognized by His Father* the young hero stands behind a table laid for a feast, but the critic in the *Journal des artistes* was not pleased. He took pains to "point out" that "the plateful of roast ribs used to hide Theseus' private parts is a rather ludicrous idea."

could have been said of Delilah if a prudent policy of the schools did not prohibit the use of female models in the pupil's *loges;* they had to be content, for Delilah, with a draped dummy."

These paintings are the entrance examination papers, so to speak, of the Prix de Rome winners in painting; those in the architectural exhibition "Paris-Rome-Athens" are final examination papers, the work completed in the last years of the architect's stay in Rome and sent back to Paris (and so known as the *Envoi*).[6]

For both architects and painters the Prix de Rome was the high road to fame and a brilliant career, but life at the Villa Médicis was no bed of roses. The candidates, French citizens only, of course, had to be unmarried; if, once successful, they married during their tenure, their pay and allowances were cut off. They could not leave Rome without the director's permission; they ate all meals in common—no guests allowed. They were forbidden to keep anyone in the house overnight "whoever it might be and whatever the reason,"[7] and the doors of the villa were locked at midnight. It sounds like the regime of a Cambridge college in the 1930s except that, unlike Cambridge undergraduates, the *pensionnaires* had a program of work laid out in detail for each year, and failure to complete any section of the program meant that money was held back until the work was done. But for the architects the third and fourth years brought an opportunity for release from this confinement; these were the years devoted to the study and *"restauration"* of an ancient site, in Italy (the Pantheon, Hadrian's Villa, the Baths of Caracalla, and Pompeii) during the first part of the century and, after 1845, for one *pensionnaire* each year, in Greece or Asia Minor.

The Western discovery of Greece had, of course, begun long before 1845. Stuart and Revett published *The Antiquities of Athens Measured and Delineated* in several volumes from 1762 to 1794 (the French translation appeared during the years 1808 and 1822). French travelers and artists had explored the ruins of Athens and published ac-

---

6. For a study of the architects' "entrance exam papers"—the projects entered for the Prix de Rome competition—see D. D. Egbert, *The Beaux-Arts Tradition in French Architecture Illustrated by the Grands Prix de Rome* (Princeton: Princeton University Press, 1980).

7. From the *Règles d'ordre* of the Academy, reproduced (with much other interesting matter) in Georges Brunel, *Correspondance des directeurs de l'Académie de France à Rome* (Rome: Edizioni dell'elefante, 1979), 1:151.

counts of their travels; there had even been, in 1829, a scholarly expedition to the Peloponnese "undertaken by order of the French government" which resulted in a splendid publication, the *Expédition scientifique de Morée.*[8] The new interest in the original models, the true sources of the classical artistic canons, combined with the almost universal enthusiasm aroused by the Greeks' heroic struggle for independence, finally achieved by 1833, might have been expected to affect the program at the Villa Médicis long before 1845. That it failed to do so was almost entirely the responsibility of the permanent secretary of the Académie des Beaux-Arts in Paris, a gentleman with the awesome name of Antoine Chrysostome Quatremère de Quincy.

His opposition stemmed partly from his distrust of the Romantic movement in art and literature (Greece in the early nineteenth century was thought of as an exotic if not Oriental country) and also from a bitter opposition to the consequences, for classicizing architects, of the discovery of color on ancient Greek architectural members. A sculptor himself, he accepted the evidence for polychromy on Greek sculpture but drew the line firmly on the architectural front. "Architecture," he wrote in his *Dictionnaire historique d'architecture* (1825), "insofar as its forms derive their value from an order of things independent of matter, has no need of *colors* in order to fulfill its true purpose."

In 1828 Henri Labrouste, who was many years later to design the Bibliothèque Sainte-Geneviève in Paris, broke precedent by choosing a Greek temple complex at Paestum in southern Italy for his *Envoi*, but in 1833 Victor Baltard was refused permission to prepare his *Envoi* in Greece. In 1846, however, the French government, intent on establishing a French cultural presence in Greece, opened the Ecole française d'Athènes for scholars and archaeologists, and in the following year a place was made available there for a student of architecture from the French Academy in Rome. This was the beginning of a long series of *Envois*—the last in 1936–37—from Greece and Asia Minor.

The catalogue *Paris-Rome-Athens*[9] consists of a 215-page block of illustrations, color as well as black and white, of all the *Envois* that

---

8. The principal illustrations were collected and issued separately in a magnificent, outsize edition by the Bank of Greece (Athens, 1975).

9. *Paris-Rome-Athens: Travels in Greece by French Architects in the Nineteenth and Twentieth Centuries* (Houston: Museum of Fine Arts, 1982).

dealt with ancient Greek sites. It reproduces with complete success the colors of the paintings but what it cannot do is convey any impression of their size. Tournaire's *restauration* of the sanctuary at Delphi, for example, is six feet five inches high by almost twelve feet long; Hulot's view of Selinus from the south is over three and a half feet by fifteen feet eight inches; Nénot's panorama of Delos is four feet by thirteen feet six inches and Bernier's façade of the Mausoleum is ten feet high and six and a half feet across.

Furthermore, when these huge drawings are washed in the startling colors that the architects favored more and more as the century moved on, the effect is overwhelming. In fact, faced with Loviot's (1879) re-creation of Athena standing four feet high in a cross section of the Parthenon, looking for all the world like an odalisque in fancy dress posed against the décor of a Second Empire *maison de passe*,[10] or his red, white, and blue version of a corner of the Parthenon entablature, complete with Lapith, centaur, and winged gryphon—all the horns of Disneyland loudly blowing—the dazed visitor whose image of Greek art has been based on the texture of Pentelic marble gilded by time finds himself wishing he could recall the banished shade of Antoine Chrysostome Quatremère de Quincy.

Loviot, of course, went too far, as even his contemporaries realized, but that color was used on classic Greek buildings, as background for sculpture and in its own right on the entablature, no one now doubts. But no one can believe that it was laid on in such garish hues and with such a lavish hand. Martin Robertson speaks for informed modern opinion in his discussion of the use of color on the Parthenon frieze. "There is a world of difference between the schematic archaic colouring and the sophisticated pictorial treatment of the early Hellenistic reliefs but they have this in common, and the Parthenon frieze will have had it, too, that the character of the marble is not obscured but glows through and harmonizes the colours."[11] In the *restaurations* of Loviot and still more in Blavette's phantasmagoric

---

10. For a colored, double-page spread illustrating the *restauration*, see *The Architecture of the Ecole des Beaux-Arts*, ed. Arthur Drexler (New York: Museum of Modern Art, 1977), pp. 298–99. The exhibition on which the book is based was reviewed by Ada Louise Huxtable in the *New York Review of Books*, 27 November, 1975.

11. Martin Robertson and Alison Frantz, *The Parthenon Frieze* (New York: Oxford University Press, 1975), p. 10.

vision of the Hall of the Mysteries at Eleusis (1844) with its frescoes of swirling serpents, the paint totally obscures the nature of the material beneath it; it might, for all the eye can see, be stuccoed brick or plywood.

It was, however, precisely these bizarre visions that caught the fancy and helped mold the taste of the Parisian *nouveaux riches* of the Second Empire. But they also had their effect closer to home. The red, vermilion, green, bright blue, and gilt on the classicizing façade of the Philadelphia Museum (1928) would never have seen the light of day but for the authority of the Ecole des Beaux-Arts, which, from the mideighties on, attracted large numbers of American architects to its courses.

The polychrome extravaganzas of Loviot and company are certainly the most dazzling items in the exhibition. But they are not typical. Most of the *Envois* keep a fairly tight reign on the urge to leave no stone unpainted; they direct attention to the structural elements of the buildings as well as the ornamentation and, when they do use color, prefer dark Pompeian reds to the poster palette of Loviot. Many pictures of unrestored sites, especially those drawn before the availability of photography, are valuable historical documents—Paccard's 1845 drawings of the Parthenon, for example, or Boitte's 1864 meticulously detailed studies of the Propylaea after Beulé's 1853 excavations. The architects, in fact, had from the first worked hand in hand with archaeologists and when the great excavations began—Delphi and Delos were both projects of the Ecole française—the Prix de Rome architects were on hand to record the present and recreate the past.

Tournaire's 1894 *Envoi*, nineteen items covering the great French dig at Delphi, is a treasure both from the historical and the artistic point of view. His surveys, though recently revised and brought up to date in Volume II (1975) of the *Fouilles de Delphes*, still remain, as the catalogue puts it, "the necessary basis of any study of Delphi." Two large watercolors offer a view of the excavations at different stages: November 1894 in plan, the same month in 1893 in elevation. In 1893 the work has gone far enough up the slope to uncover the base of the temple of Apollo; behind and above it are the still undemolished houses of the village of Castri. (The villagers, protesting so violently that at one point Greek soldiers with loaded rifles surrounded the site, had been given new houses, at French expense, on the site now covered with hotels and restaurants.) Among the scattered stones in the excavated area one of the two twins, Cleobis or Biton, is lying on the ground (the other was not found until the next year); the bronze charioteer had not yet come to light (he was much farther up the slope, north of the theater) but the general layout of the lower part of the sacred precinct is clear to see.

Tournaire's *restauration*, over six feet high and twelve feet long, is based on the excavations and the ancient authorities; it is perhaps the most convincing restoration of an ancient religious site ever attempted. With its buildings and statues crowding the zigzag path up to the temple, smoke rising from the great altar on one side of it and the theater's row on row of stone benches rising behind the other, the painting reminds us forcibly how deceptive ruins can be, what false perspective moonlight and a broken column can create. This Delphi is bursting with human figures, a Cecil B. DeMille crowd scene, but on closer inspection it becomes clear that the figures are not human. The few human beings in the painting are members of a procession just starting on the way up through the sanctuary from the lower right; the figures that jam every pediment, roof, wall, and base are statues of gods and heroes.

Tournaire's vision of a huge architectural complex filled to bursting with marble and bronze statues is a jarring reminder of one feature of ancient city life that we tend to underestimate. The unwary visitor to Barletta in southern Italy is apt to be disconcerted by the presence on the sidewalk of a larger-than-life bronze Roman emperor (identity unknown), but the ancient Greek or Roman city dweller spent his days in a forest of such statuary—gods, heroes, and later deified emperors watched his every move. "This place is so full of divine presences," says the bawdyhouse-keeper Quartilla in Petronius' *Satyricon*, "that it's easier to find a god than a human being."

Delphi was not the only large complex site to attract the Prix de Rome architects. Defrasse produced an impressive panorama of the great spa at Epidaurus (1891–93); Laloux did the same for the German excavation at Olympia (1883). With Pontremoli's study of Pergamon (1895) the new emphasis on architectural organization of civic space rather than individual monuments came to full maturity. Pergamon was a carefully planned Hellenistic city, built on terraces descending from a hilltop. Temples, altars, and the agora were fitted neatly around a steeply banked theater that overlooked the plain;

and much lower down was the largest gymnasium ever built in the Greek world.

Four of the last five *Envois,* completed between 1904 and 1937, show the same interest in town planning; they reconstruct (some of them with a large measure of creative imagination) ancient Selinus, Delos, Priene in Asia Minor (another planned Hellenistic city), and Lindos on the island of Rhodes. The one exception is a fresh approach to the Acropolis at Athens; it is mentioned here because Nicod's delicately colored painting of Athens at the foot of its Acropolis, as it was in 1912, will both delight and sadden those who know only the sprawling, shapeless megalopolis that now spreads out from the Acropolis as far as the eye can see through the polluted air.

These *Envois* were, of course, only the beginning of an architect's career; the Prix de Rome conferred enormous prestige and its winners returned to Paris destined for a successful career in both public and private building. Their thoroughly academic training, however, had not prepared them for the new building materials the nineteenth century was to provide—materials which, like cast iron and, later, steel, called for engineering skills that the Ecole, in true Aristotelian fashion, considered beneath the dignity of an artist. As a result the list of their commissions as fully fledged architects is limited, with few exceptions, to ecclesiastical and state buildings, especially to maintenance and restoration of historic monuments (the Louvre, Versailles, Fountainbleau, etc.). There are, however, some famous Paris monuments that were designed by Prix de Rome architects: Charles Garnier (1852–1853) built the Paris Opéra; Albert Thomas (1875) was responsible for the façade of the Grand Palais on the avenue d'Antin; Laloux (1883) for the Gare d'Orsay. All these buildings bear the stamp of the classical tradition to which their designers had devoted so much study and it is no accident that almost all of the Prix de Rome architects spent at least some and many of them all of the final years of their careers teaching at the Ecole des Beaux-Arts.

The gulf between architects trained almost exclusively in classical drawing and engineers who calculated weights and metal stress grew wider as the nineteenth century moved on; education at the Ecole tended to steer the student not so much to designing real buildings as to producing fancy projects that would catch the eye of the Prix de Rome judges. One Prix de Rome architect, in fact—Gauthier (1810)— was so negligent of purely material factors, so intent on "an order of things independent of matter," that a church he designed in his native city of Troyes threatened to collapse as it neared completion. (He was unable to pay the huge fine imposed on him and died in prison.) But the new construction methods and materials could not be ignored forever; in the Paris of the Tour Eiffel even the commissions of the Prix de Rome winners could not be executed exclusively in the cut-stone masonry that was the only monumental building material the classically trained architect thought proper. When they did use metal, however, most of them managed to conceal it. Though Labrouste made brilliant use of metal structures on the interior of his Bibliothèque Sainte-Geneviève, Garnier saw to it that in the Paris Opéra the iron beams were masked by masonry; the only metal visible is that of the gates in the façade.

The Beaux-Arts Prix de Rome style, an eclectic classicism often dignified with the label Neobaroque, became the reigning fashion in Paris and remained so for most of the Second Empire and the Third Republic, but its influence can also be seen in New York—in the Public Library, the Metropolitan Museum, and Grand Central Station. From the middle of the eighties large numbers of American architects had followed courses at the Ecole, but the Beaux-Arts obsession with ancient Greece had been transferred to this continent much earlier. The architectural schools of MIT (1866) and Columbia (1881) both based their curriculum on the Ecole des Beaux-Arts model, and the Chicago World's Fair of 1893, a panorama of classical fantasies, proclaimed the triumph of Greek architecture seen through the distorting lens of Paris.

It was in that same year and in the same city that Frank Lloyd Wright received his first commission; Le Corbusier, born six years earlier in Switzerland, was to settle in Paris in 1917; in 1919 Gropius founded the Bauhaus at Weimar and launched the International Style. By the third decade of this century the functional emphasis was dominant; the new builders of the house and the city had no place for ornamentation in their severe vision. The Beaux-Arts style was abandoned and though the Prix de Rome competitions were still held and the winners dispatched to Rome until the riots of 1968, the *Envois* lost interest for everyone except the academicians who had made them a requirement in the first place. The abolition of the Prix de Rome itself seemed to be the final slab closed over the tomb of that Greek ideal which through its Roman and Renaissance adaptations and finally through the rediscovery of its original forms had haunted the vision of Western builders from the moment the last stone of the Parthenon was put into place.

Reports of its death were, however, exaggerated; as Horace said of nature, you can pitch it out with a fork but it will keep running back. The Beaux-Arts tradition is back in the limelight again; this exhibit is of more than antiquarian interest. Barbara Rose, in the introduction to the catalogue, sums up the situation: "Obeying what Max J. Friedlaender, writing of style, referred to as 'the grandfather principle,' Post-Modernism, in relation to the International Style, appreciates and emulates elements of the Beaux-Arts tradition, in particular its later historical eclecticism, in a manner that makes the drawings of the Prix de Rome winners especially relevant to the contemporary eye." And just as one World's Fair, that of Chicago in 1893, heralded the full emergence of the Beaux-Arts style in this country, its resurrection is signaled by another World's Fair—New Orleans 1984. Charles Moore's *Wonderwall*, which has been described by Paul Goldberger in the *New York Times*[12] as a "2,400-foot-long, 10-foot thick, three-storey-high meandering collection of urns, towers, columns, domes, chimneys, gazebos, pediments, busts, cupids and animal sculptures," looks like classical ornamentation run riot. And another Moore creation at the fair, the Centennial Pavilions, appears to the same critic as "a collection of gazebo-like pavilions that seem to float on a man-made lagoon. They are decorated in the ornate style of the Beaux-Arts but painted in a happy combination of purple and salmon, and so they become a kind of cartoon-like fantasy of a great Second Empire palace." Although he might, to quote Housman, have felt like Sin when she gave birth to Death, Loviot, if he could see that happy combination of purple and salmon, would be forced to recognize his own progeny.

The nineteenth-century Prix de Rome painters have no such spectacular evidence of resurrection to show but they are nevertheless as timely in their reappearance as their architectural colleagues. The modern turn away from abstract form coincides with the revival of interest in nineteenth-century painting, which is reflected not only in exhibitions and scholarly studies but also in the art market, where

12. May 13, 1984.

even the soppy Hellenic daydreams of Sir Lawrence Alma-Tadema are now commanding robust prices.

Near the beginning of Anthony Powell's *Dance,* four canvases of Mr. Deacon (long since deceased after falling downstairs at the Brass Monkey) are displayed for sale in a junk shop in north London. They all belong "to the same school of large, untidy, exclusively male-figured compositions, light in tone and mythological in subject." One of them, upside down, exhibits "a forest of inverted legs, moving furiously towards their goal in what appeared to be one of the running events in the Olympic games." They were "finally knocked down for a few pounds" but "bidding was reasonably brisk: possibly on account of the frames." But in the final volume of Powell's saga a young art dealer opens (in 1971) a Deacon Centenary Exhibition (the *Boyhood of Cyrus* is sold "within an hour of the show opening") and a critic writes solemnly of "his roots . . . in Continental Symbolism" and the "seminaturalistic treatment of more than one of his favorite renderings of Greek or Roman legend." As so often happens, life is imitating art, fact trailing behind fiction.

The Scorpion's Sting

In ancient Greek the word "epigram" meant nothing more than "inscription," its exact Latin equivalent. It was a statement "written on" something, originally something other than paper: an elegiac couplet naming the dedicator carved on the base or leg of a statue dedicated to a god, commemorative verses chiseled in the stone of a funeral column. The tomb of the Spartans killed at Thermopylae, for example, was inscribed with the famous elegiac couplet: "Stranger, tell the Spartans that we lie here, obeying their orders." And the base of the statue of the Athenian tyrannicides proclaimed, in the same tightly organized verse form, their name and title to glory: "In truth a great light shone on the people of Athens when Harmodios and Aristogeiton killed Hipparchus." The epigram says much in little. It has to, for cutting an inscription in bronze or marble is a laborious and expensive process; our word "lapidary" (formed from the Latin word for "stone") alludes to the material constraints that made for concision.

With the spread of literacy in the fifth and later centuries B.C., the epigram became a literary genre. Although concision remained its hallmark, its subject matter widened to include not only imaginary dedications and epitaphs for poets and other figures long since dead, but eventually almost every aspect of social and private life: love poems (some of the most exquisite were later attributed, falsely, to Plato), prayers, philosophical reflections on life and death, literary criticism and polemic, and satire (doctors were a favored target).

The satiric epigram, especially the "short poem ending in a witty or ingenious turn of thought to which the rest of the composition is intended to lead up" (as the Oxford English Dictionary defines it), did not come into fashion in the Greek world until the first century. At about the same time, this particular form found its classic Latin voice in the fifteen hundred or so epigrams of a poet born in the Roman province of Spain, Marcus Valerius Martialis, known to the English

This essay originally appeared in the *New Republic,* February 1, 1988.

poets of the sixteenth and seventeenth centuries, who admired and imitated him, as Martial.

Martial had his Roman predecessors, whom he mentions in the preface to his first collection, which was issued in A.D. 85–86. Among them was Catullus, whose extant corpus of 116 poems contains, besides the passionate love poems for which he is best known, scurrilous attacks on his contemporaries (Julius Caesar among others); compliments, jokes, and exhortations addressed to friends and enemies; sexually explicit vignettes of the activities of persons who may or may not be fictitious; and anecdotal sketches of life among the younger Roman aristocrats—what in his introductory poem he calls, with ironic self-deprecation, *nugae*, "trifles." Martial describes his poems with the same word, and his concerns are similar, with two significant exceptions. There are no passionate love poems in his book, and, unlike Catullus, he makes no attacks on public figures. The Republic had long since been replaced by the Principate, and the only acceptable comment on a ruling emperor was flattery, a commodity that Martial supplied with a lavish hand for the delectation of the emperor Domitian (A.D. 81–96).

Domitian's assassination in 96 brought to an end a reign of terror that the historian Tacitus, who lived through it, described, in words that bridge the centuries, as "the extreme of slavery, when the informer robbed us of the interchange of speech and hearing. We should have lost memory as well as voice, if it had been as easy to forget as to keep silence." When, with Domitian's successors, the era of "the five good emperors" began, Martial apologized in an epigram for his obsequious adulation of the tyrant. Imagining that the usual fulsome compliments come asking to be written up, he tells them their day is done: "I am not going to call anyone master and god; there is no longer any place for you in this town." It is a witty apologia, but it did him no good; out of favor, he retired to end his days in the provincial Spain he had left for Rome as a young man.

Politics and love aside, Martial's range is very wide. J. P. Sullivan, one of the editors of a new anthology of Martial translations,[1] speaks of his "witty, yet almost Dickensian, depiction of Roman life." And it is true that to read his epigrams is to take a tour of ancient Rome—

---

1. *Epigrams of Martial Englished by Divers Hands*, ed. J. P. Sullivan and Peter Whigham (Berkeley and Los Angeles: University of California Press, 1987).

from the newly built Colosseum to the slave market, from the bookshops where Martial's epigrams are on sale ("Near Caesar's Forum there's a shop. . . . Look for me there") to the usually meager fare of the table of the literary patron, not to mention the brothels and the beds of sexual partners locked in every conceivable position and combination. His poems, to quote Sullivan, are a gallery of "satiric portraits and sketches of patrons and clients, dandies, upstarts, fortune hunters, connoisseurs, dinner cadgers, lawyers, schoolmasters, doctors, debtors, bores, poisoners, nymphomaniacs, hypocritical intellectuals and the like."

Martial was an author much read and enjoyed in the ancient world. Unlike Catullus, whose text depends on a single manuscript (now lost) that turned up in thirteenth-century Verona, Martial survived the Dark Ages in an impressive number of copies. He was among the first of the classics to appear in print (in 1471) and was a prime favorite of poets and translators in Renaissance France and England. Sullivan points out that the skillful wit of his compliments to sovereigns and patrons recommended itself to sixteenth and seventeenth-century poets; "they too knew the mechanics and requirements of power and patronage." And as a model for the short witty poem, a favorite medium of, among many others, Donne, Harrington, Prior, and Herrick, Martial had no rival.

He was also one of the authors included in the famous French series of classical editions made for the Dauphin *in usum serenissimi Delphini*, the eldest son of Louix XIV. The editors, concerned for the presumed innocence of the royal pupil, relegated all the obscene epigrams to an appendix, an expedient that, as Byron remarked in *Don Juan*, "saves, in fact, the trouble of an index: For there we have them all at one fell swoop." When, two and a half centuries later, the editor of the Loeb Classical Library edition of Martial faced the problem of providing a prose translation of the offending items he fell back on the elegant Italian version of Giuspanio Graglia.

The sexually explicit epigrams, which cluster particularly thick in Book XI (recently issued in a scholarly edition, with prose translation),[2] leave nothing to the imagination. "I wish he were less nauseous," Macaulay wrote, echoing Byron's ironic "all those nauseous

---

2. N. M. Kay, *Martial Book XI: A Commentary* (New York: Oxford University Press, 1985).

epigrams of Martial." And in fact the obscene poems (about one-tenth of the corpus) range from the raunchy to the disgusting, from *Penthouse* to *Hustler* and beyond. This was an obstacle to the appreciation of Martial in Victorian times; but as the editors of this selection put it, "this side of Martial does interest the modern audience because of the increasing sexual frankness of our own literature and a greater curiosity about subjects formerly kept from historical and critical inspection."

That curiosity will be fully satisfied by this volume. This is no "gelded Martiall"—John Donne's indignant dismissal of a bowdlerized selection edited by a Jesuit in 1599. The "mainly modern" translators (among them such well-known practitioners of the art as Dudley Fitts, Tony Harrison, Rolfe Humphries, James Michie, Peter Porter, and Peter Whigham) unblushingly supply Anglo-Saxon four- and five-letter equivalents for the crude terms of what Martial is pleased to call *Romana simplicitas*, "Latin blunt and direct," in Sullivan's translation. Interestingly enough, in view of the modern rediscovery of the "other Victorians," the most repellently disgusting poem of the lot (XI 61) is translated (and expanded) in elegant Swinburnian rhythm and revolting detail by the Victorian litterateur George Augustus Henry Sala.

These poems reveal prejudices that were characteristic of the Roman male animal, but will scarcely recommend them to educated readers today. The persona of the epigrammatist is not averse to playing the active role in a homosexual coupling, especially with a handsome slave boy, but he expresses loathing for a grown man who assumes the passive role. He regards lesbian love as a monstrous aberration (it is manless adultery); and in heterosexual relations he expects oral favors from his female partner, but regards a man who would reciprocate as the lowest of degenerates. His views of the married state are summed up in a couplet that runs, in James Michie's elegant version: "Wives should obey their husbands. Only then / Can women share equality with men."

When one adds to all this the fawning adulation of the poems addressed to the powerful, the whining tone of his complaints about the meanness of his patrons, and the tedious repetition of some of his themes and rhetorical tricks, there seem to be grounds for asking whether Martial deserves to be reissued for the modern reader. An affirmative answer is suggested by the number and the quality of the poets who have translated him; in addition to the modern poets listed above, this volume offers versions of Martial by Byron, Cowley, Harrington, Leigh Hunt, Johnson, Jonson, Pope, Pound, Stevenson, and Swift.

An even stronger argument for Martial's importance is the strength and spread of his influence on English poetry. Sullivan's introductory essay deals especially with the presence of Martial in the poetry of the sixteenth and seventeenth centuries, and goes on to remark that what won his admirers was above all the quality the Augustans knew as "wit." "It is scarcely an exaggeration," he writes, "to claim that the lineal descendants of Martial's biting elegiac distichs are the couplets of John Dryden and Alexander Pope."

The wit is best displayed in those epigrams that reflect the lapidary origin of the genre; in these the scorpion sting in the tail is most deadly. The couplet on married life quoted above is a brilliant example; the point is not clear until the very last word, which fulfills expectation by completing the tight metrical pattern but defies it by its paradoxical sense. *Inferior matrona suo sit, Prisce, marito* ("Inferior let the wife be, Priscus, to her husband"). *Non aliter fiunt femina virque* ("Not otherwise are wife and husband") *pares* ("equal"). That last word was unpredictable and yet, once heard, seems inevitable.

Since English verse, unlike Latin, is not marshaled in strict quantitative patterns, the precision of the Latin elegiac couplet, which gives such rhythmic emphasis to the closing syllables, has to be obtained by the skillful use of rhyme. This was an imperative of the Augustan heroic couplet. But the Augustans were not the only poets to share the legacy of Martial; the sound of his voice can be heard in every age of English poetry. Belloc, Blake, Burns, Byron, Coleridge, Graves, Hardy, Hood, Hopkins, Housman, Kipling, Landor, Moore, Rossetti, and Yeats—these are some of the poets whose names appear in the index of writers at the back of Geoffrey Grigson's invaluable *The Faber Book of Epigrams and Epitaphs,* and their indebtedness to Martial is plain to see.

Byron's epitaph for Castlereagh, for example, is a brilliant specimen of the sting in the tail provided by an explosive final rhyme. "Posterity will ne'er survey / A nobler grave than this; / Here lie the bones of Castlereagh. / Stop, traveller, and piss." Martial would never have launched such a missile against a real person, but he would have admired the ferocious whiplash of that last word. Byron, of course, knew his Martial well, but the tradition can be seen at work even in the efforts of anonymous epigrammatists, like the one who wrote, on the wall of a U.S. Army latrine during the Second World War, some lines that expressed the deepest feelings of most of the combatants. "Soldiers who wish to be a hero," it ran, "Are practically zero, / But those who wish to be civilians, / Jesus, they run into millions."

This anthology is long overdue. It is a generous selection: about four hundred of the epigrams in modern translations and an appendix of some forty older versions for comparison. And it covers every aspect of Martial's oeuvre. Though the scorpion epigrams predominate (as they should), there is much besides: longer poems dealing with life in Rome or the country (where Martial had a rural retreat), affectionate addresses to friends, literary and social gossip—poems that even Macaulay (who, characteristically, "learned about 360 of the best lines") praised for their "rapid succession of vivid images." Martial himself can be cited for a review of his book: "Good work you'll find, some poor, and much that's worse; / It takes all sorts to make a book of verse."

On Poets & Poetry

Subversive Activities

The nearest English equivalent of the word Herodotus used to describe his account of the Persian War and its antecedents, *historiai*, is "enquiries"; the Greek verb *historein* means "to ask questions." In recent years history has begun to ask questions about people it once took little or no notice of; to concern itself, for example, with "the short and simple annals of the poor" and the "destiny obscure" of the neglected and oppressed. The history of blacks in America has become a flourishing academic industry, that of women all over the world and throughout the centuries an even wider field of research and publication, and "gay history," of which Louis Crompton's *Byron and Greek Love*[1] is a distinguished specimen, seems, to judge from the wealth of literature cited in his footnotes, to be following in their wake.

Such approaches to history have produced important work; new and significant data have been amassed, which often throw fresh and revealing light on the established record. But since these studies are for the most part undertaken by scholars who share the race, sex, or inclination of the group they are investigating, it is only natural that they sometimes reflect the bias in the minds of their authors. This can manifest itself in a failure to view the new data in historical perspective, in a tendency to base broad generalizations on evidence which, given the nature of historical records prior to the twentieth century, is often inadequate, and finally in a polemical tone that puts the reader on his guard. No historian, of course, has ever been totally free of partiality to a cause, class, or nation, but the best of them have tried to be so, and sincerely thought they had succeeded. Macaulay, for example, would have been surprised and indignant if he had lived long enough to hear himself credited with the creation of the "Whig theory of English history."

This essay originally appeared in the *New York Review of Books*, November 20, 1985.

1. *Byron and Greek Love: Homophobia in Nineteenth-Century England* (Berkeley and Los Angeles: University of California Press, 1985).

It is a pleasure to be able to report that although Crompton, as a cofounder of the Gay Caucus for Modern Languages, is clearly a committed witness, his book exhibits none of the characteristic flaws of sectarian history. He is, to be sure, too ready to find specific personal references in the works of the imagination (Byron's Thyrza, for example, is unequivocally identified with Edlestone, the choirboy at Trinity College, Cambridge, with whom he had a deep romantic attachment), but this is an error historians, by the nature of their calling, are prone to; the real danger facing a gay historian, a failure to distinguish between affection, romantic friendship, and sexual passion when expressed in the idiom of a different age, Crompton is fully aware of and gracefully avoids.

Unlike some modern critics who, faced with new evidence, have come to obviously exaggerated conclusions about Byron's sexual ambivalence ("basically homosexual," for example), Crompton is measured in his judgment, recognizing that "Byron's heterosexual impulses were fully as real as his homosexual ones and, if we take his life as a whole, more persistent and significant." But, though the book's structure is a narrative account of Byron's homosexual inclinations and encounters and their effects, its real novelty and importance lie elsewhere, in the matter announced in the subtitle. With a dispassionate authority and in a wealth of detail Crompton explores some little-known and very unpleasant features of one of the most richly documented periods of English history—the age of Keats, Shelley, Wordsworth, Coleridge, Castlereagh, Jeremy Bentham, and Byron.

It is of course no news that Byron's vigorous career as a rival of Don Juan Tenorio was punctuated by homosexual attachments of varying intensity. Crompton acknowledges his debt to Peter Quennell's *Byron: The Years of Fame* (1935) and the later studies which dealt with Byron's relationships with his Harrow schoolmates and with Edlestone, as well as his affairs with fifteen-year-old boys on his first and also on his last visit to Greece. Crompton attempts "to shape this deluge of new material" (much of it scattered through Leslie Marchand's great edition of Byron's letters and journals) "into a narrative." And he adds new and notable evidence, in particular a letter from his Cambridge friend Charles Skinner Matthews to Byron at Falmouth on his way to Greece (1809) and another which reached Byron at Malta on his way back (1811), both of them here printed for the first time. The earlier letter, a reply to one of Byron's, leaves no doubt whatever, if indeed any still remained, about the import of Byron's cryptic references to Georgia, hyacinths, and *"Plen.* and *optabil.-Coit.,"* an abbreviated quotation from Petronius which was Byron's usual phrase for a satisfactory sexual encounter.²

Matthews writes to Byron and Hobhouse in the tone of a professor congratulating his pupils on their progress in what he calls *"ma méthode,"* compliments Byron on his "first efforts in *the mysterious*, that style in which more is meant than meets the Eye," takes it that the hyacinths Byron speaks of "culling" at Falmouth "will be of the class polyandria and not monogynia," and wishes for both of them in their travels in the East "all the success which in your most methodistical fantasies you can wish yourselves."

The second letter, a reply to one of Byron's now lost, asks for more details on what must have been an account of Byron's exploits in the East and then reports Matthews's own sexual inactivity: *"Quant à ma méthode,* my botanical studies have been sadly at a stand." There can be no reasonable doubt that Crompton is justified in his claim that the three men "share what today would be called a gay identity, based on common interests and a sense of alienation from a society they must protect themselves from by a "special 'mysterious' style." The "common interest" was a love of boys, the "Greek love" of Crompton's title; Hyakinthos was a boy love of the god Apollo.

The final paragraphs of Matthews's second letter gave Byron an account of the arrests and punishments of homosexuals in England during his absence: some of what the press of the day called "miscreants" had been exposed in the pillory to the fury of the mob, others hanged. "That which you get for £5," writes Matthews, jocularly, referring to the easy availability of homosexual pleasures in Greece and Turkey, "we must risque our necks for; and are content to risque them."

That men were regularly hanged for homosexual relations in nineteenth-century England—sixty in the first three decades of the century and "another score under naval regulations"—will come as a surprise to most readers; it was in fact the "discovery of an unprece-

---

2. Leslie A. Marchand, ed., *Byron's Letters and Journals*, Vol. 1, *"In My Hot Youth"* (Cambridge: Harvard University Press, 1973), pp. 206–7; Gilbert Highet identified the quotation *"plenum et optabilem coitum"* (*Satyricon* 86) for Marchand; Crompton points out that in its Petronian context it clearly refers to homosexual coupling.

dented number of executions of homosexuals in England in the statistical reports" of the period that first drew Crompton's attention to his subject. Hanging, however, was reserved for those unfortunates in whose cases solid evidence of sexual intercourse was proved (or confessed); where "evidence both of penetration and emission" was not available, the arrested men were charged with "assault with the attempt to commit sodomy" and given the lesser sentence of exposure in the pillory. Contemporary accounts of what this meant for the victim strongly suggest that hanging might have been preferable. Of one survivor of this ordeal a journalist eyewitness remarked: "The head of this wretch when he reached Newgate was compared to a swallow's nest. It took three buckets of hot water to restore it to anything like a human shape. Though much battered and bruised, the fellow is in no danger, but he is at present totally blind."

Crompton quotes extensively from a contemporary pamphlet which describes the ordeal of six men sentenced to the pillory in 1810. What he justifiably calls a "semilynching, which was supposed to stop short of killing" (though in fact the victims did not always survive) was organized by the police, who escorted the prisoners through a hostile mob armed with balls of mud and brickbats. They arrived at the pillory looking like "bears dipped in a stagnant pool"; once secured, they were exposed to the ministrations of "upwards of fifty women who were permitted to stand in the ring, who assailed them incessantly with mud, dead cats, rotten eggs, potatoes, and buckets filled with blood, offal, and dung." The newspapers reported the event in graphic detail; their editorials, far from expressing sympathy for the victims, declared that if any of them died from the effects of their punishment they would die "unpitied" and "justly execrated," or else complained that the pillory was too merciful a sentence and demanded the death penalty.

The wretched sufferers on the gallows or in the pillory seem to have been exclusively working-class men; persons higher up on the social ladder who were arrested usually managed to avoid punishment and escape to the Continent, like the Bishop of Clogher in Ireland who, caught *in flagrante delicto* with a guardsman in 1822, jumped bail and left England for good. Even mere suspicion based on gossip could drive a man into exile; William Beckford, the rich and famous author of *Vathek*, felt himself constrained to leave England for ten years and was still treated as a social pariah when he returned.

Crompton's thesis is that one of the reasons Byron went into self-imposed exile was his fear that rumors of his homosexual escapades might draw down on him the ostracism of his peers and the vicious rage of the street mobs who, infuriated by the escape of Bishop Clogher, attacked and pillaged the episcopal palace. That such rumors were abroad is clear from notes in Hobhouse's diary; their source was Byron's rejected mistress Lady Caroline Lamb, to whom Byron seems to have confessed that, as Lady Byron put it, "from his boyhood on he had been in the practice of unnatural crime." Given the universal "homophobia"[3] which Crompton has so copiously documented for the period, fear of exposure on this score may well have been as urgent a motive for Byron's abrupt departure from England as the scandal of his broken marriage and his affair with his half-sister Augusta.

It is a remarkable paradox that an England which was in many ways the most liberal country in Europe could condemn homosexuals to the rope and the pillory at a time when on the Continent the medieval laws that made sodomy a capital offense had been totally repudiated, as in revolutionary France, or allowed to fall into disuse, as in Catholic Italy. Reform of the criminal law, imposed by such enlightened despots as Catherine in Russia, Frederick in Prussia, and Grand Duke Leopold in Tuscany, was not even contemplated by the British parliaments of the eighteenth century. As for the manic hatred for sexual deviants that inspired both the mobs at the pillory and the editorial writers at their desks, Crompton explains it as caused partly by English xenophobia and partly by the activities of the Society for

---

3. Until the subject could at last be discussed objectively in the press and in books, there were no words in the English language for homosexuals that were not derogatory. The words that eventually came into use were, however, linguistically inelegant, to say the least. "Homosexual" is an ugly hybrid, half Greek, half Latin; it was taken over from the Germans, who had coined the word as early as 1869. (Crompton mentions an American coinage which never became current—"similisexualism"; it is all Latin but obviously too much of a mouthful for common use.) "Homophobia" is all Greek but unfortunately it doesn't mean what it is supposed to. The Greek prefix "homo-" means "alike"; "homogeneous" means "of the same kind" and so "homophobia" should mean something like "sharing the same fear." The word has been formed by false analogy with such words as "xenophobia," but since the only alternative (used once by Crompton) seems to be "antihomosexualism" it will probably remain in use, all the more so since those unacquainted with the classical languages will take the prefix "homo-" for the vulgar abbreviation of "homosexual" often heard in common speech.

the Reformation of Manners, which, in the opening decades of the eighteenth century, made homosexuality the main target of its propaganda and its network of pious informers. The Napoleonic wars and especially the threat of French invasion after the renewal of hostilities in 1803 did nothing to lessen public virulence against what was considered an un-British vice.

And yet, as Crompton himself seems at times to feel, this is not an adequate explanation for the deep roots and long duration of English prejudice on this subject. The Napoleonic wars ended with victory in 1815 but the rate of executions went up; the death penalty was not rescinded until 1861, when it was replaced by life imprisonment, and sexual relations between men were not decriminalized until 1967. Given the frequency of homosexual attachments among upper-class Englishmen who attended public schools and all-male universities in the century and a half between Byron's departure and the Wolfenden Report of 1957, one can only wonder why legal redress came so late. Perhaps the brake on reform was fear of the rancorous antagonism of the lower classes that made possible the atrocity of the pillory and that manifested itself as late as 1895 when a mob attacked Oscar Wilde on his way to prison. Even so one might have expected that as the years went by the laws would be allowed to fall into oblivion. What happened, however, was exactly the opposite: arrests for homosexual offenses reached the number of three thousand as late as 1952. What these archaic laws did encourage, of course, was blackmail. How many prominent men with a reputation to defend paid up to silence male prostitutes or rejected lovers we shall never know, but there is good evidence, discussed in detail by Crompton, that one of the causes of Castlereagh's suicide was the threat of blackmail on this count. "I am accused of the same crime as the Bishop of Clogher," he told King George IV.

Almost as hard to understand as the slowness of legal reform is the fact that in spite of the universal public abhorrence of homosexuality the Greek and Latin classics continued to serve as the basic text of upper-class education. Plato's *Phaedrus* and *Symposium*, to name only two of the best-known dialogues, make no bones about what kind of love is under discussion; Horace's *Odes* often mention boys as objects of love, desire, or mere pleasure, and even Virgil, as Byron jocularly points out in a famous stanza of *Don Juan*, blotted his otherwise clean copybook in his second eclogue, which deals with Corydon's passion for Alexis. Horace and Virgil the schoolmasters could manage by selective assignment or expurgation; even as late as 1930, I read Juvenal in an edition entitled *The Satires of Juvenal,* which contained only thirteen of the extant poems—one of the missing, Satire XI, is the complaint of a homosexual prostitute which goes into scabrous detail about the unpleasantness of his duties. And in 1961, to the amazement of the American classical establishment, the Oxford University Press brought out an edition of Catullus from which, to quote the preface, "a few poems which do not lend themselves to comment in English have been omitted." The "few" number 32 out of a total of 116; 13 of them are concerned with carnal homosexual relations.

Plato, however, is not so easy to handle; consequently, as Crompton points out, he almost entirely disappeared from the British educational curriculum in the eighteenth and early nineteenth centuries. The Greekless reader, too, was spared the cultural shock Plato's early dialogues would have given him; the only available translations were thoroughly bowdlerized. John Stuart Mill published a partial translation of the *Phaedrus,* excerpted "in such a way as to leave no hint" of the presence of homosexuality in the text even though, as Crompton justly remarks, the theme "is woven into the very warp and woof" of the dialogue. And when Shelley, in 1818, embarked on his translation of the *Symposium,* prefaced by an essay "upon the cause of some differences in sentiment between the antients & moderns with respect to the subject of the dialogue," he knew that he was treading dangerous ground. He did not, in fact, publish the translation and when his widow decided to do so she was prevailed upon by Leigh Hunt to change "unacceptable words like 'lover' into 'friend,' 'men' into 'human beings,' and 'youths' into 'young people.'" What is more, the speech of Alcibiades in which he describes his unsuccessful attempt to seduce Socrates was omitted. The essay, of course, was suppressed entirely; its full text in fact did not become available to the general public until the classical scholar James Notopoulos included it in his *Platonism of Shelley,* published in 1949.

Fear of legal action and censorship, not to mention the certainty of social ostracism, enforced the conspiracy of silence until late in the twentieth century; protest, even rational discussion of the subject, could only be private. A most eloquent private protest and an eminently rational discussion were the work of a contemporary of Byron (one for whom, incidentally, Byron had no respect), the jurist and philosopher Jeremy Bentham.[4] In 1774, almost two centuries before the recommendations of the Wolfenden Committee were incorporated in the law of the land, Bentham wrote the first of a series of notes, essays, and projected books on this subject, the latest of them dated 1825, eight years before his death at the age of eighty-four. As a hedonist and utilitarian he could see no reason to punish "a crime, if a crime it is to be called, that produces no misery in Society." But he never dared publish a word of his voluminous writings on this theme, in spite of frequent resolutions to do so, recorded in his notes; his opinions remained unread until 1931, when C. K. Ogden published some extracts in his edition of Bentham's *Theory of Legislation.*

Crompton obtained from the library of University College in London, where Bentham's papers (along with his well-preserved and fully dressed corpse) are stored, more than five hundred manuscript pages of his reflections on homosexuality and the law. "Composed over a period of fifty years," they were "remarkably far-ranging in their perspectives, analysing the subject from a legal, moral, psychological and even literary point of view." Crompton gives a generous sample of this fascinating material (indeed his book might well have been titled "Byron, Bentham, and Greek Love"); the most sensational item is Bentham's proposed sequel to a book he published under a pseudonym in 1823, *Not Paul but Jesus.*

The published book was a general challenge to St. Paul's right to set himself up as a spokesman for Christ; it made no mention of his denunciation of homosexual love, though Paul's Epistle to the Romans (1:24ff.) was the New Testament text on which the Church based its condemnation of homosexuality—"vile affections . . . against nature. . . . men with men working that which is unseemly." Bentham treated this subject, however, at length and in detail in the unpublished manuscripts of what was to have been the sequel—three hundred pages of notes which "seem to have been written helter-skelter and then reorganized under chapter headings." After a philosophical rejection of asceticism in general Bentham draws a contrast between a true ascetic, St. John the Baptist, and an anti-ascetic, indeed, antinomian, Christ, a figure "strikingly similar to the portrait William

---

4. Presented with a copy of Bentham's *Springs of Action* during his final trip to Greece, Byron threw it to the floor and exclaimed: "What does the old fool know of springs of action; my —— has more spring to it."

Blake was elaborating at almost exactly the same time in his unfinished poem 'The Everlasting Gospel.'" Christ, who nowhere specifically condemns love between men, was, in Bentham's view, perfectly capable of rejecting Mosaic law on this point as he did on others.[5] But Bentham goes much farther and wonders whether the references to the "beloved disciple" in the Gospel According to St. John may not suggest "the same sort of love as that which appears to have had place between David and Jonathan," a love which he has earlier characterized as sexual. He even sees in the "young man, having a linen cloth cast about his naked body" mentioned by St. Mark in his account of the arrest of Jesus in Gethsemane (Mark 14: 50–52) a *cinaedus* (the Greco-Roman word for a homosexual prostitute) and a "rival or a candidate for the situation of rival to the Apostle."

It is understandable that Bentham shrank from publishing these opinions but, though Crompton does not mention it, he was not the first to hold them. Christopher Marlowe, according to one of his accusers, said that "St. John was a bedfellow to Christ," and according to an unsigned deposition in the British Museum about Marlowe's "monstrous opinions" (thought to be in the handwriting of Thomas Kyd), he "would report St. John to be our saviour Christ's Alexis . . . that is, that Christ did love him with an extraordinarie love." According to this same source, Marlowe also anticipated Bentham's low estimate of St. Paul; he told the anonymous informer "that for me to wryte a poem of St. Paul's conversion as I was determined to do would be as if I should go write a book of fast and loose, esteeming St. Paul a jugler."

From his hedonist and utilitarian viewpoint Bentham can see nothing wrong in a relationship that does no harm to others, but he fails to appreciate one social aspect of the matter, the fear that besets heterosexual parents that those placed in authority over their preadolescent sons as teachers or trainers may, if homosexually inclined, seduce or even molest them. "SCOUTMASTER BETRAYS TRUST," ran a famous (though possibly apocryphal) headline in Britain's prewar mass-circulation Sunday paper, *The News of the World*; "INCIDENT IN RAILWAY CARRIAGE." The *News* was a scandal sheet prized for its ver-

---

5. Leviticus 20:13. "If a man also lie with mankind, as he lieth with a woman, both of them have committed an abomination: they shall surely be put to death."

batim reports of proceedings in the divorce courts, but that headline gives pithy expression to a real concern. In Matthews's 1811 letter to Byron the list of arrests for sodomy includes "a sandman for pedicating one of his boys" and "John Cary Cole, usher of a school, for ditto with some of his pupils."

Even the ancient Athenians, who took love affairs between grown men and adolescent boys for granted, were concerned about this matter; Solon the lawgiver, we are told by a fourth-century orator, regarded teachers with suspicion and drew up elaborate regulations to ensure that teachers and gymnastic trainers would never be alone with a boy.[6] And today that issue of homosexuals as teachers in school is, in some parts of the country, a matter for acrid controversy—in which the problem of heterosexual men teaching young girls is scarcely mentioned.

Bentham rather lightheartedly dismisses this thorny subject; according to Crompton, he "is willing to believe there may be some advantage in such a relation." But this is probably an over-reaction against the raw malevolence of his contemporaries. Bentham's rational discussion of the entire problem is a welcome contrast to the venomous rhetoric of the public prints and a wholesome relief from the record of barbarous punishments. Crompton's discovery and presentation of this arresting material is an important contribution to English social history. It is also timely. As anxiety about the AIDS syndrome assumes the proportions of a national panic and voices charged with biblical indignation begin to suggest extreme measures, the book will serve as a salutary reminder of the barbarities into which blind prejudice against an unpopular minority can plunge an otherwise progressive society.

6. Aeschines, *Against Timarchus*, 9ff. The statement is all the more remarkable since the speaker later announces that he has been and still is a "lover" (i.e., of young men).

Closet Modern

Whewell's Court, a rather dowdy nineteenth-century Gothic annex of Trinity College, Cambridge, lies across the road from the splendid main gate of the college, the entrance to Great Court. Coming from St. John's, Trinity's next-door neighbor, I often had occasion to cross the road to Whewell's, on my way to visit my friend Michael Straight, whose rooms were on a staircase at the far end of the court, facing Sidney Street and Jesus Lane. Sometimes, in the afternoon, I would pass, in one of the narrow courts or even narrower passages between them, a white-haired old gentleman wearing a stiff stand-up white collar and black elastic-sided boots, who was proceeding in the opposite direction; his eyes were fixed directly forward on some far-off object—a look that promised brusque refusal of any attempt at contact and that strangely resembled what I later came to call, with fellow soldiers, the "thousand-yard stare." This was the Kennedy Professor of Latin, A. E. Housman, out for his long afternoon walk, which often brought him back through the four courts of St. John's (in 1934 it had only four) on his way home to his rooms in Whewell's Court.

His rooms were in fact on the same staircase as Michael Straight's, and that was not the only strange propinquity offered by Whewell's Court. One early evening, bounding down the stairs three steps at a time, full of whiskey and late for Hall at St. John's, I narrowly missed crashing into a slight figure of a man who nervously slipped through a door as I and my companion tumbled past. "Do you know who you almost knocked over?" said my friend as we reached the ground. "That was Ludwig Wittgenstein."

The only contact between Housman and Wittgenstein recorded by Norman Page in his witty and discriminating *A. E. Housman: A Critical Biography*[1] is a request by Wittgenstein, "stricken with diarrhoea," for "permission to use Housman's lavatory"—which was re-

---

This essay originally appeared in the *New York Review of Books*, March 15, 1984.

1. New York: Schocken, 1988.

fused. This incident is understandable only in the light of Housman's ferocious defense of his privacy and the fact that in 1934 (and this may still, for all I know, be true) the older buildings of the Cambridge colleges were barbarously short of toilet facilities. In St. John's I spent my first year in rooms that were more than one hundred and fifty yards of unheated corridor and staircase away from the nearest available plumbing.

One important aspect of his privacy Housman guarded to the last—"Others have held their tongues and so can I." It seems impossible to decide, on the basis of existing evidence (and there does not seem to be more to come), whether he was ever a practicing homosexual; whether he ever tasted, as E. M. Forster hoped he did, of the "stolen waters he recommended so ardently to others," though in fact the poem Forster refers to was not published until after Housman's death. Many critics and at least one biographer have leaped to conclusions on this point; Page, though he regards Housman's illicit pleasures as more likely than unlikely, is admirably judicious and states firmly that "we cannot give them a local habitation and a name without crossing the ill-guarded frontier separating biography from romantic fiction." The Venetian gondolier Andrea (who had only one eye); the companion on motor trips in France who was "amiable . . . though not of much education"; the collection of pornography (including Swinburne's *Whippingham Papers*)—none of this is hard evidence for physical indulgence of Housman's undoubted homosexual bent. The most suggestive item is a document dating (probably) from May 1932; it is (according to Page), "a list of fifteen consecutive days of the week . . . ; beside each is written a numeral, the only numerals employed being 0, 3, 9, and 10; beside all those except the ones with a 'zero' notation is a French noun indicating some masculine avocation or attribute—sailor, boxer, dancer, negro. (In one case *danseur* is queried.) In the margin the phrase '10 in 15 days' is written." Page finds it "difficult to accept" the conclusion of an earlier biographer—that these notations "include 'a note of the price paid on various occasions' for the services of male prostitutes" (and indeed if that is what the figures indicate one wonders about the chaps that got only 3),[2] but the entry does bring to mind an item in Auden's 1929 journal—a list of names headed "Boys had. Germany 1929."

2. In letters to the *New York Review* some other explanations of these numbers were offered. Professor Hugh Lloyd-Jones also rejects the idea that "these numbers

About the homosexual fixation of Housman's emotional nature, however, there is no doubt at all; his life was set on its strange course by an apparently unrequited passion for his athletic fellow student Moses Jackson. After their Oxford days, Housman, a junior clerk now in the Patent Office, roomed with Jackson and his brother in London; after three years he moved away to rooms of his own. Jackson left for India to become principal of a college at Karachi and returned two years later to marry; Housman was not invited to the wedding and learned of it only after Jackson returned with his bride to India. He retired in 1911, but moved with his family to Canada, where he died of cancer in 1923. We have no letters of Housman to Jackson (though his last letter to his dying friend exists—unpublished—in private hands) and no letters from Jackson.

But Housman himself made no secret of the fact that Jackson was "the man who had more influence on my life than anyone else," and the tortured repression of his love, the pain caused by its rejection, and the private revolt against the society that condemned it are themes easily recognizable in his poetry, even in the two books published in his lifetime. This was apparent to kindred spirits long before the poems published by Laurence Housman after his brother's death made it clear for all to see. Lowes Dickinson, for example, wrote to congratulate Housman on *Last Poems* (1922): "What they say appeals to something very deep in me. And deep calls to deep." And E. M. Forster, who "had loved *A Shropshire Lad* since Cambridge days," came to the conclusion that "the poems concealed a personal experience . . . the author had fallen in love with a man."

It is likely, though there is no evidence to prove it, that the psychic disruption caused by his discovery of his real feelings for Jackson had something to do with Housman's disastrous performance in "Greats"; Arnold and Newman both got Seconds and Auden a Third, but Housman actually failed and left Oxford without a degree. The news that his father was dying undoubtedly played its part and so perhaps did his contempt for the approach to scholarship represented

---

represent the price paid to each person. . . . surely they tell us what mark—you would say grade—Housman gave him, the maximum being ten." and Mr. Alan Bell, of Oxford, suggests that the figures refer "to the time of day. . . . Whatever Housman did with the *danseur, boxeur, marin, Niçois* or others, he did it either after luncheon or after dinner, at 3 P.M. or 9 to 10 P.M."

by "Greats." (Of Jowett, the declared enemy of "specialized research," he was later to write in his notebook: "Jowett's Plato: the best translation of a Greek philosopher which has ever been executed by a person who understood neither philosophy nor Greek.") Whatever the reasons, Housman went into the examination rooms totally unprepared.

He was of course not the first nor the last to do so. Many an Oxford or Cambridge undergraduate has spent the pleasant spring months of his last year idling on the river, staying up late with friends, and staving off the awful prospect of disaster with apocalyptic visions—the world may come to an end, war may break out. When the examination date came and the world was still there and at peace, some few made away with themselves, as Housman apparently was tempted to do. "For me, one flowery Maytime," he wrote later, "It went so ill that I / Designed to die." But most have managed to scrape a Second or a Third by filling sheet after sheet with shameless guesswork and barely relevant material cunningly combined with what solid stuff they could summon from the well of memory.

Housman didn't even try. On some papers he wrote "practically nothing." "Short and scrappy . . . practically no answers at all," was how one of the examiners later remembered his philosophy papers. "Proud and angry dust" are the words he used much later to describe human nature, and the adjectives certainly describe his own character. He was too proud, too angry to make the ignominious effort that would have allowed the examiners to give him a Third and his degree. It was, as Page aptly puts it, "a complete act of academic suicide." He spent the next fifty years vindicating that pride by scholarly publications that made him, in Auden's phrase, "the leading classic of his generation" (and not just of his own) and venting his anger, in deadly concentrated invective that made the verbose scurrilities of Milton and Salmasius look like child's play, on fellow scholars who presumed to exercise his chosen profession of textual critic and failed to live up to his Olympian standards.

"The intellect of man is forced to choose / Perfection of the life, or of the work," said Yeats; in Housman's case perfection of the life was denied him by the nature and object of his love but there can have been few men who devoted themselves with such fanatical energy to the alternative. The next fifty years seem in fact somewhat unrewarding from a biographer's point of view: ten years in London working as a clerk by day and in his spare time writing classical papers which won him an international reputation; nineteen years of teaching and scholarly publication at University College, London; twenty-four years as Kennedy Professor of Latin at Cambridge—the only relief from unrelenting hard work occasional summer trips to Europe.

And yet, as Page points out, "Housman's biographer cannot complain of a shortage of material." The trouble is that much of this material is either suspect or trivial. "Only the most naive," Page goes on, "will treat with uniform respect all that has appeared in print, or be duped by the delusion of total recall enjoyed by so many memoirists and retailers of anecdote." His own intention is "to bring into play a sympathetic skepticism" and this he does with skill and discretion. As for the trivia, his policy is "anti-inflationary"; too many modern biographies, he complains, are "dropsical with fact, fat books out of which slim books are seeking to escape." He has tried "never to give a fact simply for the sake of giving a fact" and though he fears that he may have sometimes, though not deliberately, broken his own rule, the reader will be hard put to find any instances. Page's account of Housman's life—one chapter on the Patent Office years, "a ten-year exile from the academic world"; one on University College and two on Cambridge—is a remarkable achievement.

There are still some dark areas (we have very few letters, for example, from the period before Housman assumed the professorship at University College), but Page's Housman is a fully convincing portrait of an extraordinary man, who combined two talents so opposed that if we did not know that the formidable editor of Juvenal, Lucan, and Manilius was also the poet of *A Shropshire Lad*, we would hardly have guessed the truth. This account of his life, his "long fools'-errand to the grave," supersedes all previous biographies, not only because "most of the material in this book has never appeared in print and some of it has been available only recently" but also because Page writes with the critical acumen, wit, and elegance the subject imperiously demands.

Page's subtitle, "A Critical Biography," is justified not only because he is critical of the sources in his biographical section but also because he devotes more than a quarter of his book to a discussion of

Housman's work, both the scholarship and the poetry. Though he is quite right in his claim that "it is possible to exaggerate the arcane nature" of Housman's scholarly pursuits and, further, that "the nature of textual criticism is more easily grasped by the non-specialist than that of, say, nuclear physics," he is of necessity dependent in his assessment of Housman as a classical scholar on the pronouncements of experts. He ends his Chapter 7, "The Scholar," with a quotation, four and a half pages long, from the balanced appreciation written for the centenary of Housman's birth by Shackleton Bailey, whose work on the letters of Cicero, on Propertius and Horace, is more than sufficient warrant for his authority in this matter. Shackleton Bailey sees Housman's main achievement as the reversal of a scholarly trend toward defending manuscript readings at any cost, torturing meaning and coherence out of unlikely phrases, "construing, as the phrase goes, through a brick wall."

But what Bailey admires most is "Housman's unremitting, passionate zeal to see each of the innumerable problems in his text not as others had presented it or as he might have preferred it to appear but exactly as it was." On Housman's notorious ferocity in print he points out that it was not directed against minor errors. "His *saeva indignatio* was nearly always reserved for pretentious incompetence, intellectual fraud, meanness of spirit, and that compound of the three which makes men band together, with cries of mutual encouragement, round a fashionable totem." And he adds that Housman's denunciations were hardly ever wrong. "Robinson Ellis *had*, among scholars, the intellect of an idiot child, Francken *was* a born blunderer, marked cross from the womb and perverse, van Wageningen's commentary *does* most resemble a magpie's nest."

No one doubts Housman's eminence as a scholar and a textual critic but some have complained of the narrow focus of his interests and in particular of his decision to devote thirty years of his time to an edition of Manilius, an Augustan poet whom Housman himself called "tedious." Page dismisses Auden's charge—"deliberately he chose the dryasdust"—as "missing the point about Housman's scholarship in his anxiety to make a point about his masochism." But the fact that "an editor of Manilius was certain to suffer less competition, and less anxiety during a long-term undertaking that he might be beaten to the post" can hardly have been the reason for Housman's choice of Manilius; if ever a man had no fear of competition in his chosen field, it was Housman, whose contempt for his rivals was bottomless. Page quotes Housman telling Robert Bridges that Manilius "writes on astronomy and astrology without knowing either. My interest in him is purely technical" and adds his own comment, that strong literary interest can be a positive handicap for a textual critic.

That is a formula worthy of Housman himself, but it goes too far. The textual critic must in the last analysis fall back, as Housman never tires of emphasizing, on judgment not technique, and this judgment is literary: it is, or should be, informed by an almost instinctive grasp of what an author would be likely to write, based on an intimate acquaintance with every aspect of his style, meter, and content. And there is in fact no reason in the world why the textual critic should prefer the second-rate author to work on; Richard Bentley's great work was an edition of Horace. When Housman wrote to his London colleague and friend Arthur Platt: "If you prefer Aeschylus to Manilius you are no true scholar; you must be deeply tainted with literature," he was indeed speaking with "characteristic irony" but he was probably joking, too (all his other letters to Platt were destroyed by Mrs. Platt after her husband's death as "too Rabelaisian").

The fact is that before he accepted the Latin chair at University College his critical faculties had been brought to bear on some of the greatest poets in the canon; almost one-third of the 421 pages of the first volume of his classical papers (1882–97) is devoted to Aeschylus, Sophocles, Euripides, Horace, Ovid, and Propertius. And these papers are much more than "purely technical." Though few of the emendations he proposes appear in modern texts, his diagnostic flair is superb. He angrily reproved those who compared him to his idol Bentley but his work on the text of the Greek tragedians brings to mind his words about Bentley, who could "strike his finger on the place and say *thou ailest here, and here.*" When I think of what Housman might have done for the improvement and elucidation of our texts of Aeschylus, Sophocles, and Euripides instead of devoting thirty years to the verses of an astrological hack, I am tempted to use his own words against him: "The time lost, the tissues wasted . . . are in our brief irreparable life disheartening to think of."[3]

---

3. Professor Lloyd-Jones, who is preparing a new Oxford text of Sophocles, disagrees vehemently (*New York Review of Books*, June 14, 1984). Housman's notes on Greek tragic texts, he writes, "are learned and ingenious but they are not very

"Scholarship," Housman said in his 1911 inaugural lecture at Cambridge, "is not literary criticism; and of the duties of a Latin chair literary criticism forms no part." In the Cambridge of 1911, as Page points out, this was not so strange a statement as it would be if made today. Academic literary criticism was at that time, some years before Leavis and Richards began to transform the English School at Cambridge, "no more than a hazy, undisciplined attempt to communicate 'appreciation' or aesthetic response"—Quiller-Couch's vapid outpourings on Shakespeare, for example.

Though he rejected literary criticism as part of his duties, Housman claimed to have great respect for literary critics but he believed that they were hard to find, appearing, he suggested later in the same lecture, "once in a century, or once in two centuries." The eighteenth century had seen the birth of a literary critic, Lessing, who was also a classical scholar. Such a "purely accidental conjunction" was not likely to occur again soon—"and if so early a century as the twentieth is to witness it in another person, all I know is that I am not he." This may be false modesty (one never knows with Housman); Page finds that though "an unwilling critic he was not an inept one" and cites an interesting judgment on Addison's prose. But Housman's comments on modern writers present a different picture. He advised his friend and publisher Grant Richards against publishing Proust: "I have not finished Proust's book but I have read enough to form the opinion that an English translation would not sell." He found little to admire in Hopkins: "His manner strikes me as deliberately adopted to compensate by strangeness for the lack of pure merit." On the other hand he pronounced Masefield's feeble plays (*The Tragedy of Nan and Other Plays*) "well worth reading; they contain a lot that is very good." And he thought Edna St. Vincent Millay "the best living American poet" and her inane sonnet sequence "Fatal Interview" "mighty good."

Such verdicts are perhaps not surprising from a poet who admired Matthew Arnold above all and praised Coventry Patmore and, later, Blunden, Blunt, and Bridges; "we must remember," Page writes, "that he was a late-Victorian poet," and he cites Philip Larkin's "tentative conclusion" that "perhaps there is more of a mid-Victorian in Housman than is generally realized." It is all the more astonishing

---

often *right*." I defer to this judgment, but still think Housman could have found an author worthier of his talents than Manilius.

that in the best of his poetry there is nothing old-fashioned; its dominant note, stoic acceptance of a faulty if not malevolent universe, rings as true today as when he first sounded it.

There was, inevitably, an initial reaction against the widespread popularity of his poetry. Even before Housman's death Ezra Pound had opened fire with a typically slashing article in the *Criterion;* Housman had not been dead a month when Cyril Connolly published a devastating assessment in the *New Statesman.* Conrad Aiken, David Daiches, and Edith Sitwell among others all added their voices to the chorus of denigration; Orwell and Auden admitted the power of Housman's enchantments but thought them effective only on the young. The wheel has since come full circle. Page points out that the 1979 edition of *The Oxford Book of Quotations* (the first substantial revision since 1941) includes almost twice as many passages from Housman as the previous edition; it may be added that it contains ninety citations from Housman's verse as against ninety-seven from T. S. Eliot, seventy from W. B. Yeats, sixty-nine from Auden, and fifty-three from Hardy.

Page explains his decision to separate the detailed discussion of Housman as a poet from the biographical chapters, a decision "not lightly taken." The "biographer's dream . . . to integrate the life and work so successfully that the latter can be seen and felt as flowing naturally from the process of living" is an unattainable ideal in the case of Housman, "for whom art was separate from daily life, a consciously different, secret activity, running in quite another direction from his public existence." In any case, it is impossible to date many of the poems, and there are some that were started early and completed late. An example of the pitfalls that await the incautious literary historian is the exquisite poem "Parta Quies," which reads like an epitaph for Jackson or for Housman himself, and in which one critic saw signs of "mature style"; it was printed first in an Oxford magazine in 1879, when Housman was twenty years old. But Page does not really need to apologize for his separate treatment of the poems: for such a procedure he had an august model in Samuel Johnson, whose classic *Lives of the Poets* deal first with the life and then move on to a critical assessment of the works.

Page's short but masterly analysis of Housman's themes and diction uncovers a poet very different from the sentimental romantic dismissed by the critics of the decades that followed his death: a poet who "wrote from an urgent personal need to find expression for the inexpressible." Page quotes with approval one dissentient voice in the critical chorus—John Peale Bishop, who wrote in 1940: "There is always something that is not clear, something not brought into the open, something that is left in doubt." This is not so true of course of the poems Housman did not publish in his lifetime. In some of them—"He would not stay for me," for example, or "Because I liked you better / Than suits a man to say"—the real situation has what Page calls "the immediacy of a diary entry . . . it is preserved in the memory like an old photograph; a perfectly shaped monument to that moment." In other poems—"Oh, were he and I together / Shipmates on the fleeted main," for example—"the circumstantial world," as Page puts it, "has undergone a dreamlike transformation," though "the code is not hard to decipher." In some, in fact, the message is almost in the clear, as in the bitter, beautiful poem that begins "Crossing alone the nighted ferry" and ends with Housman's assessment of his own lifelong devotion to Jackson as well as his final declaration of independence: ". . . the true sick-hearted slave, / Expect him not in the just city / And free land of the grave."

But in the two volumes published in his lifetime (1896 and 1922) Housman "objectifies certain preoccupations in order to be able in his poems to work out problems and attitudes . . . that he was unable or unwilling to communicate to anyone in direct and literal terms." He was not, Page claims, a "poet of nature and landscape," not even a "regional poet" (he insisted he did not know Shropshire well): "his real landscapes are of the heart." His themes are death, exile, and love, and to present these themes "by impersonation" he creates "certain recurring figures or roles of which the most prominent are the soldier, the lover, the rustic, the exile and the criminal."

Page's brilliant exploration of the way these figures are exploited, to express by "indirection" the poet's own "unuttered, unutterable anxieties and yearnings," is a convincing demonstration of Housman's true stature as a poet, one whose best work derives its strength from a "quality of controlled passion—an intensity held in check by lexical precision and the formal discipline of verse." If Housman's ghost could return to read this sensitive, subtle, and enlightening exposition, he might well temper the severity of his strictures on literary critics. But he would also be delighted to find that printers, like scribes, are blunderers still and that one of his most beautiful stanzas, cited expressly for that reason, is disfigured by a hideous misprint which renders a line unintelligible. Readers who fancy themselves as textual critics may try their hand at emending "On acres of the seeded grasses / The changing burnish beaves" before checking the text in *Last Poems XL*.

Siegfried Sassoon

The European war of 1914–18 was not only the end of an era; it was also, as Paul Fussell demonstrated in his brilliant analysis of its literature and legacy, *The Great War and Modern Memory*, a catastrophe that has haunted the Western imagination ever since. The apocalyptic visions of Verdun, the Somme, and Passchendaele were stamped indelibly on the minds and disturbed the dreams of the soldiers who had fought there; they weighed heavily also on the spirits of the young men who were granted a last-minute reprieve by the unexpected German collapse in the last half of 1918. The senior schoolboys who had expected to spend 1919 in the trenches as short-lived subalterns celebrated their escape in riotous parties (it was the generation of Evelyn Waugh and the Bright Young Things); and they wondered how, if the war had gone on, they would have measured up—like Christopher Isherwood and his friends who (as he tells the story in *Lions and Shadows*) devised dangerous trials of skill and daring, on fast motorcycles for example, to serve as The Test. But the next generation, the war babies of 1914–18, was obsessed by the Great War as well; its literature was the preferred reading of their adolescence and it was the war that furnished their earliest memories. My own date from 1917; I was barely three years old. I remember a Lee-Enfield rifle leaning up against a haversack, gas mask, and helmet in our living room; my father was on twenty-four-hour leave from Flanders on his way to Italy, where his regiment was to stiffen the Italian front, which had crumbled at Caporetto. And I remember too being carried across a London street in bright moonlight to the shelter of an underground taxi garage; in the sky the long arms of the searchlights hunted for zeppelins. My generation grew up treasuring such memories, but even if we had wanted to ignore the Great War, school would not have let us. Every eleventh of November we stood silent in class for

This essay originally appeared in *Grand Street* 2, no. 4 (Summer 1983).

two minutes; every Empire Day we waved Union Jacks and sang "Land of Hope and Glory" to Elgar's tune; and every Friday we turned up in class in khaki uniforms and the afternoon was devoted to the activities of the Cadet Corps. The boys became troops and the masters turned into officers, which many of them had in fact been in what it was fashionable to refer to as "the late unpleasantness."

As we read the memoirs and poems of the war's survivors we were numbed by the appalling tales of mass slaughter and by the blind folly of the generals who ordered it. Naturally we adopted the standpoint of the rebels. "My God, Joynson-Hicks" was, at my school, a code phrase expressing amazement at the latest idiocy of those in authority; it was the beginning of a sentence attributed to Field Marshal Sir Douglas Haig, commander of the British forces in France. As his horse skidded in the mud of his Headquarters courtyard, well to the rear of the Passchendaele offensive, he is supposed to have asked his aide: "My God, Joynson-Hicks, did I really send men to fight in this?" In fact, the speaker was one General Kiggell, an officer on Haig's staff; he was in a car, not on a horse, and his interlocutor's name is unknown. But myth is more potent than fact and we were not alone in our belief that the words were Haig's. And in any case, the point of the story, true or not, was all too well taken: the nightmare slaughter in the mud had been organized by generals who had little or no idea of conditions at the front.

For us, the "Staff" was the villain of the piece but our heroes were not the pacifists—Bertie Russell in Brixton Prison or the Bloomsbury crowd, obsessively intent (as the Woolf diaries and correspondence reveal) on keeping themselves and all their precious acquaintances exempt from the fate of their generation. We admired the men whose protest against the war came from direct experience of it: Wilfred Owen and Robert Graves, Henri Barbusse and Georges Duhamel. But above all, for the direct rage of his war poems and the hallucinatory clarity and deceptive simplicity of his *Memoirs of an Infantry Officer,* we admired Siegfried Sassoon.

Owen's war poetry was the voice of the tragic Muse—"the poetry," he wrote himself, "is in the pity"; we knew and loved those poems—"Exposure," "Strange Meeting"—but more to our taste as schoolboys, and purpose as adolescent rebels, was the angry satiric note Sassoon was master of. In *Siegfried's Journey,* written many years later, he speaks of his surprise at discovering that he had "a hitherto unpredictable talent for satirical epigram. Nothing I had written before 1916 showed any symptom of this development. It was as if I had suddenly found myself to be an expert boxer without having undergone any training." He could not "ascertain that his method was modelled on any other writer. . . . I merely chanced on the device of composing two or three harsh, peremptory, and colloquial stanzas with a knock-out blow in the last line." For the English reading public of 1917 these last-line surprises must indeed have been a jab to the solar plexus; "The One-Legged Man," for example, looks with joy and satisfaction at the landscape, his home, and his wife, and thinks: "Thank God they had to amputate." Nor was much comfort to be derived from the bitter irony of "Does it Matter?"—"Does it matter?— losing your sight? . . . / There's such splendid work for the blind; / And people will always be kind." For us, growing up as the twenties turned into the thirties, and sensing, more keenly with every passing year, that our Friday afternoon exercises in khaki were one day to turn into the real thing, the satiric poems were of more immediate appeal, especially those that made a ferocious onslaught on the complacent acceptance of mass slaughter at the front by staff officers safe in the rear. "The General": ". . . 'cheery old card,' grunted Harry to Jack . . . / But he did for them both with his plan of attack." Or "Base Details": "If I were fierce, and bald, and short of breath, / I'd live with scarlet Majors at the Base, / And speed glum heroes up the line to death." We saw ourselves as the troops and our master officers as the staff; this was deplorably unjust, but adolescence is not noted for justice in its attitude toward the older generation. We even identified ourselves in fantasy with the returning soldiers who in "Fight to a Finish" fix bayonets at the victory parade and turn on the "Yellow-Pressmen . . . At last the boys had found a cushy job" while their lieutenant takes his "trusty bombers . . . to clear those Junkers out of Parliament." The poem served us as an apocalyptic vision—a schoolboy massacre of the elders of the tribe—which many years later I was astonished, and by this time appalled, to see spectacularly staged in the last scenes of Lindsay Anderson's *If*. We were of course to feel Sassoon's anger genuinely not as schoolboys but as soldiers, for it is true of every war that much as he may fear and perhaps even hate the enemy opposing him, the combat infantryman broods with deep and bitter resentment over the enormous number of people in his rear who sleep safely at night. One of Barbusse's squad in *Le feu* comes back from leave in the rear unable to say anything but "*Y en a trop*"—"There's too many of 'em."

Later we read Sassoon's prose, the three volumes that described the experiences of a fictional "Sherston" from boyhood up to the Armistice of 1918; *Memoirs of a Fox-Hunting Man, Memoirs of an Infantry Officer,* and *Sherston's Progress.* These books are a remarkable exercise in the autobiographical mode. Sherston speaks throughout in the first person and the experiences are clearly Sassoon's, yet some significant distortions of fact justify a view that Sherston is enough of a fiction to enable its creator to write about himself without self-consciousness; to cite one striking instance, Sherston is not a poet. This deliberate distancing of "I" from self is reinforced by the self-deprecating humor natural to a man looking back over more than a decade at the thoughts and actions of his youth. The result is a narrative in which one never for a moment feels that Sherston is Sassoon putting himself in the best possible light; the narrative has both the compulsive credibility of fiction at its best and the authenticity of an eyewitness account.

His *Memoirs of a Fox-Hunting Man* carries the epigraph, "This happy breed of men, this little world," and it does indeed confine itself, for three-quarters of its length, within the narrow limits of the literary territory staked out by Robert Smith Surtees. The reader who is not a native will have to get used to such unfamiliar properties as loose-boxes, main-earths, point-to-points, dog-foxes, main-rides, and a parrot that its master has taught to ejaculate, "Tear 'im and eat 'im." The book charts the stages of a young man's initiation into the tribal rites of the English country gentry; hesitant and shy at first, he makes his way, by his headlong recklessness as a rider, to victory in the race for the Colonel's Cup and wins the friendship of a young Master of Hounds whom he idolizes. This is a world in which women rarely make an appearance and never an impression; in which, apparently, nobody has to work for a living (Sherston himself, like Sassoon, lives off an inheritance); in which the events of the greater world, in London, in Paris and Berlin, might just as well be happening on another planet as the riders jump the fences and the cricket match goes endlessly on in the long English summer afternoons. These chapters are an elegiac evocation of that now unimaginable world "before the war"; Sassoon might be saying, substituting his own date for Talleyrand's 1789, that those who had not lived in the years before 1914 could have no idea of *les plaisirs de la vie*. London, Paris, and Berlin, however, do interrupt the game; the last words of the book see Sherston in the trenches just before dawn. "I remembered that it was Easter Sunday. Standing in that dismal ditch, I could find no consolation in the thought that Christ was risen. I sploshed back to the dug-out to call the others up for 'stand to.'"

In *Memoirs of an Infantry Officer* Sherston struggles to achieve recognition among soldiers as he once did among fox hunters. "Six years before," writes Sassoon, "I had been ambitious of winning races because that had seemed a significant way of demonstrating my equality with my contemporaries. And now I wanted to make the World War serve a similar purpose, for if only I could get a Military Cross I should feel comparatively safe and confident." Get it he does, for "conspicuous gallantry during a raid on the enemy trenches" during which "he remained for one and a half hours under rifle and bomb fire collecting and bringing in our wounded." Those are the words of Sassoon's official citation, which are not reproduced in *Memoirs of an Infantry Officer*, where Sherston gives an unrhetorical account of a pointless, badly prepared raid of which "the only result" was "two killed and ten wounded"; one of the dead was Corporal O'Brien, whom Sherston had made a second dangerous trip across no-man's-land to rescue. The decoration was officially awarded on June 30, the eve of the great Somme offensive of 1916, a battle in which the British casualties reached the gruesome number of sixty thousand in one day. Sherston goes into the battle still untouched, feeling, for example, "no sympathy" for a fellow officer who was stunned into terrified paralysis by the barrage; he distinguishes himself by an insane single-handed bombing raid on a forward enemy trench. But he records the look of that disastrous battle (here Sherston is reproducing Sassoon's diaries), the blind movements of the troops stumbling innocently into deadly fire—"many walked casually across with sloped arms"—and as his company is relieved by inexperienced New Army troops his mood sobers. Sassoon looks back at Sherston. "Visualizing that forlorn crowd of khaki figures . . . I can believe that I saw then, for the first time, how blindly war destroys its victims. The sun had gone down on my own reckless brandishings, and I understood the doomed condition of these half-trained civilians who had been sent up to attack the Wood."

As the attacks grind remorselessly and bloodily on and Sherston, after a spell of illness in England, returns to take part in the Arras fighting of 1917, disenchantment with the war builds up until, returned wounded to England in 1917, he makes his famous statement, which is read out in the House of Commons and printed in *The Times.* "I am making this statement as an act of wilful defiance of military authority, because I believe that the War is being deliberately prolonged by those who have the power to end it. . . . I believe that this War, upon which I entered as a war of defense and liberation, has now become a war of aggression and conquest." Instead of haling him before a court-martial the army authorities diagnosed shell shock and sent him to a rehabilitation center in Scotland where he was treated by the man who became his father figure, W. H. R. Rivers; it was in Scotland, as we learn from the later, autobiographical *Siegfried's Journey,* that Sassoon made the acquaintance of Wilfred Owen, whose poems he later edited (this is not mentioned in *Memoirs,* since "Sherston," as Sassoon puts it in *Journey,* "was denied the complex advantage of being a soldier poet"). Eventually, rated fit for duty, he was sent to the Middle East and then returned to France in 1918, to be wounded for a second time; *Sherston's Progress* ends with a visit from Rivers to his hospital bed in London.

The publication of *Siegfried's Journey* in 1945 cast a new retrospective light on the trilogy, especially the last part of it, for in this book Sassoon, writing in his own person, covers again the ground from 1916 to 1918 (and then carries the story on to 1920). This time he writes as a poet and discusses the composition of his poems, the reaction to their publication, the hardening of his resolve to make his protest. That protest was purely negative; he had no suggestion about what should be done to end the war; he spoke vaguely of "negotiations." But we now know that Germany would not have agreed to give up her hold on Belgium, an essential condition for Britain, and Sassoon himself, writing in 1945, says: "in light of subsequent events it is difficult to believe that a Peace negotiated in 1917 would have been permanent. I share the general opinion that nothing on earth would have prevented a recurrence of Teutonic aggressiveness."

Now, with the publication of *Diaries 1915–18,* edited and introduced by Rupert Hart-Davis,[1] we have a different kind of perspective

---

1. *Siegfried Sassoon: Diaries, 1915–1918, ed.* Rupert Hart-Davis. (London: Faber & Faber, 1980).

on the Sherston trilogy; these diaries are the raw material Sassoon drew on, adapted, rejected, or amplified as he looked back on the war after ten years of peace. Fussell, in the third chapter of his book, has revealed the "thematic architecture" that underlies "Sherston's" apparently artless narrative; Sassoon's diaries, written at white heat on the spot, enable us to see the architect at work. For the most part, in the trilogy he expands, especially by the addition of conversation; Sherston's account of his exploit in the Somme battle, a riveting four pages in *Memoirs,* covers less than a paragraph in the diary, which has no word of an essential feature of the later account, the death of Lance-Corporal Kendle. Sometimes, however, the diary is more vivid than the later account; Sassoon's first impressions have been toned down in Sherston's *Memoirs,* as in the description of the raid for which he won the M.C. When the Germans start to shoot down into the crater where O'Brien lies wounded and Sherston is trying to reach him, it is only in the diary that we can hear the authentic tone of the frontline soldier's indignation at what seems to be personal vindictiveness on the part of the enemy—"The bloody sods are firing down at me at point-blank range." One is reminded irresistibly of Joseph Heller's Captain Yossarian: "They're trying to kill me."

The persona of Sherston dictated the exclusion of poetry from the trilogy but the diaries are full of it; here we can see many of the poems in first draft, at the moment of composition, in their context— both those later published and some that appear to have remained buried in the diaries. Sometimes this context sheds light on poems that seemed ambiguous or puzzling. "The Kiss," for example, can be read as a romantic hymn to rifle and bayonet: "To these I turn, in these I trust—Brother Lead and Sister Steel." It was inspired, however, by an enthusiastic lecture-demonstration of bayonet fighting by "a great brawny Highland Major." Sassoon wanders off to the woods. "A pigeon cooed. Phrases from the bayonet lecture came back to me. . . . 'The bullet and the bayonet are brother and sister . . . get your bayonet into his kidneys; it'll go in as easy as butter. . . .' I told the trees what I had been hearing, but they hate steel. . . . And a blackbird's song cries aloud that April cannot understand what war means." This passage from the diary suggests that the ferocious wish for a successful bayonet thrust with which the poem concludes may be that of the Highland Major but is certainly not the poet's.

Sassoon speaks often of his own concerns as a poet. He was shown, for example, Robert Graves's manuscript poems—"some very bad, violent and repulsive. A few full of promise and real beauty." Later he passes startlingly prescient judgment: "a magical name for young poets in 1980, if only he survives this carnage." Unfortunately the diaries that would have told us of his friendship with Owen (recreated from memory in *Siegfried's Journey*) were lost (or were never written); the crucial period at the rehabilitation center which followed the publication of Sassoon's protest against the war is undocumented.

Poetry, however, was not the only side of Sassoon that was suppressed in Sherston; the war diaries reveal clearly enough that the poet's tenderest feelings were for those of his own sex. His references to women, in poetry as in prose, are few and generally contemptuous; "they are outside my philosophy," he told a questioner. His affection for some of his fellow officers is stronger than the normal bond between soldiers who have shared privation and danger and even than that which links English schoolboys. "So I wrote his name in chalk on the beech-tree stem, and left a rough garland of ivy there, and a yellow primrose for his yellow hair and kind grey eyes, my dear, my dear"—this is a lover's grief for a fallen comrade. And when he remarks of a private soldier, Jim Linthwaite, whom he sees working on a punishment detail in a blue jersey, "Something drew me to him when I saw him first . . . and I've loved him ever since (it is just as well he's not in my present company)," he shows a commendable self-knowledge. In the *Diaries 1920–22*[2] he carries on two affairs, one with "Gabriel," a painter, in England, another with "P.," a twenty-six-year-old man he had met in Rome in 1921 and with whom he travels to Italy in the last months of 1922. Both relationships are unsatisfactory; neither man is Sassoon's intellectual equal and perhaps the continual annoyance and the disappointment he expresses have something to do with the fact that he hands out quite large sums of money to both of them from time to time. The shallowness of the connection is apparent from the fact that they are interchangeable: "Gabriel will step into P.'s shoes for the winter."

The problem posed by his sexual orientation dominates most

---

2. *Siegfried Sassoon: Diaries, 1920–1922*, ed. Rupert Hart-Davis (London: Faber & Faber, 1981).

of the introspective passages of these diaries; it also furnishes a theme for "the masterpiece that I'll be writing five, ten, fifteen, or twenty years hence. . . . It is to be one of the stepping-stones across the raging (or lethargic) river of intolerance which divides creatures of my temperament from a free and unsecretive existence among their fellow-men. A mere self-revelation, however spontaneous and clearly-expressed, can never achieve as much as—well, imagine another *Madame Bovary* dealing with sexual inversion, a book that the world *must* recognize and learn to understand! . . . That such a book will be written, in English, I do not doubt. This century will produce it. May I live to read it, even though it be by another hand than mine." A few months later he thought that he had begun to write it himself; he had 13,500 words of a story he called his "Schumann Concerto"—"the biggest sustained effort" of his life. In the entry for June 9, he identifies it with the *Madame Bovary* of the earlier passage; he has already told us that the germ of it was the thought of "Jim Linthwaite and his blue jersey." But his later footnotes prick the bubble. The story was "overwritten and artificial in expression . . . no good at all." And on the prediction that this century will produce the "masterpiece" in question he wryly remarks, in a footnote added nineteen years later: "Nothing would surprise me now. But I am still awaiting the masterpiece. Homosexuality has become a bore; the intelligentsia have captured it." To which one is tempted to say, "Amen."

There are of course other matters discussed in these diaries: there are poems (many of which were to appear in the privately printed *Recreations*, an edition of seventy-five copies) and there are accounts of meetings with poets and writers—among them W. H. Davies, Edmund Blunden, Walter de la Mare, E. M. Forster and, above all, Hardy—that display the acute observation and the admirable style of the autobiographical writings. But too many of the entries are brief records of meetings, meals, concerts, visits to the theater. "If the ensuing pages are tedious and trivial . . . ," he says in the first entry; quite a few of them are. Many such items could have been omitted with no loss to the reader's understanding of the more interesting material. The diaries proper are preceded by five pages from a manuscript that was evidently designed to continue the autobiography from the point where *Siegfried's Journey* ended. It is admirably written and the reader's first reaction is to wish that he had finished the job instead of leaving the diary in its present state. But then, of course, we would not have had the frank revelations the diary contains. And, in spite of its occasional dry patches, it is an absorbing document.

But Sassoon's fame will always rest on his idyllic re-creation of his fox-hunting youth and his nightmare evocation of the war. And in the Second World War, though by that time I had not thought of him for years and did not even know whether he was still alive, I was suddenly and violently reminded of all that he had meant to me when I was young. In the spring of 1944 I took a bunch of officers, American, British, and French, out into the woods somewhere in Leicestershire for demolition training. We were all preparing to jump into occupied France when the invasion began, to arm and train the Maquisards and direct their activities along lines useful to the advancing Allied forces. When we reached a suitable clearing I instructed the class in the technique of cutting down trees with Primacord so as to make a roadblock; we wound up the proceedings with a demonstration of the smoke grenade. I lashed two of them to one of the newly created stumps and tied a cord to the pins; we all backed off well to leeward. As I pulled the pins I saw out of the corner of my eye a gray-brown shape streak at full speed across the edge of a wood. A few seconds later the clearing was invaded by baying hounds in full pursuit and at that precise moment the grenades detonated, enveloping the pack in an impenetrable cloud of gray-white smoke. With agonized yelps and barks the hounds ran in all directions as the smoke poured relentlessly out; above the noise of the hounds we could now hear horses whinnying and screaming, men shouting curses. As we stood speechless with astonishment at the unforeseen results of our military exercise, a horseman, in pink coat and black cap, came charging through the smoke screen, pulled up his red-eyed, coughing horse and roared at me: "What the bloody hell do you think you're doing?" Before I could answer (but what could I have said?) the horse bolted, out of control, and took its blaspheming rider with it. And I remember thinking: "Siegfried should have seen this."

W. H. Auden

Auden, says Randall Jarrell, "wrote, then, some of the strongest, strangest, and most original poetry that anyone has written in this century; when old men, dying in their beds, mumble something unintelligible to the nurse, it is some of these lines that they will be repeating." If so (for what they are mumbling might also be late Yeats), it will be, as Jarrell says, early Auden—poems written "at the beginning of the thirties." It is not that Auden's poetic vein was worked out by the time he settled in America; on the contrary, the New York years were richly productive and (though Jarrell had nothing but hard words for much of it) the quality of the later poetry would be more than enough to establish Auden's position as a major figure, even if it stood alone. But what he wrote and published in the 1930s was extraordinary, not only for its strength and strangeness, but also for its effect: it fired the imagination of a whole younger generation which had grown up with middle-class expectations only to find itself facing a devastated economy at home and the apparently irresistible rise of Fascist regimes abroad. For the industrial workers, especially the three million unemployed, the situation was desperate, but even for the young graduates of the universities, most avenues were closed. I left Cambridge in 1936 with a B.A. in classics; I still remember my interview with the University Employment Board. "You have, of course, put your name down with Gabbitas and Thring?" was the first thing I was asked. Gabbitas and Thring—an authentic name, though it sounds like something from *Bleak House* (it appears in Auden's *Letter to Lord Byron* as "Rabbits-arse and String")—was the agency that placed graduates of the older universities at boys' boarding schools teetering on the verge of bankruptcy (like Auden's school at Helensburgh, "the headmaster partially blind, his wife growing gradually mad in a canvas shelter in the garden") or wildly remote and run by the headmaster's wife (like the one where Evelyn Waugh swam out

This essay originally appeared in *Grand Street* 1, no. 2 (Winter 1982).

to sea to put an end to a miserable existence but ran into a school of jellyfish and turned back). I could not face the prospect of teaching classics in a boys' school and said so; the ensuing silence was broken by a hesitant voice which asked whether I had ever considered taking Holy Orders. I had not. And the third member of the board, pulling at his white mustache, said, in a hearty tone: "What about the army?" They promised to get in touch with me "if anything suitable should turn up."

For those of us who left school for the university or the university for the real world in the early thirties, Auden was our prophet crying in the wilderness. He could express, in the meters of Burns and with the savage indignation of Swift, our rage against the loud-voiced, servile apologists of the so-called National Government—"A host of columbines and pathics / Who show the poor by mathematics / In their defence / That wealth and poverty are merely / Mental pictures, so that clearly, / Every tramp's a landlord really / In mind-events." He could evoke, in images drawn from some dark well of the unconscious, our inchoate fears—"When the green field comes off like a lid / Revealing what were much better hid, / Unpleasant." He gave us love songs for an unstable time—"Lay your sleeping head, my love / Human on my faithless arm" (though not all of us realized that both the participants in this idyll were male). He wrote the pastorals of the dead industrial landscape: "our city—with the byres of poverty down to / The river's edge," "harvests rotting in the valleys," "Smokeless chimneys, damaged bridges, rotting wharves and choked canals." Above all, he gave us images and mythic prototypes for what we saw ahead—the war that we feared was inevitable and the struggles that would be needed if the world was ever to be set right: the sentry, the spy, the conqueror, the frontier, control of the passes. Even the obscurity of so many of his lines was, in our eyes, no defect but a virtue; it marked the verses as the proper vehicle of dark prophecies and also infuriated the elders of the tribe. This poetry was ours: the word suited to the time. The *kairos*, to use Auden's title for a later poem, had found its *logos*.

It turned out that we were "wrong from the start." The voice we took to be that of a poet committed to public causes, spokesman of a critical and radical generation, was powered not by social conscience or devotion to a political ideal, but by purely private anxiety and anguish, stemming from what the other poet the dying old man might be mumbling called "the foul rag-and-bone-shop of the heart." Though Auden was the unacknowledged legislator and unappointed laureate of our generation, who celebrated in impressive odes unofficial heroes—Yeats, Freud, Henry James—he meant exactly what he said in the epigraph to *The Orators:* "Private faces in public places / Are wiser and nicer / Than public faces in private places." His only connection with Communism was a title, "A Communist to Others," attached to a poem beginning "Comrades"; he later suppressed the title and changed the first word to "Brothers." He was not even a Socialist; in fact the various visions of the just city that emerged from his early writings are dim prospects which seem to owe more to D. H. Lawrence than to Karl Marx. And he was never for one moment bothered by the problem which gnawed at the conscience of English left-wing intellectuals all through the period: personal and social relationships with the working class, the focus of Orwell's abrasive and typically honest brooding in the second part of *The Road to Wigan Pier.* Auden's only contacts with the workers seem to have been commercial sex transactions with the unemployed Berlin youth—"I like sex and Pieps likes money; it's a good exchange." He was thus exemplifying, in a literal fashion its author could hardly have foreseen, Marx's famous dictum that capitalism had "put an end to all . . . idyllic relations and left no other bond between man and man than . . . callous cash payment."

Edward Mendelson, in the first chapter of his *Early Auden,*[1] presents what must be accepted as the definitive statement on the youthful poems and their reception.

> Like Byron, he became famous in his early twenties. Like Byron, he became famous for a style he later renounced. . . . The poems were taken as fragments of an activist allegory whose key, though hidden, really did exist. Auden's readers, while agreeing in this view, divided into two hostile camps: those who complained that the key was a private myth or private joke reserved for a coterie of cronies and insiders, and those who felt *they* were the insiders . . . and proceeded to fill the gaps in his broken pattern with their own political and psychological enthusiasms. . . . Readers hailed or denounced him as a spokesman; he never wrote as one.

1. New York: Viking, 1981.

All this should have been clear by the end of the decade, but it was not. I remember a poetry reading in New York City, some time early in 1939, where Auden's rendering of "Our hunting fathers" drew enthusiastic applause from the largely left-wing audience; what they were saluting was the echo of Lenin in the final lines—"to hunger, work illegally, / And be anonymous"—with no inkling of what Mendelson rightly calls the "dire statements" of this "very pessimistic text" which is Auden's "darkest and most compressed statement of the way we really live—abandoned by Eros to our own devices." What should have alerted Auden's hearers was his enthusiastic reading of a poem by Kipling, "The Gods of the Copybook Headings," a poem which could justifiably be subtitled "Barry Goldwater's Hymn"; it traces the law of fang and claw from the Ice Age down to the present (a historical survey which may be the model for the opening sections of *Spain* and *In Time of War*) to assert the necessity for hard work, individual initiative and a fat defense budget, with side swipes at the graduated income tax ("robbing selected Peter to pay for collective Paul") and the Welfare State (". . . and the brave new world begins / When all men are paid for existing and no man must pay for his sins"). Perhaps the audience's failure to read this plain signal was due to its unfamiliarity with Auden's exotic accent and delivery: the voice of a half-mad Oxfordshire curate with occasional notes suggestive of a sheep in extreme distress.

Mendelson, who, as Auden's literary executor, reedited the poems written before 1941 in *The English Auden* (he restored the original versions and included whole poems Auden had decided to suppress), has now, in *Early Auden*, explicated them in magisterial fashion, setting them firmly in their literary and biographical context, elucidating their notorious obscurity with new insights based not only on unpublished material in Auden's papers but also on fresh, perceptive analysis of texts, prose as well as verse, which have not been given their due attention. One of those reprinted in *The English Auden* is "Writing," an essay which Auden "prepared for a children's encyclopedia early in 1932." As Mendelson remarks, its context may explain why it has been neglected in the critical literature. It is a remarkable document which not only "offers a premature exposition of the central themes of structuralist literary theory and its successors," but also announces "three elements" which "form an inseparable cluster in Auden's early poems—the unbridged gulf, the lost wholeness, the threat of violence."

Mendelson pursues these main themes through the enigmatic poems of the early years, as he traces Auden's journey from attempts to "find the abstract language that would be appropriate to the private acts of the mind" to the search for "the different language that might constitute a group." But the struggle to break out of loneliness resulted, to begin with, in the most disconcerting of his early poems, *The Orators*, which is, as Mendelson puts it, "an account of everything a group ought not to be." This work certainly has a "pungency and extravagance that he never equalled," but even Mendelson's sympathetic and sensitive reading, drawing on Auden's own discussions in letters and in print, fails to make it any more lucid than it seemed when it appeared in 1931; it still reads, in Mendelson's own phrase, "like an expressionist autobiography." Nevertheless, this is by far the most revealing discussion of *The Orators* that has yet appeared, and the chapters covering the poems written (and unfinished) up to June 1933 are rich in persuasive readings of Auden's search for "a poetic language of choice and community." They are also invaluable for their discussion of unfinished and unpublished work, especially what Auden called his "epic": two-fifths of a projected three-thousand-line poem which "took its outline from Dante—a guided spiritual journey through darkness into light—and its verse from Langland" and would have been an "anatomy of modern England."

Mendelson chooses June 1933 as a watershed (Part Two is headed "The Two Worlds, June 1933–January 1939") because of the "vision of *agape*" (as Auden later characterized it) which inspired the poem beginning "Out on the lawn I lie in bed / Vega conspicuous overhead / In the windless nights of June"; he felt himself "invaded by a power which, though I consented to it, was irresistible and certainly not mine. For the first time in my life I knew exactly . . . what it means to love one's neighbor as oneself." Both the vision and the poem were, like Auden's early essay on language, premature. "His vision of *agape* pointed the direction he would later follow. But the vision faded, and 'A Summer Night' accurately foresaw a time of loneliness and separation." And the poem itself was "an early gesture of allegiance to the Augustan literary tradition that would unmistakably—in the rhymed octosyllabic couplets of *New Year Letter*—become his real home." From this point on, though "Auden had no hope of altering the divisive loneliness that was his main subject, in his work after June 1933 he both explored his division and sought to resolve it."

The rest of Mendelson's book is best described in his own elegant summary. After a chapter offering

> a sketch-map of the central rift in Auden's landscape, the frontier between the private and public worlds . . . the chapters that follow describe his various projects for overcoming this frontier . . . a concise list of these projects might read something like this: *Erotic*—joining the two worlds through sexual love and personal growth, *Redemptive*—saving mankind from its divisions by personal example and direct cure, *Didactic*—teaching an audience, through parables, to unlearn hatred and learn love, *World-historical*—allowing the problem to be solved by determined forces working on an international scale, and *Escapist*—abandoning the problem altogether and finding comfort on an island of refuge.

Those who know their poet will recognize the rightness of these categories and in his exploration of them Mendelson combines sureness of critical understanding with brilliant choice of illustrative material to make this book the indispensable guide to early Auden. Particularly remarkable is the discussion of the sonnet sequence *In Time of War*, for which Mendelson makes, and justifies, the large claim that it is "Auden's most profound and audacious poem of the 1930s, perhaps the greatest English poem of the decade."

Mendelson's book leaves Auden at the end of the "low dishonest decade"; Humphrey Carpenter's *W. H. Auden: A Biography*,[2] covers the subject from the cradle in York to the grave in Kirchstetten. This is not, as the author points out, an "authorized" biography, undertaken at the request of the executors, but it draws on previously unpublished writings now in their charge (the acknowledgements contain a handsome tribute to Mendelson for his role as "active collaborator") as well as on the widely scattered printed sources. This life costs considerably more than the shilling of Auden's well-known line, but it does contain "all the facts"—as many, that is, as are ever likely to be known. Carpenter is a skillful biographer; he has woven the sometimes sordid, always interesting and often puzzling evidence into a consistently fascinating, convincing narrative pattern. Auden was one of the tribe of English eccentrics as well as a great poet and a caustic

---

2. Boston: Houghton Mifflin, 1981.

wit; the material is rich and Carpenter makes brilliant use of it. The book is full of surprises—I was astonished to read that Auden proposed marriage to the recently widowed Hannah Arendt in 1970—and unforgettable scenes. My favorite is Auden presiding over the dinner table in his Brooklyn "boarding house" (among the boarders were Carson McCullers, Benjamin Britten, Paul and Jane Bowles): "We've got a roast and two veg., salad and savory, and there will be no political discussion."

However, Carpenter does not confine himself to "the facts." His book is all the more illuminating because he treats the work as well as the life and often demonstrates vital connections. In his preface, "Auden and Biography," he takes note of his subject's well-known objections to the genre—literary biographers, he said, were "gossip-writers and voyeurs calling themselves scholars"—and records Auden's attempts to suppress letters in order "to make biography impossible." He counters this with Auden's own delight in the biographies and letters of literary figures as well as the contradictory fact (contradictions were typical of Auden) that he published a great deal of autobiographical material himself. In fact, Carpenter did not need to take a defensive position; anyone who was really worried about future biographers would have never left such a mass of material for them and would certainly have got rid of the 1929 journal which contains a list of names under the heading "Boys had. Germany 1928–29." One of Auden's heroes, Henry James, also wished to "frustrate as utterly as possible the post mortem exploiter," but he went about it in resolute fashion. In 1909, James "gathered his private papers [the account is Leon Edel's], forty years of letters from his contemporaries, manuscripts, scenarios, old notebooks, and piled them on a rubbish fire in his garden. . . . A great Anglo-American literary archive perished on that day." One can only conclude that Auden was beyond caring or even that he wanted the truth known. After all, it was he who had written: "At last the secret is out, as it always must come in the end."

Auden was insistent on the point that biography "throws no light whatsoever upon the artist's work," though he did believe that "more often than most people realize, his works may throw light on his life." He was wrong about biography; Carpenter's account illuminates many a passage in the work. I had never understood, for example, why the lines dealing with Joseph's reception of the angel's news in

For the Time Being moved with such passionate energy and expressed such desolate suffering—

> Caught in the jealous trap
> Of my empty house I hear
> As I sit alone in the dark
> Everything, everything,
> The drip of the bathroom tap
> The creak of the sofa spring.
> The wind in the air-shaft, all
> Making the same remark
> Stupidly, stupidly,
> Over and over again . . .

Was Auden simply imposing a starkly modern realism on a sacred tale, as Pasolini did in the opening sequences of *Il Vangelo secondo Matteo*? It turns out that the anguish was real; its deep source is Auden's realization that the "marriage" to Chester Kallmann, on which he had built such hopes, was not made in heaven, that "Certainty, fidelity / On the stroke of midnight pass / Like vibrations of a bell." And this revelation, for one reader at least, does exactly what Auden claimed biography could not do for the writer: "No knowledge of the raw ingredients will explain the peculiar flavor of the verbal dishes he invites the public to taste." And far from demeaning the poem, this insight into its genesis enhances its poignancy.

There is apparently no poet ready to write an elegy for Auden, as he did for Yeats and Freud, but these two books will do much to keep alive the memory of the man and the meaning of his work. And it is to be hoped that Edward Mendelson will go on to explore with the same penetrating intelligence, the same critical finesse, the work of "the Auden of later years—the avuncular, domestic, conservative, High Anglican poet of civilization" who, in Mendelson's words, "became the most inclusive poet of the twentieth century, its most technically skilled, and its most truthful."

Forster's Later Years

On October 1, 1925, E. M. Forster wrote his name in a large bound notebook which had come down through two generations of his family almost untouched; its first owner, Bishop Jebb of Limerick, had filled only eighteen of its more than four hundred pages before he bequeathed it to his chaplain, Forster's grandfather. From 1925 to 1965 Forster used it as a commonplace book, a repository for a wide variety of entries: extracts from his reading in English, French and, occasionally, Latin, reports of his dreams and of casual conversations overheard, self-analysis, reflections on contemporary as well as classical writers, reactions to current events and notes on his own health. First published in an expensive facsimile edition in 1978, it has now been reissued and edited with meticulous and illuminating notes by an expert on Forster, Philip Gardner, who first made his acquaintance in the 1950s as an undergraduate at King's.[1] Roughly this same period, the second half of Forster's long life span of ninety-two years, is documented also by the second volume of *Selected Letters of E. M. Forster (1921–1970)*,[2] which, like the first volume, is scrupulously edited and annotated by Mary Lago and Forster's biographer P. N. Furbank. Both books contain material Forster did not intend to publish; together they enable us to listen to the two private voices, one speaking to friends and the other to himself, of a great writer, who, with all his novels behind him (*A Passage to India*, the last to be published in his lifetime, came out in 1924), became a renowned critic, reviewer, broadcaster, essayist and public figure.

This was the Forster of my generation; to those born during and just after the First World War everything written before 1914 seemed to belong to an almost mythical world—"before the war"; only *Passage to India* sounded a contemporary, indeed a prophetic, note. Our

---

This essay originally appeared in *Grand Street* 5, no. 4 (Summer 1986).

1. *Commonplace Book* (Stanford: Stanford University Press, 1985).
2. Cambridge: Harvard University Press, 1985.

Forster—the Forster of the thirties—was the critic whose reviews in *Time and Tide* and the *Listener* never failed to delight as well as instruct, but he was also president of the Committee for Civil Liberties who in that capacity denounced the government's oppressive Sedition Bill and also appeared in court, together with thirty-eight other writers, prepared to testify in favor of Radclyffe Hall's novel *The Well of Loneliness*, which the Home Secretary had suppressed as obscene. The magistrate refused to admit their evidence, which must have come as something of a relief to Forster and many of the others who, like him, had no high opinion of the book's literary quality. In a letter to Hugh Walpole, he speaks of it as "the tedious Well." Its author had made life difficult for him by insisting, according to Virginia Woolf, that he come out publicly in praise of its "artistic merit—even genius" and had "scolded him like a fishwife."

Some years later, while in the fifth form at school, I was asked by a fellow student if I would make copies of an extract from *The Well of Loneliness* which had recently come into his possession. I would be paid sixpence per copy, the price, in those days, of a package of ten good cigarettes. He proposed to sell them at a higher price which he did not see fit to disclose. He already had other copyists enrolled; the work was to be done during prep. Curiosity about a notorious book, the subject of raucous jokes on the music-hall stage and still rawer jokes on the street, and the natural inclination of the English schoolboy to subversive activities were powerful incentives, and I joined the scriptorium, to be presented with a three-page handwritten text which was a steamy, explicit description of Sapphic copulation. I made only three copies, for the entrepreneur had overestimated the market; not long afterwards he was expelled from school, for reasons never made public but apparently as a result of some enterprise not connected with the *samizdat Well of Loneliness*, for no member of the scriptorium was summoned to the headmaster's study. Many years later, when the book was finally published in England, I leafed through it, only to find that compared with the lurid prose I had helped to disseminate it was chaste as the driven snow. Forster would have appreciated the irony: the Home Secretary, a man with the Gilbertian name of Joynson-Hicks, had become, by his suppression of a book he considered obscene, unwitting midwife to the birth of something really pornographic.

Forster's political activity was not confined to opposing censorship. As the world situation grew more menacing after Hitler's seizure of power, he associated himself with the political Left that was trying to organize an international Popular Front against Fascism. In June 1935, he went to Paris to speak at a congress of writers organized by André Malraux, which was under Communist control, as Forster was quite aware. He wrote later to J. B. Priestley, asking him to join the International Association of Writers: "It's so important that people whose main interests are not political should take part. Otherwise the thing will degenerate into a Communist stunt." In July 1937 he was in Paris again, this time at the invitation of Gilbert Murray, for a session of the League of Nations' Institut International de Co-opération Intellectuelle. It must have been during this visit that he went to the Paris Exposition on which he wrote an essay for the fourth issue of John Lehmann's *New Writing* (1937). It headed a table of contents that included John Cornford's last poems, as well as poems by Auden, stories by V. S. Pritchett and Ignazio Silone among others, and Stephen Spender's report on the writers' congress held at Valencia in Republican Spain.

That summer of 1937 was the last carefree holiday season Europe was to enjoy for many years; the Exposition, in which the major European powers were represented, seemed to offer the image of a continental balance of power, an assurance of stability. Paris was still the exhilarating city of the Front Populaire, though the original alliance of Socialist and Communist parties was fast disintegrating. The Spanish Republic was still successfully holding the line against Franco and his German and Italian backers. The Soviet Union still seemed the best counterweight to Hitler's military buildup, its alliance with France the guarantee that Hitler would not undertake a major war. There were dark patches in this hopeful picture. The destruction of Guernica by the Luftwaffe suggested that Hitler might in fact be preparing for all-out war, and the French Right was beginning to come out openly for surrender—*Mieux vaut Hitler que Staline* was the message of a poster that had started to make its appearance on the walls of Parisian streets. Above all, the attitude of Neville Chamberlain's government in Britain, openly pro-Franco and almost as openly in favor of major concessions to the Nazis, aroused suspicions of betrayal that were to be spectacularly and tragically confirmed at Munich a year later. But it was still possible, in that summer of 1937, to hope for the best, as I and so many of the young English visitors did, and the crowds that poured through the exhibition space in the shadow of the Tour Eiffel were in a festive mood, determined to enjoy to the full what was destined to be the last of those displays of technical progress and industrial power, which, since Victorian times, had proclaimed the unchallenged economic and political predominance of Europe.

The axis of the exposition buildings was a confrontation; the German and Russian pavilions, of approximately equal size, seemed to be straining to get at one another. A gigantic worker and his only slightly less gigantic wife on the pinnacle of the Soviet building strode manfully toward the Nazi emblem opposite, holding aloft crossed hammer and sickle. Inside, the Soviet pavilion was a crowded collection of tractors and airplane engines, of graphs and statistical charts, relieved only by photographs of collective farms and paintings of Stakhanovite miners. One entire wall was covered by a painting showing the full presidium of the USSR descending the steps of a government building, Comrade Stalin front and center, the rest identified in the caption at the base of the huge canvas.

The initial reaction of Forster to this crowded display was one of disappointment. "The solid and ardent pair," he writes, referring to the figures on the roof, "ignore good taste. . . . Their aims are moral, their methods disciplinary. Passing beneath their sealed up petticoats and trousers we enter a realm which is earnest cheerful instructive constructive and consistent, but which has had to blunt some of the vagrant sensibilities of mankind and is consequently not wholly alive." He goes on however to compensate for this faint praise with some rather sentimental imagery. "The Soviet pavilion is a nudge to the blind. It is trying . . . to dodge money and wipe away the film of coin and notes which keeps forming on the human retina." Later in the year a different kind of Soviet wiping away took place; as many of the individuals featured on the mass portrait disappeared from public view into Stalin's prisons, their images were removed from the painting and replaced by those of their successors. But Forster, like most of us at the time, was willing to give the Soviet Union the benefit of the doubt, something which was hardly possible for Nazi Germany.

About the German pavilion, a sort of dark cathedral which, hung with Wagnerian canvases, focused the worshiper's devotion on Zeiss lenses and ball bearings, Forster has only a phrase, it "presents Valhalla in a telephone box." But he waxes eloquent on the Italian pavilion. Forster's Italy, the Italy of *A Room with a View* and *Where Angels*

Fear to Tread, was now the concentrated essence of all that he most abhorred—imperialist expansion, industrialization, coercion. His opening sentence leaves no doubt about the depth of his feelings. "Satan. Unexpected but unmistakable he appears in the great entrance court of the Italian pavilion." This dramatic evocation refers to the equestrian statue of Mussolini, a heroic nude, which soon had to be moved out of the entrance court and fenced off; French workers had taken to giving one of their number a leg up so that he could report to the world what, if anything, was to be seen between Il Duce's marble legs. Forster does not mention (it was probably too much for him) the relief frieze, modeled on that of the Parthenon, which celebrated the conquest of Abyssinia, though when he writes of Mussolini (whom he never dignifies with his name), "He sprays savages with scent," he is obviously referring to the Italian use of poison gas against Abyssinian tribesmen. "He presses a button and a bull bursts" is another of the actions Forster ascribes to "Satan," and this is a reference to one of the most extraordinary presentations of the exposition: the pavilion of the Spanish Republic. There was very little in it but two things no one could forget: a fountain of mercury, the product of the mines at Almadén, not yet overrun by Franco's troops, and Picasso's *Guernica*, "a terrifying fresco . . . Bombs split bull's skull, woman's trunk, man's shins." Forster draws a contrast between this "huge black and white thing called 'Guernica'" and the Van Goghs he had described earlier in the essay, "the pictures of potatoes and miners who have eaten potatoes until their faces are tuberous and dented and their skins grimed and unpeeled." Picasso's fresco "is indignant and so it is less disquieting than the potato feeders of Van Gogh. Picasso is grotesquely angry, and those who are angry still hope." Van Gogh, on the other hand, had written "Sorrow is better than joy" on the white walls of his cell. "Every now and then," Forster writes, "people have preferred sorrow to joy, and asserted that wisdom and creation can result only from suffering."

But the Paris Expo was not all so depressing or menacing; Forster enjoyed himself in the Park of Attractions. "The crowd was what journalists call 'good-humoured'; and I, a journalist, was part of it. . . . Oh, the French! Why are they so good at organizing these lighter happinesses?" The Park of Attractions did offer a rich menu of amusements—Forster mentions the scenic railway, shooting galleries, balloon rides and "a booth marked *Perversités. Images Troublantes"*—but there was also, for the foreign visitor, the constant entertainment provided by the behavior of the crowds. Though not even the French were able to make jokes about Picasso's *Guernica*, everything else was a target for those devastating comments Parisian bystanders are famous for. Their reactions to the British pavilion, for example, which featured Dalton china, handmade fishing flies and an enormous blown-up photograph of Neville Chamberlain fishing in a Scottish stream were a revelation of the infinite propensities of the French language for abusive ridicule and a delight to the British students who shared the French opinion of the Prime Minister. And then there were the rumors. A long line outside the Argentine pavilion one morning was certainly not a tribute to the rather dreary objects it housed; *"distribution de biftec gratuit"* was the explanation offered by the people in the queue. Another day people lining up outside the charming but modest Danish pavilion offered a different explanation (which, unlike the other, turned out to be true): *"il y a un W.C. gratuit."*

Forster had begun his report on the Expo with a description of the model of our world revolving in the astronomical section of the Palais de la Découverte: "Its colouring, its general appearance, accord with the latest deductions. The result is surprising. For not even France, not even Europe, is visible. There are great marks on the surface of the model but they represent clouds and snows, not continents and seas." It is on this same note that he ends the essay. "Meanwhile and all the while, the Earth revolves in her alcove, veiled in wool. She has sent samples of her hopes and lusts to Paris; that they will again be collected there, or anywhere, is unlikely, but she herself will look much the same as soon as one stands a little back in space." In spite of his genuine devotion to the cause of civil liberties, his opposition to censorship, his participation in the writers' congress and his hatred of war and the Fascist regimes which glorified it, he was himself, to use his own famous description of Cavafy, "standing at a slight angle to the universe."

His Bloomsbury friends in fact did not take his role as a public figure seriously. He had asked the Woolfs to accompany him to the congress in Paris. Virginia, in her diary for June 13, 1935, writes: "Morgan divined that we would not come to Paris. Always divines the meaning & then flits off. . . . M has a razor edge to his mind. And he can't get on with 'Bloomsbury' & feels, I guess, unattached & thus takes on public work, which depresses him."

He had of course been very close to "Bloomsbury" once, but in the years after the first war he had drawn apart. "I don't belong automatically," he had noted in his commonplace book in 1929, "—from 1916 the gulf was bound to widen." They are, he writes, "essentially *gentlefolks*, would open other people's letters, but wouldn't steal, bully, slander, or blackmail like many of their critics, and have acquired a culture in harmony with their social position. Hence their stability. . . . Academic background, independent income, continental enthusiasm, sex-talk and all, they are in the English tradition." And a year later he records: "Visit to Virginia, prospects of, not wholly pleasurable. I shall watch her curiosity and flattery exhaust themselves in turn. Nor does it do to rally the Pythoness."

The Pythoness, over the years, had recorded some rather acid impressions of Forster; she was especially contemptuous of his homosexual bent and his friends and lovers. In her diary for April 4, 1930, she describes an "atmosphere of buggery" at a party where Forster was among those present: "an atmosphere entirely secluded, intimate, & set on one object; all agreed on what they liked. . . . A photograph of Stephen Tennant (Siegfried Sassoon goes to the same tailor) in a tunic, in an attitude, was shown about; also little boys in a private school. Morgan became unfamiliar, discussing the beauties of Hilton Young's stepson. . . . This all made on me a tinkling, private, giggling, impression. As if I had gone in to a men's urinal." And in 1933, in a letter to Quentin Bell (December 21) she reports on the "great sorrow" among the "Lilies of the Valley," her name for the homosexual poets and writers who had "set up a new quarter in Maida Vale." Their great sorrow was the defection of Siegfried Sassoon; "he's gone and married a woman and says . . . that he has never till now known what love meant . . . this greatly worries the Lilies of the Valley, among whom is Morgan, of course, who loves a crippled bootmaker; why this passion for the porter, the policeman and the bootmaker?" The bootmaker has never been identified and is presumably the product of Virginia's imagination, but there were indeed two policemen among Forster's lovers, with one of whom, "Bob" Buckingham, he established a relationship that lasted from 1930 until he died, in Buckingham's house in Coventry, in 1970. This side of Forster's life, though obviously common knowledge in Bloomsbury, was carefully concealed from the public; the only novel he wrote which dealt openly with the subject, *Maurice,* completed in 1914 but revised continuously until 1960, was shown in manuscript to selected friends but not published till after his death. Posthumous, too, was the publication of short stories with a homosexual theme: "The Life to Come," "Arthur Snatchfold" and "Dr. Woolacott," which T. E. Lawrence, who read it in manuscript, expressed such admiration for that Forster replied: "It is the experience of a lifetime to get such praise. . . . What you have written has the effect of something absolute on me." Forster was reticent about others too. His biography of "Goldie" Lowes Dickinson made no mention of his homosexuality, though it was notorious and can easily be read between the lines of his once fashionable book, *The Greek View of Life.* "The EMF Goldie thing," Virginia wrote in her diary for October 2, 1934, "to me quite futile." There were however good reasons for discretion. The "Goldie thing" had been commissioned by Dickinson's family and in any case it was not until 1967 that homosexual acts between consenting adults were decriminalized. And Forster had no illusions about popular opinion on the subject. Writing to Christopher Isherwood in 1933 about *Maurice,* he says: "Yes, if the pendulum keeps swinging in its present direction, it might get published in time. But the more one meets decent and sensible people, of whom there are now a good few, the more does one forget the millions of beasts and idiots who still prowl in the darkness, ready to gibber and devour. I had a truer view of civilization thirty years ago, when I regarded myself as hiding a fatal secret."

In his commonplace book, however, and in letters to kindred spirits, Forster feels no need for restraint. One of the most remarkable of the letters was written to W. J. H. Sprott in 1932, after Bob Buckingham, Forster's close friend since 1930, had married. Forster is a man in torment. "I think I ought to write, but it hurts me, it seems like blaming my lover and beloved. . . . I can hardly ever see him. Dear Jack, it is as I feared, and worse—the woman is domineering, sly and *knowing* and at present she seems to have got him down." To which a note is appended: "I don't mean that he has 'refused' or is likely to." Luckily this mood passed, and Forster and May Buckingham became good friends. Forster and Bob still had their meetings in town or on trips; he stood godfather to their son Robin Morgan and though he can still complain, in 1940, that Bob does not come to see him often enough—"May has got you placed just where you don't like to suggest it, yourself, as being unfair to her. . . . I do not blame her, but I do blame you for not standing up against feminine technique better than that"—he can also speak up for her. "Hope you won't sacrifice May too much to Robin, and chaw up her flower bed again. She has a life to lead, too, and has to spend a good deal of it looking out of the back door." And in April 1961, when he had a heart attack and thought he was dying, they were at his bedside; "Bob and May were to my right and left" he recorded later in his commonplace book, "I was not surprised and liked touching them; Bob's little finger pressed mine and pursued it when he shifted. This I shall never forget."

Many of the letters are addressed to fellow writers and artists, and these letters often have the special interest that attaches to discussions of work in progress. Those addressed to Benjamin Britten, Eric Crozier, Robert Trevelyan and Lionel Trilling about the libretto for the Britten opera *Billy Budd* give a lively picture of the gestation of the text; and Forster's suggestions to Christopher Isherwood about the staging of *Ascent of F6*, as well as his critique of the stage version of *A Passage to India* in a letter to its adapter Santha Rama Rau, show him as an acute critic of the theater. More important than all these, however, are the letters to and about the Greek poet Constantine Cavafy.

In his *Pharos and Pharillon* (1923), Forster had published translations by George Valassopoulos of three of Cavafy's poems; they "attracted attention," as he wrote to the poet in a request for more. It is characteristic of Cavafy that he did not reply, which prompted Forster to send a letter signed "Yours inconsolably, Fellow-poet," which ran: "All mourn, all deplore / Both Gentile and Jew, / That they hear no more / From you." More poems did arrive eventually and Forster managed to place them in periodicals; one of the most beautiful of them, "Ithaki," appeared first in Eliot's *Criterion*. Forster "tinkered up" the Valassopoulos translations, but it is clear that he had no sure grasp of modern Greek. When one poem, "Mia nychta" ("One Night"), came without a translation he asked Valassopoulos whether it was "erotic." (It happens to be about the intoxicating memory of a night of love in a sordid room over a working-class taverna.) Robert Liddell, in his *Cavafy: A Critical Biography* (1974), quotes from a letter Forster wrote to him an account of his attempt to "make out the poems with the aid of Valassopoulos' translations" and his own knowledge of ancient Greek as well as coaching from the poet himself, whose first reaction was negative. "'You cannot *possibly* understand my poems, my dear Forster' and then he began to lead me through one of them, *The City*, I think, and: 'But good—my dear Forster, very good indeed . . . you have seen the point . . . good.'"

Forster's plan for a complete edition of Cavafy (who died in 1933) was pursued with vigor but came in the end to nothing. It was a sore disappointment to him; writing in 1945 to William Plomer, he concludes an account of his efforts and their frustration with the words: "Deep behind it all is Cavafy, whom I loved, and what is best done for his immortality." Later still, in a letter to George Valassopoulos about Marguerite Yourcenar's 1958 translation, he writes: "How very proud I am, George, that I ever got to know him; it is certainly one of my 'triumphs.'" It is typical of Forster's reverence for friendship that he sees his "triumph" in the personal contact rather than in his success in bringing the poems to the attention of the English-speaking literary world and so contributing not a little to the establishment of Cavafy's immortality.

Letters to women are not so numerous as those to men; they are addressed mainly to two correspondents of long standing: to Florence Barger, the wife of his undergraduate friend at King's, and to his mother. To Florence he had confided the details of his affair with the Alexandrian tram conductor Mohammed El Adl; "she was my confidante," he later wrote Plomer, "and as sometimes happens to people when they are confided in, she became very broad-minded; less so in later years, but a heroine and a darling always." His letters to her in 1921 are about his reunion with Mohammed, who was dying of tuberculosis. Florence was his confidante only up to a point. "I told her all about myself," he writes to Plomer, "up to 1921—i.e. the year Mohammed died, and she has made something sacred and permanent for herself out of this, which fresh confidences would disturb." In his mother, on the other hand, he did not confide at all; his letters to her, which in earlier days were long, frequent and remarkable, especially those written from abroad, for their detailed descriptions of places and occasions, grow rarer after they both moved to Abinger, even though after 1925 he spent one or two nights a week in his Bloomsbury flat. Forster resisted the advice of friends who urged him to cut loose from his mother, though he often complained of her overbearing ways. One letter to her, written from the 1917 Club in London some time in June 1922 expresses, in mock baby talk, his profound dissatisfaction. "Dearest Mummy—Poppy is safely arrived and now he is going to write a disagreeable letter. He wants to ask Mummy to try not to interfere with him so much. If he wants to take his clock to London, let him take it—if he doesn't want to put little books into an envelope, don't put them back in it—if he loses his glove, accept the fact & etc. Each thing is so trivial by itself that it is absurd to mention it, but they all add up to a loss of independence." Forster himself later added to this letter the comment: "Poppy kicks."

The Pythoness, as usual, had some hard words to describe the situation, referring, in a letter to the composer Ethel Smyth dated September 1930, to Forster's "old mother, whose sister, son, daughter and husband he is. They share a Surrey house; and live like mice in a nest." Forster himself had even harder words. In 1937, writing to J. R. Ackerley, he summed up the relationship in what, for him, were extraordinarily brutal terms, though characteristically he tempers them by a recognition of how much he owed his mother. "Although my mother has been intermittently tiresome for the last thirty years, cramped and warped my genius, hindered my career, blocked and buggered up my house, and boycotted my beloved, I have to admit that she provided a sort of rich subsoil where I have been able to rest and grow." In 1930 he had written in his commonplace book a scenario for a novel. "Idea of mother and son. She dominates him in youth. Manhood brings him emancipation—perhaps through friendship or a happy marriage. But the mother is waiting. Her vitality depends on character, and asserts itself as the sap drains out of him. She gets her way and reestablishes his childhood, with the difference that his subjection is conscious now and causes him humiliation and pain. Is her tyranny conscious? I think not. Could the same relationship occur between father and daughter? No. A ruthless writer might make something of this. But two people pulling each other into salvation is the only theme I find worthwhile."

His mother died in 1945, "peacefully, as I was spooning her some lunch," he wrote to Bob Buckingham. "I think there was something deeper between us than I knew, for the shock is worse than I expected. I can't explain—or could explain all too well, being a writer—

but it has to do with the greatness of love and one's own smallness." His mother's death marked the end of an era for him in more ways than one: the lease on the house at Abinger in which the two of them had lived since 1924 had run out some years earlier and the landlord now asked Forster to leave. In his commonplace book he drew, in 1946, a detailed plan of the kitchen garden at the Abinger house with the caption: "the year I was driven out after it had been cultivated for 70 years." Luckily, his old Cambridge college, King's, made him an honorary Fellow and offered him a home, where he spent the rest of his life.

From this point on the commonplace book changes character. The rich citations from his reading yield place more and more to personal reminiscences, records of dreams and reflections on his physical and intellectual state, while the citations he does make seem more closely related to personal concerns than was the case in the early years. The entries for 1926, for example, quotations from and notes on Sterne, Defoe, Swift, Richardson, James, Dickens, Melville and other novelists are his homework in preparation for the Clark Lectures at Cambridge, which were issued later as *Aspects of the Novel*.[3] In 1930 he is busy with analysis of Corneille's drama and criticism as well as the poetry and prose of Dryden and Johnson, turning later to Boileau, then to Wordsworth and Coleridge. In his essay "Bishop Jebb's Book," he wondered what the original owner of his commonplace book would have thought of his use of it: "scribbling notes about Marx, . . . copying extracts from Madame de Sévigné." But this lighthearted description of his jottings gives no hint of the riches the book contains. His quotations are always striking passages and they are accompanied by an informal commentary that shows Forster at his critical best. On a passage of Boileau, for example, he complains of the "dreary remark" that "Big writers are above jealousy: *C'est un vice de la médiocrité.*" He adduces Coleridge's *Biographia Literaria II*, "who also pretends that geniuses are 'of calm and tranquil temper in all that related to themselves.' What's the evidence? I believe nearly all writers are jealous and *all* sensitive to praise or blame, though their reactions aren't obvious e.g. jealousy may emerge as nervous altruism." And to Wordsworth's claim that he employed the "language

---

3. New York: Harcourt Brace, 1927.

really spoken by men," Forster objects: "*But* he never employs or discusses dialect (C. says he does in the Sailor's Mother but no) or slang. His country folk have taken emetics, and only a standardized dulness survives, as of school teachers' school children and their parents established in the Lakes by some Central authority."

During the war years he took to reading the Church Fathers and produced "a few notes on late 3rd and early 4th century events. . . . I have (May 1942) been seeking in that period *not* an explanation of our disaster, but wisdom with which to bear them." The parallel between the England of 1942 and the fall of Rome is, however, "queered," as he puts it, "by the existence of Christianity and the attendant denunciation of sex." He expresses respect for Augustine's intelligence but finds it "difficult to follow" his opinions on sex: "what he thinks is wrong in copulation is not the semen but the pleasure attending its emission" and is delighted to discover that the real name of Augustine's heretical opponent, the British monk Pelagius, who denied the doctrine of original sin, was Morgan, meaning "born by the sea" (for which *pelagius* is a rough Latin equivalent). This is indeed a remarkable coincidence, for Forster too did not believe in original sin; at this point in his commonplace book he wrote a jocular couplet about "my namesake" who "bye-passed a great deal of nonsense": "Pelagius says that whether you're saved or whether in Hell you burn / Is nothing to do with the Church, my boy, but purely your own concern."

Forster in fact seems to have had no sense of sin at all, especially in the matter of sexual pleasure, and he finds it hard to understand the hysterical emphasis on continence and virginity that is omnipresent in the writings of Augustine and still more in the writings of "that detestable Father" Jerome. In this area he is an anarchist, and it is interesting that besides copying out dicta of Marx and Engels (from a French Marxist anthology), he also made a series of extracts from Bakunin: "Every State, like every theology, assumes man to be wicked. . . . There cannot be a good, just and moral State." These are very close to Forster's own deepest convictions. Of Carr's biography of Bakunin, from which he quotes these maxims, he writes: "All presented by Carr as sordid and absurd, and best so presented, leaving the reader to strike the match and make Bakunin a light in the darkness. For he is that." Fourth-century heretical theologian and nineteenth-century Russian anarchist might seem a strange tandem, but Forster combines the Pelagian sense of man's fundamental innocence with Bakunin's abhorrence of the state, while rejecting the Christianity of the one and the will to violence of the other.

Augustine's attitude toward the fall of Rome he finds it difficult to divine but finally decides that he was "not as upset as Jerome." From Hodgkin's *Italy and Her Invaders* he extracts passages recording Jerome's reaction, noting that he quotes Virgil's line about the fall of Troy—*Urbs antiqua ruit, multos dominata per annos* ("An ancient city falls, that ruled for many years" in Robert Fitzgerald's version)—a line which, Forster remarks, "I myself was to read 1500 years later, after seeing the Docks on fire from my roof in Chiswick."

The war ended, but victory and the arrival of the Labour government brought him little comfort. He had always thought of himself as a democrat and a progressive. "I belong to the fag-end of Victorian liberalism," he wrote just after the war. In 1940, commenting on a passage of Acton about Western civilized values, he wrote in his commonplace book, "Yet my duty is plain enough: to talk this nineteenth-century stuff with a twentieth-century voice and not to be shoved out of believing in intellectual honesty and the individual." But by 1947 his mood had changed. "I have always wanted to share my advantages with others," he writes, "but now I am asked to give up advantages so that others may have things I don't want; to help build a world I should find uninhabitable. It is a severe demand. The generous-minded of the past century—Shelley and the Liberals—have not appreciated its irony. They have assumed that, once the chains had fallen, art, scenery, passionate personal love, would become popular. One is placed in the equivocal position of the aristocrat who believes in real goods—for they are real—and is tempted to defend them against democracy. The town here [he was writing this in Cambridge] is bitter against the university for preserving their joint amenities and preventing industrial development."

Industrialization and the disappearance of the countryside had long been high among his concerns even before the war, but the effects of the war and the rapid urbanization of the English countryside which followed it appalled him. A visit to a wartime farm run by a government agency prompted him to write: "This was 'Rockingham Forest' once. Seen in the bright sun, it glowed as the English countryside of the future—one huge food-tub from which the lorries will proceed to the mills." And in 1960 he wrote: "Still the bird sings, our companion about to leave us, though it does not know this and though most men do not know it. It has sung in human earshot for millions of years." Already in 1955 he had recorded a bleak vision of the future. "The man-modified surface of the earth is on its way to being man-destroyed. After which will come the man-modification of the waters and the destruction of their contents (dead fish from Pest Control in the Cam). Assuming present processes continue—though it is a risky assumption—nothing will be allowed to survive that does not conduce to human comfort, and the nature of human comfort will be decided by applied scientists."

He could no longer believe in progress, but to the end he retained his belief in "intellectual honesty and the individual." The honesty is painfully evident in the later sections of the commonplace book where he records the evidence of his physical decay (a coldly objective catalogue of bodily malfunctions dated 8–7–48 leaves nothing to the imagination) and the weakening of his mental faculties—the loss of memory, of the power to concentrate. But there is no sign that he wishes for death; the last two entries in the commonplace book are Clemenceau's answer when asked what he would do now that he was old—"I am going to live till I die" ("I like this answer," says Forster)—and a quotation from Philo denigrating sense perception as opposed to the life of the mind, on which Forster comments: "Transcribed with some trouble at the age of 86 and not with complete approval. I would like sense-perceptions to attend me to the end." Apparently they did, for there is an entry in his unpublished diary (quoted by Gardner in his preface to the commonplace book) for June 6, 1967, which runs: "I am probably close to the end of my own life, which has been a successful one and to the end a happy one. And now for dinner!" And the final entry in the commonplace book, dated November 1968, is: "How it rains!" As indeed it does in Cambridge in November; the rain, whipped by winds off the North Sea, sweeps across the Backs where Forster had so often walked, across the Fellows' garden where in 1959 he had spent the morning "sunbrowning . . . reading *Il Gattopardo*," and storms against the pinnacles of Henry Sixth's Chapel, where, for once, the death of a Fellow of King's would not be marked by a memorial service: "Since at 85 I may have to die soon," he had written in the book, "I should like to emphasize that I am still not a Christian and don't want even a memorial service in our friendly chapel." His death was commemorated, in appropriate fashion, for he was a lover and connoisseur of music, by a concert given in the Hall of the college which had housed him as a young student and then, with a generosity which would hardly be possible in the government-regulated Cambridge of today, gave him a home for the last quarter-century of his life.

ESSAYS
The Modern World

From Madrid to the Garden of the Finzi-Contini

Everybody but Shakespeare

The Narrative History of the Spanish Civil War, 1936–1939 is the subtitle of Peter Wyden's book, *The Passionate War*.[1] The article seems a trifle presumptuous and the adjective would once have seemed redundant; but the Muse of history has in recent years turned statistician-sociologist and some qualification was necessary to give the reader a signal that this book is the most old-fashioned kind of history imaginable. Like the book of the Father of History, the Greek Herodotus, it is an account of a war told mainly through the stories of individual actors and sufferers. The readers will find here no profound analysis of the causes or indeed of the politics of the war—for that he must go to Burnett Bolloten and Hugh Thomas; what he will find is a fast-moving sequence of dramatic scenes, each one centered on an individual, and all of them skillfully linked in a narrative which, however selectively, does cover the progress and the main events of this complicated conflict. Many of the separate scenes are, or contain, good stories—the French have a word for it: *histoire anecdotique*—but Wyden insists that this is not a "docudrama." It is, he says, "the most painstaking possible reconstruction based on interviews and an extraordinary outpouring of records, diaries, histories, autobiographies, letters, all sifted and cross-checked to avoid any avoidable inaccuracy. . . . All sources are cited in detail in the source notes."

These sources are for the most part firsthand accounts (though some of them have been filtered through later compilers; many of them are based on interviews with survivors. For his earlier book, *The Bay of Pigs* (1974), Wyden used not only documents extracted from official United States sources and interviews with Cubans who had taken part in that ill-fated adventure; he had also the brilliant idea of asking Fidel Castro for his side of the story and was regaled with a lengthy and fascinating account of the operation from the other side.

This essay originally appeared in the *New Republic,* August 8, 1983.

1. New York: Simon & Schuster, 1983.

For this new book he has landed no comparable big fish but the net was spread wide and the catch is impressive.

He cites interviews with Serrano Suñer, Franco's brother-in-law (who was caught in Madrid and escaped by a miracle), with no less than ten former flyers and artillery officers of the Nazi Condor Legion, with more than a dozen members of the American Lincoln Brigade, with Martha Gellhorn, with the widow of Merriman, commander of the Lincolns and Hemingway's model for Robert Jordan, with Claud Cockburn, with the Spanish officials who transferred the gold of the Bank of Spain to Russian ships at Cartagena, with a nun who was condemned to death and saw her Mother Superior shot in Madrid, with a former member of a Franco firing squad, with a man who helped bury the burned corpses after the killings at Badajoz and a woman who searched for her brother's body in the streets of Toledo as the victorious Moors were let loose on the civil population, as well as with a host of minor characters including the writer of this review. Wyden cites correspondence with survivors and also papers deposited in research libraries, Louis Fischer's at Princeton, for example, letters of Martha Gellhorn to Eleanor Roosevelt at Hyde Park, a Hemingway manuscript of a fundraising speech for Spain in the John F. Kennedy Library.

The individual figures who hold the stage for a page or two (many of them, of course, like Hemingway, more than once) number about one hundred and fifteen. Over eighty of these protagonists are supporters of the government; some thirty are on the rebel side. This disproportion does not necessarily reflect a bias (though Wyden, like so many of his actors, is for the Republic, in spite of its many faults); it is much more likely to be a consequence of his method, for the plain fact is that the Republican cause attracted many more noteworthy and picturesque personalities than the other side. ("They may have won all the battles," runs a Tom Lehrer ballad, "but we had all the good songs.") Some thirty-five of these pivotal figures are Spaniards; the rest are foreign volunteers, newsmen or just plain visitors. "Everybody was there but Shakespeare," a Canadian veteran said to Wyden, and on the Republican side the international visiting list is indeed stupendous. Malraux, Koestler, Orwell, Hemingway, Martha Gellhorn, Spender, and Auden everyone has heard of, but it will come as a surprise to many to run into Simone Weil (invalided out of an anarchist column in Aragon after spilling boiling olive oil from a cooking pot over herself); Barbara Tuchman (four years out of Vassar, a correspondent for *The Nation*); Emma Goldman (who at the age of sixty-seven finally saw anarchism in action at Durrutti's headquarters) and Josephine Herbst (a member of Hemingway's exclusive club on the dangerous side of the Hotel Florida). The Franco side had no such magnetism for literary and Bohemian personalities; it attracted professionals like Adolf Galland, who rose to become commanding general of Hitler's fighter arm, and von Thoma, who later commanded Rommel's tanks in North Africa, Luigi Barzini Sr., correspondent for Mussolini's *Popolo d'Italia* and Kim Philby, working for the London *Times* (but reporting also to the Russians).

Wyden, of course, is a professional too, and the narrative is fast-paced and absorbing. But the book also makes some important contributions to the evidence for the history of the war and explores some of its most controversial features. The slaughter of prisoners at Badajoz, for example, the first major town captured by Franco troops against determined resistance, was reported at the time by one foreign eyewitness, the Portuguese journalist Mario Neves, who was allowed in by the Franco general Yagüe since Portugal's dictator Salazar was backing Franco to the hilt. Wyden has corresponded with Neves to gather some new details of his nightmare tour of the city while the first round of executions was in progress; he has secured (and reproduces) a still from the French newsreels showing a huge heap of burned corpses outside the bullring; and he has interviewed an unemployed Portuguese laborer who was hired to bury these same corpses in a ditch forty meters long, ten meters wide, and one and one-half deep and who saw, in a grim preview of the Nazi death camps, a stack of gold fillings from the victims' teeth piled up on the side of the grave.

On another Franco massacre over which charge and denial have been exchanged ever since, the destruction of Guernica, Wyden is noncommittal. Guernica was destroyed, no doubt about that—85 per cent of its buildings collapsed and the civilian casualties were at least two thousand—but controversy still rages about the objectives of the Luftwaffe officers who planned and carried out the raid. It was assumed by the civilized world at the time that this was the first attempt to implement the theories of the Italian strategist Douhet—that a war could be won simply by flattening the enemy cities from the air and so destroying enemy morale. The defense made by the Germans, at the time and since, is that their objective was a strategic bridge just east of the town; its destruction would have cut off the retreat of the government forces on the Viscaya front.

Wyden quotes only secondary sources here; they are all based, as they must be since the question is German intentions, on suspect sources, the pilots themselves. The planner of the operation, von Richthofen, who later commanded the Stukas in Poland, became a field marshal and finally died of a brain tumor in 1945, wrote in his diary after the raid, when the Nationalists entered the city: "Guernica literally razed . . . bomb craters visible in the streets . . . *ganz toll—* simply fabulous!" Naturally he did not write that his intention was to flatten the town and break the Basques' morale, but he doesn't mention the bridge which later was put forward as the real objective; he merely laments that since the Franco troops did not move in fast enough after the raid, it was "only a complete technical success." Wyden, in the end, leaves the matter open to doubt. But since that same Luftwaffe went on to do exactly the same thing at Rotterdam and Coventry (and tried to do it too at London); since, in spite of the fact that forty-three aircraft dropped one hundred thousand pounds of bombs on a target undefended by either flak or fighters, the bridge remained undamaged; and since, in addition, one-third of the bomb load consisted of incendiaries, useless against a bridge, this seems to be a case of bending over much too far backward in an attempt to be fair.

"History calls it the Spanish Civil War," says Wyden in a short prologue, "but it was no more a Spanish war or a civil war than the Vietnam war was a struggle between North and South Vietnam." Opinions may differ about how far the Vietnam war was a war between North and South Vietnam but though it is true that, as Wyden goes on to say, "in Spain the world was choosing sides for the years to come," the combatants and the casualties were overwhelmingly Spanish. The massive reprisals, most of them on the Franco side, were also in the Spanish tradition; even Farinacci, one of Mussolini's most brutal lieutenants, wrote to his *Duce:* "It is a sort of contest to see who can massacre more people, almost a national sport." And the barbarous ferocity of those reprisals was also recognizably Spanish; one cannot imagine a more suitable series of symbolic illustrations for this war than *Los desastres de la guerra,* Goya's macabre images of the war of 1808–13.

Franco was indeed the ally of Hitler and Mussolini but when the World War came he did nothing for the Italians and he thwarted Hitler's pet scheme to take Gibraltar from the landward side; he may have been a "fascist" of some kind (whatever that elastic term can still convey after so many decades of loose use) but, unlike Hitler and Mussolini, he did not create a mass movement, and also, unlike them, he was a professional soldier—his revolt, in fact, was a classic Spanish *pronunciamiento*, a military takeover. Someday the history of the war will be written by a Spaniard who can see it impartially from a national perspective and give it tragic form, but that day will not come soon; the wounds are very deep and will be slow to heal. Meanwhile, the story will continue to be told by outsiders, who naturally feature the foreign intervention.

Wyden, just as naturally, favors the American participation (just as Hugh Thomas, in the first edition of his authoritative book, found that he had "given too much attention . . . to the role of the International Brigades, particularly the British contingent"). Wyden begins and ends his book with incidents from Alvah Bessie's fine account of his service in the Lincoln Brigade; much space is devoted to the career of Merriman, the Berkeley economics instructor who commanded the Lincoln Brigade and died in the retreat from Aragon;[2] two fascinating sections deal with the career of Robert Gladnick, a Russian-born New York seaman, who started out with the Lincolns and ended up a member of a Soviet tank squadron. And a great deal of space—too much, for my money—is devoted to the doings of Ernest Hemingway.

It is of course true that Hemingway wrote a magnificent if flawed novel about the war (the main flaw being the hero's mushy romance with the little "rabbit" Maria); it is true, too, that he did much by his writing and speaking for the Republican cause and that he risked his life in Spain persistently (and often needlessly). But his assumption of the role of combat-wise veteran, which was widely accepted by his peers, had no basis in fact; he had never, strictly speaking, been in combat at all. As an ambulance driver in Italy in World War I, he operated behind the lines; the one time he went to the trenches, to dis-

2. See now Marrion Merriman and Warren Lerude, *American Commander in Spain: Robert Hale Merriman and the Lincoln Brigade* (Reno: University of Nevada Press, 1986).

tribute cigarettes, he was badly smashed up by a huge trench mortar bomb; in spite of his wounds, he carried an injured companion to safety. All his experience after that was as a war correspondent—in Turkey in 1921, and in Spain. I am not denying that war correspondents have to be brave men—their casualty list is warrant enough for their courage—but there is one vital distinction between war reporter and soldier: the one can come and go as he pleases and where he chooses, the other goes and stays where he is ordered. The reporter can choose his risks; the soldier cannot. The soldier is in it for the duration; the only way he can get out is on a stretcher or in a bag. And he lives with the sure knowledge that if it goes on long enough his turn will come; the strong, the skillful, the lucky—it will take them all.

"Do you not see," says Achilles to Lycaon, whom he is about to kill, "what a man I am, how huge, how splendid . . . ? / Yet even I have also my death and my strong destiny, / and there shall be a dawn or an afternoon or a noontime / when some man in the fighting will take the life from me also." In *Dispatches*, Michael Herr's extraordinary book on the Vietnam war ("It's the Rolling Stones go to Nam," a young veteran of the war told me), there is the story of the puzzled young marine who can't believe that the reporters came to his outpost on Mutter's Ridge of their own volition: "You mean you guys *volunteered* to come over here. . . . You guys *asked* to come here?" He cannot bridge the gulf between the harsh necessity of his own exposure to mutilation and death and the condition of a "hopeless fool who could put himself through this thing when he had choices . . . who had no more need of his life than to play with it in this way."

The other side of this coin is the marine who, seeing a group of correspondents leave for the rear, says bitterly: "I hope those guys get killed." There is hardly a combat infantryman who has not at some time or other felt at least a trace of that same deadly resentment as he watched privileged visitors go back to where a man can stand up. Hemingway was a great writer and, in some areas, especially that of honor among men, exquisitely sensitive; he must have been conscious of this gulf between himself and the fighting men and tried to bridge it by displays of bravado, some of them quite simply silly.

Still it was to be expected that Wyden would give us a lot of Hemingway; he is very good copy. And in any case this imbalance does not detract from the value of the book, which is meant, after all, for

American readers and especially for the young, to whom the Spanish Civil War, if they have heard of it at all, is ancient history. It was so even in the 1950s, as I learned to my astonishment at Yale, where an undergraduate came up to me at a party and said, hesitantly and as if he could not believe what he was saying: "I was told you fought in the Spanish Civil War." When I answered that I had and asked him why he was interested he looked at me with a reverent expression that made me feel like one of the Elgin Marbles and said: "Sir, that's my thesis!" Wyden's book will bring ancient history to life for those who have a vague feeling that there was a Spanish *something* war (was it Civil or American?) and provide themes for argument to all those who in their salad days, whether in arms or at home, followed the fortunes of Spain and, in Herbert Matthews's phrase, left their hearts there.

Remembering Madrid

"The onlooker," in the words of the English sportsman's adage, "sees most of the game." As a minor player in the defense of Madrid in November 1936 (a twenty-one-year-old member of the machine-gun company of the Bataillon Commune de Paris, Eleventh International Brigade) I was at the time sublimely ignorant of most of the military events and political issues described and discussed in two recent books on the Spanish civil war, Don Kurzman's *Miracle of November: Madrid's Epic Stand 1936*[1] and Burnett Bolloten's *The Spanish Revolution: The Left and the Struggle for Power During the Civil War.*[2]

Kurzman traces the march of the Nationalist troops from Seville to Madrid and the "miracle" which occurred in early November, when, deserted by their government and written off as lost by the foreign press corps, the Madrileños stopped dead in its tracks the Franco spearhead of Foreign Legionnaires and Moroccans who were already inside the western suburbs of the city. Bolloten covers the whole course of the three-year war; he is concerned with the politics of the war and in particular the Spanish Communist Party's relentless progress from an initial position of insignificance (40,000 members before the war) to a membership of a quarter of a million and total control of the civil and military machinery of the Republic.

Bolloten's book is a monument of historical scholarship. He was a correspondent in Spain during the war and has spent the rest of his life trying to understand what he saw there; from 1962 to 1965 he was director of research in the subject at Stanford and a large part of his unrivaled collection of source material is now deposited at the Hoover Institute. His footnotes demonstrate an awesome mastery of sources in all the languages of Europe (including Russian); the notes

This essay originally appeared in the *New York Review of Books,* November 6, 1980.

1. New York: Putnam's, 1980.
2. Chapel Hill: University of North Carolina Press, 1979.

and bibliography alone make his work an indispensable tool for any further research on the subject and a superb analytical index will make such work easy.

The book is "a vast revision and expansion" of an earlier version (1961) which was entitled *The Grand Camouflage*. Its thesis, extended and buttressed by new evidence in the present edition, was that the popular reaction to the military uprising of July 1936 was in effect a spontaneous social revolution which left industry in the hands of the unions and the land in possession of the peasants. (It was soon to be collectivized under the leadership of the Anarchist party and unions, the FAI and CNT, who were the real organizers of the revolution as they were of most of the undisciplined militia columns which constituted the popular army.) The "camouflage" of Bolloten's title was the propaganda campaign of the Communist Party which attempted to convince the Western democracies that this revolution had not in fact taken place. This propaganda was paralleled by action which gradually at first and then with almost complete success reversed the course of the social revolution in order to win the support of the Spanish middle classes and also to create a professional disciplined army.

This was a controversial thesis when the first edition was published; it seems now, with the solid documentation this revised and expanded version offers, to be firmly established. Bolloten recreates with brilliantly chosen quotations, precise references, and judicial impartiality the stages of the long political struggle through which the Spanish Communists, backed by the prestige of Russian aid (and saddled with the accompanying Russian "advisers") imposed their priorities on the governments of Azaña, Caballero, and Negrín, and hammered the undisciplined militia columns into a regular army. In the final stage, the Communists reduced to political impotence their stronger opponents, the Socialists and Anarchists, and liquidated the weaker leftist POUM in a Barcelona street battle which George Orwell, a soldier in a POUM militia column, described in his brilliant *Homage to Catalonia*.

It is a grim and occasionally sordid story, all the more depressing because Bolloten is so intent on the politics of the war that his discussion of the repressive tactics of the Communist Party and the activities of the Stalinist secret police is not balanced by an account of what was achieved at the fronts: the heroic record of the new Republican army at Brunete, at Teruel, and on the Ebro. Nevertheless, in its chosen sphere, the book is a landmark. As Raymond Carr says in his foreword, it is "a mine that will be worked over by subsequent historians."

No one can now question the truth of Bolloten's reconstruction of the facts but there is one vital question that he does not address: what alternative was there? The social revolution may have been (for some people) Paradise Now, but it was a fools' paradise; without an efficient army its days were numbered. The people who had made it proved incapable of fighting the kind of war Franco was waging against them. Anarchist columns, operating under what they called "libertarian discipline," had shown almost superhuman courage in the fight against the military revolt in Barcelona but facing experienced troops in the field they were soon outmaneuvered and outflanked, whereupon they ran like rabbits; and the columns of the Socialist party did not do much better.

The Communists owed their prodigious growth in membership and influence to the simple fact that they had (for the moment) only one objective: to create an army that could win the war. And in their formation and training of the Fifth Regiment (not a "column") they showed how it could be done. It was obvious to anyone not blinded by anarchist illusions or blinkered by the traditional socialist distrust of militarism that they were right. And this is the real reason why people as unlikely as the lifelong Socialist Alvarez Del Vayo, the aristocrat Constancia de la Mora, and the ultraconservative General Miaja joined their party—why they became, as Bolloten so clearly shows, the party of the middle classes.

But a Republican army, no matter how efficient, could only buy time; it could not win the war. Franco's revolt had from the beginning depended on German and Italian help; the volume of deliveries soared as the months went by. The Nazi Condor Legion (mostly air force and technical experts) had 14,000 veterans at its victory parade in Berlin in May 1939 and the Italian forces, mainly infantry, numbered 50,000 by mid-1937. The Italian tanks, guns, and planes were more remarkable for their quantity than for their quality; not so the German materiel—the Stuka divebomber and the 88-mm. cannon, later to be the GI's nightmare in Italy and France, both had their trial runs in Spain. Russian supplies, coming by sea from Black Sea ports, were of high quality and arrived, at first, in great quantity; but deliveries by sea were sporadic and after mid-1937 were cut off by Italian naval action.

The Republic could not hope to win the war unless France and England came to its help.

It was the firm conviction of the Spanish Communists and Liberals (and the hope of Joseph Stalin) that the Western powers would finally draw the line against Fascist aggression somewhere in Europe, a move which would almost automatically bring them in behind the Spanish Republic. When the Czech situation came to crisis point in summer 1938, Juan Negrin, who had become premier in May 1937, was convinced that the Republic was saved. He could not have imagined that Chamberlain would cold-bloodedly sell the Czechs down the river, still less that as late as July 1939 Horace Wilson, Chamberlain's closest collaborator, would try to sell the Poles down the river, too. This offer, however, came too late; Hitler had already arranged to settle Poland's hash in a deal with Stalin. The Communist Party's policy (which was of course that of its Russian "advisers") turned out to be based on an illusion. But there was no alternative; all the Republic could do was to win time and hope. And without the creation of an efficient army there would have been no time at all.

Apart from the regiments created by the Communists, the Republican forces consisted of "columns" of varying strength and political persuasions, but most of them were Anarchist formations. In Bolloten's book the Anarchists are treated with great sympathy and respect. They deserve the sympathy in the light of what happened to them at the hands of the Communists; but as defenders of the Republic in the field they were somewhat less than satisfactory. To say that Anarchist columns were not an effective combat force is an understatement; they were capable at times of almost insane bravery and much given to dramatic gestures, but they could not be relied on. Nobody in Madrid felt easy with an Anarchist formation on his flank.

Their gestures, though, could be endearing. The ship which took the first elements of what was to become the Eleventh Brigade out of Marseille in early October 1936 sailed without lights by night and came into Alicante harbor in the morning without a flag. A destroyer detached itself from the Royal Navy squadron, which was presumably there to enforce the nonintervention agreement and deny arms to Spain (only to the Republicans, of course). On the destroyer's bridge a signal light winked on and off frenetically; "They're telling us to show our colors," said one of our small English group, an ex-sailor. Our ship took no notice and the destroyer came round again; this time she fired a shot across our bows. From below our decks three heavily bearded men emerged with a flag; they ran it up and as it broke we saw that it consisted of two triangles, one jet black and the other a blazing red. We had never seen it before and neither had the British Navy; the destroyer captain must have searched his identification manual in vain, for it was the flag of the Federacion Anarquista Iberica.

Later, at Madrid, I saw something of the best troops the Anarchists could field, the column which Buenaventura Durruti had brought from Catalonia. He was the one Anarchist commander who realized that libertarian discipline was a recipe for military suicide; he offered instead the slogan "the discipline of indiscipline" and a rudimentary chain of command. These troops, in late November, were in one of the University buildings across from our own position in Filosofia y Letras and I once had to work my way over to them via a shallow trench in order to discuss passwords and patrol routes for the night—the only time supplies could come up or patrols move in the crazy-quilt pattern of the University front. Once inside the building and identified as an *Internacional* I was treated to a riotous welcome. Plied with cigars, chorizo sausages (moldy green on the outside as usual), and wine (drunk Spanish fashion, head back, the bottle tilted at exatly the right angle 18 inches above the wide-open mouth), I was peppered with questions about the Internationals (did we have officers?) and England (how strong were the English Anarchists?).

They refused to believe that there was in fact no English Anarchist party, but accepted my later (and rather lame) explanation that it must have gone underground after its leader Peter the Painter (*Pedro el Pintero* sounded very authentic) had been killed by Winston Churchill in the Siege of Sydney Street (I did not of course tell them that this had happened in 1910). They taught me how to shout their slogan—"*Viva la CNT, viva la FAI*"—and I was sent off with many hearty slaps on the back. Needless to say, the passwords we had arranged were quickly forgotten and they fired on our supply columns that night; luckily they were not noted for their marksmanship.

But the Anarchists were not always so amusing. On November 17, Durruti's men gave way before a determined Franco assault and left a gap in the line, perilously close to the heart of Madrid; the buildings they had lost had to be retaken by the Internationals, room by room, at terrible expense. And when Durruti led them back into the line he was shot dead and the column disintegrated. Most of his men went

Madrid to the Garden of the Finzi-Contini 255

back to Catalonia to join the Anarchists' columns which sat almost inactive on the long Aragon front month after month while Franco, at his leisure, made three more unsuccessful assaults on Madrid and then turned north to overrun the Basques in the spring of 1937. But some of Durruti's men went to Madrid to act as self-appointed police, hunting for fifth-columnists and spies.

It was in that capacity that I met them again. Convalescing from a wound in the brigade hospital (it was, of all places, the majestic Hotel Palace) I was invited to share a bottle of Scotch (a rare item in Madrid) with some fellow Englishmen, Claud Cockburn the journalist and J. B. S. Haldane the scientist among them. Late at night I walked back to the Palace, through the blacked-out streets, the town silent under the monotonous drone of bombers overhead. As I turned a corner, I was suddenly pushed against the wall and felt the muzzle of a weapon pressed agonizingly hard into my belly. Opposite my eyes was a bearded dark face, the mouth smelling of garlic, sour wine, and harsh Spanish tobacco. The mouth opened and said one word: "*¡Diga!*" ("Speak!") Luckily I knew what to say and said it very loud and clear: "*Viva la CNT, viva la FAI.*" The pressure on my navel was released and the mouth kissed me on the cheek as its owner and his companions slapped me on the shoulders and hailed me as a *compañero*. They escorted me home. As we parted I asked Garlic-mouth: "What would you have done if I had said '*Viva la Republica*'?" He burst out laughing. "I'd have pulled the trigger, *hombre*. That's what the Fascists say."

Madrid in the winter of 1936–37 was a remarkable place. The word *epic* has often been used of the events of that time but there was also a surrealist quality to it; I have often thought since that Luis Buñuel, if he had been there, would have felt quite at home. Just down the road from the front line the cafés of the Granvia were serving coffee and *pasteles,* those incredibly sweet pastries the Madrileños are so fond of; the subway was running and so were the streetcars. "You can take a streetcar to the front line," the Madrileños never tired of telling us, "but don't take the Metro, you might come up on the wrong side." This may well have happened in the first few days of the battle; it was some time, for instance, before the Republicans cut the telephone connections between the city and the enemy-occupied suburbs, Carabanchel and Usera. On the Puerta del Sol the bootblacks were still at their trade, dodging into doorways under an occasional shell or a burst of fifth-column sniping; and ragged little men sidled up to the passers-by opening their jackets to give a glimpse of whatever contraband they were peddling. One of them once whispered to me, as he made the familiar gesture, "Strookey-laike," and I went on, assuming it must be some Spanish brand of filthy postcard—until some days later we were issued a ration of cigarettes which came in a dark green package labeled Lucky Strike.

Haldane's visit to Madrid was another instance of this bizarre blend of the practical and normal with the terrible and absurd. He had been sent for to give advice on protective measures against the possibility of gas attack. The Italians had used it in Abyssinia and it was feared that Franco might try to end the stalemate at Madrid by a whiff of chlorine, to break the Republican front. Over Claud Cockburn's whiskey, Haldane outlined for us the problem and his solution.

The problem was: how to manufacture, in short order, enough gas masks for the thousands of troops on the front line in a city which had none of the necessary raw materials—no rubber, for example, no factories, and hardly any skilled labor. "The problem," he announced, "must be rephrased in more practical and positive terms: how to make a working gas mask quickly and in quantity out of whatever materials are available in Madrid." What, he asked us, is the one thing available in quantity and cheaply in Madrid? The answer—empty wine bottles. The problem therefore was really: to make a gas mask out of an empty wine bottle. Very simple. Stuff it with charcoal and bore a hole in the bottom; troops will hold it in their mouths and breathe through the filter. We sat in stunned silence for a while and then someone asked: "What about their noses?" Haldane had the answer ready: troops would be issued one wooden clothespin apiece to close the nostrils. It would probably have worked all right and the spectacle of soldiers breathing through a wine bottle with wooden clothespins on their noses would have been a perfect subject for one of Goya's disturbing etchings, *Los Caprichos*.

Gas was never used, but after the failure of the initial thrust at the city, Franco gave his Luftwaffe pilots carte blanche to bomb Madrid into surrender; meanwhile the German batteries in the Casa de Campo fired high explosive shells into Madrid at all hours of the day and night. But the population, the first to be subjected to what history had in store for Rotterdam, London, and Hamburg, refused to be intimidated. "*¡Madrid que bien resistes!*" ran the song heard everywhere, "*Madrid que bien resistes los bombardeos.*" And how well they resisted! The small boys in the street played a game: holding hands in a circle they sang, to the tune of Disney's Big Bad Wolf, "*¿Quien tiene miedo de trimotor?*" "Who's afraid of the trimotor?" (the three-engined Italian Caproni bomber). At the end of the chant they would yell "*¡Yo!*" ("*I* am") and run laughing in all directions pursued by the boy who had been designated "it," who with extended arms and making ferocious noises played the part of the Italian bomber.

This is the Madrid Dan Kurzman undertakes to recreate in *Miracle of November*. But he comes nowhere near suggesting the unique atmosphere and mood of that time and place: the pervasive, blind fear of what Franco's troops would do if they won, a fierce pride in the fact that for the first time the apparently irresistible advance of European Fascism had been stopped, and stopped by a miracle of military improvisation, the exhilarating feeling that if we could do this we could do anything—what Malraux in his novel *L'espoir* called *l'illusion lyrique*—and the grim business of feeding men into the meat-grinder battle going on week after week in the Casa de Campo (the former royal park) and the University City. It is perhaps not really Kurzman's fault; it would take a great writer to do it. Hemingway didn't try; Robert Jordan's Madrid is the Madrid of mid-1937—Gaylord's hotel and the cynical witticisms of Karkov (Koltsov); Malraux's section on Madrid, except for that perfect phrase, is one of the least impressive sections of *L'espoir*.

But Kurzman has at least a good title; what happened in November was indeed a miracle, something for which no fully satisfactory explanation has ever been offered. In the opening days of the month the Republican forces, though bolstered now by newly arrived Russian tanks and numerically superior to the Franco spearheads, had been pushed back in disorder to the outskirts of the city; with them came the population of the villages, driven by fear of the Moors. On November 6 the government, headed by the Socialist Largo Caballero, left for Valencia, abandoning Madrid to its fate. (One of the more popular Anarchist gestures was to arrest four of the ministers on their way and threaten to shoot them as deserters.)

Madrid was left in the charge of a middle-aged, fat, bald-headed, owl-like general called Miaja; his orders clearly implied (though they did not explicitly say) that he was to surrender Madrid on the best terms possible. He seemed like the logical choice for the job; his military career had been, even by Spanish standards, undistinguished and furthermore his sympathies were thought, on good grounds, to be with the other side. He had been, before the war, a member of the Union Militar Española, a secret organization dedicated to "protecting Spain from the Communist tide," which had Franco and Mola on its membership list; and he had expressed his conviction that a Franco victory was inevitable.

But Miaja surprised everyone. He turned to the Communists and their Fifth Regiment for support and in what must have been the most down-to-earth speech of a war that was fought to the sound of florid slogans told his hastily formed Defense Committee to be *machos,* that everyone not ready to die in Madrid should leave at once. On more than one occasion during the weeks to come, he went to the front lines and stopped a retreat by standing under fire and screaming: "Cowards! Die with your General Miaja!" at the astonished troops. What inspired him to play this unexpected role no one knows. It was probably just the characteristically furious Spanish reaction to the insult to his self-esteem he sensed in the part Caballero had cast him for.

However Miaja was only one man and the Fifth Regiment was only 60,000 men even at its peak in December. What saved Madrid from Yague's spearheads on November 7 was the manning of the front in the western and northwestern sectors by the civilian population of Madrid and the militiamen who in their panic flight from Talavera had thrown away the rifles sent by Mexico, the Republic's only disinterested ally. Summoned by their unions and political parties they went out, two and sometimes three men to one rifle, to face the Moors and the legionnaires of the *Tercio* in the battered houses of suburban Carabanchel and the hastily dug trenches in the Casa de Campo. In Carabanchel the Moors were stopped; the same men who had been outflanked and routed all the way from Badajoz to Talavera and beyond were now fighting in the Madrid streets where they were at home and where the enemy's capacity for disciplined maneuver was useless. And in the trenches, among the holm-oak trees and gently undulating hills of the Casa de Campo, they fought Yague's main thrust to a standstill.

The miracle here was the sudden change from demoralization to desperate courage. Once again, there is a partial if not fully satisfactory explanation to hand. These men were reacting to the sheer terror inspired by the Franco forces; surrender was simply unacceptable. They expected no quarter; in fact they thought that if they lost this battle those who were shot quickly would be the lucky ones. It is still a matter for dispute how many Republicans were machine-gunned in the bullring at Badajoz in August but the Madrileños believed the figure was in the thousands; they believed, too, that when the Franco forces took a town they shot anyone who had ever belonged to a union or a political party of the left or center, all Jews and Freemasons, and anyone with a bruised right shoulder (the telltale aftermath of firing a Spanish Mauser—it has a kick like a mule). They believed all this because it was mostly true and in any case they had all listened to the obscene ravings of General Queipo de Llano on Radio Sevilla, describing in lurid detail what his beloved Moors would do to the Reds first and their wives afterward. La Pasionaria sent the Madrileños to the front with the famous slogan, "Better to die on your feet than live on your knees." But they had a grimmer slogan, unpronounced but ringing in their heads: "Better to die fighting than up against a wall or drenched in blazing gasoline."

When I was wounded in front of Boadilla del Monte in mid-December 1936 I was helped over some rough patches on my way to the dressing station at Las Rozas, some seven kilometers away, by a teenage Spanish *miliciano* who was less badly hurt. At one point we heard automatic fire very close and from the wrong direction. My young friend pulled out an enormous Smith & Wesson pistol. "Don't worry," he said. "If the Moors come I'll shoot you first and myself afterward." The offer was perfectly serious and was gratefully accepted. I could not help thinking, in the slightly delirious way wounded people have, of the Tennyson poem we had learned by heart in school: Sir Richard Grenville's dying words to his crew in an Elizabethan sea battle off the Azores—"Fall into the hands of God / not into the hands of Spain." This universal fear of being taken alive was one of the constituents of the miraculous rebirth of morale in what seemed to be Madrid's final hour; not for the last time in this century a policy of deliberate terror proved, to use the cliché of a later war, "counterproductive."

One more contribution, not to the miracle of November 7 but to the fact that the fruits of that unexpected victory were not lost, was the arrival, on November 8, of the Eleventh International Brigade. The importance of the Brigades in the struggle for Madrid has been a controversial matter ever since; the Franco historians have naturally exaggerated it, the Republicans have played it down. Obviously the Eleventh Brigade did not "save" Madrid; the city had saved itself on the seventh, but the arrival of the Eleventh on the eighth and of the Twelfth some three or four days later made an important and possibly decisive contribution to the continued success of the defense in the bloody weeks to come.

Accounts of the Eleventh Brigade's role in the fighting are wildly contradictory and most of them riddled with factual error. Vincent Brome's *The International Brigades* (1966) quotes an account of the Boadilla engagement which I wrote in 1937 and goes on to say that John Cornford and Ralph Fox were killed in the course of it. In fact, John was killed some weeks later, on the Cordova front, and Fox was never in our unit at all. The two small English sections, one in the French battalion of the Eleventh, the other in the German battalion of the Twelfth, are repeatedly assigned to the wrong formations (in Brome, for example, and even in the first edition of Hugh Thomas's authoritative history of the war)[3] and every account I have seen of the famous march of the Eleventh along the Granvia on the morning of November 8 is packed with purely mythical detail. Typical is the description in Robert Colodny's otherwise carefully researched book. "Dressed in corduroy uniforms with blue berets, carrying rifles, steel helmets hanging from their belts . . . each section preceded by its officers, carrying swords and revolvers. Behind rolled a small convoy of trucks loaded with machine guns and ammunition. At the rear trotted two small squadrons of French cavalry."[4] Kurzman repeats most of this and has us actually "in steel helmets" and V. B. Johnston[5] specifies seven trucks.

I saw no cavalry on the Granvia; we had come during the night by slow train from Vallecas, east of Madrid, and there were no horses on that train. What would cavalry be doing inside Madrid anyway? And why *French* cavalry? Had they ridden all the way from France? As for the trucks, if there were any, I and my unfortunate companions in the

3. *The Spanish Civil War* (London: Eyre & Spottiswoode, 1961).
4. *The Struggle for Madrid: 1936–1937* (New York: Paine & Whitman, 1958).
5. *Legions of Babel: The International Brigades in the Spanish Civil War* (University Park, PA: Hoover Institution Publications, 1967).

machine-gun company of the Commune de Paris battalion had been cheated of our rights; we were carrying on our sore shoulders the immensely heavy barrels, mounts, and ammunition of some obsolete French machine guns we had been issued the night before. The officers (who were in any case not officers but elected "*responsables*") carried no swords and there was not a helmet in the whole battalion; I was still without a steel helmet when I was hit six weeks later. We had no corduroy uniforms; mine was the discarded dress uniform of a *chasseur alpin*, jet black with silver facings (which had to be ripped off before I went into action). The only correct item in these canonical descriptions of the march down the Granvia are the rifles and the berets, but they were black, not blue. Clio, the Muse of history, seems, on this occasion, to have been replaced by Calliope the epic Muse.[6]

Estimates of the numbers, equipment, and training of the brigade are also divergent and mostly mistaken. The three battalions of the Eleventh are credited with numbers ranging from 1,700 to 3,500; the likeliest figure is 1,900 but no one will ever know for certain, since the brigade went into action without records, without proper identification papers. The only statistic history agrees on is the butcher's bill: more than 50 per cent losses by November 23, when Franco called off the first offensive. The English section was typical; we were sixteen strong on November 8 and by December 31 eight were dead and three were badly wounded.

Our equipment was nothing to write home about; Kurzman's "poorly armed" is a more accurate estimate than the *armamento y*

---

6. The earliest source quoted for this description of the march seems to be Geoffrey Cox's *Defence of Madrid* (London, 1937). Cox was the Madrid correspondent of the London *News Chronicle* and he was in Madrid in November. I can only surmise that he saw us through a romantic haze (or a haze of a different kind—it was the barman at his hotel who told him that the brigade was marching by). Perhaps what he saw was the Twelfth Brigade, which arrived a few days later; they *did* have corduroy trousers (according to Esmond Romilly, *Boadilla* [London: Hamish Hamilton, 1937; reprinted 1971], p. 55) but no steel helmets. John Sommerfield, who carried a St. Etienne just ahead of me in the march and who wrote an eloquent account of it a few months later (*Volunteer in Spain* [London: Lawrence & Wishart, 1937]) has this to say about the uniforms and equipment we were issued before leaving for Madrid: "Some got extraordinary dark-blue short coats, some ammunition belts, some caps, some vests, some boots, some bayonet frogs, some scarves, some gloves. Everybody got *something* and no one got everything. We marched off looking like a bunch of scarecrows." (pp. 49–50).

equipo . . . de calidad y nuevos of Colonel Martinez Bande's official history.[7] Our rifles were '03 Springfields, mostly of the 1914 vintage; on the packing cases from which we had extracted them just before leaving for Madrid we saw the stamps and labels which told of their odyssey from one trouble spot to another—the letters IRA prominent among them. The machine guns we carried on the march through Madrid were utterly useless; they had been identified the previous night by "Grandpère" (our oldest Frenchman) as the Saint Etienne gun which was quickly replaced in the opening weeks of the 1914 war. It was a contraption of startling complexity, activated by a spring mechanism which looked like a huge Swiss watch.

As we worked on these museum pieces, we were interrupted by a general, who turned out to speak English. He said his name was Kléber and he promised us Lewis guns, the British light machine gun of the First World War. He was as good as his word; we had them twenty-four hours later. They were efficient weapons, though they had a remarkable number of stoppages; when they jammed, a complicated diagnostic process, not easily learned in training and harder to practice under fire, had to be gone through with deliberate care. Eventually, the Lewis guns were replaced by Russian water-cooled guns of the type we had seen in the movie *Chapayev*—basically a Vickers World War I model, but mounted on a wheeled metal carriage with a steel shield plate for the gunner. They had been designed to be pulled by horses but there were no horses in the Casa de Campo and we lugged their immense weight up and down through the leafless trees, cursing the day we had been born. But in action they proved their worth.

Apart from the weapons we had practically no equipment at all; some of us had a canteen, most of us a knife and all of us a blanket, usually of inferior material, rolled and slung over one shoulder and tied at the thigh with string. It was our only defense, a poor one, against the bitter cold of the Madrid plateau. We shivered and froze in the trenches until one night, withdrawn from the fighting in the Casa de Campo, we were quartered in a building which had evidently been, once upon a time, the royal stables. We were happy to sleep on straw but before we dozed off one of the French discovered a huge

---

7. José Manuel Martínez Bande, *La marcha sobre Madrid*. Monografías de la guerra de Liberación, No. 1 (Madrid: Libreria Editorial San Martin, 1968), p. 153.

closet full of horse blankets. They were of the softest, warmest wool we had ever run our hands over and there were enough for all of us. They were the kind of blanket that is put on the horse after racing, with a hole for the tail at one end and a long hood with huge lined apertures for the eyes at the other. My last memory of the night is the sight of two drunk Frenchmen, their faces concealed in the drooping horse heads, playing stallion and mare for the benefit of the company—*Los Caprichos* again.

The cold was beyond anything we had expected to experience in what a huge bullet-ridden poster in one of the University buildings called Sunny Spain; at the dawn stand-to we had to avoid touching the metal parts of the guns—the frozen metal would latch on to the skin and rip it off. We learned, from the Spaniards, to wrap woolen scarves around our bellies next to the skin; we crammed on to our shivering limbs every stitch of clothing we possessed and all the shirts, socks, and sweaters we had brought or could acquire. It was not until thirty years later that I saw, in the Prado, Goya's *Winter* panel, and recognized, in its padded, shivering, loaded peasants, hunched forward against the cold, the portrait of Madrid's November soldiers. The cold was so intense that the canned Russian butter which was distributed in chunks with the morning drink of *café con leche* laced with brandy could be kept in one's pocket and chewed on like toffee throughout the morning. (The other memorable piece of Russian aid was a canned meat, eaten cold of course, which consisted of tiny limbs, legs, and breasts, of an animal no one could identify; it was certainly not a bird, it was not rabbit either, and no one knew what to call it until some Parisian wit—obviously not a Party member—christened it for us. *"C'est du gosse en conserve"*—canned baby.)

There is also disagreement about the degree of training of the Eleventh and Twelfth Brigades: "ill-trained" (Kurzman), "military efficiency" (Brome), "superior efficiency" (Bolloten), "well-trained and equipped" (Hills).[8] As usual, the truth is somewhere in between the extremes. One thing is certain: the training we were given at Albacete, the Brigade base, was a farce. There were no arms to train with, not a single rifle, and so the staff fell back on the classic bourgeois-imperialist recipe for keeping idle troops out of mischief: close-order drill. Our section was put through its paces in British drill by a

---

8. George Hills, *The Battle for Madrid* (New York: St. Martin's Press, 1977).

former Guardsman; with the battalion we did French drill; sometimes our instructor was a German and we got a taste of the Prussian method; what we liked most was when someone decided we should conform to local custom and do Spanish drill—it was, compared to the Prussian, a sort of ballet.

Every now and then we were taken on a route march, along dusty roads across the baked Murcian hills, greeted on the way by peasant families perched on carts loaded down with black grapes. One march was particularly memorable. It seemed to go on forever, and to the foul-mouthed complaints of the French our company commander (a roly-poly ex-Legionnaire known, inevitably, as Bouboule) replied with exhortations to be patient—we were going to see something worthwhile. Finally, at the base of an unusually steep hill, he stood by the side of the road and told us, proudly, what it was. "Look out when you get to the top—*vous allez voir un pendu.*" And sure enough, once over the hump of the hill, we saw, hanging from a limb of a sickly looking tree, a corpse, still dressed in blue overalls and dirty-white rope-soled sandals. Whether he had been a "Fascist" or a "Red" there was no means of telling; he had been there a long time and the birds had finished with him. It was Goya again—a scene from *Los Desastres de la Guerra.* Bouboule, it turned out later, had sent scouts out all over the countryside to find a *pendu* for us. It made us wonder about the quality of the "training" in the Legion's base at Sidi-bel-Abbès.

But "ill-trained" as we were, we were light years ahead of the Spanish Republican soldiers. We had a fair number of ex-professionals in our ranks; the French had, most of them, done their military service; the Germans who were not veterans of the First World War (it had ended only eighteen years before) had, many of them, fought in anti-Nazi paramilitary organizations in the streets of German cities. And in our own tiny English section, the Oxford-Cambridge contingent (Cambridge 3, Oxford 1) had all been to schools which maintained a Cadet Corps, subsidized by the War Office. These were very efficient training units for the production of future infantry officers; training at my London school, for example, included range-firing on the Lewis gun.

But that was not all. We came from countries which had been through the 1914–18 war and we had learned, from what little our fathers would tell us, from the books which described life in the trenches and from the films and plays which attempted to recreate it, what modern war was like. Spain had not been in a major war since Napoleon's time and even in that war her major contribution had been the *guerrilla,* who crippled the French in the rear while Wellington hammered them from in front. The twentieth-century Spaniard had grown up with a vision of war which seemed to be derived from the medieval epic of the Cid and the contemporary bullfight; war was a sort of *corrida* which separated the *machos* from the cowards. We had a startling instance of this the very first time we came under fire.

It was on November 8. After our painful march through Madrid we had finally got the load off our backs and were sitting down to rest outside the Philosophy and Letters building at the western end of the University City. Some young *milicianos* had come over to talk to us, to ask where we came from: were we Russians, and if so, where were our tanks? All this in broad daylight, on a ridge line (the ground sloped down almost precipitously to the west); no one had any idea the enemy could see us. How could he? The newspapers carried a communiqué announcing heavy attacks repulsed in the area of Navalcarnero, some thirty kilometers away. It soon became apparent that this communiqué had been concocted by the same visionaries who later astonished the world by announcing that our glorious troops had advanced without losing a single foot of ground—a formulation unrivaled until, in a later war, the United States Air Force introduced the "preplanned protective reaction."

As we talked and exchanged cigarettes our ears were suddenly assailed by a sound which, starting as a sort of screaming whine, soon ceased to be a sound at all but was rather an immense, intolerable pressure on all the senses at once; we could feel as well as hear the swift approach of something huge and violent, as if a loaded freight-car were flying full speed straight at us. It was our first experience of incoming artillery and partly from animal instinct and partly also from training, we threw ourselves down and hugged the earth, waiting, in abject terror, for the explosions. When they came (it was a salvo of three) they burst below us on the escarpment. We turned over to see the Spaniards, white-faced and obviously shaken, but still standing upright. One of them caught my eye. "*¡Cobardes!*"—"Cowards!" he said triumphantly; it was the fulfillment of the Spanish male dream, to be seen facing the bull while others ran away. He did not, however, enjoy his triumph very long. The sound started again, louder and more intense this time—the enemy had got the range. The shells burst on the ridge. No one was hurt but when I looked up I saw the *milicianos* were stretched out prone, gone to ground and trying to claw their way into the earth like infantrymen born.

Apart from the fact that they supplied a much needed supplement of what our G.I.s, in a later war, cynically referred to as "warm bodies," the Brigades furnished a salutary example. "The *miliciano* began to learn; he started to pick up soldierly habits. Every 'international' became, without realizing it, a teacher," wrote the Socialist Zugazagoitia.[9] Many of the *milicianos* had of course been in action before, but it was the wrong kind of action—haphazard advance followed by disorganized if not chaotic retreat. They learned from us not to use up scarce ammunition unless there was a clearly visible target and one within range, that machine guns should be fired in short bursts and not in one continuous barrel-heating belt-exhausting rattle, and above all, that it was not cowardly to dig as deep a hole as you had time and energy for.

Nearly all accounts of the Brigades (and Bolloten's and Kurzman's are no exception) speak of them as a purely Communist organization, though few writers go as far as Hills. According to him the Eleventh Brigade consisted of Germans, Poles, Hungarians, and Yugoslavs despatched from the Soviet Union where, as refugees, they had long been an embarrassment to Stalin, and of Frenchmen and Belgians recruited by Comintern agents. This statement is pure official Franco propaganda swallowed whole. The Germans of the Edgar André battalion of the Eleventh came most of them from exile in France, where they had spent their time trying to avoid the hounding of the French police; many of the Poles also came from France—from the grim little towns of the northern French coal fields, where their fathers had been settled after the First World War to replace the French miners killed in the slaughterhouse of the Western Front. And if "Comintern agents" were responsible for recruiting the Frenchmen of our battalion, they must have been Trotskyite saboteurs.

There was a core of convinced Communists all right (who did not,

---

9. Julian de Zugazagoitia, *Historia de la guerra de España* (Buenos Aires, 1954), p. 144 (cited by Martinez Bande, p. 153).

of course, need to be "recruited") but the rest were a heady mixture of ex-Legionnaires, unemployed workers, kids just out of the *lycée*, and the inevitable contingent, in a French unit, of semialcoholics. The French made such a nuisance of themselves in Albacete, in fact— their idea of an evening's entertainment was expressed by the invitation *allons chanter dans les bordels*—that we were soon moved out to the small village of La Roda, where the ingredients for such a program were nonexistent. Later, at Madrid, where we once spent a miserable twenty-four hours in a perfume factory which directly faced the towering Hopital Clinico, from which the Moorish snipers were looking down our throats, the *soulards* of the battalion distinguished themselves by drinking the bay rum and clinical alcohol they found on the factory shelves; when we were withdrawn we had to carry them out with us, dead to the world. But they had fought well when sober and our crazy Bouboule died leading a desperate bayonet charge in the Casa de Campo.

It is true that as time went on it was the Comintern which organized the transportation and controlled enrollment. It also carried out political purges in the ranks. Of this last activity I was quite unaware and had in fact been invalided out of Spain before it went into high gear. As a result it was a long time before I was able to accept the fact, so memorably dramatized in Hemingway's *For Whom the Bell Tolls* (and later confirmed by the French Communist party itself) that André Marty, the grand old man of the Black Sea mutiny, who had been such a benevolent presence at the base (he spoke a little English and did our small group some favors), had turned into a paranoid inquisitor and executioner—the "butcher of Albacete."

As for transportation, it was natural that an organization used to clandestine work should take charge of operations that involved illegal movement in and through Fascist countries as well as illegal transport across frontiers. But the first brigades, the Eleventh and Twelfth, were different. Some of the men, like my friend John Cornford, had been in Spain from the beginning, long before the Brigades were formed; of the others, most came unprompted, many at their own expense[10] and some at the risk of their lives. Auden had the words for it:

10. Esmond Romilly (who ended up in the German battalion of the XIIth Brigade) rode a bicycle from Dieppe to Marseille, losing his money and passport on the way (*Boadilla*, p. 18).

> They clung like burrs to the long expresses that lurch
> Through the unjust lands, through the night, through the alpine tunnel
> They floated over the oceans.
> They walked the passes; they came to present their lives.

The miracle of November prolonged the war but it turned out to be merely a postponement of the final defeat; to little Peterkin's question one could only give old Kaspar's answer. It could even be argued (and it no doubt has been) that it would have been better for Spain if Franco had indeed ridden a white horse into the Puerta del Sol on November 7, as Radio Lisbon triumphantly announced at the time; the war would soon have been over and the sufferings of the Spanish people would have been cut short by two years. But it might have gone otherwise. Madrid's November showed that Fascism was not after all irresistible; it sent the British and French, who had sat impotently by while Mussolini conquered Abyssinia and Hitler reoccupied the Rhineland, a clear signal: this is the time to draw the line and Madrid is the place to do it.

If the Baldwin government had given Léon Blum the go-ahead signal to open the frontier to arms shipments or if Blum had had the guts to defy London and open it anyway, the Republic might have been saved; Madrid might have been the turning of the tide and become, as the banners in its streets proclaimed, *la tumba del Fascismo*. But when, in 1937, Baldwin was replaced by Chamberlain, that hope, if it had ever existed, was doomed. Backed by his sinister Foreign Secretary Halifax (alias Irwin alias Wood) and sure that he could manipulate for his own ends the dictator he always toothily referred to as "Herr Hitler," the new prime minister moved swiftly along the path which brought the Wehrmacht to the Channel and the Luftwaffe over England.

The consequences for France were even worse. Blum's pusillanimous abandonment of the Frente Popular government in Spain undermined the strength of his own Front Populaire, and the morale of the French working class was steadily eaten away as the long-drawn-out betrayal went on. The soldiers mobilized in 1939 to fight Fascism across the Rhine had no confidence in their leaders and were conscious of the potential enemy on their southern flank. When the blow came, they collapsed. The German triumph of 1940 was a victory, as historians have since demonstrated, not of superior numbers and materiel, but of superior morale. In the summer of 1940 I listened, on Long Island, to the radio bulletins which announced the incredibly swift disintegration of the French Army. With me was Gustavo Durán, a Republican general who had fought all through the war and escaped from Spain in the last days. As the dismal rout of the French ended in surrender he suddenly burst out, with that characteristic Spanish combination of pride and contempt: "Three weeks! They lasted only three weeks! And *we* resisted for almost three years."

Durán was not the only one to leave Spain in the last days of the war. Over the French frontier there came, on foot and just ahead of Franco's pursuit, somewhere between 350,000 and 500,000 Republican Spaniards. When France declared war on Hitler, some former soldiers of the Republican Army fought in the Foreign Legion; 14,000 of them were taken prisoner by the Nazis in Belgium and shipped off to Mauthausen and other concentration camps—10,000 died there. Under Vichy the Spaniards were conscripted to work for the German Todt organization but it was not long before they became the backbone of the Resistance in southwestern France. Others managed to escape and come back to France with Leclerc's armored division. By the war's end 60,000 Spanish Republicans had taken part in the battles against Hitler's armies. When Germany capitulated in 1945 they were confident that the Allies would now exert pressure to bring down the Franco regime (which had, after all, sent a division to fight with the Nazis in Russia).

For a moment it seemed as if their hopes might be fulfilled. There were indeed contingency plans for intervention of some kind in Spain under consideration in late 1944. They have never, to my knowledge, been referred to in print and I can speak of them only from personal experience, with no knowledge of how extensive they were or what higher headquarters were involved. The facts are these. In early October 1944 I was a captain in the United States Army, attached to OSS, awaiting reassignment in London after a mission (Operation Jedburgh) to the French Maquis which involved arms supply by air and fairly large-scale guerrilla operations against the German army of occupation. We were all expecting to be returned to Washington and, from there, since there seemed to be no future for guerrilla operations in Europe, to be assigned to the China-Burma-India theater.

One day I was called into the office near Grosvenor Square and introduced to a colonel I had never seen before. I was told to stand by for a possible mission in Europe and warned that it was Top Secret. Since there was no place left in the ETO for our type of operation except Germany I asked for some more information; I was not prepared to jump into the Black Forest and start looking for the German resistance movement. "It's not Germany," I was told. And if the mission were approved, I would be on the training staff for a large special detachment stationed in England; I might or might not go in with them. "Go in where?" I asked stubbornly. "Just think hard," said the colonel. "I'll give you a hint, though—you've been there before."

A few days later I was called in again and told that the mission had been scrubbed. And furthermore that I was to forget that it had ever been mentioned. "Let this out," I was told, "and we'll lock you up and throw the key away." Later I heard from a British Jedburgh officer who had been born in Argentina and spoke fluent Spanish that he, too, had been tapped for the mission and had actually seen a training camp for Spaniards, many of them Basques. He was glad the project had been scrubbed. "Terrifying people," he said. "Frightened the hell out of me."

Higher headquarters had ruled out support for guerrilla operations against Franco. Perhaps it was just as well. Only a month later the Spanish Republican exiles took matters into their own hands; armed with supplies that had been parachuted to them in the French Resistance, a force of some 2,000 invaded the Basque country. They seized sixteen villages and held them for ten days against the 45,000 troops Franco sent in. But the general insurrection which they had hoped to provoke showed no signs of life and they had to withdraw. Later, as it gradually became clear after the war that the Western Allies had no interest in their cause, they turned to guerrilla operations again but were no more successful. Their courage, skill, and sacrifice were all to no avail, for they could not command the widespread sympathy and support which are the guerrilla's base.[11] The Spanish people had had enough of violent action; before too long Franco was able to exploit the Western Allies' need for cold-war bases and lay the foundation for the "economic miracle" of the sixties, which significantly narrowed what Gerald Brenan (*New York Re-*

---

11. For a full account see Luis Stein, *Beyond Death and Exile: The Spanish Republicans in France, 1939–1955* (Cambridge: Harvard University Press, 1979).

view of Books, 27 September, 1979) called "the huge gap between the working man's income and that of even the modest bourgeois which . . . made the real problems of Spain insoluble."

The amnesty that was proclaimed after Franco's death came too late for the exiles, who had fought Fascism so long, so well, and on so many fronts; history had passed them by. "History," so runs the conclusion of Auden's poem, "History, to the defeated / May say Alas but cannot help or pardon." In 1965, when he published his *Collected Poems,* he excluded "Spain 1937" because of these lines—"this wicked doctrine," he called it. But the Republican exiles could have told him it was the bare, bitter truth. It still is.[12]

12. For an exchange of letters on this essay with William Herrick, see the *New York Review of Books,* April 16, 1981, p. 41.

The Spanish Tragedy

July 1986 was the fiftieth anniversary of the outbreak of the Spanish civil war. The war began as a rebellion of the Spanish Army generals against the country's democratically elected government, and ended three years later with the establishment of General Francisco Franco Bahamonde as dictator, a position he was to hold until his death in 1975.

Seen in retrospect, the war was the almost inevitable product of irreconcilable antagonisms within Spanish society that only a strong regime could hope to control. Instead of a strong government, however, the election victory of the Frente Popular in 1936 brought to office a cabinet of liberal republicans from minority parties, dependent for its continued existence on the cooperation of the Socialists and the as yet small Communist party. The Popular Front was threatened by forces that did not recognize its authority. On the right stood, among others, the Falange, a Fascist party on the Italian model, and the Carlist Requetes, fanatically devoted to the monarchy and the Catholic Church; on the left, a strong and widespread Anarchist movement which proclaimed its intention to abolish not only the state but also the Catholic Church—and in fact burned many churches. Small wonder that two of the most impressive books on the politics of Spain in the twentieth century are entitled *The Spanish Labyrinth*[1] and *The Spanish Cockpit*.[2]

Yet though its causes were so deeply rooted in circumstances peculiar to Spain (Basque and Catalan aspirations to autonomy added another unique complication), this war became, within days of its outbreak, the passionate concern of many people in Western Europe and America who had little or no understanding of its complex ori-

This essay originally appeared in the *New York Review of Books*, March 26, 1987.

1. By Gerald Brenan (Cambridge: Cambridge University Press, 1943).
2. By Franz Borkenau (London: 1937; Ann Arbor: University of Michigan Press, 1963).

gins. The military rebels were supported and supplied by Hitler and Mussolini from the very beginning—German and Italian planes made possible the first military airlift in history, the transportation of Franco's Moorish mercenaries from Africa to the mainland. The Madrid government represented the electoral victory of the Frente Popular, a left-to-center coalition like that which had brought the Socialist Léon Blum to power in France in the same year. So Spain became the first battleground of the anti-Fascist war, a place where the advance of Fascist power in Europe unopposed and in fact at times actively encouraged by the British government, might be given a serious, perhaps even decisive, setback.

"*Madrid sera la tumba del Fascismo*" was a slogan launched when Franco's Moors and foreign legionaries were stopped dead at the edge of the city in November 1936; it was the hope, a not irrational one, of all progressive opinion in the West. It was not to be, of course; the French, cowed by threats from London that if they sold arms to the Republic they would have to face the consequences alone, joined Great Britain on the Nonintervention Committee, which "was to graduate," as Hugh Thomas[3] puts it, "from equivocation to hypocrisy." The British and French left the Republic to fight a professional army, backed by German and Italian weapons, specialists, and troops, with a rabble militia, without officers and heterogeneously armed, and dependent for heavy armament on Soviet shipments over the long sea route from Odessa through waters patrolled by Italian submarines, warships, and planes.[4] The wonder is that the Republic survived so long; if it had managed to survive six months longer, in fact, it might have been saved at the last moment by the outbreak of the European war in September 1939.

The long, heroic resistance of the Republic aroused in its time the enthusiastic admiration of liberal and left-wing circles in the West. This was true above all of writers, who were especially sensitive to the threat of Fascism, both abroad and at home. "Our prerogatives as men," Louis MacNeice wrote in a poem addressed to Auden in 1936,

3. *The Spanish Civil War*, new ed. (New York: Harper & Row, 1986).
4. For Italian sinking of supply ships (not only Russian but also British, French, Greek, and Danish) see ibid., pp. 740ff. Mussolini boasted in September 1937 that he had sunk nearly 200,000 tons (Thomas, p. 743) and by October, according to Thomas (p. 745), "the blockade of the Mediterranean was now almost complete."

> Will be cancelled who knows when.
> Still I drink your health before
> The gun-butt raps upon the door.[5]

Later, recalling a visit to Spain just before the war broke out, he wrote of leaving the country,

>   . . . not realising
> That Spain would soon denote
> Our grief, our aspirations;
> Not knowing that our blunt
> Ideals would find their whetstones, that our spirit
> Would find its frontier on the Spanish front,
> Its body in a rag-tag army.[6]

MacNeice spoke for an entire generation of writers, British, European, and American; the war was midwife to an abundant and talented literature, a "burst of creative energy," as Hugh Thomas puts it in his definitive history of the war, "which can be argued as comparable in quality to anything produced in the Second World War."

The fiftieth anniversary has revived interest in this struggle that now seems so remote even to those who took an active part in it. In Washington, for example, a conference organized by the Smithsonian Institution's Museum of American History recently discussed the impact of the war on the American political scene and in particular the role of the Abraham Lincoln Battalion. It was addressed by historians and veterans (one of them, Professor Robert Colodny, was both) and concluded with a screening of a remarkable film, *The Good Fight*, which through interviews with veterans and contemporary photographs and newsreels recreates the atmosphere of the time and explores the motives of the participants.

Similar conferences are being planned or already announced at more than one university; meanwhile a number of new books on the war and an important reissue of an old one have already appeared, and there are no doubt more to come. The reissue is Hugh Thomas's basic history, *The Spanish Civil War*. It was first published in 1961; in 1977 a "revised and enlarged edition" incorporated the new material,

---

5. *The Collected Poems of Louis MacNeice* (New York: Oxford University Press, 1967), p. 75.
6. Ibid., p. 112.

much of it published in Spain, which had come to light in the interval. Now Harper and Row has produced what it calls a "third edition," with a "new preface by the author." There is indeed a new preface—less than two pages in length—but otherwise the text is unchanged from the 1977 edition. The misprints remain uncorrected (two lines missing and two repeated on page 862, for example) and so do slips of the pen (a remark of Orwell attributed to Auden on page 653).

More important, no notice is taken of material published after 1977 that calls for correction or addition. In his account of the arrival of the Eleventh International Brigade at Madrid in November 1936, for example, Thomas has the march led by "a battalion of Germans with a section of British machine-gunners, including the poet John Cornford." In fact, Cornford and the present writer were in the 2nd Battalion, the French "Commune de Paris."[7] This error was corrected in an article published in the *New York Review of Books* in 1980 (see pp. 260ff.). As for additions, Peter Wyden's book *The Passionate War* (see pp. 245ff.) provides new evidence about the massacre of prisoners by Franco's troops at Badajoz in 1936, a subject for bitter controversy ever since the first reports of these mass shootings in the bullring reached the outside world.

Still, even though it is regrettable that the opportunity to bring it up to date was not seized, Thomas's book is the fullest and best one-volume nonpartisan history of the war in English.[8] Starting from the overthrow of the monarchy in 1931 Thomas constructs a clear and skillfully paced narrative which gives equal weight to the military, political, and economic aspects of the conflict. His analysis of the dissension on both sides is illuminating and fair-minded, though on rereading I detected a somewhat disproportionate admiration for the way Franco succeeded in manipulating his warring constituencies to his own advantage, unlike the unfortunate Republic, which resorted to armed repression in Catalonia in 1937 and in its final days was un-

---

7. Thomas has confused our section with the English group (of which Esmond Romilly was a member) that served in the German Battalion of the Twelfth Brigade. They arrived at Madrid several days later.

8. Gabriel Jackson, *A Concise History of the Spanish Civil War* (London: Thames & Hudson, 1980) is also worth consulting. Anthony Beevor's *The Spanish Civil War* (New York: Bedrick, 1983) is a much fuller treatment, especially notable for its expert discussion of the military operations. (Beevor was trained at Sandhurst and served for five years as a regular officer in the British Army.)

able to prevent the military commanders at Madrid from surrendering unconditionally and so ending the war.

A subtle bias perhaps shows itself in the fact that victims of repression are either "shot" or "executed" in Franco territory whereas in the Republic they are usually "murdered." The distinction may stem from Thomas's generalization that "though there was much killing in rebel Spain, the idea of *limpieza,* the 'cleaning up' of the country from the evils which had overtaken it, was a disciplined policy of the new authorities and a part of their program of regeneration"; whereas "in Republican Spain most of the killing was the consequence of anarchy, the outcome of a national breakdown, and not the work of the state." Since the "national breakdown" had been mainly provoked by the rebellion of the military authorities and since the policy of *limpieza* entailed what Thomas calls "a wave of executions which began in 1936 and continued, if the truth be known, until 1941 or 1942,"[9] this summary is, to say the least, disingenuous.

It is true that in Franco territory the killings were carried out by men in uniform, but that is hardly warrant for the distinction between "execution" and "murder." Given the scale and difficulty of the undertaking, however, these are minor lapses; the task of maintaining an impartial tone in a field where controversy rages on almost every point (Thomas's bibliography includes nearly nine hundred publications) must have been exacting in the extreme and one can only admire the careful weighing of the evidence and its full citation, which make this book still, for the English-speaking world, the standard history of the war.

The illustrations in this edition of the book, unlike those in the first, consist entirely of photographs of the leading personalities on both sides, and since one of Thomas's strong points is his incisive delineation of character—his portraits of Franco, Manuel Azaña, the Republican president, and the Anarchist leader Durruti, for example, are particularly memorable—this seems appropriate. But the war was the first to be fully documented by photographers. "This," said a Catalan official to Claud Cockburn, "is the most photogenic war any-

---

9. Jackson's figures for executions and reprisal killings (as revised downward in his 1980 paperback edition) are: 20,000 on the Republican side, "committed mostly during the first three months of the struggle," and on the other side "the Nationalists, counting the entire time from July 1936 to the end of the mass executions in 1944, liquidated 150,000 to 200,000 of their compatriots."

one has ever seen." The visual aspect of it is handsomely covered in a collection of more than three hundred and fifty illustrations: *The Spanish Civil War: A History in Pictures.*[10] They are arranged chronologically from the fall of the monarchy in 1931 to the collapse of the Republic in 1939; the first photograph shows triumphant Republicans standing on an overturned equestrian royal statue and the last a Republican soldier interned in France, giving a light to a sentry through the wire. These images of the war come from both sides of the lines and they are supplemented by a generous selection of those posters which, in the hands of the Republican artists, marked a new level in the techniques of visual propaganda.

There are unfortunately very few pictures from what was regarded at the time as the epic phase of the war, the defense of Madrid in November and December of 1936. There are photographs of bombs and artillery shells exploding in the Madrid streets, but none of the fighting in the Casa de Campo and the University City, except for one, labeled "posed picture," which shows soldiers sitting and standing up, firing out of the open windows of what is supposed to be one of the university buildings. Never, I suspect, was a picture more posed.[11] In our building, Filosofía y Letras, we fired our Lewis guns through holes we had made in the brickwork just above floor level and moved on our hands and knees below the level of the windows until we managed to barricade them with huge volumes we found in the basement (some of them dealt, in German, with Indian religion and philosophy). It is not that photographs of this part of the front were unavailable; the December 1936 issue of *Life* magazine had a number of pictures that showed the strange landscape of the Ciudad Universitaria, a world of half-ruined buildings fronting great bare expanses of grass and concrete on which nothing living was to be seen. And the film *Mourir à Madrid* has a sequence shot in the Philosophy and Letters building at night which shows International Brigade troops repelling an attack.

This is a minor complaint, however, that of a veteran who finds his own battles slighted; on the whole this is a splendid selection. And it is preceded by an introduction by Raymond Carr, a thoughtful

10. Introduction by Raymond Carr (New York: Norton, 1986).
11. The same picture appears in Beevor's book with the caption: "Rebels defend the telephone exchange in Barcelona, 1936." This may well be right; the men in the picture look like regular Spanish Army personnel.

and judicious assessment of the causes, course, and effects of the war by a noted authority on modern Spanish history.

The impact of the war on writers and intellectuals was, as Carr says in his introduction, "tremendous." That impact is the focus of two new anthologies: *Spanish Front: Writers on the Civil War* edited by Valentine Cunningham [12] and *Voices Against Tyranny: Writing of the Spanish Civil War* edited by John Miller.[13] Cunningham is a tutor in English literature at Oxford and has previously edited an anthology entitled *Spanish Civil War Verse*,[14] which included much material that had not been previously published or collected; the book is remarkable for its informed and penetrating critical introduction. His new anthology contains more prose than verse; this is understandable since, as he remarked in the preface to the earlier collection, many of the poems in it "deserve . . . to be known only to readers with a particular interest in the literature of this war."

In the new volume there is much that is familiar—poems by Auden, Spender, George Barker, and John Cornford, prose extracts from Koestler, Orwell, Bernanos, Regler, and Esmond Romilly's *Boadilla*, perhaps the most moving of all the eyewitness accounts by combatants. But there is also much that is unfamiliar and very good to have. There is, for example, a previously unpublished letter of Stephen Spender to Virginia Woolf, written in April 1937 after a visit to Spain, which urges her to discourage Julian Bell from joining the Brigades and laments the fate of those volunteers who "should never have joined" and find themselves unable to stand the stress of combat. (Not that they were shot as deserters, which would have been their lot in the 1914 war; they were, to quote Spender, "quite well treated in a camp.")

There is also a letter from Simone Weil to Georges Bernanos; she has just read *Les Grands Cimetières sous la lune*, his terrifying account of the Fascist massacres on Majorca, and writes that she has had an experience herself "which echoes yours." Not that the killings carried out by the Anarchists, one of whose columns she had joined, were on the scale of those organized by the Italian Fascist Rossi on Majorca; but, as she puts it, "numbers are perhaps not the main thing in such

   12. New York: Oxford University Press, 1986.
   13. Introduction by Stephen Spender (New York: Scribner's, 1986).
   14. Harmondsworth: Penguin, 1980.

matters. The real point is how murder is regarded." Also included is Anthony Blunt's dismissal of Picasso's series of etchings *Sueño y mentira de Franco* as the work of "a talented artist struggling to cope with a problem entirely outside his powers" and the heated correspondence, including a rebuttal by Herbert Read, which followed the publication of Blunt's article "Picasso Unfrocked" in *The Spectator.*

One novel feature of this anthology is its emphasis on the role of women in the war. "The fairly well-known male story of concerned male artists and writers," Cunningham says in his introduction, "has now to be supplemented by the story of engaged women writers and artists."[15] A section captioned (rather strangely) "Women Writing Spain" includes items from Virginia Woolf ("Remembering Julian"), Rosamond Lehmann, and Sylvia Townsend Warner, as well as a moving account of the work of a British medical unit in the Republican Ebro offensive in 1938. It is a memoir, previously unpublished, written by Nan Green, a nurse in the unit, whose husband, serving in the British Battalion, was killed in the course of that operation.

Cunningham has obviously tried hard to find writing from adherents of the Fascist cause but the pickings are slim. Evelyn Waugh's reply to the *Left Review* questionnaire—"If I were a Spaniard I should be fighting for General Franco"—and Roy Campbell's scurrilous poem addressed to Azaña are well known. Cunningham has, however, unearthed one real gem: Hilaire Belloc's account of his interview with Franco just before the fall of Catalonia. Belloc is deeply moved by the site of their meeting, the "Marches of the Ebro, where Charlemagne first established the Christian bastion against that attack which threatened to destroy, to overwhelm, all the Christian thing." The attack in question was the advance of Islam, the "violent flame" by which "Christendom of the east and of the Mediterranean had been three-quarters overrun." Franco was "one who had fought that same battle which Roland in the legend died fighting and which the Godfrey in sober history had won when the battered remnant, the mere surviving tenth of the first Crusaders, entered Jerusalem."

Belloc is apparently unaware of the fact that it was Franco who brought Islam back to Spain more than four hundred years after Isa-

---

15. The film *The Good Fight* has a similar emphasis; some of the most impressive figures among the veterans who appear in it are women—two nurses (one of them black) and a truck driver.

bella la Católica had broken its power at Granada. The key units of the Army of Africa which advanced on Madrid were the *Regulares*, Moorish mercenaries originally recruited to fight against their own people in Morocco;[16] their "established battle-rite of castrating the corpses of their victims [was] usually," says Thomas, "restrained by their commander General Yague."[17]

The other anthology of writers, *Voices against Tyranny*, is a smaller book and its excerpts are most of them much longer than those in Cunningham's book. There is some duplication in the two volumes but prominent among the items peculiar to this volume are a story by Hemingway, "The Butterfly and the Tank," which first appeared in *Esquire* in 1938, a story by Dorothy Parker which remained unpublished until 1986, when it was printed in *Mother Jones*, an extract from Salvador Dali's autobiography with a typically idiosyncratic view of the war, and a fascinating chapter from the autobiography of Luis Buñuel, which was published in 1983.

In an article about the winter fighting in Madrid published some years ago (see pp. 250ff.) I remarked on the surrealist quality of life in the city in those days and surmised that Buñuel, if he had been there, would have felt quite at home. It turns out that he was in fact in Madrid when the rebellion began and stayed there until September; he then left for Paris, where he had been assigned to work with the Republic's ambassador. But he did not feel at all at home in Madrid. "I," he writes, "who had been such an ardent subversive, who had so desired the overthrow of the established order, now found myself in the

---

16. Franco had used the Moors in Spain before—in the ferocious repression of the revolt in Asturias in 1934, where they were allowed to rape as well as kill indiscriminately.

17. Thomas, p. 375 n. 1. The other component of the Army of Africa, which relieved Toledo and reached the outskirts of Madrid in November, was the *Tercio*, the Spanish foreign legion. It consisted mainly of Spaniards, though there was also a large Portuguese contingent. According to Beevor (p. 52), it was "composed in large part of fugitives and criminals." There were also some French in the legion, as I found out at Madrid. At one point in the fighting in the University City we were in trenches very close to the enemy; they began to shout insults and threats at us in what was clearly, judging from its expert profanity, native French. When I asked our Frenchmen of the Commune de Paris Battalion what Frenchmen would be doing in the Spanish foreign legion, they said: "Our legion will take foreigners in with no questions asked, but if you are a Frenchman on the run from the police, you have to go to the Spaniards."

middle of a volcano, and I was afraid." He was torn between his "intellectual (and emotional) attraction to anarchy" and his "fundamental need for order and peace."

The overwhelming majority of the writers represented in these two anthologies express themselves in favor of the Republic and against Franco, and liberal intellectual opinion has over the years tended to agree. That position has recently come under attack. In an article published in the *New Criterion,* "But Today the Struggle: Spain and the Intellectuals,"[18] Ronald Radosh, a professor of history at Columbia University, dismisses the Republican cause as one which, in the light of what is now known about Russian interference and manipulation, should be wholly repudiated by intellectuals. "In 1986, those who still respond to the Spanish Civil War as 'our cause' have no excuse."[19]

It is of course true, as is evident from many of the texts collected in Cunningham's anthology, that many writers and intellectuals who initially supported the Republic had second thoughts later, George Orwell prominent among them. Yet even though the role of the Russian-directed political police in the last year or so of the Republic's life has been common knowledge for at least twenty years (Radosh has no new evidence to show), few, if any, of those who once championed the Republic, with rifle or with pen, have seen fit to repudiate the cause entirely, any more than Orwell did.

Even some of those who fought in the International Brigades have had to recognize, sooner or later, unpleasant truths that they had no inkling of at the time. I am myself a case in point. I fought, with John Cornford, in the machine-gun company of the French Battalion of the Eleventh Brigade at Madrid in the winter of 1936. When, some years later, Hemingway's *For Whom the Bell Tolls* appeared, though full of admiration for the novel and the remarkable illusion it creates of Spanish character and even of Spanish speech, I was outraged by its portrayal of the French Communist official André Marty as a mur-

18. October 1986.
19. Radosh's particular target is Alfred Kazin's article, "The Wound That Will Not Heal," *New Republic,* August 25, 1986. In an article published in the *Washington Post* (April 6, 1986), "My Uncle Died in Vain Fighting the Good Fight," Radosh also portrays the U.S. volunteers in the Lincoln Brigade of the Republican Army as, at best, simple-minded dupes of Stalin's Machiavellian designs.

derous, incompetent fanatic. I had known him at Albacete in October 1936, when the Eleventh Brigade was being formed and had found him a kindly patron of our small English section (there were only twenty-one of us), which tended to get overlooked when equipment, and for that matter rations, were distributed. I expressed my indignation about Hemingway's caricature (for so it seemed to me then) to friends in New York and one of them suggested that I write an article about Marty as I knew him. I did, and it was published in the *New Masses* in November 1940. There was nothing in it that was not true but what I had not realized was that the Marty I knew in October had in fact become, long before the war ended, exactly the kind of murderous witch-hunter who makes such an unforgettable impression on the readers of Hemingway's novel.

When, much later, I recognized the justice of Hemingway's indictment, I felt considerable embarrassment about the article I had published. But I found this no reason to repudiate the entire Republican cause. War is an ugly business at best; as Thucydides said long ago, it is a teacher of violence and reduces most men's tempers to the level of their circumstances. It brings out the worst in some men and the best in others. And in most of those who fought for the Republic it brought out the best.

According to Radosh, the Spanish Republic had become, well before the end of the war, "what its enemies called it, a puppet of Moscow"—the phrase is that of the historian of the Comintern, E. H. Carr.[20] There is some exaggeration here—the repeated attempts of Juan Negrin, the Socialist doctor who became president in 1939, to negotiate a peace in 1938,[21] for example, were quite contrary to the Communist party's policy. But it is true that by late 1937 the Communist party and its Comintern and Russian "advisers" were in firm control of the Republican Armies and were exercising civilian political control through a Russian-style secret police. This state of affairs had come about not only because the Soviet Union was the Republic's sole source of modern weapons but also because the Communist party, an insignificant minority when the war began, had won widespread support by its capacity for organizing an army that, unlike the

---

20. *The Comintern and the Spanish Civil War* (New York: Pantheon, 1984), p. 31.

21. See Thomas, pp. 821, 848.

militia columns of the opening days of the war, could fight successfully against regular troops.

But it does not follow from this, as Radosh and others seem to believe, that a Republican victory would have resulted in a Spain comparable to the present Soviet satellites in eastern Europe. "The meaning of Soviet domination," he writes in a letter to the *Nation*,[22] "was succinctly explained by Dolores Ibarruri, who, speaking from her sanctuary in the Soviet Union in 1947, said, 'Spain was the first example of a "people's democracy."'" But such a development is beyond belief. If the Republic had won the war, the need for Soviet arms and a disciplined army would have vanished and so, inevitably, would the dominance of the Communist party.

The Party was already unpopular, to say the least. One of Togliatti's dispatches to Moscow, explaining how it was possible for General Casado, against Communist opposition, to end the war in 1939 by surrendering the Madrid front, speaks of "an explosion of all the hatred for our party and spirit of revenge of anarchists, provocateurs, etc., etc. . . . The p[arty] was surprised by this wave of repression, which moreover highlighted our weaknesses, especially in relation to our links with the masses."[23] Indeed, the success of Casado's coup is in itself a comment on the weakness of the Party's hold over the armed forces. And in any case the idea of Republican Spain as a "people's democracy" like Hungary or Czechoslovakia is ridiculous. Those countries have been held down only by the presence and on occasion the active intervention of Russian troops. Stalin had more to worry about than Spain in 1939 and the early forties, and in any case he did not have the capacity to maintain an army of occupation there over a long and vulnerable sea route. And even if he had tried he would have had to reckon with the recalcitrant opposition of the Spanish character to any form of control.

Thomas opens his history with a quotation from Angel Ganivet which explains much about the war that may seem strange to readers brought up in more or less disciplined societies. "Every Spaniard's ideal," it runs, "is to carry a statutory letter with a single provision, brief but imperious: 'This Spaniard is entitled to do whatever he feels like doing.'" It is relevant, too, that now, under the democratic mon-

22. December 27, 1986.
23. Carr, p. 99.

archy, the Communist party is once more what it was at the beginning of the civil war, a minority party.

The fact that continued Soviet control of a victorious Republic would have been beyond Stalin's powers negates Hugh Trevor-Roper's argument, cited by Radosh in that same letter to the *Nation,* that Stalin, "friendly to Hitler and hostile to the West . . . might have provided the Germans with the transit through Spain that Franco steadfastly refused." And a victorious Republic would certainly not have sent, as Franco did, a crack infantry division to fight by the side of the Wehrmacht in Russia.

In his *New Criterion* article Radosh's main concern is with the intellectuals and particularly the writers who supported the Republic. He spends much of his space dealing with the case of Stephen Spender, which he finds "particularly instructive." Spender, in his introduction to Miller's *Voices against Tyranny,* points out that "much of the literature of the Spanish Civil War written on the Republican side seems to show that the writers of it felt that there was a 'truth' of 'Spain' that remained independent of, and survived the mold of, Communism into which successive Republican governments were forced." Radosh is skeptical of any such "truth" and cites against its existence the case of Spender himself. He compares the letter Spender wrote to Virginia Woolf in 1937 with his remarks about John Cornford, printed in a review Spender wrote in 1938.

The letter states that "everything one hears about the International Brigade in England is lies" and complains of "the lies and unscrupulousness of some of the people who are recruiting at home." He hopes that Virginia's nephew, Julian Bell, will not join the brigades: "The qualities required apart from courage, are terrific narrowness and a religious dogmatism about the Communist Party line, or else toughness, cynicism and insensibility. The sensitive, the weak, the romantic, the enthusiastic, the truthful live in Hell there and cannot get away." He goes on to denounce the lie, which he attributes to the *Daily Worker,* the British Communist newspaper, that "people can leave the Brigade whenever they like. On the contrary, one is completely trapped there." He mentions the particular case of his "greatest friend" who "collapsed" on the fourth day of the Jarama battle. Returned to base at Albacete he tried to escape, was caught and sent to a "labor camp." Spender's request to have him attached to himself as a secretary was refused.

It is true that before mid-1937, when the brigades were formally inducted into the Republican Army, there was some confusion about the term of the enlistment of foreign volunteers. Esmond Romilly was allowed to go home after the almost complete annihilation of the British unit of the Thaelmann Battalion of the Twelfth Brigade at Boadilla in December 1936 and I, wounded in the same engagement, was also sent home, though it is true that I had, as a result of the wound, nerve damage in my right arm and shoulder and would have been of no use as a rifleman. As a matter of fact, one young man who shot himself in the foot the first time we came under artillery fire was also sent home; in the British Army in the 1914 war he would have been court-martialed.[24]

When, however, the British contingent, no longer a handful of men lost in a French or German unit, became the British Battalion, the rules had to be tightened up. The Spaniards were in for the duration, and the German and Italian soldiers of the brigades, as well as the men from other countries that had reactionary regimes, had no home to go to. It would have been disastrous for morale if one national section had enjoyed the privilege of pulling out at will. Spender recognizes, in the letter, that "the discipline is not so bad as that of Capitalist armies; deserters are not shot but quite well treated in a camp."

As for the qualities required for life in the brigades, "narrowness and religious dogmatism about the party line" were rare, and courage, toughness, cynicism, and insensibility are the hallmark of seasoned combat veterans the world over. They have to develop insensibility to the sight of what metal can do to human flesh, and they very soon develop a cynical view of the wisdom of higher headquarters and the rhetoric of politicians. In the film *The Good Fight* one veteran of the Abraham Lincoln Brigade talks with sarcastic vigor about people who came out to Spain and urged the volunteers to fight against Fascism. "What the hell did they think we were doing?" he asks indignantly. And the British Battalion, which after being bled white in the Jarama battles then spent month after month in the trenches there, adopted with enthusiasm a song written by one of their number which shows little of that religious dogmatism about the party line Spender complains of. It is sung to the tune of "Red River Valley" and the first verse goes:

24. See also the case of Keith Scott-Watson in Cunningham, p. 323.

286   THE MODERN WORLD

> There's a valley in Spain called Jarama,
> That's a place that we all know so well,
> For 'tis there that we wasted our manhood
> And most of our old age as well.[25]

The terms of Spender's letter are clearly inflated and sentimental; the vision of the brigades as Hell for the weak, the sensitive, and romantic reminds one irresistibly of so many English accounts of the sufferings of a boy with an artistic soul at a public school. His letter is the understandable reaction of a man of keen sensibilities, who had always had pacifist leanings, to the harsh realities of war, a reaction compounded by concern for a close friend who was, as he puts it, "hopelessly caught in the machinery" and for whose plight he felt himself to some extent responsible.[26]

Radosh contrasts this letter with a passage from Spender's review of a volume commemorating John Cornford, published in 1938. Cornford is there described as one who exemplified "the potentialities of a generation" that was fighting "for a form of society for which it was also willing to die." "How," asks Radosh, "are we to judge a writer who says one thing to a friend in private and quite the opposite to an innocent and credulous public on such a momentous issue?"

I cannot myself see that there is any cause to reproach Spender in this matter. He was writing about two very different men; his friend who collapsed under the strain of combat and a man of whom he says, earlier in the review, that his own writing and the essays about him give "a picture of a character so single-minded, so de-personalized, that one thinks of him, as perhaps he would wish to be thought of, as a pattern of the human cause for which he lived, rather than an individual, impressive and strong as his individuality was." In a part of the letter to Virginia Woolf that Radosh ignores he had written:

---

25. For later, official occasions, such as veterans' reunions, for example, a cleaned-up version was concocted; its first verse runs: "There's a valley in Spain called Jarama, / It's a place that we all know so well, / It is there that we gave of our Manhood, / And most of our brave comrades fell." Cunningham prints both versions in full (pp. 43–44).

26. For a full account of Spender's friend and his attempts to get him out of Spain, see Spender's autobiographical *World within World* (New York: Harcourt Brace, 1951) (references under the heading "Jimmy Younger" in the index). The young man was eventually sent back to England.

"For people who can face all this, the Brigade is all right." John Cornford could face "all this," and more.

How much Radosh is out of touch with the material he is using is clear from some of the remarks he makes on these texts. "When Spender wrote the letter to Virginia Woolf," he wonders, "was he secretly hoping that she would show it to Cornford before he made the fatal decision to join the battle, as Cornford wrote, 'whether I like it or not'?"

It is hard to know where to begin unraveling the compacted tangle of Radosh's errors here. John was already six months dead when Spender wrote his letter. And to anyone who knew John, the idea that he would pay any attention to advice from Virginia Woolf is ludicrous; in any case there is no reason to think that they ever met. Radosh was probably thinking of Julian Bell when he wrote "Cornford" but this is no mere slip of the pen, as is clear from his quotation from Cornford's letter; it is a mistake which betrays a disturbing unfamiliarity with the evidence. And that quotation, "whether I like it or not," has nothing to do with joining the brigades; it comes from a letter written from Catalonia in August 1936 when John was already fighting with a POUM column on the Aragon front. He speaks of feeling lonely and thinking of using his press card to get back to Barcelona. "But the question was decided for me. Having joined, I am in whether I like it or not." Radosh does not quote the next words; they would clash with his image of the "martyred John Cornford." They are: "And I like it. Yesterday we went out to attack, and the prospect of action was terribly exhilarating."

Radosh has a slapdash way with quotations; one more example. He cites from Orwell (his major, and quite inappropriate, example of a writer who turned his back on the Republic) a harsh dismissal of John Sommerfield's *Volunteer in Spain* as "sentimental tripe." The full sentence reads: "Seeing that the International Brigade is in some sense fighting for all of us—a thin line of suffering and often ill-armed human beings standing between barbarism and at least comparative decency, it may seem ungracious to say that this book is a piece of sentimental tripe."[27] He wrote these words in July 1937, after

27. Cyril Connolly, on the other hand, found the book "short, modest, and readable . . . an admirable account of the sensations of fighting, a true picture of what war feels like" (Cunningham, p. 19).

his return from Barcelona. In 1942, in his essay "Looking Back on the Spanish Civil War," he wrote, "If it had been won, the cause of the common people everywhere would have been strengthened."

Radosh is careless about his facts, too. In support of his statement that Stalin "purposely never gave the Republic enough arms with which to win" he describes the Russian materiel that reached Spain in October 1936 as "tanks, planes, and artillery . . . of a limited caliber—no match for the heavy equipment supplied by the Germans and Italians." Thomas has a different story to tell.[28] The fighter planes which arrived in October were the "fastest in Europe . . . technically superior to their German and Italian equivalents." The ten-ton tanks (T-26) "were heavily armored, cannon-bearing machines, of a more formidable type than the three-ton Fiat Ansaldos and six-ton Panzers Mark I . . . which had no cannon, only machine guns." And the Russian antitank guns were "superior to any German models then available." (In fact, Franco's munition factories used them as a model rather than the German product.) As for quantity, even though after the closing of the sea route by Italian naval action in mid-1937 supplies could reach the Republic only when the French government from time to time opened the frontier, Stalin delivered 900 tanks as against 200 sent by Hitler and the 150 sent by Mussolini, and 1,000 aircraft as compared to the 1,200 sent by the Fascist dictators. Stalin was no philanthropist but in the matter of heavy equipment he obviously delivered what he had been paid for.

Radosh spends much of his time castigating British and American intellectuals and writers for their blindness and hypocrisy but the only Spanish writer he pays any attention to is Garcia Lorca and then only to quote Salvador Dali to the effect that Lorca's death "was exploited for propaganda purposes" and that "personally the poet was 'the most apolitical person on earth.'"

The implication is that Lorca's murder was not something that could be blamed on the Nationalists; it must have been an accident or the result of a private quarrel. This is of course rubbish. Certainly Lorca was not a political figure like his friend, the Communist poet Rafael Alberti, but he had enough counts against him to be shot ten times over by the standards of what passed for justice in Fascist Spain. He was the brother-in-law of the Socialist mayor of Granada (who

---

28. Thomas, pp. 455–56.

was also shot); he was the director of an experimental traveling theater—La Barraca—which had been created by the left-wing student organization FUE; he was the author of a famous ballad which cast as the villains of the piece the Guardia Civil, the hated militarized police whose black patent-leather hats are to be seen on so many photographs of Spanish peasants on trial for their lives or being led off to be shot.[29]

As if this were not enough, he had, in the months preceding the rebellion, delivered the speech of welcome at a banquet for Alberti (who had just returned from the Soviet Union); he had signed, together with Alberti, Luis Cernuda, and Manuel Altolaguirre a manifesto demanding the release of the Brazilian revolutionary Luis Carlos Prestes; he had attended a banquet in honor of Malraux and other French writers at which the crowd sang the "Marseillaise" and the "Internationale." He had also, in an interview published in the widely read Madrid newspaper *El Sol*, referred to his home town Granada as "an impoverished, cowed town, a wasteland populated by the worst bourgeoisie in Spain today."[30] He was, of course, a poet, not a political figure, as he himself said more than once,[31] but he had clearly identified himself with the Republican cause and so signed his own death warrant.

He was not the only writer to proclaim his loyalty to the Republic. One of the few souvenirs I still have of my time in Spain is a tattered bundle of issues of a literary magazine published in Valencia in 1936 and 1937. *Hora de España*, it is called; among the contributors are Rafael Alberti, Manuel Altolaguirre, José Bergamín, Luis Cernuda, Rosa Chacel, Juan Domenchina, Leon Felipe, Juan Gil-Albert, Ja-

---

29. In "Romance de la Guardia Civil," one of the most famous poems in his collection, *Romancero Gitano*, the Guardia Civil are credited with "a patent-leather soul" (*alma de charol*), which may be a sarcastic allusion to their description as "the soul of Spain" by General Sanjurjo, their commander under the monarchy.

30. See Ian Gibson, *The Death of Lorca* (London: W. H. Allen, 1973), chapter 4, "Garcia Lorca and the Popular Front."

31. Just before leaving for Granada in July he said, speaking of a poet who had dedicated himself entirely to politics, "I shall never be a politician. I am a revolutionary, because there is no real poet who is not a revolutionary. . . . But I shall never be a politician, never!" ("Yo nunca seré politico. Yo soy revolucionario, porque no hay verdadero poeta que no sea revolucionario. . . . Pero politico no lo seré nunca, nunca!") José Luis Cano, *Garcia Lorca: Biografía illustrada* (Barcelona: Ediciones Destino, 1962), p. 124.

cinto Grau, Jorge Guillen, Miguel Hernández, Antonio Machado, and Emilio Prados—an honor roll of modern Spanish literature. With the fall of the Republic all of them went into exile, with the exception of Hernández, who died in a Franco jail in 1942. Spanish writers knew what Franco's Spain stood for, they knew that when Millán Astray interrupted Unamuno's repudiation of the Nationalist cause at Salamanca with the cry, "Death to the intellectuals! Long live Death!"[32] he was only putting into words the deepest feelings of Franco and his supporters.

Some of the foreign volunteers knew enough about Spain to share the feelings of its writers, but for most of them the decisive element in their decision to go to Spain was the fact that Franco was supported by Hitler and Mussolini. For those in Western Europe and America who viewed the steady advance of fascism with growing apprehension, and the spineless acquiescence in fascist aggression of the British and French governments with contemptuous anger, the resistance of the Spanish people to the military rebellion was an inspiration and a challenge. And for those who came from what Auden in his famous poem called "the unjust lands," Spain was the place where after years of clandestine, anonymous activity, of isolation and eventual exile in countries that were far from hospitable, they could at last face their enemy in the open, as soldiers, rifle in hand. The Republic, with all its faults and weaknesses, and even in its final phase of subjection to Communist control, was still on the right side of the major war that was in the making and so soon to come. The American volunteers of the Abraham Lincoln Brigade were known to the FBI as "premature anti-Fascists"; it was an accusation but it is a designation that all those who fought for the Republic can accept with pride. We were ahead of everybody else in something that had to be done.

That we lost was a tragedy for Spain, which was condemned to forty years of stifling obscurantist dictatorship. "History to the defeated," Auden wrote, "May say Alas! but cannot help or pardon." He suppressed the poem in later editions of his collected poems and once wrote on a copy of the pamphlet in which it first appeared, "This is a lie." Radosh approves: "Auden subsequently—to his honor—repudiated" the poem. But Auden was wrong to do so; what he had written

---

32. "Muera la inteligencia! Viva la muerte!" The last three words are the battle cry of the foreign legion, of which Franco was once commander.

is the bitter truth. Ask the Cuban exiles, the Hungarian freedom fighters, the Czechs, the survivors of the half a million Spaniards who fled from Franco's firing squads over the French frontier in 1939. Radosh goes farther even than Auden; he will not have history even say "Alas!"[33] But Albert Camus summed it up for all of us who still mourn the Republic. "It was in Spain," he wrote in 1946, "that men learned that one can be right and yet be beaten, that force can defeat spirit, that there are times when courage is not its own reward. It is this, no doubt, which explains why so many men, the world over, feel the Spanish drama as a personal tragedy."[34]

33. For an exchange of letters on this essay with Professor Radosh see the *New York Review of Books,* June 25, 1987, pp. 52–53.

34. Preface to *L'Espagne libre,* cited in Frederick R. Benson, *Writers in Arms* (New York: New York University Press, 1967), p. 302.

One Woman's War

"A gifted, sincere and I think rather charming young woman . . . wants more than anything to meet you," Virginia Woolf wrote to Ethyl Smyth on January 16, 1936. The young woman was "Marchesa Iris Origo, daughter of Lady Sybil Lubbock (Villa Medici Florence)," and Virginia arranged a tea party for the meeting later on in the month. It is a far cry from the Bloomsbury of 1936 to the Italy of 1943; the opening sentence of the Marchesa's diary for January of that year runs: "The first refugee children have arrived." This record, written down day by day, goes all the way to July 5, 1944. At that point the Germans have retreated to the north, leaving devastation behind them; the Allied armies have followed on their track, "and now," the entry begins, "at once, we must begin again. On the first day Antonio set the men to reaping."

The diary[1] is an extraordinary document. It was printed exactly as it had been written down, without editing or retouching. "I felt at the time," the Marchesa writes, "and feel now, that any interest this diary might have would come from its being an immediate firsthand account. I put down each day's events as they occurred as simply and truthfully as I could."

Even at the best of times, keeping a diary regularly can be a demanding discipline, often evaded by procrastination and sometimes simply forgotten, but 1943–44 in Val d'Orcia was not the best of times. "During the most eventful periods . . . it was often difficult to find time to write at all. Some passages were hurriedly scribbled at night, others with twenty children in the room—and some in the cellar during the shelling." The diary was not only demanding, it was dangerous.

This essay originally appeared in the *New Republic,* June 4, 1984.

1. *War in Val D'Orcia: An Italian War Diary* by Iris Origo was first published in England in 1947; it was reissued in an American edition, with an introduction by Dennis Mack Smith (Boston: David R. Godine, 1984).

During the first few months . . . it usually lay among the pages of the children's picture books; since I believed that the nursery bookshelf would probably be one of the last places to be searched. Later on most of it . . . was buried in tin boxes in the garden. But the current pages were naturally always in the process of being written even up to the end, with the Germans in the house and (since even in times of danger the careless remain careless) were apt to be lying about in undesirable places.

It was a wonder that it was written to start with, and a wonder too that it survived; German paratroops, the last occupiers of the house, stole everything that took their fancy and deliberately destroyed much of sentimental and personal value. "Every drawer of my writing desk has been ransacked and stained or torn-up photographs, torn out of their frames, strew the floors." But survive it did, to preserve a record of war seen from below, by the civilians whose homes and places of work are its theater and who are themselves regarded by the combatants as an obstructive nuisance at best and at worst a victim to assuage the frustrations of defeat, or—as in the case of the Moroccans of the French *Corps Expéditionnaire,* who in the Val d'Orcia raped girls and women, including an old woman of eighty—to serve as the prize of victory.

When the diary begins, the writer realizes that events have taken a decisive turn. The refugee children are from Genoa, one of the first targets of the Allied air raids: "everyone in Italy is saying: 'Now it's come, now it's our turn.'" But she has no premonition of what is still in the future—of the German occupation of Italy, the massive destruction inflicted by Allied air raids and the stubborn fighting on the ground, of the final days with German artillery batteries round her house and paratroopers manning machine guns in the garden. In January 1943 the Italian Army, though in retreat, was still fighting in Libya; it seemed inconceivable that the war would come all the way to La Foce, the Origo estate in the Val d'Orcia, south of Siena. The estate, as the Marchesa explains in an eloquent preface, was large— fifty-seven farms centered on the villa—and was worked on the Tuscan system known as *mezzadria:* "The landowner builds the farm house and keeps it in repair; he supplies the money to buy half of what is needed to cultivate and improve the land. He pays for half of the stock of cattle. When harvest comes, owner and farmer share the crops." This institution, ubiquitous in Tuscany since the thirteenth century, was not destined to survive the war and its aftermath. It was swept away in the breakdown of traditional relationships caused by the war and was in any case not compatible with the mechanization of agriculture. But its remarkable longevity speaks volumes for its efficiency. It was, Iris Origo says, "a partnership," and as the pressures of war, defeat, and German occupation mounted, the partnership at La Foce became very close. "Together we planned how to hide the oil, the hams and cheeses, so that the Germans would not find them; together we found shelter and clothes for the fugitives who knocked at our door."

For the first seven months (January to July 1943) the diary is a fascinating account of the disintegration of the Fascist regime as defeat in Africa was followed by invasion of the homeland, of the ineffectual maneuvers of the monarchy and the army in a situation that called for courage and decision, and finally of the German occupation, which made all Italy, from Sicily to the Po, a battleground, a land of blown bridges, shattered buildings, and mine fields. For the postwar visitor to Italy it is almost impossible to imagine what the country looked like in the last two years of the war. In Florence, for example, the Germans, as they abandoned the city in 1944, blew all the bridges across the Arno except the Ponte Vecchio. To make that bridge impassible for vehicles, they dynamited all the buildings on its approaches, from Piazza della Signoria on the one side and from just below Piazza Pitti on the other, creating two mountainous piles of rubble, the debris of medieval palazzi. The Arno could be crossed only by foot on a *passarella* propped on the piers of what had been Ponte alla Carraia, and on wheels over a Bailey bridge put across by the engineers in the area of Le Cascine. Other cities were even more battered, especially those which had already served as targets for the Allied air forces when the German demolition squads took over the work of destruction.

By September 12 German troops had arrived in Montepulciano, the town closest to the Origo estate. And from this point on the main preoccupation of the Origos is the constant stream of men and women on the run who pass through the valley: British prisoners captured in Africa and left to their own devices when their Italian guards went home; Italians from units that surrendered to the Germans, escaping internment in Germany; Italian Jews avoiding the S.S. round-up squads; Italian youths fleeing conscription or forced labor—not to mention Moroccans from the French Expeditionary Force, Brazilians, and "Boers who can speak no European language at all" (presumably Afrikaans-speakers from the South African Armoured Division). There were even Austrian deserters from the German Army on their way north. All of them were sheltered, fed, hidden (one Jewish family in a Catholic convent), or sent on their way to the frontiers or to try to pass through the lines, with directions, food, and clothes.

Such generosity to fugitives was widespread in rural Italy. There were some seventy thousand Allied P.O.W.s in Italy at the time of the surrender and nearly half escaped either via France or Switzerland or else by crossing the front to rejoin their own troops. The British general O'Connor wrote to the Marchesa after the war, "the Italian peasants and others behind the lines were magnificent. They could not have done more for us. They hid us, escorted us, gave us money, clothes and food . . . all the time taking tremendous risks." The Origos, too, were taking tremendous risks. They soon became aware that their hospitality was no secret. "Do you realize," the Marchesa is asked by two English escapees, "that for the last fifty miles everyone whom we have asked for help has sent us on to you? Hadn't you better be careful?" Five days after the entry recording this conversation she writes: "Spent the morning trying to alter the date of birth on the identity card of a young deserter who turned up this morning and firmly demanded this service—with the same confidence with which others have asked for a clean shirt or some food."

It was not long before a threatening article appeared in the official Fascist paper of Siena. The Origos successfully turned for aid to, of all people, the German consul and vice-consul at Florence, Wolff and Wildt, who "have probably done more than any Italian in the last few months of the occupation, to save innocent people from the Germans." Another German is mentioned in the same tone—Heydenreich, the archaeologist responsible for preserving the art treasures of Tuscany. Besides moving the bronze doors of the Battistero back to Florence from the tunnel where they had been stored, he succeeded in having Siena declared a "hospital city" protected from bombing. "He speaks with respect and liking of his opposite members of the Allied Commission, Kenneth Clarke and Woolley . . . a queer, comforting conversation, a reminder of eternal values which may outlast the present madness."

But the present madness was far from over. Rome fell to the Allies on June 5, 1944; and on that same day German officers appeared at La Foce to requisition quarters for troops. The front was moving closer. The situation was complicated by the presence in the woods of partisans who, in this area, seemed to do very little to hamper the Germans but endangered everyone by their presence and occasional small actions. Before long, however, the villa was occupied by paratroops—"the most complete set of ruffians I have ever set eyes on"—and as the artillery fire reached a crescendo and the Germans demanded the cellar where the Origos and the children had taken shelter, they started out to walk eight miles on mined roads through shell fire to refuge in Montepulciano. They were "sixty in all, of whom four were babes in arms and twenty-eight others children." (One of the babes in arms was the Marchesa's daughter, barely one year old.) They all got there safely, but the events of the days of battle prompted a bitter but just reflection in the diary.

> This glimpse of a tiny segment of the front increases my conviction of the wastefulness of this kind of warfare, the disproportion between the human suffering involved and the military results achieved. In the last five days I have seen Radicofani and Contignano destroyed, the countryside and farms studded with shell holes, girls raped, and human beings and cattle killed. Otherwise the events of the last week have had little enough effect upon either side; it is the civilians who have suffered.

But our last glimpse of the Origos is at the work of reconstruction.

> In Chianciano, where Antonio is working all day, the problems are numerous: lack of diesel oil for the threshing, of water, of light, of sugar and salt and soap, of all medicines or hospital supplies, of any transport. . . . I have formed a women's committee, have issued an appeal for old clothes of any sort and hope to set up a work room to prepare babies' layettes etc.

It is hard to remember, as one reads the closing paragraphs of the diary, that the writer who so quietly assumes fresh burdens after such terrifying experiences is the woman who was brought up in wealthy homes on Long Island and in London, who spent fourteen years in the Villa Medici, Cosimo's country retreat outside Florence, moving in wealthy aristocratic society, and who was later to write brilliant books about Leopardi, Bernadino da Siena, Byron and his Countess Guiccioli, and Francesco Datini, the merchant of Prato. *Noblesse oblige*, wrote the Duke de Lévis, who belonged to an aristocracy that had failed signally to live up to the precept and paid for that failure, most of them, with their heads; it was clearly the unspoken creed of the Origos, as they brought their farmers and their families, as well as the refugee children, through eighteen months of hardship and danger and finally led them to safety through the fire of the battle itself.

The Triumph of the Italian Jews

GETO—the word stood out in large black capitals against the small print of a poster on the wall of the Gesuati Church when I was in Venice a few years ago; it turned out to be the name of a film which was to be given a special showing in the Camera di Commercio.[1] More familiar in its nondialect form "ghetto," the word prompts images of fifteenth-century Frankfurt or twentieth-century Warsaw, but it was Venice that provided a name for the urban prisons in which the Jews were confined for many centuries. Since Venice is a city of small islands connected by bridges, nothing was easier than to post sentries on the bridges and isolate one of the islands in the northern sector of the city, an industrial site where there had been a foundry—it was done in 1516.

On the screen, watched by an overflow audience, a series of haunting images traced the three-hundred-year history of the ghetto, as the camera focused on the original decree, still in the archives, which established its regulations; ranged through the rich interior of the "Spanish" synagogue, designed by Longhena, the architect of the great church of La Salute; moved along the bricked-up windows facing the canal and the outside world and then climbed the stories which had been piled on stories as height was made to serve for space. Release came only with the arrival of Napoleon's troops, who brought in the modern age. But the film ended, as it had begun, somberly: newsreel footage that showed the solemn commemoration, in the ghetto itself, of the Italian Jews murdered by the Nazis. And in the ghetto now (it is still called by that name though no guards stand on the bridges) Venetian children kick their soccer ball against a high brick wall on which, below the crowning fringe of triple barbed wire, are fixed seven bronze bas-reliefs, images of the Holocaust.

This essay originally appeared in the *New York Review of Books*, August 18, 1983.

1. Directed by Alberto Castelloni and Paolo Borgonovi, 1982.

Italian Jewry had never occupied a conspicuous place in the consciousness of the rest of the world. There was no mass emigration, like that from Russia and Poland, no organized anti-Semitic movements, as in Germany and the Austrian Empire, no sensational *affaire* like the Dreyfus scandal in France. Indeed the Jewish presence did not loom large in the Italian consciousness either; Jews had been in Italy as long as anyone else (there are Jewish catacombs in Rome as well as Christian), and, above all, unlike their northern coreligionists, they had no separate everyday language.[2] When in the early nineteenth century the gates of the ghetto were flung open (everywhere except in papal Rome, where they stayed closed until 1870 in that crass world of ignorance and corruption immortalized in the Romanesco sonnets of Belli), the Italian Jews rejoined the mainstream of Italian life and culture from which they had been separated since the Renaissance. By the beginning of the twentieth century, to quote Stuart Hughes's *Prisoners of Hope*,[3] they "appeared fully integrated into the national life. Still more, their leading personalities constituted a special and respected variety of elite." Many of them left far behind them not only the memory of the ghetto but also their religion; often, indeed, they had half forgotten their Jewish ancestry. They were to be brutally reminded of it by the anti-Semitic decrees of 1938 and the arrival of the S.S. murder squads in 1943.

The Silver Age of the Italian Jews (Stuart Hughes's subtitle) is a fifty-year period that began in 1924, the year of the murder of Matteotti and the consolidation of Mussolini's dictatorial power. A silver age must have a golden predecessor, and Stuart Hughes finds it in the

2. George Jochnowitz, professor of linguistics at the College of Staten Island, pointed out, in a letter to the *New York Review of Books*, that there is in fact a "Judeo-Italian . . . related to Italian as Ladino is to Spanish and Yiddish is to German." Widely spoken "a hundred years ago . . . it is dying today." He draws attention to the first chapter of Primo Levi's *The Periodic Table*, "Argon," which is "in part devoted to a discussion of the vocabulary of the Jews of Turin." Stuart Hughes also refers to that chapter and quotes Levi's characterization of the "language his family had spoken" as "the dialect of the Christians surrounding them . . . intermixed with terms taken over from the Hebrew."

It is still true, however, that these linguistic phenomena, which are more like dialectal variations than a "separate everyday language," are not really comparable to the Yiddish of the northern European Jews, which is a language, and has a literature, fully distinguished from German.

3. Cambridge: Harvard University Press, 1983.

years between 1906 and the mid-1920s, "two decades in which Jews loomed largest in the national life." (There had been a still earlier golden age: the Renaissance years before the Counter-Reformation and the establishment of the ghetto, years in which the Jewish population of Italy "reached its all-time high" and "Italy's Jews felt themselves least reviled, most respected, closest to acceptance by the majority.")

The modern golden age gave Italy two prime ministers of Jewish descent, Sonnino and Luzzatti, and two dozen Jewish members of the Senate; Jews constituted only one-tenth of 1 percent of the population but 8 percent of university professors and 6.7 percent of the names listed in the *Who's Who* of the period—there were even Jewish generals and naval officers. But in one field, that of literature, they had not made their mark. This was to be the achievement of the silver age that followed 1924, and it is with six writers of the period, all of them Jewish or part Jewish, that Stuart Hughes is concerned. Their names are inscribed high on the honor roll of modern Italian literature: Italo Svevo, Alberto Moravia, Carlo Levi, Primo Levi, Natalia Ginzburg, and Giorgio Bassani.

"What would lead a non-Jew to write of Italian Jewry?" Stuart Hughes asks himself in the opening sentence of his book. The reason is "quite personal": he "suddenly realized" that nearly half of the Italian acquaintances he had made over "a number of years of sustained and close contact with Italy" were of Jewish origin. It was a fact they had neither suppressed nor emphasized; when it surfaced "it was conveyed matter-of-factly, in a tone neither of boasting nor of apology." So too with the writers; their biographical sketches sometimes did not mention the matter at all, though "in most cases this identification still seemed important to them."

Stuart Hughes was intrigued by the possibility that the study of this Italian situation might contribute to ("or even transcend") the "debate on assimilation versus Jewish identity. . . . It might . . . be possible *both* to be highly assimilated *and* to treasure one's Jewish heritage." Since his experience "suggested that the residual sense of Jewishness was a very *private matter*," he turned from individuals to literature as "the best and possibly the only avenue to understanding. It seemed plausible that even with writers who spoke scarcely at all of their Jewish origins or associations, one might pick up echoes and resonances of a tradition extending back for more than two thousand years."

"What is left of identity"—so Stuart Hughes poses the question—"when both language and religion are gone?" For the first two writers on his list, Svevo and Moravia, the question imposes itself peremptorily; they are in fact figures "so uncertain about their Jewishness" that "possibly . . . they do not belong in our story at all." Both were baptized Catholics (Svevo as a grown man, Moravia at birth); Moravia, whose Jewish father was an atheist, grew up without Jewish memories or associations. Svevo (whose real name was Schmitz) attended a school run by a rabbi in his native Trieste (then part of Austria) and, later on, a boarding school near Würzburg which catered mainly to the sons of German-Jewish businessmen; his pen name Italo Svevo recognizes his German (Swabian) education as well as his ambition to be an Italian writer. But, though he helped James Joyce, his English teacher and friend, "with the specific details . . . needed for composing a Jewish character" (Joyce in turn rescued him from obscurity by vigorously promoting his third and last novel, *La coscienza di Zeno*), there is no overt trace of his Jewish heritage in his published work. Critics have, however, seen "cryptic-Hebraic . . . theme and tonality" in the self-defeating, self-deprecating passivity of his protagonists, their sense of futility and premature assumption of old age (the "hero" of *Senilità* is in his thirties).

Stuart Hughes proposes a different reading of the last novel: he finds a "more cheerful tone" to the "self-denigration" of Zeno, whose failures in love and business turn out to be a kind of success and whose inability to give up smoking (a leitmotif of the book) is in the end accepted with humorous indulgence. "If, then, we are to view Zeno as a crypto-Jew," Stuart Hughes writes, "it is as a Jew with a style of humor familiar to us all from countless folk anecdotes . . . the ostensibly self-denigrating Jew who in the stories he tells on himself invariably manages to come out on top." He is "a person not without hope."

In Moravia, as in Svevo, Stuart Hughes finds "echoes . . . of familiar Jewish themes . . . the ingrained sorrow, the weariness of a life not yet lived, epitomized by the conviction of *senilità*"; but the hope which he detects in the ironic self-denigration of Zeno is missing. From the first novel *Gli indifferenti* (1929) to the late *La noia*, which appeared in 1960 (the English title *The Empty Canvas*[4] does not do justice to the Italian word, which covers a broad range of negative mental states from boredom to dislike), his protagonists "lingered behind Svevo's Zeno in the shallows of despair: despising themselves, they clutched at sexuality as the only form of salvation they knew." Moravia himself, in an inteview, described his personality as the product of a "curious amalgam" (presumably a reference to his Jewish father and Dalmatian mother) which had "determined" in him "an excess of sensitivity." Stuart Hughes recognizes the importance of a painfully sick childhood in the creation of a conviction of "the impossibility of taking action," but lays more stress on the Jewish strain in Moravia's ancestry as the root of what he himself described as "the central theme" of his books and his life—"the problem of action" in the sense of "contact with reality."

This may be right as far as the novels are concerned but it should be remembered that Moravia is also the author of *Racconti romani* and *Nuovi racconti romani*, two dazzling collections of very short stories about Roman life written, most of them, for the third page of the Italian newspapers. In these pages the people of the Roman streets come to life in all their color, cruelty, cynical humor, and savage energy; there is no problem of contact with reality here. It is as if the air of his native city had somehow lightened the burden of Moravia's heritage; the themes here are not Jewish but Roman. These stories are a prose equivalent of that other great street drama of Roman life, the 2,269 sonnets of Giuseppe Gioacchino Belli.[5]

They date, however, from the post-war years; Moravia's influence on the younger generation of Jewish-Italian writers was exerted through the novels and especially *Gli indifferenti*, with its scathing portrayal of the moral squalor of bourgeois (and Fascist) Italy. Primo Levi read it as a young man, and it was by reading and rereading this novel that Natalia Ginzburg taught herself to write. Moravia, though as a well-known dissident he had to go into hiding in 1943, emerged unscathed from the ordeal of the German occupation. The two younger writers, however, felt the full brunt of the Nazi terror in their own persons: Primo Levi survived ten months in Auschwitz and Natalia

---

4. Trans. Angus Davidson (New York: Farrar, Straus & Cudahy, 1961).
5. The best introduction to Belli in English is still Eleanor Clark's brilliant essay in *Rome and a Villa* (New York: Doubleday, 1952).

Ginzburg's husband Leone, frequently imprisoned by the Mussolini regime, died, probably murdered, in a German prison sometime in the winter of 1943–44.

One of Leone Ginzburg's older associates in the anti-Fascist movement was the painter and political activist Carlo Levi. He is famous for one book;[6] it is the fruit of a period of exile, under the Fascist regime, in the poverty-stricken, arid, ruined lands of the Mezzogiorno. The village to which he was confined for the duration of the Abyssinian war (Gagliano is the name he gave it) lies southeast of the small town of Eboli. Eboli, the peasants told him, was where Christ stopped; he did not get as far as Gagliano. They had given Levi a title for the famous book which he wrote about them later, as he waited, hidden in German-occupied Florence, for the arrival of the Allied armies. In this book "he managed," says Stuart Hughes, "what three generations of . . . professional students of the area, far more qualified than he, had failed to accomplish": he awakened his fellow northerners (he was born in Turin) to the "bitter realities of the Italian South." His Jewish identity is hardly mentioned; it surfaces only occasionally, as when the village priest, asking him to play the organ at a Mass, speaks tactfully of a "different faith."

Stuart Hughes finds in Carlo Levi's work a familiar Jewish theme, however: "the age-old theme of exile." Perhaps, too, his sympathetic understanding of that alien peasant world, which in a famous passage he linked to Virgil's *"humilem . . . Italiam,"* "low-lying Italy" (as it appeared to the Trojans on their ships), and to Dante's *"umile Italia"* (so different from the imperial vision Mussolini struggled to impose), a world "hedged in by custom and sorrow, cut off from History and the State, eternally patient" owes something to ancestral memories of another confined and forgotten world, the ghetto.

"With Primo Levi," Stuart Hughes writes, "we come at last to a 'real' Jew." Born, like his unrelated namesake Carlo, in Turin, he studied to become a chemist only to find his way barred by the anti-Semitic laws of 1938, which made him an alien among his fellow students and professors. What had been a "cheerful little anomaly" became overnight a source of embarrassment; forced back on the Jewish tradition in which he had been raised but to which, like others

---

6. *Christ Stopped at Eboli. The Story of a Year,* trans. Frances Frenaye (New York: Farrar, Strauss & Co., 1947).

of his generation, he had paid little more than lip service, he began "to be proud of" the "impurity" for which he had been cast out. By 1943 he had joined a partisan band in Piedmont; he was arrested when the group was rounded up by the Germans in December of that year. He incautiously identified himself as "an Italian citizen of Jewish race" and was soon on his way to Auschwitz. He was still alive when the German guards marched their prisoners west through the snow before the advancing Russian columns; too weak to march, he was left behind in the January cold of 1945 to wait for the Russians, who arrived ten days later. It took him nine months of wandering in Eastern Europe before he found his way back over the Brenner Pass to Italy.

In 1947 he published his account of the ten months in Auschwitz, *Se questo è un uomo*,[7] which became "one of the classics in the genre" of concentration-camp memoirs. It was originally rejected by the publisher Einaudi, whose founder, Giulio, had been a member of an anti-Fascist group in Turin; the reader who had advised him against publication was none other than Natalia Ginzburg. It was not until 1958 that Einaudi reversed this decision; from then on the firm published all of Levi's writing.

The initial rejection is understandable. The book shows no trace of hatred for the German people, not even for the administrators of the death camps; it is almost as if Levi had dismissed them as nonhuman. In fact, twenty-two years after the war's end, when his former boss at the Buna chemical factory, where he had worked while an inmate at the camp, suggested a "friendly reunion," his reaction "in the German of the concentration camp" was "*Der Mann hat keine Ahnung*"— "He hasn't the faintest idea."

Levi offered his book not as one more account of unspeakable suffering but as a "serene study of certain aspects of the human soul"; it was prompted, as Stuart Hughes puts it, by a "compulsion to plumb the depths of unparalleled human experience." It certainly plumbs the depths: the cowed, silent shame of the prisoners as one of their number, the last resister, the last man of courage, is hanged; the total collapse of morale and human norms of feeling in the ten days of waiting for the Russians as the sick men froze or starved to death; the old

---

7. Trans. Stuart Woolf, as *If This Is a Man* (New York: Orion, 1959) and as *Survival in Auschwitz* (New York: Collier, 1961).

Jew who prays in thanksgiving to God that *he* has not been marked for death in the "selection" that has just taken place—"If I were God," Levi comments, "I would spit out [his] prayer upon the ground."

For Levi and his fellow Italian Jews—"gentle, educated, defenseless," no good at manual labor, unfit for the dog-eat-dog struggle to survive that was the rule of the camps—the old man's thanksgiving "for a special favor bestowed from on high smacked of a notion of Judaism they had abandoned three generations ago" for an "ecumenical humanism" that "admitted of no limitations on a universal claim to sympathy." Levi remembers in Auschwitz the speech Ulisse makes in Dante's *Inferno* as he urges his crew to embark on a final voyage into uncharted waters: "fatti non foste a viver come bruti, / ma per seguir virtute e conoscenza." Though he and his companions are, in fact, in hell and living like brute beasts, he finds some reason for his sufferings in the idea that like Ulisse, he "is embarked on an ultimate voyage beyond the limits of the human," that he is, through suffering, pursuing "virtue and knowledge" that will enable him to "deepen . . . understanding of an evil so vast and irreparable that it had pervaded the lives of one and all." Later he can sum up his wartime experience as "the awesome privilege of our generation and of my people."[8]

Still another Levi of Turin (unrelated to the other two) grew up to be a writer: Natalia, the youngest of the five children of Professor Giuseppe Levi, three of whose four sons were active, like their father, in the anti-Fascist movement. Her education, which she looked back on as marked by "inattention, incoherence, absurdity, and an absolute absence of any . . . defined and precise ideology," left her with-

---

8. In his last book, *The Drowned and the Saved* (trans. Raymond Rosenthal [New York: Summit Books, 1988]), completed just before he committed suicide, Levi's mood has hardened. In what Cynthia Ozick (*New Republic*, March 21, 1988) calls "much less a book of narrative and incident than it is full of siftings of the most sordid deposits of the criminal imagination—the inescapable struggle of a civilized mind to bore through to the essence and consequence of degradation and atrocity," Levi explores the depths of suffering and humiliation inflicted on the inmates of the camps and indicts not just the Nazis, but the German people— "those I had seen from close up, those from among whom the S.S. militia were recruited, and also those others, those who had believed, who not believing had kept silent, who did not have the frail courage to look into our eyes, throw us a piece of bread, whisper a human word."

out religious instruction, and her isolation as the youngest in a formidable family inspired in her a "melancholy . . . motionless, limitless, incomprehensible, inexplicable, like a sky way up high, black, brooding, and deserted." As she described her apprenticeship later, she trained herself to write "without feminine . . . sentimentality"; she "wanted to write like a man." She created a distinctive narrative style which Stuart Hughes brilliantly sums up as marked by "a dry factuality, the cool stance of an external observer, with an undercurrent of suppressed rage." (She herself expressed the wish that "every sentence should be like a whipping or a slap.") The style was to serve her well as, with the news of her husband's death in prison, she entered the years of solitude and "irremediable . . . sorrow."

The milieu of her early fiction is not Jewish; she had a strange conviction that her background made her unfit for the profession of literature—she could not think of a "writer who was at one and the same time Jewish, of a middle-class family, son of a professor, and raised in Piedmont." The early stories and novels, in fact, are set in a vague locale which could be anywhere, and the characters, often not given names until near the end of the tale, might be anyone—anyone, that is, afflicted by the brooding sense of loneliness, of the fragility of human happiness, which was the legacy of her difficult childhood and the bitter loss of her husband. "Why have we ruined everything?" is the refrain of the lovers in *Voices in the Evening* (1961).[9]

Her only long novel *Tutti i nostri ieri* ("All Our Yesterdays"), published in 1952,[10] deals with the vicissitudes of an Italian family in the war years; the two Jewish characters, a "Turk" and a Polish Jew from Warsaw, are both peripheral foreigners. And in the novella *Sagittario* (1957) there is a Jewish character, a doctor, who is also a Polish refugee. It is as if the author found it impossible to deal in the fictional mode with her own people; in *Voices in the Evening* there are no explicitly Jewish characters at all. But finally, in 1963, she confronted her own experience in *Lessico famigliare* (*Family Sayings*):[11] the story of her family with "gaps and omissions," which needed to "be read as though it were a novel."

---

9. Trans. D. M. Low (New York: Dutton, 1963).
10. Published in English as *A Light for Fools*, trans. Angus Davidson (New York: Dutton, 1957).
11. Turin: Einaudi, 1963. Trans. D. M. Low (New York: Dutton, 1967).

The links connecting the episodes and personalities are those characteristic expressions which in every family are preserved as cherished souvenirs of personality or memorable incident; the book is a "lexicon" of "those ancient phrases, heard and repeated an infinite number of times in our childhood. . . . One of these would make us recognize one another, in the darkness of a cave or among millions of people." In this autobiography, a classic of the genre, the "only book" which, by her own account, she wrote "in a state of absolute freedom," she found what Stuart Hughes calls "precisely the tone she needed, a tone of delicate irony veined with cordial affection." It is a heroic as well as a delicately comic family chronicle. The Levi home was a nucleus of anti-Fascist activity—it was the base, for example, for the spectacular operation that smuggled the Socialist statesman Filippo Turati out of Italy to safety in Corsica. But the sad note is still there: the arrival of Jewish refugees from abroad stirs fears for the future, ancestral fears, soon to be justified, of persecution and exile.

Of the other main theme Stuart Hughes finds in these writers, *senilità*, there is no trace in Natalia Ginzburg's writing; that was the malaise of the older generation. But she contributed a third theme—"again a variant on something eternal": the family, in this case a family in which "private life and public concerns were inextricably entangled." It was a family history to which she would look back in memory for support and of which she could feel proud.

No such source of moral strength was available to the last of the six writers, Giorgio Bassani, whose family belonged to the upper bourgeoisie of Ferrara. The Jewish families of Ferrara had an almost unique distinction: they were large-scale landowners (a consequence of their role as suppliers of capital for the drainage and reclamation of the Po delta in the nineteenth century). Most of them were supporters of Fascism during the 1920s but their treatment after 1938 was no different from that meted out to the anti-Fascist Jewish families of Turin. Young Bassani, at the age of twenty-two, was suddenly excluded from his accustomed world of social acceptance, tennis, and the pursuit of pretty blondes; he had to break his engagement to a Catholic girl and later became a teacher in the now segregated Jewish school. He also became an active anti-Fascist and later worked against the regime under an assumed name in Florence and Rome.

After the war, he published three volumes of poetry, but the series of stories and novels that were eventually to be retouched and joined together as *Il Romanzo di Ferrara* (1974) began with the publication in 1952 of the bitter story *"Una lapide in Via Mazzini"*; it appeared in the famous magazine *Botteghe oscure,* of which Bassani was then editor. He also worked for the publishing firm of Feltrinelli and it was he who accepted for publication Tomasi di Lampedusa's great Sicilian novel *Il gattopardo,* after it had been rejected by Einaudi.

Bassani, "alone among his contemporaries, celebrated his Italian Jewish heritage as the underlying and pervasive theme of his work." Though many of the stories concern relations between Jews and non-Jews (relations which Stuart Hughes sums up as "a riddle of irremediable misunderstanding"), the focus of the stories is always on the Jewish protagonist, the Jewish milieu. In the development of Bassani's themes, Stuart Hughes sees him progressing through four phases: "initially through depicting ambiguous relations between Jews and non-Jews; then through setting up an alter ego, for whom he next substituted his own person; in the end through creating a self-contained all-Jewish preserve in which a single lofty, enigmatic figure epitomized the subtleties and the perplexities of Italian Judaism."

That figure is the seventy-three-year-old patriarch Professor Ermanno Finzi-Contini; the novel in which he appears, *Il giardino dei Finzi-Contini* (1962, English translation 1965),[12] is the work that made Bassani's name familiar to American readers, and many who did not read the book saw the tragic, beautiful film that De Sica based on it (1970). The Finzi-Contini family, rich landowners "with their palatial residence close to the city walls," were "obsessed with their own privacy"; they had restored for their personal use a small abandoned synagogue of the "Spanish" rite and had not been seen in public for five years or so when the anti-Semitic laws were promulgated in 1938. The professor then put the tennis court in his huge gardens at the disposal of young coreligionists excluded from the local club, and so the narrator, a young man hopelessly in love with the professor's blonde daughter Micòl, became a member of the charmed circle.

The narrator is admitted not only to the tennis court but, after his exclusion from the municipal library, to the magnificent collections in the professor's private study; he is admitted, too, into the professor's

---

12. Turin: Einaudi, 1962. Trans. Isabel Quigly (London: Faber & Faber, 1965).

"intensely private vision of Judaism in the contemporary world," a secret plan in which the narrator was to have a part, to become, in fact, "one of the shining lights of Italian Jewry." This vision is never revealed except by vague hints. For the narrator's father, a physician and freethinker who thinks of himself as a "modern Jew," the family's self-absorbed, withdrawn existence is merely "misplaced pride, a covert anti-Semitism," but the narrator knows that it is in fact a way of dodging urgent pressure to join the Fascist party, as many Ferrarese Jews had done.

In 1938, when the regime reveals its anti-Semitic program, the family leaves its private synagogue and rejoins the Jewish community for Rosh Hashana; "We're all in the same boat now," says Micòl—as indeed they are. But for the moment it seems almost as if the professor, at any rate, welcomes the new segregation laws; at the family dinner table, the first time the narrator is invited to share their meal, the new situation is greeted with "elegantly sarcastic . . . comments, . . . well-bred hilarity." It may be, Stuart Hughes suggests, that the professor saw this resegregation as conforming to his secret plan; perhaps "deep in his heart [he] nourished a nostalgia for the ghetto." For those invited to share it, the garden, for a few years, offered "an oasis of serenity in a world of desperation"; for the narrator its "mere recollection spelt 'paradise.'"

It was to end, of course, in the hell of deportation and the camps. Bassani leaves this to the imagination, merely stating the fact in the prologue, but no one who saw it will ever forget the sequence in De Sica's film in which the family, three generations of it, is herded into the local schoolrooms with the rest of Ferrara's Jewish population by an officious Italian usher—"*Prego*," he says imperiously, "*prego*"—as jackbooted SS troopers pace the corridors.

Two of Bassani's major characters appear in stories set in postwar Ferrara; neither finds it possible to reinsert himself in the new society. They both leave, one by shooting himself, just at the time when life seems to be returning to normal; "It is as if," says Stuart Hughes, "the anti-Semitic laws were a 'time bomb' whose delayed action could destroy even those who had apparently come through unscathed." The protagonist of the late novella *L'airone* (*The Heron*, 1968),[13] a land-

13. Milan: Mondadori, 1968. Trans. William Weaver (New York: Harcourt Brace & World, 1970).

owner (though not on the scale of the Finzi-Contini), escapes the worst consequences of the persecutions by marrying a non-Jew of a socially lower order, transferring his property to her and moving to Switzerland. In 1947, tied to a wife and daughter he does not love, afraid of rebellious sharecroppers on his estate whom he has denounced to the police, he goes off hunting in the marshes. A heron is brought down by his guide and he watches it drag itself about mortally wounded; it is no good to eat, the guide explains, but can be stuffed and used as an ornament. The landowner represses an impulse to put the wounded bird out of its misery; to have done so, he suddenly thinks, would seem like "shooting, in a sense, at himself."

Later, back in town, he remembers the heron—it too had felt "hemmed in on all sides without the slightest possibility of escape." The sight of stuffed birds in a taxidermist's window clinches his resolve; the birds were more beautiful now than when they were alive—they glowed with "a perfection of . . . beauty . . . , final and imperishable." Before he shoots himself he recalls that he has regularly paid his annual dues; no one could raise objections to his burial in the Jewish cemetery. "It was," says Stuart Hughes, "as though his suicide might restore him, in a sense deeper than he could possibly think or express, to the company of his fellow-Jews . . . as though what remained of his Judaism could be saved through death alone."

The early story "*Una lapide in Via Mazzini*" is equally uncompromising. As a workman, in August 1945, starts to mount on the walls of the synagogue in Via Mazzini a plaque inscribed with the names of 183 Jewish citizens of Ferrara who are presumed dead in the camps, he is interrupted by a strange figure, a man dressed in bits and pieces of all the uniforms of Europe, who gives his name as Geo Josz, one of those inscribed on the stone. The narrator clearly speaks as a citizen of Ferrara, occasionally switching from third-person description to first-person plural; the tone of voice is that of a reasonable, solid citizen who has survived the vicissitudes of Mussolini's regime, the German-dominated Republica di Salò, and the dangerous period of partisan *epurazione*—he wants no further trouble, just a return to normal.

Geo Josz is a disturbing element from the beginning; subtle nuances in Bassani's fluid prose, so apparently colloquial, so elegantly structured, convey the narrator's feeling of unease, almost annoyance, at this unexpected reappearance. Josz does little to improve the atmosphere: he asserts roundly that the plaque will have to be "done over again," he even doubts that it should be put up at all. He treats one of his uncles, who had joined the partisans from his hiding place in the country, with distrust, almost hostility; he greets with hysterical joy the one who had been the most prominent Fascist among the Ferrara Jews and with him settles into an "instinctive understanding," a tacit "pact" to forget the past.

But in May of the next year he meets on the Via Mazzini one Count Scocca, a figure who was "for all of us, without exception, the symbol of the blessed days *entre deux guerres,*" an impoverished aristocrat who had been on the payroll of Mussolini's secret police, the OVRA, and director of the Ferrara section of the Italo-Germanic Cultural Institute. No one knew what passed between them but the conversation ended with two slaps on the count's face, administered by Geo. Had the count asked after his family? Whistled a snatch of *Lili Marlene?* No one knew.

But from that point on Geo Josz became a real pest; he appeared in public wearing the rags he had first turned up in and would sit in the principal café, opposite the former Fascist officials who were now coming out of the closet (Ferrara was "returning to normal"), and show pictures of his relatives who had died in the gas chambers. And suddenly, one day, he disappeared, never to be seen again. The narrator by this time is not only baffled but almost indignant. One thing is clear: not only does he feel no responsibility for what Josz and the other 182 have suffered, he has not even the slightest idea of the enormity of that suffering. *Der Mann hat keine Ahnung.* . . .

But then in a sudden moment of illumination, he understands the riddle. Geo and the count had met at twilight, the hour when "things and people who before seemed perfectly ordinary to you, may suddenly show themselves for what they really are." Geo must have asked himself: "What am I doing with this man? Who is he? And who am I, answering his questions and so playing his game?" He answered with two slaps on the cheeks. But he might have answered, says the narrator, "with a demented, inhuman howl, so loud that the whole city . . . could have heard it and shuddered."

"Prisoners of hope," Stuart Hughes's title, is a phrase used by the rabbi of a small town in Piedmont to comfort his son. "Many times," he said, "Jewish optimism is born of despair. Only for prisoners of hope is there a sure tomorrow." Even Bassani's dark vision in *The Heron* was balanced by the story "Necessity Is the Veil of God," which he put first in the last volume of his consolidated *Romanzo*. It is a short evocation of a victim of the Holocaust, a woman whose husband, together with his parents, was sent off to the death camps. But she had borne a son and that son, in 1945 as the survivors gathered in the synagogue, "seemed the very personification of life that eternally ends and eternally begins again."

Stuart Hughes sums up the "overarching theme" of his book as "the eternal hope of a people whose sufferings have likewise been eternal." At times it must have seemed that the hope was illusory. Yet there is one remarkable statistic which suggests otherwise, that the "ecumenical humanism" implicit in Primo Levi's rejection of the old man's prayer was not confined to enlightened Jews. Of the 36,000 Jews caught in Nazi-occupied Italy, just under four-fifths were saved, an "apparent miracle, surpassed only by the record of Denmark." And much of the credit goes to the Italian people whose behavior, at the time of the great Rome roundup, was described in a Gestapo report as "outright passive resistance which in many individual cases amounted to active assistance."

The years between 1924 and 1974 may indeed have been a silver age for the Italian Jews, but for Italian prose literature the age was golden. This distinguished book, which combines the expert skills of a seasoned historian with the understanding of a literary critic steeped in the language and literature of his subject, offers a challenging interpretation to those who already know these writers, and will serve as a masterly introduction for those whom it will inspire to make their acquaintance.

ESSAYS ANCIENT & MODERN

Designed by Martha Farlow

Composed by G&S Typesetters, Inc., in Meridien

Printed by Edwards Brothers, Inc., on 50-lb. Glatfelter B-16.

www.ingramcontent.com/pod-product-compliance
Lightning Source LLC
Chambersburg PA
CBHW021530030725
29115CB00030B/368